Strategic Adjustment and the Rise of China

A VOLUME IN THE SERIES

Cornell Studies in Security Affairs

edited by Robert J. Art, Robert Jervis, and Stephen M. Walt

A list of titles in this series is available at www.cornellpress.cornell.edu.

Strategic Adjustment and the Rise of China

Power and Politics in East Asia

Edited by

ROBERT S. ROSS
AND ØYSTEIN TUNSJØ

Cornell University Press

Ithaca and London

Cornell University Press gratefully acknowledges receipt of a
subvention from the Norwegian Institute for Defence Studies which
aided in the publication of this book.

First published 2017 by Cornell University Press

Printed in the United States of America

Library of Congress Cataloging-in-Publication Data

Names: Ross, Robert S., 1954– editor. | Tunsjø, Øystein, editor.
Title: Strategic adjustment and the rise of China: power and politics in
    East Asia/edited by Robert S. Ross and Øystein Tunsjø.
Other titles: Cornell studies in security affairs.
Description: Ithaca; London: Cornell University Press, 2017. |
    Series: Cornell studies in security affairs | Includes bibliographical
    references and index.
Identifiers: LCCN 2016057396 (print) | LCCN 2016059916 (ebook) |
    ISBN 9781501709180 (cloth: alk. paper) | ISBN 9781501709197
    (pbk.: alk. paper) | ISBN 9781501712760 (ret) |
    ISBN 9781501712777 (pdf)
Subjects: LCSH: China—Foreign relations—21st century. |
    East Asia—Foreign relations—21st century.
Classification: LCC DS779.47 .S79 2017 (print) | LCC DS779.47
    (ebook) | DDC 355/.033051—dc23
LC record available at https://lccn.loc.gov/2016057396

Contents

List of Contributors   *vii*

Acknowledgments   *ix*

Introduction   *1*
ROBERT S. ROSS AND ØYSTEIN TUNSJØ

PART I. POWER AND POLITICS IN THE EAST ASIAN TRANSITION

1. Domestic Politics and Nationalism in
    East Asian Security   *15*
    RANDALL L. SCHWELLER

2. U.S.-China Relations: *From Unipolar Hedging
    toward Bipolar Balancing*   *41*
    ØYSTEIN TUNSJØ

3. Perception, Misperception, and Sensitivity:
    *Chinese Economic Power and Preferences after the
    2008 Financial Crisis*   *69*
    DANIEL W. DREZNER

4. Two Asias? *China's Rise, Dual Structure, and the Alliance
    System in East Asia*   *100*
    WANG DONG

PART II. JAPAN, SOUTH KOREA, AND THE RISE OF CHINA: *NATIONAL SECURITY AND NATIONALISM*

5. Protecting the Status Quo: *Japan's Response to the Rise of China* 137
    IAN BOWERS AND BJØRN ELIAS MIKALSEN GRØNNING

6. Popular Nationalism and Economic Interests in China's Japan Policy 169
    JAMES REILLY

7. China's Rise and Security Dynamics on the Korean Peninsula 196
    CHUNG-IN MOON

PART III. GREAT POWER RELATIONS AND REGIONAL CONFLICT

8. Threading the Needle: *The South China Sea Disputes and U.S.-China Relations* 233
    M. TAYLOR FRAVEL

9. The United States and China in Northeast Asia: *Third-Party Coercion and Alliance Relations* 261
    ROBERT S. ROSS

    Conclusion: *East Asia at the Center: Power Shifts and Theory* 285
    ØYSTEIN TUNSJØ

    Index 299

Contributors

Ian Bowers is an assistant professor at the Norwegian Defence University College and the Norwegian Institute for Defence Studies.

Daniel W. Drezner is a professor of international politics at the Fletcher School, Tufts University, a nonresident senior fellow at the Brookings Institution, and a contributing editor at the *Washington Post*.

M. Taylor Fravel is an associate professor of political science and member of the Security Studies Program at the Massachusetts Institute of Technology.

Bjørn Elias Mikalsen Grønning is a research fellow at the Norwegian Defence University College and the Norwegian Institute for Defence Studies.

Chung-in Moon is a professor at the Department of Political Science, Yonsei University, and chairman of the Presidential Committee on Northeast Asia Cooperation Initiative, Republic of Korea.

James Reilly is a senior lecturer in Northeast Asian politics in the Department of Government and International Relations at the University of Sydney.

Robert S. Ross is a professor of political science at Boston College and an associate at the John King Fairbank Center for Chinese Studies, Harvard University.

Randall L. Schweller is a professor of political science and a Joan N. Huber Faculty Fellow in social and behavioral sciences at Ohio State University.

Øystein Tunsjø is a professor of international politics at the Norwegian Defence University College and the Norwegian Institute for Defence Studies.

Wang Dong is an associate professor and the director of the Center for Northeast Asian Strategic Studies at Peking University.

Acknowledgments

The editors are grateful to the Norwegian Embassy in Beijing, and to the Norwegian Ministry of Foreign Affairs and Ministry of Defence, for the financial support that made this project possible. They also appreciate the assistance and staff support from the School of International Studies, Peking University, which contributed to the success of the conference in Beijing in 2013, and the Norwegian Institute for Defence Studies, which hosted a second conference in Oslo in 2014.

Strategic Adjustment and the Rise of China

Introduction

Robert S. Ross and Øystein Tunsjø

In the aftermath of the Cold War, East Asia experienced considerable stability, despite the determined rise of China and its consequences for regional security and economic affairs. Maritime territorial disputes existed, but they had not fundamentally affected U.S.-China relations. China's market had developed a major role in the region's economic growth. Nonetheless, with the exception of brief and intermittent regional tension focused on North Korea's nuclear program and Taiwan's independence movement, cooperation was the norm, competition remain muted, and the regional economy continued to reflect the post–World War II economic order.

Since 2009, however, U.S.-China strategic competition and regional instability have become more pronounced.[1] The Sino-Japanese maritime disputes in the East China Sea over the Diaoyu/Senkaku Islands and the maritime disputes in the South China Sea over the Paracel Islands and the Spratly Islands have become sources of heightened U.S.-China tension and of widespread concern for the prospect for long-term regional stability. There has also been heightened U.S.-China strategic competition on the Korean Peninsula, with implications for South Korea's effort to maintain cooperative relations with both a rising China and its ally, the United States. In regional economic affairs, there has been U.S.-China conflict over China's initiative to establish a multilateral regional investment bank and the implicit competition between U.S. and Chinese proposals for regional free trade arrangements. These security and economic developments have contributed to increased bilateral U.S.-China tension, and they have created

---

1. For a discussion of international reaction to China's "assertive diplomacy" in 2009–2010, see Michael D. Swaine, "China's Assertive Behavior—Part One: On 'Core Interests,'" *China Leadership Monitor* 34 (2011), http://www.hoover.org/research/chinas-assertive-behavior -part-one-core-interests.

heightened policymaking dilemmas for all of the smaller East Asian countries.

This volume focuses on the underlying sources of these recent challenges to the regional order; the implications of these developments for China, the United States and the region's smaller states; and the challenges these states have encountered in developing policy responses that contribute to both their national security and regional stability. The contributors to this volume understand that the most significant factor contributing to heightened regional instability has been the rise of China. Although China has yet to catch up to the United States in security affairs, and its future is uncertain, it is clear that after nearly thirty-five years of economic growth and military modernization, China now plays a more significant role in East Asian economic and strategic orders and poses a greater challenge to U.S. leadership. This development in U.S.-China great power relations has required strategic adjustment throughout East Asia and it is central to the growing instability and tension throughout East Asia.

The Rise of China and the Regional Order

The recent development of regional instability has not reflected short-term developments that can be remedied simply with improved policymaking. Rather, heightened great power competition and regional instability reflect the rise of China and the fundamental changes underlying the U.S.-China relationship. After thirty years of economic and military modernization, China's economic and military rise have reached a new stage allowing for both greater economic activism and greater defense of its sovereignty claims and resistance to adverse regional security trends.

Rising China has not closed the gap in U.S.-China maritime capabilities; the U.S.-China power transition has yet to become a threat to great power peace. Nonetheless, incremental improvement in Chinese maritime capabilities, including an increasing number of naval and coast guard ships, has allowed China to be more active in regional maritime affairs.[2] The Chinese Navy now spends more time at sea, and it conducts increasingly large and sophisticated exercises in other countries' coastal waters and in the vicinity

---

2. For analysis of Chinese naval modernization, see, for example, Peter Dutton, Andrew S. Erickson, and Ryan Martinson, eds., *China's Near Seas Combat Capabilities* (Newport, RI: China Maritime Studies Institute, U.S. Naval War College, 2014), https://www.usnwc.edu /Research—Gaming/China-Maritime-Studies-Institute/Publications/documents/Web -CMS11-(1)-(1).aspx; and Michael S. Chase, Jeffrey Engstrom, Tai Ming Cheung, Kristen A. Gunness, Scott Warren Harold, Susan Puska, and Samuel K. Berkowitz, *China's Incomplete Military Transformation Assessing the Weaknesses of the People's Liberation Army (PLA)* (Santa Monica, CA: RAND, 2015).

of disputed maritime territories as well as enhanced surveillance of U.S. naval operations throughout the South China Sea.

Whereas until recently the Chinese Navy did not have the capability to operate within the U.S. maritime sphere of influence, it now operates in the East China Sea and the South China Sea, regions critical to U.S. security and alliance stability. On the Korean Peninsula, China's military modernization, its increased economic importance to South Korean prosperity, and its growing responsibility for constraining North Korean belligerence contributes to growing Chinese impact on peninsular security affairs.

Similarly, in international economic affairs China has yet to close the gap in economic power between it and the United States. Nonetheless, incremental changes in Chinese economic capabilities have affected regionwide economic policymaking. Many East Asian countries have experienced increased dependence on the Chinese market, including Japan and South Korea, reinforcing trends in security affairs. Moreover, China's expanding foreign aid budget has put pressure on the regional economic order. Commensurate with its greater economic capabilities, China has sought a leadership role in the regional economy, posing challenges to the established U.S.-led regional trade and banking orders.

Gradual rates of change among the great powers necessarily affect great power relations and small power alignments and thus the regional security order.[3] This process can occur well before a rising power achieves parity with an established power. Incremental changes in relative power can effect a state's security and policymaking long before a power transition reaches a critical stage, suggesting greater likelihood of a great power war. In these circumstances, relative shifts in great power capabilities compel small states to reconsider their relationship with the established great power.[4] Small states may bolster their traditional alignments, or they may decide to improve relations with the rising power.[5]

As small powers experience the greater relative capabilities of the rising power, great power competition will increase. The rising power seeks greater

3. Robert Gilpin, *War and Change in World Politics* (Cambridge: Cambridge University Press, 1983).

4. Robert L. Rothstein, *Alliances and Small Powers* (New York: Columbia University Press, 1968); Hans J. Morgenthau, *Politics among Nations: The Struggle for Power and Peace*, fifth ed. (New York: Knopf, 1978), chap. 12; Annette Baker Fox, *The Power of Small States: Diplomacy in World War II* (Chicago: University of Chicago Press, 1959), 187; Michael I. Handel, *Weak States in the International System* (New York: Cass, 1990), 183–87; George Liska, Nations in Alliance: The Limits of Interdependence (Baltimore: Johns Hopkins University Press, 1968), 27. Cf. Stephen M. Walt, *The Origins of Alliances* (Ithaca, NY: Cornell University Press, 1987).

5. For a discussion of the contingent nature of small state response to changing great power relations, see Jack S. Levy, ""Balances and Balancing: Concepts, Propositions, and Research Design," in *Realism and the Balance of Power: A New Debate*, ed. John A. Vasquez and Colin Elman, (Upper Saddle River, NJ: Prentice Hall, 2003), 139–40.

influence over a revised regional security order commensurate with its improved relative capabilities. The established power, on the other hand, will seek to consolidate the regional status quo by maintaining its military advantages and resisting small power realignment. This is what Hans Morgenthau described as "the pattern of indirect competition" in balance of power politics. This process can entail vital and nonnegotiable interests over the alignment of small states and over spheres of influence.[6] Such indirect competition over the alignment of smaller regional states has been the primary focus of this stage of great power conflict in the power transition in East Asia rather than direct U.S.-China competition in bilateral arms races and defense spending.

There has been incremental change in relative U.S. and Chinese capabilities. This has elicited concern throughout East Asia regarding the great power balance and the implications for the respective security of all countries in the region. There has thus also been greater competition among the great powers over the regional order, as they see to advance their respective interests vis-à-vis the smaller regional states during a period of changing great power capabilities and regional instability.

But relative change among the great powers does not mechanically cause great power war. The extent of great power tension and regional instability is ultimately indeterminate, reflecting the convergence of multiple factors, including not only changes in the distribution of power among the great powers but also such domestic factors as nationalism and leadership.[7] Nationalism and leadership have been fundamental to policymaking since the Napoleonic era, and they have interacted with structural change to contribute to the power transition wars from the Napoleonic Wars through World War II in Europe and East Asia. The combination of international structure and domestic politics will similarly influence the course of East Asian international politics in the twenty-first century. This understanding of the multiple sources of great power conflict is fundamental to the neoclassical realist perspective on international politics, and it is a perspective shared by the contributors to this volume.[8]

6. Morgenthau, *Politics among Nations*, chap. 12.

7. Jonathan Kirshner, "The Tragedy of Offensive Realism: Classical Realism and the Rise of China," *European Journal of International Relations* 18, no. 1 (2012): 53–75. Cf. John J. Mearsheimer, "The Gathering Storm: China's Challenge to US Power in Asia," *Chinese Journal of International Politics* 3, no. 4 (2010): 381–96; Robert Gilpin, "The Theory of Hegemonic War," *Journal of Interdisciplinary History* 18, no. 4 (1988): 591–613.

8. On neoclassical realism, see, for example, Gideon Rose, "Neoclassical Realism and Theories of Foreign Policy," *World Politics* 51, no. 1 (1998): 144–72; Steven E. Lobell, Norrin M. Ripsman, and Jeffrey W. Taliaferro, eds., *Neoclassical Realism, the State, and Foreign Policy* (New York: Cambridge University Press, 2009).

Power, Politics, and Policy Adjustment

Recent developments in the rise of Chinese power and in U.S.-China relations have required strategic adjustment on the part of all East Asian countries. Both the United States and China have had to adjust to China's expanded capabilities and to the new bilateral distribution of regional power. The region's smaller countries have also faced pressures for policy adjustment. As China rises, they experience pressures to adjust their strategic alignment among the great powers to advance cooperation with China but also to sustain cooperation with the United States.

But, as suggested by the neoclassical approach to international politics, these adjustment challenges are exacerbated by the politics of policymaking. Nationalism is a prominent feature of policymaking throughout East Asia, and the combination of international and domestic pressures in policymaking is reflected in conflicts over maritime territorial disputes and in the broader range of regional security issues created by the rise of China.

NATIONAL SECURITY AND STRATEGIC ADJUSTMENT

Greater deployment of China's improved maritime capabilities in the vicinity of other countries inevitably makes those countries more apprehensive about their security. But this dynamics also poses a challenge to Chinese policymaking. China can be more active in pursuing its interests, but its capabilities can also contribute to greater regional apprehension and resistance. Moreover, because improved Chinese capabilities raise security concerns among U.S. allies, China's more active defense of its interests also challenges U.S. security in East Asia. The rise of Chinese power requires national adjustment to these new realities for China to both defend its regional interests and to maintain a stable regional environment.

But the rise of China has also required strategic adjustment on the part of other countries, including the United States. Improved Chinese maritime capabilities and more active Chinese defense of its maritime interests have challenged U.S. security and its commitment to its strategic partnerships, and it has encouraged U.S. alliance consolidation with Australia, Japan, and the Philippines. But a forceful U.S. response can elicit Chinese concerns for U.S. "containment" of China and thus a Chinese pushback, contributing to regional tension and diminished U.S.-China cooperation. U.S. coercive diplomacy vis-à-vis China can also encourage destabilizing policies from U.S. allies and "entrapment" of the United States in its conflicts with China, thus challenging U.S. interests in both bilateral U.S.-China cooperation and regional stability.[9]

---

9. For a discussion of this dilemma in alliances, see Glenn H. Snyder, "The Security Dilemma in Alliance Politics," *World Politics* 36, no. 4 (1984): 461–95.

For its smaller neighbors, responding to China's rise requires reconsideration of the implications of the changing U.S.-China balance for their respective security policies, including their strategic alignment between the great powers and their own defense spending.[10] This can be a difficult process. South Korea's dilemma has been particularly acute, as it has been the focus of U.S.-China "indirect competition." Seoul's effort to avoid antagonizing Beijing by restraining its cooperation with the United States has encountered U.S. pressure to consolidate U.S.-South Korean alliance cooperation, including U.S. pressure on South Korea to begin alliance cooperation on missile defense. The Philippines has gyrated between cooperation with the United States and China, similarly reflecting the challenge of managing the rise of China. Japan, on the other hand, has resisted the rise of China. It has strengthened its defense postures and its alliance cooperation with the United States.

In economic affairs, the United States and the smaller East Asian countries have similarly struggled to adjust to China's economic rise. As China insists on a regional trade order and multilateral banking leadership commensurate with its growing economic importance, the United States has perceived challenges to its regional economic leadership. Unsuccessful U.S. opposition in 2014–15 to East Asian countries' participation in the Chinese-sponsored Asian Infrastructure Investment Bank (AIIB) has reflected U.S. perception of a Chinese challenge to U.S. regional leadership. Smaller East Asian economies have labored to adjust to this competition between the established U.S. and emerging Chinese regional economic orders. Australia and South Korea experienced considerable U.S. pressure to resist joining the AIIB, but they did nonetheless join as "founding members."

East Asian countries have also experienced pressure from the United States and China as each has pressured smaller economies to join their respective free trade agreements. The United States encouraged countries to join its Trans-Pacific Partnership (TPP) and China has encouraged countries to join its Regional Comprehensive Economic Partnership (RCEP).

But as countries struggle to adjust to rising powers, policymakers frequently respond not only to their country's changing strategic circumstances but also to the pressures of domestic politics on policymaking. The contributors to the volume understand that security policy is not a mechanical response to international circumstances; national security and domestic politics combine to determine policymaking.

In contemporary East Asia, the importance of domestic politics in shaping countries' policy responses to a rising China has been particularly prominent. The regionwide growth of mass nationalism has constrained policymakers'

---

10. For an early discussion of this process in East Asia, see Robert S. Ross, "Balance of Power Politics and the Rise of China: Accommodation and Balancing in East Asia," *Security Studies* 15, no. 3 (2006): 355–95.

flexibility in mitigating conflict associated with the rise of China, the changing regional order, and the increased salience of maritime territorial disputes lest they appear to be sacrificing their country's security and sovereignty. Elite nationalism has also contributed to the development of regional tension.

DOMESTIC POLITICS, NATIONALISM, AND POLICY ADJUSTMENT

The neoclassical perspective is thus especially helpful for understanding contemporary East Asia, as nationalism has become an increasingly influential force in policymaking. Nationalism has been an especially prominent factor in Chinese policymaking, where it has affected China's management of U.S.-China conflicts of interest and of the territorial disputes with Japan and in the South China Sea.[11] Yet throughout East Asia nationalism has also affected how China's neighbors have responded to its rise. Regarding the region's maritime disputes, mass nationalism in the Philippines and Vietnam have also made moderation of conflict and negotiated solutions to sovereignty conflicts exceptionally difficult. In Japan, elite nationalism has contributed to heightened Sino-Japanese tension. Nationalism and policy instability among U.S. allies has challenged U.S. ability to moderate regional tension and to maintain cooperation with China.

Regionwide nationalism has also contributed to the hardening of strategic alignments in an increasingly polarized East Asia. Nationalism has bolstered Japan's effort to resist rising China with greater regionwide military activism, increased funding for its navy, and consolidation of U.S.-Japan alliance cooperation. Domestic politics has also affected economic relations in East Asia, as publics throughout the region have responded to national interest conflicts with economic nationalism, further exacerbating political relations in East Asia. Tension in Sino-Japanese and Sino-Vietnamese relations have, in part, reflected the impact of economic nationalism on diplomacy.

China's Rise and East Asia's Response: The Structure of This Volume

The impact of the incremental rise of China on East Asian international relations is the focus of this volume. Every state in East Asia has experienced greater Chinese power. But each has responded in unique ways, reflecting the particular impact of the rise of China on its security and the unique

---

11. For a discussion of the impact of nationalism on Chinese foreign policy in 2010, Robert S. Ross, "Chinese Nationalism and Its Influence on Foreign Policy," in *China across the Divide*, ed. Rosemary Foot (Oxford: Oxford University Press, 2013), 72–96.

domestic setting of its foreign policymaking. The impact of China's rise on the regional order will reflect the sum of the distinct adjustments of particular countries.

In chapter 1, Randall L. Schweller works within the neoclassical realist tradition to examine the role of nationalism in foreign policymaking and the implication for the international politics of East Asia. Schweller argues that whereas as the rise of China is an important structural factor necessarily affecting states' security policies throughout East Asia, China's rise does not determine these states' security policies. Rather, domestic politics ultimately determines how a state responds to changing security circumstances. In particular, nationalism can drive states to adopt more belligerent policies than warranted by their strategic environment, thus contributing to heightened bilateral conflicts and regional tension. Schweller argues that, in contemporary East Asia, rising China sets the context of policymaking, but domestic politics has been the primary factor shaping policy. Elite transitions and domestic uncertainty in China, Japan, and North Korea have all contributed to regional uncertainty and heightened tension. From this neoclassical realist perspective, China's assertive diplomacy reflects as much China's domestic social and political instability and nationalism as it does China's rising capabilities. But Schweller also observes that nationalism is not limited to China. A "clash of nationalisms" is developing in East Asia. Nationalism in Japan and elsewhere in East Asia is contributing to a heightened region-wide tension.

In chapter 2, Øystein Tunsjø discusses the impact of the rise of China on the great power structure and the gradual transformation of the international system from post–Cold War U.S. unipolarity to U.S.-China bipolarity. Tunsjø develops a hedging framework for analysis and argues that whereas hedging had characterized regional diplomacy under U.S.-led unipolarity, under emerging bipolarity balancing is becoming the dominant security policy for the United States, China, and the smaller regional powers. Since 2009 this tendency toward balancing behavior has been reflected in China's "assertive diplomacy," in the U.S. "pivot" to East Asia, and in the security policies of the smaller regional powers. Tunsjø examines the traditional sources of great power capabilities to observe China's emergence as the world's second great power. While China has yet to establish strategic parity with the United States, Tunsjø points out that the distribution of capabilities in the contemporary international system is roughly similar to the bipolar U.S.-Soviet Cold War structure. He then examines the impact of the emerging U.S.-China bipolar structure for East Asian security affairs and strategic adjustment throughout the region.

In chapter 3, Daniel W. Drezner examines the impact of the rise of the Chinese economy on the international economic structure. He observes the rapid growth of the Chinese economy, but his analysis reveals that China has yet to challenge the United States as the anchor of the global financial system: the renminbi remains negligible in international financial transactions. Indeed, since the 2007–8 global financial crisis, the U.S. dollar has expanded its importance relative to the renminbi in global finance. Drezner's analysis suggests that the renminbi is far from becoming a significant international reserve currency and that the United States will continue to dominate the regional financial order. In trade relations, however, Drezner establishes the significant importance of the Chinese market for economies throughout East Asia. In this respect, the rise of the Chinese economy has enabled China to challenge the United States as the sole economic great power in East Asia, with implications for the regional trade order. The implicit competition between the Chinese-sponsored RCEP and the U.S.-sponsored TPP reflects this emerging balance in U.S. and Chinese regional economic competition.

In chapter 4, Wang Dong addresses the impact of the rise of China on growing U.S.-China regional competition. Following Drezner's analysis, Wang observes that the rise of the Chinese economy has challenged U.S. market dominance in East Asia. In regional security affairs, China has also achieved noticeable gains vis-à-vis the United States but, following Tunsjø's analysis, its strategic rise remains in its early stages. Thus the United States continues to dominate the strategic order in maritime East Asia. Wang observes that this distinction between the region's economic and strategic structure has created a great power "dual structure" in East Asia comprising an "Economic Asia" and a "Security Asia." China has improved its economic presence in the region, promoting regionwide cooperation within Chinese-led institutions. In security affairs, it has also developed a more proactive policy, but it simultaneously acknowledges the United States as the region's dominant strategic power. In contrast to the successes of its economic activism, China's proactive security policy provoked the U.S. pivot, in which the United States has strengthened its regional military presence while developing regionwide multilateral strategic networks within its regional "hub-and-spoke" system of strategic partnerships. Wang considers various alternative future regional orders, each premised on the ability of the United States and China to adjust to the growing equilibrium in the strategic relationship between the two nations.

Chapters 5 and 6 respectively examine the strategic and economic sources of the growing tension in Sino-Japanese relations. In chapter 5, Ian Bowers and Bjørn Elias Mikalsen Grønning analyze the domestic and international sources of Japan's adjustment to the "power shift" in Sino-Japanese relations. They argue that the growth of the Chinese economy, which is now larger than the Japanese economy, and the modernization of the Chinese Navy pose a mounting challenge to Japanese security and its secure access to sea lanes of communication. They argue that China's rise, and developments in Japanese domestic politics, have produced a multifaceted Japanese strategic response to prevent China from posing a significant threat to Japanese security. Under Prime Minister Shinzo Abe's leadership, Japan has strengthened its domestic capabilities with reform of its national security policymaking institutions and relaxed restrictions on international military cooperation. The Japanese military has also strengthened its deterrent capabilities with improved surveillance and expanded arms deployments in the East China Sea. Simultaneously, Japan has bolstered U.S.-Japan alliance cooperation and developed strategic cooperation with countries in the region, including Australia, the Philippines, and Vietnam.

In chapter 6, James Reilly investigates the contribution of Sino-Japanese economic interdependence on China's moderation of the role of mass nationalism on its policymaking. Reilly argues that the importance to China of stable Sino-Japanese economic cooperation has compelled Chinese leaders to repress periodic mass outbursts of anti-Japanese nationalism before they could harm Sino-Japanese economic cooperation. But the rise of the Chinese economy vis-à-vis Japan, and Beijing's corresponding understanding that Japanese dependence on the Chinese economy has superseded Sino-Japanese interdependence, have weakened the constraints of economic interests on China's Japan policy. China's firm response to Japan's "nationalization" of the disputed Diaoyu/Senkaku Islands in 2012—including the persistence of anti-Japanese nationalism in the Chinese media and the Chinese Coast Guard's frequent presence within the disputed waters surrounding the islands—reflects a significant departure from its past policy of moderation toward the territorial dispute. Reilly thus observes that the rise of the Chinese economy has eroded the contribution of economic interdependence to stable Sino-Japanese relations, suggesting a long-term trend of greater nationalist content in China's Japan policy.

In chapter 7, Chung-in Moon examines South Korea's response to the rise of China. He establishes South Korea's growing dependence on the Chinese economy and its growing cooperation with China to manage North Korean belligerence. Moon observes that the rise of China thus creates strategic pressure on South Korea both to accommodate Chinese interests and to maintain defense cooperation with the United States, and that this policy challenge is exacerbated by politically significant anti-Japanese nationalism in South Korea. The result has been significant South Korean policy instability. The policy swings in South Korea's maneuvering between United States and China from the government of Roh Moo-hyun to that of Lee Myung-bak and then to Park Geun-hye reveal the difficulty that great power competition during a power transition imposes on a small country. Moon shows that U.S. efforts to cooperate with South Korea on missile defense and joint wartime planning have especially complicated Seoul's management of a rising China. Moreover, when South Korean leaders have tried to accommodate U.S. interests in trilateral alliance cooperation with Japan, South Korean domestic politics and anti-Japanese nationalism have blocked South Korean participation. Moon observes that as the U.S.-China competition over South Korea has intensified, there will be ever greater pressure on South Korea to "take sides." Ultimately, despite South Korean preferences to avoid taking sides, should China continue to expand its relative capabilities on the Korean Peninsula and there be unification of north and south, it may be necessary for South Korea to bandwagon with rising China.

In chapters 8 and 9, M. Taylor Fravel and Robert S. Ross examine the impact of the strategic rise of China on U.S.-China competition in Southeast Asia and Northeast Asia, respectively. Fravel addresses the U.S. management of its alliance dilemma in the context of its allies' maritime territorial disputes with China over the Spratly Islands in the South China Sea. Fravel shows that the challenge for the United States has been to respond to China's more active defense of its territorial sovereignty by reassuring its allies of its defense commitments without encouraging its allies to escalate the conflict and entrap the United States in heightened conflict with China, and thus undermine U.S. interests in regional stability and U.S.-China cooperation. This has been especially challenging in U.S.-Philippines relations. The 2012 Sino-Philippine confrontation in the Scarborough Shoal, and China's land reclamation on Chinese-occupied features also claimed by the Philippines in 2014–15, elicited heightened U.S. support for Philippine security. Nonetheless, Fravel observes that the United States has "threaded the needle," avoiding excessive and potentially counterproductive commitments to Philippine security.

In chapter 9, Robert S. Ross similarly examines alliance dynamics in U.S.-China relations in Northeast Asia. He analyzes how each nation has used third-party coercive diplomacy to compel the other to restrain its allies' challenges to great power security. A major objective of U.S. policy toward North Korea and the corresponding tension of the Korean Peninsula has been to compel China to exercise greater control over North Korea's nuclear weapons program. A major objective of Chinese policy toward Japan and the corresponding tension in the East China Sea has been to compel the United States to restrain Japanese challenges to Chinese sovereignty claims in disputed waters in the East China Sea. China and the United States have each confronted the other with the risk of "entrapment" in their respective allies' conflict. For a brief period, third-party coercion contributed to greater U.S.-China cooperation as each country adjusted its policies toward its respective ally, easing regional tension and U.S.-China conflict. But ongoing U.S.-China strategic competition elicited another round of U.S. and Chinese third-party coercion, both in Northeast Asia and in the South China Sea, with renewed great power tension and regional instability. As the rise of China continues and U.S.-China competition increases, the ability of third-party coercion to ease great power tension will likely diminish.

This volume's conclusion offers concluding thoughts regarding the rise of China and the prospects for U.S.-China cooperation and regional stability. There is considerable uncertainty regarding China's long-term trajectory. In

2014–15, China's economic growth rate was in decline and institutional reforms and macroeconomic rebalancing continued to pose significant challenges to China's leaders. Similarly, there is uncertainty regarding the United
States' ability to reduce its national debt and restrain its intervention in
local conflicts outside of East Asia. But should China continue to rise and
the United States sustain its ability to contend over the regional order, the
competition between rising China and status quo United States will intensify.
The great powers, in their effort to defend their regional security interests, will
shape the East Asian order and the prospects for war and peace.

I. POWER AND POLITICS IN THE EAST ASIAN TRANSITION

Domestic Politics and Nationalism in East Asian Security

Randall L. Schweller

A world in transition is a deeply uncertain one for both structural and motivational reasons. Emergent systems tend to encounter destabilizing and unpredictable power shifts among the system's most powerful actors; they also experience changing state motivations associated with relative power positions in flux.[1] Regarding intentions, even if a reasonable amount of certainty could be achieved regarding the present motivations of the rising powers (in today's world, China, India, and—though stumbling of late—Brazil) and those of the incumbents (the European Union, Japan, and the United States), there is no guarantee that current intentions will remain stable over time. Just as we expect people who go from rags to riches (or vice versa) to change their ambitions, rising and declining powers can be expected to expand or contract their goals as power reshuffles at the top of the international pecking order.

Both kinds of uncertainty—*structural* uncertainty about the global distribution of capabilities and *motivational* uncertainty about the goals of rising and established major powers—spring from the taproot of domestic politics. In contemporary East Asia, the rise of China and the emerging transformation of the regional security order have contributed to significant uncertainty and policy instability. But structural uncertainty and the trajectory of a state's power also crucially depend on the kinds of strategies its leaders embrace to mobilize resources (financial, productive, and human) for purposes of national security and economic growth. There is a long tradition within international relations (IR) scholarship of taking into account

---

1. Amrita Narlikar, "Introduction: Negotiating the Rise of New Powers," *International Affairs* 89, no. 3 (2013): 567.

domestic as well as material factors in the specification of national power. Kenneth Waltz himself includes political stability and competence in his list of key capabilities that determine national rankings within the global hierarchy of power.[2]

In terms of motivational uncertainty, variance in state preferences across time and space has long been attributed to domestic politics. Even the purest of systemic theories acknowledge a range of state goals and policies. Sometimes these divergences are explained through reference to system structure: states differently situated within the international system hold dissimilar aims and respond differently to comparable external incentives. Among similarly situated states, however, differences in states' goals and responses to external cues are explained not by international structure but rather by domestic politics. Specifically, national political processes serve as "imperfect" transmission belts (intervening variables) that introduce deviations (residual variance) from the predictions of systemic theory regarding rational responses to external constraints and opportunities.[3] East Asian states are subject to structural constraints and shifting distribution of capabilities, but—as the various contributions to this volume point out—their responses to the rise of China differ.

Theories of domestic politics locate the determinants of foreign policy behavior and the national interest within the state itself. They are typically stories about how internal social and political pressures hold sway over the administrative and decision-making apparatuses of the state, causing a variety of state actions and goals that may or may not be responses to external stimuli. Variation in state goals is also a consequence of how elites frame national interests and demands in different ways for different audiences.[4]

Domestic politics are particularly salient in a changing world. This is because the political environments that develop during global transitions are populated and defined by emerging powers that, though expected to show competitive international faces, are more inward-looking, if not wholly distracted by domestic politics, than outwardly focused. After all, sudden and dramatic national growth induces massive social and political dislocations. As a nation grows, therefore, it becomes increasingly essential for its leaders, continuously mediating between their national societies and the international economy, to periodically recalibrate the balance between citi-

2. Kenneth N. Waltz, *Theory of International Politics* (Reading, MA: Addison-Wesley, 1979), 131.

3. Andrew Moravcsik, "Introduction: Integrating International and Domestic Theories of International Bargaining," in *Double-Edged Diplomacy: International Bargaining and Domestic Politics*, ed. Peter B. Evans, Harold K. Jacobson, and Robert D. Putnam (Berkeley: University of California Press, 1993), 9.

4. See, for instance, Shaun Breslin, "China and the Global Order: Signalling Threat or Friendship?" *International Affairs* 89, no. 3 (2013): 615–34.

zens, states, and markets as they simultaneously encourage stable and sustained growth.[5]

We see the primacy of domestic politics in the present world transformation—one driven largely by developments in the political landscape of East Asia, which is being fashioned largely by the domestic politics of the major regional players. Consider the politics of China as it tries to manage the international challenges of its rise. Since late 2012 it has experienced a once-in-a-decade leadership transition, slowing growth, and a show trial that sentenced one of the country's best-known political personalities, Bo Xilai, to life imprisonment.[6] China's leaders understand that they must initiate sweeping domestic reforms to tackle three key internally generated problems: corruption, debt, and pollution.

Japan, for its part, has seen its politics stirred by resurgent nationalism in recent years, partly as a response to China's rise and growing assertiveness. Led since 2012 by an overtly nationalist prime minister, Shinzo Abe, Japan has pursued a far more assertive, nationalist foreign policy—one that persistently stokes patriotic fervor, expresses hawkish pride in Japan's national strength, and argues that the country has behaved no differently from any other colonial power in the last century.[7] Predictably, Japan's relations with its neighbors, especially China and South Korea, have deteriorated. In addition, Japan, like China, faces serious internal challenges that must be dealt with in the coming years. Most important, Japan is the "grayest" country in the history of the earth. Its workforce is barely over 50 percent of its population, and these workers must not only support themselves and their children but also Japan's retirees, who comprise a whopping 40 percent of the country's population. The author Bill Emmott got it right back in 1989, when he noted of Japanese economic power that the sun also sets.[8]

Meanwhile, the United States is trying to reconcile its desire to preserve American hegemony in the face of a rising China and dangerously high national debt, a war-weary public, and dwindling domestic support for anything international, much less foreign entanglements—all of which has forced the administration of President Barack Obama to develop a low-cost model for U.S. global management. In practice this means relying on

5. See Gregory Chin and Ramesh Thakur, "Will China Change the Rules of Global Order?" *Washington Quarterly* 33, no. 4 (2010): 119–38.

6. Bo's wife, Gu Kailai, received a suspended death sentence for murdering British businessman Neil Heywood.

7. See David Pilling, *Bending Adversity: Japan and the Art of Survival* (New York: Penguin, 2014); and Margarita Estévez-Abe, "Feeling Triumphalist in Tokyo: The Real Reasons Nationalism Is Back in Japan," *Foreign Affairs* 93, no. 3 (2014): 165.

8. Bill Emmott's *The Sun Also Sets* was a runaway best seller in Japan when the Japanese translation first appeared in 1991. Unlike most "scholarly" observers, normal Japanese citizens rightly sensed that something was amiss. See Bill Emmott, *The Sun Also Sets: The Limits to Japan's Economic Power* (New York: Touchstone, 1989).

economic sanctions to punish enemies, targeting terrorists with drones, fighting wars with robots and computerized weapons, avoiding unilateralism in favor of "leading from behind," and pivoting to Asia within an overall grand strategy of "selective engagement" and balancing China.[9] It also means lots of setbacks for valued U.S. foreign policy projects, as well as dubious prospects for the few "achievements" that the administration claims to have made. Most glaringly, neither of the two principal presidential candidates—Hillary Clinton and Donald Trump—supported the Trans-Pacific Partnership signed by the United States and eleven other countries on February 4, 2016, even though it has been forcefully promoted by the Obama administration as a landmark trade deal that undergirds America's strategic pivot to Asia.[10]

And reminiscent of HBO's fantasy drama *Game of Thrones*, court politics at the apex of the ruling dictatorship in North Korea took a brutal turn with the execution of Jang Song-thaek, the uncle of North Korean leader Kim Jong-un and the regime's number two man, for treason. North Korea's supreme leader has ordered the killing of no fewer than seventy officials since he came to power in 2011, according to the South Korean intelligence service. In a particularly disturbing show of Kim Jong-un's brutality, the country's defense minister, Hyon Yong Chol, was killed by firing squad using an antiaircraft gun at a military school in front of hundreds of people in Pyongyang on April 30, 2015, after the regime accused him of treason for "dozing off" during a military event.

In addition to reaffirming reports about Kim's ruthlessness and, perhaps, reducing the Obama administration's strategic patience with Pyongyang, these executions have heightened Beijing's worries about North Korean stability. One might expect that China's leadership would be even less willing to take a tough stance with Pyongyang (on, for instance, denuclearization) for fear of further destabilizing its leadership, possibly leading to the collapse of the North Korean state along its border.[11] Nevertheless, in

9. Mark Leonard, "Why Convergence Breeds Conflict: Growing More Similar Will Push China and the United States Apart," *Foreign Affairs* 92, no. 5 (2013): 130–31.

10. See Howard Koplowitz, "TPP Agreement: Where Do 2016 Presidential Candidates Stand on the Trans-Pacific Partnership?" *International Business Times*, May 12, 2015, http://www.ibtimes.com/tpp-agreement-where-do-2016-presidential-candidates-stand-trans-pacific-partnership-1918946; "TPP Trade Deal 'a Disaster,' Other Countries will 'Dupe' US—Donald Trump," *RT*, May 11, 2015, https://www.rt.com/usa/257377-tpp-deal-trump-criticism/; Dan Merica and Eric Bradner, "Hillary Clinton Comes Out against TPP Trade Deal," CNN Politics, October 7, 2015, http://www.cnn.com/2015/10/07/politics/hillary-clinton-opposes-tpp/index.html.

11. Chinese foreign minister Wang Yi stressed that China would never allow chaos or conflict on the Korean Peninsula, asserting that "China is serious on this." Wang Yi, quoted in Michael R. Gordon, "China Set to Press North Korea Further on Nuclear Aims, Kerry Says," *New York Times*, February 15, 2014.

March 2016 the fifteen-member United Nations Security Council passed Resolution 2270, condemning North Korea for its January 6 nuclear test and February 7 missile launch. Negotiated for weeks by American and Chinese officials, the language of the new resolution greatly expands the breadth and depth of previous resolutions (1695, 1718, 1874, 2087, and 2094) on North Korea, undermining the nation's ability to raise money and secure technology and other resources for its nuclear weapons program.[12] The resolution's impact will, however, ultimately depend on the political will of UN member states, particularly China, to enforce implementation.

Returning to the larger point, the magnitude of internal pressures being exerted on—and aggravated by—the political leaders of China, Japan, North Korea, and the United States makes it a good bet that domestic politics will play a significant, if not decisive, role in shaping the patterns of their foreign policies and, by extension, the dynamics of East Asian regional security.

The rest of this chapter unfolds as follows. I begin by exploring the kinds of causal explanations that are classified under the rubric of second-image theories. This is followed by analysis of how these various causal schemes can play themselves out in a regional security setting (in this case, how China's assertiveness may be the result of any one domestic political factor or a combination of them). Next, the chapter investigates the domestic determinants of state power and interests, with a special focus on nationalism. With respect to China, nationalism interacts with its growing power and status to produce a "double whammy" effect: an increasingly assertive foreign policy regardless of whether its rise continues or stalls. After surveying the various ways that domestic politics can generate aggressive foreign policies that ratchet up interstate conflict, I then consider the potential pacifying effects of domestic politics. The chapter then moves to analysis of how nationalism makes it easier for leaders to mobilize public support for military preparation and sacrifices associated with military buildups (here, nationalism promotes internal balancing behavior).[13] Conversely, nationalism and associated historical enmities interact with aspects of regional multipolarity to constrain China's rivals from aligning with each other to maintain their

---

12. Specifically, the resolution calls for inspecting all cargo going in and out of the country, banning all weapons trade, and expanding the list of individuals confronting sanctions. See Louis Charbonneau and Michelle Nichols, "UN Imposes Harsh New Sanctions on North Korea over Its Nuclear Program," Reuters, March 3, 2016, http://www.reuters.com/article /us-northkorea-nuclear-un-idUSKCN0W41Z2; Scott A. Snyder, "North Korea: Will the New Sanctions Work? On Paper, They Represent a Significant Increase in Pressure on Pyongyang," Diplomat, March 6, 2016, http://thediplomat.com/2016/03/north-korea-will-the-new -sanctions-work/.

13. States can balance internally through the buildup of their own national and autonomous military capabilities, and externally through coalitions that aggregate their capabilities with those of their allies.

security (here, nationalism inhibits external balancing behavior).[14] These "alliance handicaps," to use George Liska's term, considerably reduce the structural flexibility typically associated with multipolarity within the Asia-Pacific regional system and thereby explain the puzzling absence of a coalition to counterbalance a rising and increasingly assertive China.[15] I conclude with a brief discussion of how a clash of nationalisms in East Asia will likely unfold in the coming decade.

What Are Second-Image Explanations?

Second-image explanations are distinguished from third-image theories in two fundamental ways: they either loosen the third-image assumption of states as unitary-rational actors, opening up the "black box" to focus on what is going on inside the state, or they claim that different regime types or domestic structures cause significant variations in foreign policy responses, such that states should not be treated as billiard balls that respond to external stimuli in precisely the same ways.

When second-image variables define international relations, the overall story of international (or regional) politics will not be simple, straightforward, or even coherent from the big-picture perspective. Instead, international politics will be the fractured product of many individual and often quite complex story lines—some embedded in partisan politics, others in domestic structures and cultural values, and still others in ideas, trials, and experiences that may have occurred decades or even centuries ago.

Sometimes the decisive impact of domestic politics on international relations is obvious. What else could explain, for instance, the annual U.S.-China Human Rights Dialogue? At the completion of the most recent discussion, now in its eighteenth round, the United States government claimed to be "deeply concerned" that "Chinese authorities had tried to silence activists by targeting their family members and associates." Clearly there is no geopolitical reason for U.S. concern about how China treats its dissidents, and no compulsion in the external environment responsible for the Obama administration's uneasiness, if not alarm, over China's human rights record. For Chinese government authorities, of course, democratic activism is of great concern because of its potential domestic ramifications. During the conference, the state-run news media featured commentary from the official Xinhua news agency warning that if China embraced the democratic ideas being promoted by its liberal dissidents, the nation would undergo tur-

14. See Zoltán Búzás, "Nationalism and Balancing: The Case of East Asia," unpublished manuscript, McGill University Centre for International Peace and Security Studies, 2014.
15. George Liska, *Nations in Alliance* (Baltimore: Johns Hopkins University Press, 1962).

moil worse than that suffered by the Soviet Union after the collapse of communism; the commentary accused liberal intellectuals of "blatantly inciting
the public to serve as cannon fodder for triggering social turmoil in China"
and "creating Apocalyptic visions of China's imminent collapse and vilify-
ing the present socialist system."[16]

At other times, the effects of domestic politics are more complex, involving multiple domestic actors and causal chains composed of many
links. This is often the case for second-image theories that emphasize the
redistributive aspects of grand strategic choices, highlighting the pressures
within the state rather than the pushes and pulls *outside* it. This inside-out
approach typical of all domestic politics theories starts with the premise
that a leader's foreign policy choices are often constrained and sometimes
distorted by societal interests (e.g., those of bankers, industrialists, mer-
chants, interest groups, and the general public) that have a stake in the
nation's foreign policy.[17]

Statistical studies have shown that nations undergoing regime transitions
from authoritarianism toward democracy are most likely (compared with
stable autocracies and stable democracies) to initiate conflict with their
neighbors.[18] The reason for this rather counterintuitive finding is that demo-
cratizing states typically undergo a combustible process of rapid mass participation before effective democratic institutions have emerged to handle the
enormous pressures for political participation. With democracy taking place
in the streets (akin to mobocracy) rather than within institutionalized channels, elites resort to militant nationalist appeals in an attempt to mobilize
and steer mass support without surrendering their grip on power.

We may be seeing just such a dangerous dynamic playing itself out in
China over the next decade or so. According to David M. Lampton, China is
experiencing a tectonic shift: the pluralization and fracturing of its society,
economy, and bureaucracy, making it progressively more challenging for
China's leaders to govern.[19] The Beijing government's job is made all the
more difficult by "more densely packed urban populations, rapidly rising
aspirations, the spread of knowledge, and the greater ease of coordinating social action" as well as "by the lack of institutions that would articulate

16. Jane Perlez, "Chinese Journalist Detained in Beijing, One Day after Human Rights Talk with U.S.," *New York Times*, August 3, 2013.

17. See, for instance, Peter Trubowitz, *Politics and Strategy: Partisan Ambition and American Statecraft* (Princeton, NJ: Princeton University Press, 2011).

18. Edward D. Mansfield and Jack Snyder, "Democratization and the Danger of War," *International Security* 20, no. 1 (Summer 1995): 5–38; Edward D. Mansfield and Jack L. Snyder, "Democratic Transitions, Institutional Strength, and War," *International Organization* 56, no. 2 (2002): 297–337; and Edward D. Mansfield and Jack Snyder, *Electing to Fight: Why Emerging Democracies Go to War* (Cambridge, MA: MIT Press, 2005).

19. David M. Lampton, "How China Is Ruled: Why It's Getting Harder for Beijing to Govern," *Foreign Affairs* 93, no. 1 (2014): 74–84.

various interests, impartially adjudicate conflicts among them, and ensure the responsible and just implementation of policy."[20] A China characterized by a weaker state and a stronger but more diffuse society will require substantial political reform that includes more reliable "rule of law" mechanisms to resolve conflicts, accommodate various interests, and distribute scarce resources.

Currently, the Chinese Communist Party legitimizes its rule less on communist principles than on continued prosperity and the avoidance of social chaos, combined with appeals to nationalism. Yet as Aaron Friedberg points out, "If economic progress falters, the present government will have little choice but to lean even more heavily on nationalist appeals as its sole remaining source of support. It may also be inclined to resort to assertive external policies as a way of rallying the Chinese people and turning their energies and frustrations outward, most likely toward Taiwan or Japan or the United States, rather than inward, toward Beijing."[21] This threatening scenario would likely be realized if China continues to pluralize and fracture but fails to build the institutions and norms required for responsible and just government at home and constructive behavior abroad. Indeed, as China goes down this path, the stage will be set for the kind of hypernationalist rhetoric and reckless foreign policies that have taken root in all other great powers similarly afflicted by cartelized politics and fragmented societies.

The Second Image, State Intentions, and Regional Security

In a hypothetical world driven entirely by structural-systemic causes, there would be no uniquely American, Chinese, Japanese, Russian, or Swiss explanations for these countries' behaviors or foreign policy preferences. It is a world driven by massively intense structural incentives and constraints consistent with Arnold Wolfers's famous "house on fire" and "racetrack" analogies, where external compulsion determines behavior.[22] Structural theories of this kind must posit strict situational determinism—a "straitjacket" or "single exit" notion of international structure—that leaves actors with no other choice but to act as they did, such that no outcome can occur other than the one predicted by the theory.[23]

20. Ibid., 83.
21. Aaron Friedberg, "The Future of U.S.-China Relations: Is Conflict Inevitable?" *International Security* 30, no. 2 (2005): 30.
22. Arnold Wolfers, *Discord and Collaboration: Essays on International Politics* (Baltimore: Johns Hopkins University Press, 1962).
23. Spiro J. Latsis, "Situational Determinism in Economics," *British Journal for the Philosophy of Science* 23 (1972): 207–45.

The emergence of powerful aggressors—states that make security scarce and war appear inevitable—raises the temperature to the point where we can speak of compulsion in the external environment. In other words, third-image factors explain why people within the burning house rush to its exits. In terms of international politics, the third image provides a straight-forward prediction for how states can be expected to respond to powerful aggressors: they will build arms and form alliances to counterbalance them. Notice that the third image does not tell us how the house got on fire in the first place nor explain the actions of those who do not rush to leave the house, perhaps because they do not perceive it to be on fire. These explanations are to be found in causes that reside within the second and first images.

The second image explains how the house got on fire—that is, why certain states at certain times have expansionist aims and will threaten war to achieve those goals. Because regional security is largely a matter of the intentions of powerful states in the neighborhood and because these intentions are forged by second-image factors, assessments of the degree of security within a region are typically rooted in domestic-level causes. The key questions for regional security are: Do powerful states within the region, especially rising ones, have revisionist aims? Are they limited or unlimited? Are they assuming an aggressive or peaceful posture in their foreign relations? Are their grievances perceived by other powerful states within the region as legitimate or illegitimate? Can they be satisfied peacefully and without harm to the security of others within the region?

To see the significance of domestic politics with respect to how the house gets on fire, consider China's foreign policy over the past twenty years and its effects on regional security. Starting in the early 1990s, the core tenets of China's grand strategy emerged from Deng Xiaoping's famous "lie low, hide our capacities, and bide our time" doctrine. Consistent with this doctrine, Chinese grand strategy sought to reassure other countries about Beijing's intentions, thereby preempting any counterbalancing motives and actions against China. One of the keys to this strategy was the Chinese government's effective efforts to ensure that its foreign policy was not driven by emotional nationalist rhetoric.

From 2009 to 2010, however, a consensus emerged among Western pundits that Chinese foreign policy has taken a more strident turn in bilateral, regional, and international contexts. Discussion of China's rise among both Chinese and foreign observers (especially among U.S. analysts and media) has been dominated by the theme of a newly assertive China—one that as it grows economically and militarily more powerful becomes more comfortable politically in revealing its "true colors."[24] Some claim that China has

---

24. For examples of this type of commentary, see Michael Swaine, "Perceptions of an Assertive China," *China Leadership Monitor* 32 (2010): 10n1.

begun to assume an offensive grand strategic posture—one that arguably seeks to expand the nation's relative power, influence, and status in the world. Moreover, the "assertiveness pundits" claim that the Chinese government has been more willing to follow popular nationalist calls to confront Western powers and adopt tougher measures in maritime territorial disputes with its neighbors.[25] Typifying this new assertiveness, in November 2013 China unilaterally declared an Air Defense Identification Zone over an area of the East China Sea that covers the Senkakus, the uninhabited islands administered by Japan but claimed by China, where they are called Diaoyu. The move drew sharp criticism from both Tokyo and Washington. In its annual defense white paper, Japan's Ministry of Defense warned that China is "attempting to alter the status quo by coercive measures," including "dangerous acts that could cause unintended consequences," ratcheting up tensions in the East China Sea that could trigger an unwanted clash.[26]

Explanations of China's new assertiveness have focused on both international structure and China's domestic politics—that is, on both third-image and second-image causes. Regarding international structure, pundits claim that in the wake of the 2008 financial crisis, Chinese leaders perceived a dramatic shift in the global balance of power—an unprecedented transfer of power and wealth from west to east and south.[27] The perceived decline of American power and the onset of a more multipolar world, so the argument goes, have emboldened Chinese leaders to be "more confident in ignoring Deng Xiaoping's longtime axiom not to treat the United States as an adversary, and in challenging the United States on China's interests."[28] Here China's new assertiveness is consistent with the classical realist principle that nations expand their political interests abroad when their relative power increases. Or as Robert Gilpin explains the dynamic correlation between power and the national interest, "The Realist law of uneven growth implies that as the power of a group or state increases, that group or state will be tempted to try to increase its control over the environment. In order to increase its own security, it will try to expand its political, economic, and territorial control, it will try to change the international system in accordance

25. For examples, see Alastair Iain Johnston, "How New and Assertive Is China's New Assertiveness?" *International Security* 37, no. 4 (2013): 7–48. Johnston challenges the validity of the dominant "new assertiveness" view, which he claims has "gone viral" in the U.S. media, the blogosphere, and in scholarly work.

26. Japanese Ministry of Defense, *Defense of Japan 2014: Annual White Paper* (Tokyo: Japanese Ministry of Defense, 2014), http://www.mod.go.jp/e/publ/w_paper/pdf/2014/DOJ2014_1-1-0_1st_0730.pdf.

27. Swaine, "Perceptions of an Assertive China," 2.

28. Johnston, "How New and Assertive Is China's New Assertiveness?," 35.

with its particular set of interests."[29] In this view, China's assertiveness is a predictable consequence of its changed (i.e., more exalted) position within the international system.

If China's continued rise is predicted to cause it to behave more assertively, then naturally we should expect decelerated growth to cause it to be more reserved. This is the basic logic of "if X (growth) then Y (assertiveness); if no X (no growth) then no Y (no assertiveness)." Thus, is it safe to assume that unmanageable official corruption, an aging population, and an unsustainable economic model will slow down China's economic growth and, consequently, restrain its behavior and moderate its goals? Unfortunately, there is another, more disturbing possibility: rather than moderating Beijing's assertiveness, economic decline might intensify internal problems, making the Chinese government, for reasons discussed below, more belligerent in its foreign relations and prone to miscalculation. If so, the real danger is not managing China's rise but adjusting to a "new normal" and weathering the nation's eventual decline.

The straightforward logic of "if growth causes assertiveness, then decline causes moderation" is confounded by causes rooted in both the second and third images. At the international systemic level of analysis, history is riddled with cases of declining nations lashing out because they perceived long-term trends were against them. At the domestic level, incompetent leaders have routinely whipped up hypernationalism (national paranoia and fear of external enemies) to blunt internal opposition and distract the public's attention from the regime's economic mismanagement and other failings. This is the familiar "scapegoat hypothesis" or diversionary war theory, which takes a decidedly second-image view of a nation's foreign policy. The causal scheme goes essentially as follows: A severe economic crisis or downturn causes social unrest at home. Threatened by mass discontent and antigovernment hostility, the ruling regime tries to shore up its domestic support by searching for enemies (an out-group to target) in an attempt to (1) divert the public's attention away from the government's poor performance (its inability to solve the country's economic troubles) and (2) gain in-group solidarity and a rally-around-the-flag effect. Seen in this light, China's tough diplomacy stemmed not from confidence in its military and economic strength but from a deep sense of insecurity. As Robert Ross explains, faced with the challenges of "nerve-racking years of financial crisis and social unrest" and "no longer able to count on easy support based on the country's economic growth," China's leaders moved to sustain their popular legitimacy by appeasing an

29. Robert Gilpin, *War and Change in World Politics* (Cambridge: Cambridge University Press, 1981), 94–95; Fareed Zakaria, *From Wealth to Power: The Unusual Origins of America's World Role* (Princeton, NJ: Princeton University Press, 1998), 19–20.

increasingly nationalist public with gestures of force."[30] Growing unrest and the need to reverse a real crisis of legitimacy gave Beijing "no choice but to appease a growing cadre of hard-line nationalists who wanted to project a tough image of China to the world."[31]

A related domestic view emphasizes the rise of Chinese popular nationalism coupled with the declining legitimacy of the ruling regime. Suisheng Zhao, for instance, argues that China's post-2008 "strident turn" is explained by the convergence of Chinese state nationalism and popular nationalism calling for a more muscular Chinese foreign policy. Zhao notes, "Enjoying an inflated sense of empowerment supported by its new quotient of wealth and military capacities, and terrified of an uncertain future due to increasing social, economic and political tensions at home, the communist state has become more willing to play to the popular nationalist gallery in pursuing the so-called core national interests."[32]

Other second-image studies focus on new interest groups, such as large state-owned oil companies, and their incorporation into the foreign policy-making process.[33] Still other studies focus on changing civil-military relations in China, suggesting that, in the absence of strong central leaders, the People's Liberation Army (PLA) has increased its political influence over the decision-making process.

Nationalism and the Domestic Sources of State Power and Interests

Following the principle of Occam's razor, third-image theories should always be the analyst's first cut at a problem because they provide the most parsimonious and generalizable answers to our questions. When and only when third-image explanations (those at the structural-systemic level) fail to account for the behaviors or outcomes under investigation do we have a "puzzle" that likely requires a second-image—or some unit-level (e.g., intrastate)—variable to explain what is going on. As realists and their critics have pointed out, states do not always respond to threats in ways that realist balance-of-power theory predicts. When this occurs, there is good reason to

30. Robert S. Ross, "The Problem with the Pivot: Obama's New Asia Policy Is Unnecessary and Counterproductive," *Foreign Affairs* 91, no. 6 (2012): 72.

31. Ibid., 75.

32. Suisheng Zhao, "Foreign Policy Implications of Chinese Nationalism Revisited: The Strident Turn," *Journal of Contemporary China* 22, no. 82 (2013): 535.

33. See Yan Sun, *Chinese National Security Decision-Making: Processes and Challenges* (Washington, DC: Brookings Institution, 2013); and Linda Jakobson and Dean Knox, *New Foreign Policy Actors in China*, SIPRI Policy Paper no. 26 (Stockholm: Stockholm International Peace Research Institute, 2010), http://books.sipri.org/files/PP/SIPRIPP26.pdf.

suspect that societal constraints and pressures within the state are responsible for the puzzling behavior. Yet causes rooted in domestic politics (also known as the *Innenpolitik* tradition) are not only useful for explaining behaviors that deviate from realpolitik expectations; they also define and determine the extent of national power and interests, both of which are functions of domestic politics. Indeed, realism, thought by many to be a strictly third-image theory, has always acknowledged the domestic determinants of power and interests. Consider the matter of state power.

A country's size, population, and abundance of resources tell us something about its potential for power on a regional, continental, or world stage. That said, these measures are often poor predictors of a state's power trajectory. To be sure, there is some minimum threshold of material resources that a state must possess in order to have a viable chance of achieving some form of hegemony, whether regional, continental, or global. We may conclude, therefore, that a country's natural endowments will either permit or prevent it from entertaining realistic aspirations for hegemonic (or, simply, great power) status. They do not, however, tell us whether a state will be able to mobilize those resources and do so in a timely manner in order to respond successfully to systemic incentives and opportunities. Nor do they tell us the purposes of state action—that is, whether a nation is willing to pursue a dynamic foreign policy or aspires to some form of political hegemony. For this we need to know something about the internal or domestic makeup of the state; more specifically, we need to know whether or not there are constraints on the development and exercise of the state's potential power and whether there is a national will to amass power.

Classical and offensive realism assume that states, because they operate within a dangerous and uncertain anarchic realm, maximize their security and power (influence, territory, prestige, etc.).[34] Simply put, states expand when they can.[35] Part of "when they can" is international: advantageous moments when power realities—such as the opening of a power vacuum or the weakening of a neighbor—allow the state to expand. The other, mostly overlooked, part of "when they can" is domestic: wars are dangerous and costly undertakings, and prudent leaders can only wage them somewhat safely (in terms of the survival of their regimes, regardless of the outcome) and expect victory when their citizens viscerally identify with the territorial

---

34. For the power-maximizing assumption of classical realism, see Hans J. Morgenthau, *Politics among Nations: The Struggle for Power and Peace*, 4th ed. (New York: Knopf, 1967). For offensive realism, see John J. Mearsheimer, *The Tragedy of Great Power Politics* (New York: Norton, 2001).

35. Gilpin, *War and Change*, 23–24, 94–95. For the assumption of influence maximizing as the primary objective of states, and especially great powers, see Zakaria, *From Wealth to Power*, chap. 2.

nation-state—that is, when they perceive the state as the source of both ob-ligations and, as E. H. Carr noted of the late nineteenth century, benefits.[36]

Consistent with this reasoning, Hans Morgenthau avers, "National char-acter and, above all, national morale and the quality of government, espe-cially in the conduct of foreign affairs, are the most important . . . components of national power."[37] Similarly, Robert Strausz-Hupé concludes, "For the de-terminants of a state's behavior in international politics, realists place greater weight than do idealists on non-material factors, such as patriotism and nationalism."[38] The point is that the accumulation and projection of national power depend on the prior existence of a strong state backed by national will and unity of purpose. National power is partly a matter of territorial size, population, and natural resources. Yet nation-states that are rich in these endowments are not always powerful; a state is only as strong as its ability to extract resources from its society.[39] When we explore the internal workings of states that have failed to reach their full power po-tential, we therefore typically see domestic rot and underdevelopment due to political instability, high debt, mismanagement, corruption, bureaucratic inefficiency, and deep ethnic, religious, and regional cleavages—all of which combine to prevent the state, despite its relative abundance of material re-sources, from extracting and building its capabilities. This rot from within partly explains why we do not see hegemonic bids in the former Third World despite the fact that there is no shortage of eligible candidates.[40]

All of which is to say that the domestic-level counterpart to structural realism, especially in an age of mass politics, is nationalism. Arising in re-sponse to the problems of modernity, nationalism fastened on immutable cultural attributes as the bedrock of a new identity that would endure in times of rapid change. Nationalism, whether as a movement or an ideology, functions, according to John Breuilly, "to bind together people in a particular territory in an endeavor to gain and use state power."[41] Nationalism is, "above and beyond all else, about politics and that politics is about power.

36. Edward Hallett Carr, *Nationalism and After* (New York: Macmillan, 1945).

37. Morgenthau, *Politics among Nations*, 198.

38. Robert Strausz-Hupé, *Democracy and American Foreign Policy: Reflections on the Legacy of Alexis de Tocqueville* (New Brunswick, NJ: Transaction, 1995), 85.

39. See Randall L. Schweller, "Neoclassical Realism and State Mobilization: Expansionist Ideology in the Age of Mass Politics," in *Neoclassical Realism, the State, and Foreign Policy*, ed. Steve Lobell, Jeffrey Taliaferro, and Norrin Ripsman (New York: Cambridge University Press, 2009), 227–50.

40. See, for example, Julius O. Ihonvbere, "Nigeria as Africa's Great Power: Constraints and Prospects for the 1990s," *International Journal* 46, no. 4 (1991): 510–35; and Mohammed Ayoob, "India as Regional Hegemon: External Opportunities and Internal Constraints," *International Journal* 46, no. 4 (1991): 420–48.

41. John Breuilly, *Nationalism and the State*, 2nd ed. (Chicago: University of Chicago Press, 1994), 381.

Power, in the modern world, is principally about control of the state. The central task is to relate nationalism to the objectives of obtaining and using state power."[42] One could not provide a better description of realism at the level of domestic politics.[43] Nationalism is a natural complement to structural realist theory, its domestic-level counterpart.[44] The notion of a constant struggle among nations over issues of power, security, and prestige that animates realism is in no small part a consequence of nationalism, which "fuels interstate rivalry and by its sharp delineation of in- and out-groups, abets status rivalry, accentuates stereotyping, and deepens and perpetuates perceived grievances."[45]

Nationalism and Historical Legacies

Sometimes nationalism—and here I mean not political movements seeking to create nation-states but rather the assertive foreign policies of governments to embellish state power and the formation of public opinion in support of such policies—may be understood as the domestic counterpart of structural realism. At other times it is an unintended consequence of greedy domestic interests fighting over the redistributive issues raised by grand strategy. And still other times, nationalism is a direct outgrowth of national historical legacies.

Chinese nationalism is very much a product of the country's historical legacy "of a long and glorious past, unjust treatment at the hands of foreigners from 1840 to 1949 (and beyond), a desire to regain international respect and equality, an imperative for territorial reunification, and a wish to reaffirm their collective greatness as a people and nation."[46] A shared sense of shame and humiliation with respect to China's experience of having been a playground of foreign (Western and Japanese) intervention and encroachment is a particularly potent driver of Chinese nationalism and its current behavior.[47] Indeed, shame has been a stimulant, a call to action, for generations of

42. Ibid., 1.

43. Oddly, the literature on nationalism rarely, if ever, mentions political realism. For instance, in *Nationalism and the State*, Breuilly relates nationalism to functionalist, communications, Marxist, identity, and psychological approaches. He never once mentions realism, even though his account of nationalism is rooted in state power.

44. See John J. Mearsheimer, "Kissing Cousins: Nationalism and Realism," unpublished manuscript, Yale Workshop on International Relations, May 5, 2011.

45. Steve Chan, *Looking for Balance: China, the United States, and Power Balancing in East Asia* (Stanford, CA: Stanford University Press, 2012), 65.

46. David M. Lampton, *Same Bed, Different Dreams: Managing U.S.-China Relations, 1989–2000* (Berkeley: University of California Press, 2001), 251.

47. See, for instance, Zheng Wang, *Never Forget National Humiliation: Historical Memory in Chinese Politics and Foreign Relations* (New York: Columbia University Press, 2012).

Chinese leaders and intellectuals. Though it may sound odd to most Western ears, feeling shame was (and remains) the path to escape the bitter reality of China's humiliating past. "To feel shame is to approach courage," reads an inscription in the Temple of Tranquil Seas in Nanjing, where China signed one of its most unequal treaties with a foreign power. China "carries the self-image of a 'victim nation,' albeit a nation with aspirations finally on a path toward greatness restored. This victim complex, coupled with China's aspirations and growing power, creates a sense of entitlement—a combination that makes Beijing prickly in its dealing with the United States" and its neighbors.[48]

We see this cantankerous and touchy mood not only in Beijing's increasingly tough diplomacy but in the violent demonstrations over the past several years staged by Chinese nationalists against Japanese companies with operations in China, causing some of those companies to relocate to Vietnam. Today, more than ever, Chinese public displays of nationalism and outrage—whether set off by perceived unfair treatment by the West, U.S.–South Korea naval exercises, or insults from the Japanese—appear genuine rather than manufactured. Moreover, whereas nationalism was traditionally confined primarily to young Chinese and to some soldiers in the PLA, it has spread to Chinese businesspeople, academics, and elite politicians.[49] This diffusion of Chinese nationalism is the product of China's rise and its domestic political system becoming more participative, with different factions fighting among each other, and China's public sphere growing more dynamic, fueled by the Internet and social media. "Beyond the party's control," notes Jayshree Bajoria, "the emergence of the Internet in the last two decades has given nationalists more power to vent their anger after particular incidents. It has also brought the huge Chinese diaspora in places like Indonesia, the Philippines, Malaysia, Europe, and North America, into closer contact with those residing within China's borders," facilitating the continuous flow and escalation of nationalist rhetoric and propaganda.[50] And because social media can be used to organize large-scale, nationalist protests in Beijing and other cities against foreign governments, the continued expansion of information technologies throughout the population promises to accentuate the role of nationalism in Chinese policymaking; it also threatens to raise Chinese nationalism to dangerous and unstable levels of hypernationalism.[51]

48. Lampton, *Same Bed, Different Dreams*, 251–52.

49. Robert S. Ross, "The Domestic Sources of China's 'Assertive Diplomacy,' 2009–10: Nationalism and Chinese Foreign Policy," in *China across the Divide: The Domestic and Global in Politics and Society*, ed. Rosemary Foot (New York: Oxford University Press, 2013), 79.

50. Jayshree Bajoria, "Nationalism in China," Council on Foreign Relations, April 23, 2008, http://www.cfr.org/china/nationalism-china/p16079.

51. See Ross, "The Domestic Sources of China's 'Assertive Diplomacy,'" 80.

Given China's determination to avenge its past, there is every reason to expect that Chinese nationalism will continue to grow in lockstep with the country's increased power. This phenomenon is already evident among Chinese policymakers, military officials, and average citizens. The consensus is that China must eventually become more internationally assertive to the point where it, like the United States, is willing to intervene in the domestic affairs of other countries to protect its far-flung interests abroad.[52] Moreover, some suggest that the goal of global dominance lies at the core of China's journey from humiliation to rejuvenation. The notion of national rejuvenation, according to the conservative Chinese analyst Yan Xuetong, "conjures 'the psychological power' associated with China's rise 'to its former world status.' The concept assumes both that China is recovering its natural position and that this means being the 'number one nation in the world.' "[53]

Some prominent Japanese and Indian observers, however, believe that Chinese nationalism and the growing extroversion of its foreign policy recall Nazi Germany's quest for lebensraum and are similarly driven by a view of the superiority of the Chinese race. Along these lines, Shinzo Abe, in an address delivered to a Washington think tank in October 2010, said that "China's military strategy has rested on the concept of a 'strategic frontier'" since the 1980s, adding, "In a nutshell, this very dangerous idea posits that borders and exclusive economic zones are determined by national power, and that as long as China's economy continues to grow, its sphere of influence will continue to expand. Some might associate this with the German concept of 'lebensraum.' "[54] Likewise, a veteran Indian journalist, Rajinder Puri, called China "a corporate version of Nazi Germany" and posed the question, "Is Nazi China Emerging?"[55] There is little wonder that these perceptions come from Japanese and Indian sources, two countries most sensitive to and potentially harmed by China's growth in power. This raises the fundamental question, are these perceptions being driven by domestic politics inside China (second-image causes) or by changes in the balance of power (third-image causes)? Or, alternately, are third-image variables causing changes in China's domestic politics and shifting the tone of its diplomatic rhetoric in an increasingly nationalist direction (the second image

52. See Leonard, "Why Convergence Breeds Conflict," 129–30.

53. Yan Xuetong, quoted in Jacqueline Newmyer Deal, "China's Nationalist Heritage," *National Interest* 123 (2013), 49.

54. Hudson Institute, "Former Japanese Prime Minister Shinzo Abe on U.S.-Japanese Relations, the Capital Hilton, Washington DC, October 15, 2010: Transcript," http://s3.amazonaws.com/media.hudson.org/files/publications/AbeEventTranscript.pdf.

55. Rajinder Puri, "Is Nazi China Emerging?" *Indian Defence Review*, September 25, 2011, http://www.indiandefencereview.com/spotlights/is-nazi-china-emerging/; Deal, "China's Nationalist Heritage," 45.

reversed)? The next section discusses the second image reversed in a more benign light.

Domestic Politics and Liberal Cosmopolitanism

Thus far I have argued that the intentions and goals of states are largely a function of second-image variables. Domestic politics can explain how nationalist urges sometimes compel the state to accumulate power in a way that overrides prudent foreign policy, resulting in imperial overstretch and self-encirclement. This is a decidedly realist version of domestic politics. On the more positive side, second-image causes are also at work when domestic economic interests quell passions that seek to gin up nasty international politics—that is, when business interests tip the balance of forces within their respective countries toward those in favor of peaceful conflict resolution. This is the familiar "economic interdependence" argument rooted in nineteenth-century Manchester liberalism about how international economic relations affect domestic politics, which, in turn, recast national interests in a more pacific light.

Ironically, these peaceful "political" effects of trade are fully evident in Beijing's avowed reluctance to mix politics with economics in its relations with other countries. For instance, at the height of the anti-Japanese riots of 2005, as nationalist Chinese demonstrators were calling for a boycott of Japanese products and demanding that the Ministry of Railways not import Japanese bullet train technology, minister of commerce Bo Xilai admonished the rioters for linking economic issues with political and diplomatic ones. In a globalized economy, he argued, a boycott of Japanese products would wind up hurting China: "Boycotting products [of another country] will be detrimental to the interests of the producers and consumers of both countries. . . . This will hurt our cooperation and [economic] development with other countries."[56] Here the Chinese Communist Party emphasized the country's gains from trade to defuse a malicious and vindictive political atmosphere. In August 2012 an op-ed in *China Daily* similarly warned, "Blindly boycotting Japanese goods by giving way to sentiments could harm our own industries and exports, and reduce employment."[57] Indeed, Japan remains China's largest source of imports and foreign investment; take away this Japanese input and China's export markets collapse. Thus, if the theory of economic interdependence is correct, the logic of "mutual

---

56. Bo Xilai, quoted in Willy Lam, "As China's Foreign Policy Hardens, It Is Beijing versus All," AsiaNews.it, July 4, 2012, http://www.asianews.it/news-en/As-China's-foreign-policy -hardens,-it-is-Beijing-versus-all-25192.html.

57. Op-ed, *China Daily*, quoted in Richard Katz, "Mutual Assured Production: Why Trade Will Limit Conflict between China and Japan," *Foreign Affairs* 92, no. 4 (2013): 24.

assured production" will continue to limit conflict between China and Japan.[58]

During the 1960s and 1970s, studies of international interdependence focused exclusively on ways that greater economic links among countries altered the nature of world politics by changing the context and alternatives facing countries.[59] Beginning in the late 1970s, a new but related literature argued that international forces could decisively shape not only the external environment in which countries operate but also the internal politics of states. By affecting the interests, power, and coalitions that form in domestic politics, international interdependence exerts a significant influence on the internal politics, and hence on the foreign policies and definition of interests, of countries both large and small. This is what IR theorists call a "second-image reversed" version of the relationship between internal and external politics—one that is not simply an inside-out view but rather follows an outside-inside-out logic.[60]

In his influential work *National Power and the Structure of Foreign Trade*, Albert Hirschman described such a process in terms of the political influence effect of trade. Simply put, large and growing trade relations between big and small states will eventually change the way the smaller state conceives of its national interests, which will gradually and over time converge with those of its larger partner. Business groups, Hirschman observed, "will exert a powerful influence in favor of a 'friendly' attitude toward the state" upon which their economic interests depend.[61] On precisely how trade relations bring about foreign policy convergence, Jonathan Kirshner notes that

58. Ibid.

59. Richard Cooper, *The Economics of Interdependence* (New York: McGraw-Hill for the Council on Foreign Relations, 1968); Richard Cooper, "Economic Interdependence and Foreign Policy in the Seventies," *World Politics* 24, no. 2 (1972): 159–81; Richard Rosecrance and Arthur Stein, "Interdependence: Myth or Reality?" *World Politics* 26, no. 4 (1973): 1–27; Peter J. Katzenstein, "International Interdependence: Some Long-Term Trends and Recent Changes," *International Organization* 29, no. 4 (1975): 1021–34; and Robert O. Keohane and Joseph S. Nye, *Power and Interdependence: World Politics in Transition* (Boston: Little, Brown, 1977). See also Karl W. Deutsch and Alexander Eckstein, "National Industrialization and the Decline of the International Economic Sector, 1890–1957," *World Politics* 13, no. 2 (1961): 267–99. Deutsch and Eckstein found that the ratio of foreign trade to national income for seventeen countries peaked in 1913, sharply declined in the 1930s, and did not return to pre-1914 levels despite all efforts to expand international trade in the 1950s. They concluded that the foreign trade ratio may rise during the early stages of industrialization but decline significantly at a later intermediate stage, possibly rising once again at very high levels of economic development.

60. Peter Gourevitch, "The Second Image Reversed: The International Sources of Domestic Politics," *International Organization* 32, no. 4 (1978): 881–912; Peter J. Katzenstein, ed., *Between Power and Plenty: Foreign Economic Policies in Advanced Industrial States* (Madison: University of Wisconsin Press, 1978); Robert O. Keohane and Helen V. Milner, eds., *Internationalization and Domestic Politics* (Cambridge: Cambridge University Press, 1996).

61. Albert O. Hirschman, *National Power and the Structure of Foreign Trade* (Berkeley: University of California Press, 1980 [1945]), 29.

"when these relationships are sustained, and especially when they involve expanding sectors of the economy, over time the reshuffling of power, interests, and incentives among firms, sectors, and political coalitions will increasingly reflect these new realities. Those that favor warm relations will be empowered, and the trajectory of the 'national interest' remolded."[62] Of course, the warming effects of economic interdependence do not always triumph, as World War I infamously confirmed. But they do raise the costs of letting emotions steer the ship of state.

To Balance or Bandwagon?

If trade patterns largely determine countries' foreign policies, then states in East Asia might be expected to bandwagon with China.[63] Then again, the opposite might happen. The claim that trade "multiplies the occasions for conflicts that may promote resentment and even war" has been made often enough by self-proclaimed realists.[64] Thus, Dale Copeland points out, "interdependence—meaning mutual dependence and thus vulnerability—gives states an incentive to initiate war, if only to ensure continued access to necessary materials and goods."[65] More generally, realists claim that economic interdependence exerts only weak effects on states, "sometimes good, providing the benefits of divided labor, mutual understanding, and cultural enrichment, and sometimes bad, leading to protectionism, mutual resentment, conflict, and war."[66] The effects of economic interdependence are weak because, like politics, all economics is local. Even in today's global economy, "protectionism is alive and well," assert Ian Bremmer and Nouriel Roubini, because leaders well understand that "there is no collective economic security in a globalized economy," and so they "must worry first and foremost about growth and jobs at home."[67] No matter how intense the constraints imposed on governments by the logic of globalization, domestic

62. Jonathan Kirshner, "The Consequences of China's Economic Rise for Sino-U.S. Relations: Rivalry, Political Conflict, and (Not) War," in *China's Ascent: Power, Security, and the Future of International Politics*, ed. Robert S. Ross and Zhu Feng (Ithaca, NY: Cornell University Press, 2008), 242. See also Rawi Abdelal and Jonathan Kirshner, "Strategy, Economic Relations, and the Definition of National Interests," *Security Studies* 9, no. 1 (1999): 123–62.

63. See Sarah Kreps and Gustavo Flores-Macías, "The Foreign Policy Consequences of Trade: China's Commercial Relations with Africa and Latin America, 1992–2006," *Journal of Politics* 75, no. 2 (2013): 357–71.

64. Kenneth N. Waltz, "Structural Realism after the Cold War," *International Security* 25, no. 1 (2000): 14.

65. Dale C. Copeland, "Economic Interdependence and War: A Theory of Trade Expectations," *International Security* 20, no. 4 (1996): 6.

66. Waltz, "Structural Realism after the Cold War," 15.

67. Ian Bremmer and Nouriel Roubini, "A G-Zero World: The New Economic Club Will Produce Conflict, Not Cooperation," *Foreign Affairs* 90, no. 2 (2011): 7.

politics in the economic sphere reign supreme—at least, during normal times.[68] If and when an external threat emerges, however, national economic policy becomes too serious a business to be steered either by the impersonal forces of the global market or by the interest-group politics characteristic of a functioning laissez-faire society.[69] Rather, the potential incompatibility of public and private interests compels the state to intervene when the interests of domestic actors diverge from its own and those of the nation as a whole.[70]

If, as realists contend, issues of national security more than those of commerce drive countries' foreign policies, then we might expect states in East Asia to start balancing aggressively against China. Arguing that China's neighbors are more leery of its military rise than they are enticed by the potential economic benefits of foreign policy cooperation, Robert Ross finds that "economic capabilities alone are insufficient to generate accommodation" among dominant and subordinate states.[71] And thus, as China's military strength and power projection capabilities grow, security concerns among countries doing business with China, Ross predicts, will increasingly outweigh the benefits of trade, making states in East Asia more likely to balance than to accommodate China.

At this point in time, the debate over whether countries in East Asia will balance against or bandwagon with China is somewhat miscast. They will do both. In a region of great uncertainty, hedging strategies that combine combative and cooperative aspects will prevail.[72] The more central question is, can a regional system composed of states rationalized by nationalism be anything other than an inherently bellicose one?

Nationalism and Internal Balancing against China

According to structural realism, all states derive a general strategic interest from the structural condition of anarchy in counterbalancing the growing

68. The classic study is E. E. Schattschneider, *Politics, Pressures and the Tariff: A Study of Free Private Enterprise in Pressure Politics, as Shown in the 1929–1930 Revision of the Tariff* (New York: Prentice Hall, 1935).

69. For an impressive rebuttal to this claim, see Kevin Narizny, *The Political Economy of Grand Strategy* (Ithaca, NY: Cornell University Press, 2007).

70. Jonathan Kirshner, "The Political Economy of Realism," in *Unipolar Politics: Realism and State Strategies after the Cold War*, ed. Ethan Kapstein and Michael Mastanduno (New York: Columbia University Press, 1999), 73–75. Kirshner goes on to say that, according to realists, states "aim to establish and preserve their independence from three encroachments: those of particular domestic interests, other states, and economic forces" (75).

71. Robert Ross, "Balance of Power Politics and the Rise of China: Accommodation and Balancing in East Asia," *Security Studies* 15, no. 3 (2006): 368.

72. For hedging strategies, see Øystein Tunsjø, *Security and Profit in China's Energy Policy: Hedging against Risk* (New York: Columbia University Press, 2013).

power of a neighboring rival—especially one that appears to be bidding for regional domination. Such systemic pressures, however, must be filtered through intervening variables at the unit level. This is why neoclassical realists stress the influence of domestic politics on states' ability and willingness to undertake balancing policies. Some unit-level factors assist balancing behaviors; others impede them.

The few studies that explicitly examine the impact of nationalism on balancing find that the two phenomena complement each other. Several scholars go so far as to posit nationalism as a necessary condition for balancing behavior. For instance, Steve Chan opines, "It is not difficult to imagine that whenever and wherever sovereignty and nationalism have receded (as in contemporary Western Europe) or have never taken root (as in international systems in the pre-modern era), the motivation for undertaking balancing behavior would be more muted if not entirely removed. Conversely, wherever nationalism and sovereignty still hold strong sway (such as in contemporary East Asia), balancing behavior should be more likely."[73]

Nationalism exerts profound effects on various pivotal aspects of international politics that are essential to the realist enterprise. Key for our present purposes is nationalism's role in extracting resources from society to enhance state power. Leaders use nationalism to mobilize public support for military preparation and sacrifices. Indeed, the theory that states purposefully foster nationalism to facilitate internal balancing may be generalized to apply "to any security competition that involves 'mass mobilization,' that is, requires of society a large-scale financial, organizational, and industrial effort to produce a great military force of any kind, on sea or even in the air as well as on land."[74] Moreover, as Zoltán Búzás points out, "nationalism seems expedient for mitigating the domestic impediments to effective balancing. Through appeals to shared collective identity and common interests in the security of state and nation, nationalism can alleviate domestic causes of underbalancing, such as domestic fragmentation."[75]

Until 2013, Japanese military policy in response to the rising Chinese threat could be characterized as underbalancing, defined as a situation in which threatened countries either (1) fail to recognize a clear and present danger; or, more typically, (2) simply do not react to it; or, more typically still, (3) respond in paltry and imprudent ways.[76] Japan falls mostly into the third

73. Chan, *Looking for Balance*, 65.

74. Barry R. Posen, "Nationalism, the Mass Army, and Military Power," *International Security* 18, no. 2 (1993): 122–23.

75. Búzás, "Nationalism and Balancing," 2. For underbalancing, see Randall L. Schweller, "Unanswered Threats: A Neoclassical Realist Theory of Underbalancing," *International Security* 29, no. 2 (2004): 159–201; and Randall L. Schweller, *Unanswered Threats: Political Constraints on the Balance of Power* (Princeton, NJ: Princeton University Press, 2006).

76. Schweller, "Unanswered Threats," 159.

category. As Christopher Hughes noted in 2012, the reliance of Japan's grand strategy on the United States "has merely delayed addressing the long-term challenges of a rising China, Korean Peninsula instability, developments in East Asian regionalism, and a multipolarizing international system. Moreover, Japan's dependence on the United States is likely to be unsustainable in any case, as U.S. power progressively wanes in the Asia-Pacific region, thus only enhancing Japan's desperation that it has been constrained from fully articulating a complementary or alternative grand strategy."[77]

Meanwhile, China has been operating under the presumption of maritime military clashes, modernizing its equipment, bolstering its fleet of new lightweight warships, and preparing to launch its first domestically built aircraft carrier in the early 2020s.[78] These are worrying developments for Japan. Though Tokyo increasingly fears that Beijing could achieve military superiority, Japan is saddled with a stagnating economy, making it difficult for the country to compete with China in a real arms race.[79]

Recently, however, there are signs that Japan is shifting from a restrained hedging posture to one—in accordance with the predictions of structural realism—that looks more like "internal" balancing. The key domestic factor facilitating this shift in grand strategy is the resurgent nationalism of Japanese politics.[80] For almost seven decades, Japan's pacifist public opinion appeared as an immutable roadblock, obstructing the grander ambitions of policymakers who would otherwise push outward Japan's military role.[81] To override these antimilitaristic norms, the Abe administration has leaned on aggressive nationalism to garner domestic support for its systematic dismantlement of the postwar constraints on Japan's exercise of military power, including breaches in 2014 of the ban on the exercise of collective self-defense,

77. Christopher W. Hughes, "The Democratic Party of Japan's New (but Failing) Grand Security Strategy: From 'Reluctant Realism' to 'Resentful Realism'?," *Journal of Japanese Studies* 38, no. 1 (2012): 139.

78. Rajaram Panda notes with alarm China's expansion of military power, pointing out that China's defense budget has quadrupled in the past decade, reaching 808.2 billion yuan (about ¥12.9 trillion) for fiscal 2014, up 12 percent from the previous year. Meanwhile, Japan's defense budget stood at ¥4.78 trillion in fiscal 2014, an increase of 2.2 percent year-on-year from the ¥4.68 trillion of the previous fiscal year. See Rajaram Panda, "Japan's Defense White Paper 2014 and Coping with the China 'Threat,'" *IPRIS Viewpoints* 150 (2014), http://www.ipris.org/php/download.php?fid=797.

79. See the comments by Alexandra Sakaki in Rodion Ebbighausen, "Japan Concerned over China's 'Profoundly Dangerous' Acts," Deutsche Welle, August 6, 2014, http://www.dw.de/japan-concerned-over-chinas-profoundly-dangerous-acts/a-17834009?maca=en-rss-en-all-1573-rdf.

80. See Yew Meng Lai, *Nationalism and Power Politics in Japan's Relations with China: A Neoclassical Realist Interpretation* (New York: Routledge, 2014).

81. See Paul Midford, *Rethinking Japanese Public Opinion and Security: From Pacifism to Realism?* (Stanford, CA: Stanford University Press, 2011).

in large part in reaction to Sino-Japanese tensions.[82] Abe and his allies—pro-American conservative nationalists—want Japan to become a more reliable ally of the United States by ending the era of pacifism and taking on more of the military responsibilities that the United States expects of Japan.

In addition to renascent Japanese nationalism, public opinion data suggests that a "new" nationalism is on the rise in South Korea, encouraging the country to adopt a more assertive posture and to play a more central role in East Asian affairs. According to a survey conducted by the Asian Institute for Policy Studies, South Koreans expect China to overtake the United States as the most influential country in the world within a decade. More interesting is just how confident South Koreans are of their own nation. Over the next ten years, they expect South Korea's influence to surpass that of Japan and even to rival that of Russia, requiring a structural reorganization of East Asia that gives the Republic of Korea a more prominent role.[83] As Steven Denney and Karl Freidhoff point out, "The growing confidence among Koreans should be carefully watched, because as the confidence of the general population grows, the South Korean government will carry out policies that act on this confidence."[84]

Structural and Unit-Level Barriers to External Balancing

The question remains, however, why Japan has not formed a tight defensive alliance with South Korea against China and, possibly, North Korea. South Korea and Japan are both threatened by a more powerful and still growing regional rival, China, which neither can counterbalance solely by its own internal means. Both countries, of course, have a bilateral alliance with the United States, which is militarily stronger than China, and such an alliance may be enough to balance China. That said, there has been wide recognition of emerging global multipolarity among Japan's political leaders, who not only perceive the decline of Japan and the United States relative to China but also strongly accept "the 'rise of the rest,' in the shape of India, a resurgent Russia, a stronger South Korea, and, further afield, Brazil and a more integrated European Union."[85] These changes in the external environment—the passing from U.S. unipolarity to a more evenly distributed multipolar balance of power—provide powerful incentives for Japan and South Korea

---

82. Estévez-Abe, "Feeling Triumphalist in Tokyo," 165.

83. Steven Denney and Karl Freidhoff, "South Korea and a New Nationalism in an Era of Strength and Prosperity," PacNet no. 75 (Honolulu, HI: Pacific Forum Center for Strategic and International Studies, 2013), http://csis.org/files/publication/Pac1375_0.pdf.

84. Ibid.

85. Hughes, "The Democratic Party of Japan's New (but Failing) Grand Security Strategy," 113.

to aggregate their capabilities as a counterweight to China's growing military strength. Yet there is no discernable movement in that direction, despite strong urgings by the United States "for closer cooperation and better relations between our allies—Japan and South Korea."[86]

The reason why China's rise and associated muscle flexing has not translated into a willingness on the part of South Korea to reconsider its cold shoulder toward Japan—and thereby allow the three allies to beef up their regional security—resides in long-held resentments that date back to Japan's wartime occupation of South Korea. It is a vivid example of how unit-level factors can limit the attractiveness of certain alliances that would otherwise be made for purely strategic interests rooted in system structure. The key point is that the apparent alliance flexibility that derives from the wealth of physical alternatives that are, in theory, available under a multipolar structure (as in the Asia-Pacific region) should not be confused with the actual alternatives that are politically available to states within the system given their particular interests and affinities.[87]

This dearth of actual alternatives under multipolarity is a function of what are called alliance handicaps—that is, various impediments in the form of constraints rooted in ideologies, personal rivalries, national hatreds, and ongoing territorial disputes—to alignments that would otherwise be forged in response to immediate strategic interests.[88] These various inhibitions that in practice make alliance alternatives scarce are important because, for a multipolar balance-of-power system to operate properly, states cannot be so limited by alliance handicaps that they are unable to follow the systemic imperative to pool their resources against a dangerous shared threat—that is, to align and realign in response to shifts in power that threaten their security.[89] To an arguably unprecedented degree, alliance handicaps abound in East Asia, where nationalism, maritime and border disputes, fears of entrapment (e.g., with Taiwan in a war against China, with South Korea in a war against North Korea, etc.), competing ideologies, and especially historical

---

86. Vice president Joe Biden to Japanese prime minister Shinzō, quoted in Yuka Hayashi, Jeremy Page, and Jonathan Cheng, "Biden's Mission: Unite Japan, South Korea," *Wall Street Journal*, December 7, 2013.

87. See Glenn H. Snyder, *Alliance Politics* (Ithaca, NY: Cornell University Press, 1997), 148–49.

88. Fear of entrapment in a costly and unwanted war by virtue of an alliance tie can also impose considerable restrictions on the choice of alliance partners and, by extension, on the flexibility of alliances in a multipolar system. See Snyder, *Alliance Politics*; and Zeev Maoz, *Paradoxes of War: On the Art of National Self-Entrapment* (Boston: Unwin Hymann, 1990), chap. 7.

89. Robert Jervis, "From Balance to Concert: A Study of International Security Cooperation," in *Cooperation under Anarchy*, ed. Kenneth A. Oye (Princeton, NJ: Princeton University Press, 1986), 60.

legacies have prevented virtually any and all possible combinations of Beijing's neighbors from forming a coalition against a rising China.

A Clash of Nationalisms

As its oil platforms drill in disputed waters, China no longer speaks the language of "quiet rise." Rather, Xi Jinping's self-assured foreign policy stimulates fear in Japan, the Philippines, South Korea, Taiwan, the United States, and Vietnam. Nationalism is on the rise in the Asia-Pacific region, and it will engender discourses and practices within China that work to undermine the legitimacy of the established order. This will be true whether China's relative power continues to grow, stalls, or—worse still—contracts. Mounting nationalism within the Asia-Pacific region will also promote internal balancing among Beijing's neighbors—perhaps engendering spiraling arms competitions—but will, along with other alliance handicaps, inhibit their ability and desire to align with each other against China.

Rather than expecting current economic synergies and political accommodations to usher in full-blown policy convergence, warm political relations, and further steps toward regional integration, East Asia is more likely to witness a situation of (at best) peaceful coexistence in the form of a cold peace. But while the region's conflicts will most likely continue to simmer, they will not reach a boiling point. Outside the remote possibility of land warfare on the Korean Peninsula, East Asia's maritime geography argues in favor of naval competition but militates against land invasions and occupations. Because of what John Mearsheimer calls the "stopping power of water" and the fact that East Asia is a seascape,[90] and Robert Kaplan notes that "the spaces between the principal nodes of population are overwhelmingly maritime,"[91] the region will likely avoid the kind of great military conflagrations that took place on dry land in the twentieth century—even as heightened nationalism continues to fuel tensions and disorder.

90. Mearsheimer, *The Tragedy of Great Power Politics*, 114–28.
91. Robert D. Kaplan, *Asia's Cauldron: The South China Sea and the End of a Stable Pacific* (New York: Random House, 2014), 5.

U.S.-China Relations

From Unipolar Hedging toward Bipolar Balancing

Øystein Tunsjø

The United States and China have, during the post–Cold War unipolar period, developed extensive hedging strategies that evenly mix cooperation and confrontation in order to manage uncertainty about the sustainability of the unipolar system, China's rise, and the potential transition to a new bipolar or multipolar system. On the one hand, the United States has signaled a benign intent and encouraged China to become a responsible stakeholder in sustaining the current international order. On the other hand, the United States has developed capabilities to counter Chinese aggression and untoward behavior. China has sought to continue to rise peacefully by cooperating to ensure a benign security environment and contributing to upholding the international order that was conducive to its relative power rise. At the same time, China has mixed such cooperative approaches with a confrontational stand that ensured its own interests against U.S. dominance and power preponderance. Since 2009, however, the United States and China have gradually changed their strategies from hedging toward more balancing. Hedging strategies that evenly mix cooperation and confrontation are less warranted. The two nations still cooperate, but a more confrontational stance has been emphasized. Less uncertainty about China's rise and a transition toward a bipolar system have been important drivers behind this strategic shift.

Realist writers are correct in arguing that the United States and China incorporate balancing elements in their strategies and that China's military buildup is motivated by a desire to counter U.S. military dominance in East Asia.[1]

---

1. Robert S. Ross, "Balance of Power Politics and the Rise of China: Accommodation and Balancing in East Asia," *Security Studies* 15 (2006): 355–95; Robert S. Ross, "Bipolarity and Balancing in East Asia," in *Balance of Power: Theory and Practice in the 21st Century*, ed.

Scholars have also emphasized that most balancing is internal rather than external,[2] and China has increased its defense expenditures annually by about 10 percent for two decades. Since China has maintained economic growth of close to 10 percent during the same period, the share magnitude of the rise in China's gross domestic product (GDP) means that there is a strong cumulative effect when China has sustained defense spending of about 2 percent of its GDP. This has shifted the distribution of capabilities in the international system, and China's economic growth has been transformed into military capabilities that increasingly challenge the regional balance of power in East Asia. Yet China's internal balancing in the unipolar era is far from resembling the arms race of the Cold War bipolar system or the internal and external balancing under multipolar systems prior to the First and Second World Wars.

Since the end of the Cold War, the interaction between China and the United States, and most regional secondary states in East Asia, have not fallen squarely on the predictions of balance of power or threat theory contending that states will either balance against or bandwagon with the most powerful or threatening state.[3] Several studies have explained why the world has remained "out of balance" in the post–Cold War era.[4] Nonetheless, questions still loom about the content of the strategies pursued in the unipolar post–Cold War system when balance of power theory is not able to answer them satisfactory. In addition, there is a need for explain-

---

T. V. Paul, James J. Wirtz, and Michel Fortmann (Stanford, CA: Stanford University Press, 2004), 267–304; Stephen Walt, "Alliances in a Unipolar World," in *International Relations Theory and the Consequences of Unipolarity*, ed. G. John Ikenberry, Michael Mastanduno, and William C. Wohlforth (Cambridge: Cambridge University Press, 2011), 99–139.

2. Joseph M. Parent and Sebastian Rosato, "Balancing in Neorealism," *International Security* 40, no. 2 (2015): 51–86.

3. Kenneth N. Waltz, *Theory of International Politics* (New York: McGraw-Hill, 1979); Stephen Walt, *The Origins of Alliances* (Ithaca, NY: Cornell University Press, 1987); William C. Wohlforth, "The Stability of a Unipolar World," *International Security* 21 (1999): 5–41; Avery Goldstein, *Rising to the Challenge: China's Grand Strategy and International Security* (Stanford, CA: Stanford University Press, 2005); Denny Roy, "Southeast Asia and China: Balancing or Bandwagoning?," *Contemporary Southeast Asia* 27, no. 2 (2005): 305–22; Rosemary Foot, "Chinese Strategies in a US-Hegemonic Global Order: Accommodating and Hedging," *International Affairs* 82, no. 1 (2006): 77–94; Van Jackson, "Power, Trust, and Network Complexity: Three Logics of Hedging in Asian Security," *International Relations of the Asia-Pacific* 14, no. 3 (2014): 331–56.

4. Stephen G. Brooks and William C. Wohlforth, *World Out of Balance: International Relations and the Challenge of American Primacy* (Princeton, NJ: Princeton University Press, 2008); Nuno P. Monteiro, *Theory of Unipolar Politics* (Cambridge: Cambridge University Press, 2014); William C. Wohlforth, "How Not to Evaluate Theories," *International Studies Quarterly* 56, no. 1 (2012): 219–22; G. John Ikenberry, Michael Mastanduno, and William C. Wohlforth, eds., *International Relations Theory and the Consequences of Unipolarity* (Cambridge: Cambridge University Press, 2011); Jack S. Levy and William R. Thompson, "Balancing on Land and Sea: Do States Ally against the Leading Global Power?" *International Security* 35, no. 1 (2010): 7–43; Wohlforth, "The Stability."

ing the strategies of unthreatened states in the unipolar system. Randall L. Schweller has argued that, historically, bandwagoning is a common form of behavior among unthreatened dissatisfied and revisionist great powers.[5] But hedging, rather than bandwagoning or balancing, better explains the behavior of the United States, China, and regional states in East Asia in the post–Cold War era. The United States and China have relied on hedging strategies that on a spectrum falls between confrontation and cooperation.

Stephen G. Brooks and William C. Wohlforth have suggested that researchers "would be wise to invest their talents in investigating the novel dynamics of great power bargaining in today's unipolar world rather than seeking to stretch old analytical concepts that were created to deal with the bipolar and multipolar systems of the past."[6] The present chapter seeks to address this advice. Instead of stretching traditional concepts such as balancing and bandwagoning, it examines how the concept of hedging can be utilized to make sense of the United States and China's pattern of behavior during the post–Cold War unipolar era and how the incentives for hedging strategies decreases as a new bipolar U.S.-China system emerges.

The chapter is divided into three parts. The first part seeks to clarify, conceptualize, and theorize the meaning of hedging. The notion of hedging is increasingly invoked by analysts of international politics dissatisfied with traditional approaches and theories. However, *hedging*, a term borrowed from finance and economic theory, has too often been used as a buzzword and applied without clear meaning. The concept remains analytically opaque and insufficiently worked out in the relevant literature. The following analysis conceptualizes the phenomenon by differentiating between three types of hedging (extensive hedging, negative moderate hedging, and positive moderate hedging); contends that states hedge under conditions of high uncertainty; and identifies the conditions that favor hedging.

The second part shows how the United States and China have pursued extensive hedging that for the most part balances between cooperation and confrontation. The third part of this chapter examines more recent patterns of behavior suggesting that extensive hedging is about to change to negative moderate hedging and that signs of more confrontation and balancing measures are increasing, which corresponds with a systemic shift in the distribution of capabilities whereby U.S. unipolarity wanes and U.S.-China bipolarity emerges.

---

5. Randall L. Schweller, "New Realist Research on Alliances: Refining, Not Refuting, Waltz's Balancing Proposition," *American Political Science Review* 91, no. 4 (1997): 927–30.

6. Stephen G. Brooks and William C. Wohlforth, "Hard Times for Soft Balancing," *International Security* 30, no. 1 (2005): 107.

Part 1: Conceptualizing and Theorizing Hedging

The terms *hedging* and *hedge* have appeared frequently in government strategy papers, but a thorough examination of their meaning and usage is lacking.[7] The search for a concept able to capture state strategies that mix cooperation and confrontation has been pursued without explicit invocation of hedging. For example, a combination of engagement and containment was proposed by analysts from the RAND Corporation in 1999, who called it "congagement."[8] Aaron Friedberg's subsequent and more thorough application of "congagement" in analyzing U.S.-China policy shares features related to hedging.[9] Yet the term *hedging*, rather than *congagement*, has proliferated in analysis of international politics over the last decade. Few states can contain another state, and hedging better captures how states seek to strike a balance between cooperation and confrontation. Accordingly, *hedging* has become a term often used in academic writing and analysis,[10] and several scholars have sought to clarify and conceptualize hedging.[11]

7. U.S. Department of Defense, *Quadrennial Defense Review Report, February 6, 2006*, http://archive.defense.gov/pubs/pdfs/QDR20060203.pdf; White House, *The National Security Strategy of the United States of America*, http://www.comw.org/qdr/fulltext/nss2006.pdf; U.S. Department of Defense, *National Defense Strategy, June 2008*, http://archive.defense.gov/pubs/2008NationalDefenseStrategy.pdf; U.S. Department of Defense, *Annual Report to Congress: Military Power of the People's Republic of China 2007*, https://fas.org/nuke/guide/china/dod-2007.pdf; U.S. Department of Defense, *Annual Report to Congress: Military Power of the People's Republic of China, 2008*, https://fas.org/nuke/guide/china/dod-2008.pdf; Australian Department of Defence, *Defending Australia in the Asia Pacific Century: Force 2030*, Defence White Paper 2009, http://www.defence.gov.au/whitepaper/2009/docs/defence_white_paper_2009.pdf.

8. Zalmay M. Khalilzad, Abram N. Shulsky, Daniel L. Byman, Roger Cliff, David T. Orletsky, David Shlapak, and Ashley J. Tellis, *The United States and a Rising China: Strategic and Military Implications* (Santa Monica, CA: RAND, 1999); Peter Rudolf, "China's Rise and the United States: Perceptions and Strategy," in *China's Rise: The Return of Geopolitics?*, ed. Gudrun Wacker (Berlin: Stiftung Wissenschaft und Politik, 2006): 61–67, http://www.swp-berlin.org/common/get_document.php?asset_id=2973.

9. Aaron Freidberg, *A Contest for Supremacy: China, America, and the Struggle for Mastery in Asia* (New York: Norton, 2011), 88–119.

10. G. John Ikenberry, "Between the Eagle and the Dragon: America, China, and Middle States Strategies in East Asia," *Political Science Quarterly* 131, no. 1 (2016): 9–43; Øystein Tunsjø, "China's Rise: Towards a Division of Labor in Transatlantic Relations," in *Responding to China's Rise: US and EU Strategies*, ed. Vinod K. Aggraval and Sara A. Newland (New York: Springer, 2015), 151–74; John D. Ciorciari, *The Limits of Alignments: Southeast Asia and the Great Powers since 1975* (Washington, DC: Georgetown University Press, 2010); Øystein Tunsjø, "Geopolitical Shifts, Great Power Relations and Norway's Foreign Policy," *Cooperation and Conflict* 46, no. 1 (2011): 60–77; William H. Overholt, *Asia, America, and the Transformation of Geopolitics* (New York: Cambridge University Press, 2008), 229–30, 242, 302; Byung-Kook Kim, "Between China, America, and North Korea: South Korea's Hedging," in *China's Ascent: Power, Security, and the Future of International Politics*, ed. Robert S. Ross and Zhu Feng (Ithaca, NY: Cornell University Press, 2008), 191–217.

11. Øystein Tunsjø, *US Taiwan Policy: Constructing the Triangle* (London: Routledge, 2008), 107–18. Øystein Tunsjø, "Zhongguo nengyuan anquan de dui chong zhanlüe" [China

Elsewhere I have developed a hedging framework for analyzing China's energy security policy,[12] and Richard J. Samuels and James L. Schoff have examined Japan's nuclear strategy from a hedging perspective.[13] Despite its prevalence, however, hedging remains an elusive, underdeveloped, and improperly understood term in international relations (IR) and security studies. As Evelyn Goh has noted, "There is no satisfactory exposition of hedging as a strategy. What does hedging behavior look like?"[14] In the same vein, Samuels notes that "as yet we have no general theory of this important and ubiquitous aspect of grand theory. Our received theoretical guidance about the conditions under which states will hedge—with what instruments and with how much recklessness—remains nearly as contradictory as the history of international relations."[15]

Evan S. Medeiros has taken important steps in his pioneering work to assess the hedging dynamic between the United States and China in the Asia-Pacific region, arguing that the United States "has chosen to hedge its security bets by adopting both cooperative and competitive policies toward China's rise in Asia." Nonetheless, he contends that "the term 'hedging' is underdeveloped both in the international relations theory and the security studies literatures."[16] What some pioneers noted about a decade ago still captures the status of knowledge today. As Cheng-Chwee Kuik has noted, "despite the growing usage of hedging as an 'alternative' alignment choice

hedges its energy security bets], *Shijie jingji yu zhengzhi* [World economics and international politics], August 2008, 42–51; Cheng-Chwee Kuik, "The Essence of Hedging: Malaysia and Singapore's Response to a Rising China," *Contemporary Southeast Asia* 30, no. 2 (2008): 159–85; Cheng-Chwee Kuik, "How Do Weaker States Hedge? Unpacking ASEAN States' Alignment Behavior towards China," *Journal of Contemporary China* 25, no. 100 (2016): 500–514; Darren J. Lim and Zack Cooper, "Reassessing Hedging: The Logic of Alignment in East Asia," *Security Studies* 24 (2015): 696–727; Van Jackson, "Power, Trust, and Network Complexity: Three Logics of Hedging in Asian Security," *International Relations of the Asia-Pacific* 14 (2014): 331–56; Brock Tessman, "System Structure and State Strategy: Adding Hedging to the Menu," *Security Studies* 21, no. 2 (2012): 192–231; Brock Tessman and Wojtek Wolfe, "Great Powers and Strategic Hedging: The Case of Chinese Energy Security Strategies," *International Studies Review* 13, no. 2 (2011): 214–40; Robert A. Manning and James J. Przystup, "Asia's Transition Diplomacy: Hedging against Futureshock," *Survival* 41, no. 3 (1999): 43–67.

12. Øystein Tunsjø, *Security and Profit in China's Energy Policy: Hedging against Risk* (New York: Columbia University Press, 2013); Øystein Tunsjø, "Hedging against Energy Dependency: New Perspectives on China's Energy Security," *International Relations* 24, no. 1 (2010): 25–45.

13. Richard J. Samuels and James L. Schoff, "Japan's Nuclear Hedge: Beyond 'Allergy' and Breakout," *Political Science Quarterly* 130, no. 3 (2015): 475–503.

14. Evelyn Goh, *Meeting the China Challenge: The U.S. in Southeast Asian Regional Security Strategies*, Policy Studies 16 (Washington, DC: East-West Center, 2005). See also Foot, "Chinese Strategies"; Robert G. Sutter, *China's Rise: Implications for US Leadership in Asia*, Policy Studies 21 (Washington, DC: East-West Center, 2006); and Tunsjø, *US Taiwan Policy*.

15. Samuels, *Securing Japan*, 8.

16. Medeiros, "Strategic Hedging," 145–47.

in IR literature, it has remained an under-studied phenomenon."[17] The following analysis conceptualizes, theorizes, and operationalizes the term *hedging* in order to explain U.S.-China relations in the post–Cold War era.

HOW DO STATES HEDGE, AND WHAT DOES HEDGING LOOK LIKE?

Hedging is defined here as the development and implementation of government strategies aimed at reconciling conciliation and confrontation in order to remain reasonably well-positioned regardless of future developments.[18] States hedge by combining somewhat contradictory cooperative and confrontational strategies to produce a balanced approach in order to manage uncertainty. The degree of hedging is likely to vary over time, and it can be differentiated between extensive hedging, negative moderate hedging, and positive moderate hedging. Extensive hedging balances relatively equally between cooperation and confrontation. Negative moderate hedging is characterized by a mix of stronger emphasis on confrontational or balancing measures over cooperative approaches. Positive moderate hedging has a stronger emphasis on cooperation over confrontation. Distinguishing between negative and positive moderate hedging is important because it indicates whether cooperation or balancing intensifies and uncertainty decreases. Such analysis also clarifies and contrasts the understanding of hedging developed here with the existing conceptualization and usage of such juxtapositions as *light hedging* versus *heavy hedging*, and *hesitant hedgers* versus *active hedgers*,[19] thereby providing a more nuanced understanding of the behavior. The different forms of hedging are illustrated in figure 2.1.[20]

The degree of hedging is assumed to be determined by the perceived degree of uncertainty. When there is high uncertainty, it is expected that states evenly mix confrontation and cooperation in order to manage uncertainty. When uncertainty decreases, we expect to find more or less confrontation or cooperation and less hedging. Let us imagine that the three types of hedging behavior can be identified within the color dark gray as we describe

17. Kuik, "How Do Weaker States Hedge?"; Kuik, "Malaysia between the United States and China," 174.

18. Tunsjø, *Security and Profit*, 2. I agree with Goh that hedging states "cultivate a middle position or avoid having to choose one side at the obvious expense of another," but I have questioned the argument that only weak states pursue hedging. The United States and China are no exception in the post–Cold War pattern of hedging. See Goh, "Meeting"; Evelyn Goh, "Understanding 'Hedging' in Asia-Pacific Security," PacNet 43 (Honolulu: Pacific Forum CSIS, 2006), https://csis-prod.s3.amazonaws.com/s3fs-public/legacy_files/files/media/csis/pubs/pac0643.pdf; and Tunsjø, *US Taiwan Policy*, 110–14.

19. Kuik, "How Do Weaker States Hedge?"; Kuik, "Malaysia between the United States and China," 174; Chung, "East Asia Responds."

20. I would like to thank Therese Klingstedt for all her help in designing this figure.

Low uncertainty	High uncertainty	Low uncertainty
Strong balancing	Medium balancing	Weak balancing
90% 70%	50% 30%	10%

Negative moderate hedging   Extensive hedging   Positive moderate hedging

Weak cooperation	Medium cooperation	Strong cooperation
10% 30%	50% 70%	90%

◄──────── Balancing intensifies   Cooperation intensifies ────────►

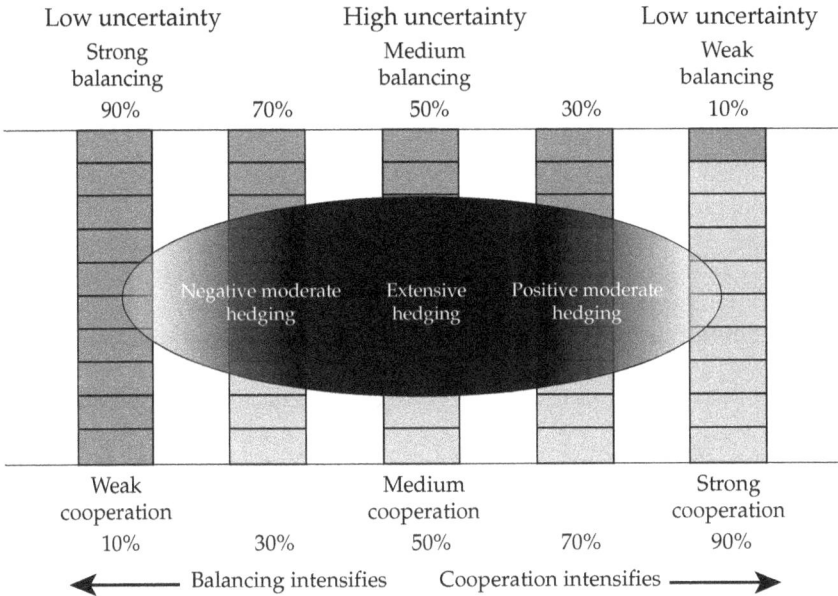

Figure 2.1. Conceptualizing hedging.

U.S.-China relations in the post–Cold War unipolar era. Relations between the two nations during most of the post–Cold War period can be categorized as extensive hedging. The period 2002–8 could be seen as an example of positive moderate hedging, whereby the United States intensified cooperation with China in order to focus on its wars in Afghanistan and Iraq and China refrained from taking advantage of this situation by supporting U.S. adversaries or behaving more assertive in East Asia as the United States was preoccupied by two wars. The contemporary shift from 2009 onward, marked by increased balancing in U.S.-China relations, provides an example of negative moderate hedging.

At one end of the low uncertainty spectrum we find strong balancing. During the Cold War, the bipolar distribution of capabilities polarized international politics and created highly predictable circumstances and low uncertainty. The United States and NATO's foreign policy toward the Soviet Union during the Cold War provides an example of strong balancing. Under such circumstances, states are unlikely to pursue hedging strategies. At the other end of the spectrum we find strong cooperation. The foreign policies of European Union member states provide an example of strong cooperation. The development of institutions, regimes, international law, norms, and interdependence has a moderating effect on anarchy in the international system, which decreases uncertainty, thereby making hedging less attractive and strong cooperation more likely.

Accordingly, we not only need to identify how states mix cooperation and confrontation in their hedging strategies (that is, how they differentiate between extensive and negative or positive moderate hedging) but also how they differentiate hedging behavior from strong balancing and strong cooperation—for example, by specifying and distinguishing between (1) actions that are hedging against uncertainty and (2) cooperative acts that do not reflect uncertainty but are intended to further other interests. The United States and China might undertake cooperative actions toward one another because each does not know how aggressive the other might be and both want to avoid a self-fulfilling spiral. But one nation's leaders might also be totally convinced that the other nation is a deadly serious rival, yet still engage in forms of cooperation that are either of mutual benefit or help reduce risks that threaten both equally, such as a "hot line" arrangement or a climate change accord. Only the first type of cooperation is considered as hedging against an uncertain future.[21] Such an analysis will facilitate a more explicit discussion of the different predictions yielded by a hedging theory and the balance of power or threat theory.

In conceptualizing what it means to hedge we need to recognize that *both* cooperative and confrontational elements are an integral part of a hedging strategy. The two elements can be evenly mixed (extensive hedging), or in some cases the pursuit of cooperation may be most important (positive moderate hedging); in others, a government might prioritize confrontation (negative moderate hedging). Joseph S. Nye, assistant secretary of defense under President Bill Clinton, had an important role in developing U.S.-China policy in the post–Cold War era, which he argues was designed as a strategy of "integrate but hedge."[22] According to Nye, the United States would support Chinese membership in the World Trade Organization but simultaneously reaffirm the importance of the U.S.-Japan security alliance and improve relations with India to counterbalance China's rise. Nye contends that such a strategy has enjoyed bipartisan support throughout the administrations of presidents Bill Clinton, George W. Bush, and Barack Obama. Similarly, G. John Ikenberry has argued that "the United States, China, and the middle states [in East Asia] are all pursuing mixed strategies of engagement and hedging."[23] The idea that U.S.-China policy should engage, hedge, or develop some form of engagement-plus-hedging strategy toward the rise of China has been the conventional view, and the term

21. I would like to thank one of the anonymous reviewers for pointing to this important distinction.

22. Joseph S. Nye Jr., "Work with China, Don't Contain It," *New York Times*, January 25, 2013, http://www.nytimes.com/2013/01/26/opinion/work-with-china-dont-contain-it.html.

23. Ikenberry, "Between the Eagle and the Dragon," 41.

hedging has fallen into common usage in official documents, statements, and academic writing.[24]

The understanding of hedging developed here more strongly emphasizes that decision makers hedge when they pursue a strategy that mixes confrontation *and* cooperation to manage uncertainty. A strategy that engages and integrates on the one hand and hedges on the other differs from the conceptualization of hedging outlined above, which emphasizes that elements of both cooperation and confrontation are inextricably linked in a hedging strategy. Hedging cannot be solely benign or antagonistic behavior; it requires decision makers to mix cooperation and confrontation. If the United States had only sought to improve relations with India to counterbalance China without seeking to integrate China into the existing U.S.-led international institutional order, then there would have been no hedging strategy. Instead, the United States would be pursuing a balancing or alignment strategy.[25]

Darren J. Lim and Zack Cooper have sought to reassess and redefine hedging "as an alignment choice."[26] While their analysis allows for a more narrow examination of some of the confrontational elements (i.e., security alignment) that are part of a hedging strategy, their reassessment throws the baby out with the bathwater. If—for the sake of argument, and in order to conceptualize—we agree that hedging is the color dark gray, which we get from mixing black (confrontation) and light gray (cooperation), then we cannot exclude cooperation or engagement from our analysis of hedging (see figure 2.1 above). If we follow Lim and Cooper, and only study the color black, then we are studying states' alignment or alliance polices, not hedging strategies or the color dark gray. Simply put, we cannot make dark gray out of black alone. We need to mix confrontation (black) with cooperation (light gray) to get hedging (dark gray). Lim and Cooper's so-called redefinition of hedging confuses hedging with alignment.[27] Hedging encompasses

---

24. See Freidberg, *A Contest for Supremacy*; Michael D. Swaine, *America's Challenge: Engaging a Rising China in the Twenty-First Century* (Washington, DC: Carnegie Endowment for International Peace, 2011), 341; Garry J. Schmitt, "Introduction," in *The Rise of China: Essays on the Future Competition*, ed. Garry J. Schmitt (New York: Encounter, 2009), vii; and David Shambaugh and Karl Inderfurth, "China and the U.S.: To Hedge or Engage," Yale Global Online, April 11, 2007, http://yaleglobal.yale.edu/content/china-and-us-hedge-or-engage.

25. As an analogy, an investor who relies on either "shorts" or "longs" is speculating, seeking simply to make a profit whether the market is bearish or bullish. A hedging investor, on the other hand, combines shorts and longs in an attempt to minimize risk and be reasonably well off regardless of market fluctuations.

26. Lim and Cooper, "Reassessing Hedging."

27. This is also the case with Jackson's study; see Jackson, "Power, Trust, and Network Complexity." Even if we adopted the view of hedging presented by Lim and Cooper, and Jackson, and only focused on the confrontational "actions," alignment is only one element—and not even the most important—of the factors that can be examined in the confrontational

both cooperative and confrontational actions as the interaction between the United States and China in the post–Cold War era demonstrates.

WHY AND WHEN DO STATES HEDGE?

The conceptualization of hedging provides a starting point for identifying how states hedge, describing what such hedging looks like, and demonstrating nuances in states' foreign policies. But such analysis does not answer why and when states hedge. Once we can point to the conditions that might compel states to hedge we can not only explain why states hedge but predict when they are likely to do so and move toward developing a new hedging theory. Hedging strategies aim to ensure against dismal outcomes in situations shrouded in uncertainty,[28] which suggests that states are likely to hedge under conditions of high uncertainty. Put differently, states are unlikely to hedge when they are certain about other states' benign intentions (increased likelihood of cooperation) or hostile intentions (increased likelihood of confrontation), and most likely to hedge when they are uncertain whether another state is a friend or a foe (more likely to strike a balance between cooperation and confrontation). Hedging is tied to how states "manage uncertainty" about other states' intentions and future behavior, but hedging does not emphasize the pursuit of cooperative *or* competitive strategies.[29] Instead, hedging is on a "more or less" instead of an "either/or"

---

realm of a hedging strategy. Internal balancing, such as arms buildup, is often more crucial. China's increased military capabilities are clearly more important in preserving and advancing its interests than its strategic partnership with Russia, its close alignment with Pakistan, and its alliance with North Korea. Nonetheless, cooperation has also been important in promoting China's interests and in avoiding a war or a conflict with the United States or its own neighbors, which has been a core objective in managing risks in the post–Cold War era through hedging. For a similar interpretation of hedging, see Ikenberry, "Between the Eagle and the Dragon," 36–37. Such imprecise usage of the term *hedging* has led others to present an inadequate analysis of the phenomenon. See Kei Koga, "The Rise of China and Japan's Balancing Strategy: Critical Junctures and Policy Shifts in the 2010s," *Journal of Contemporary China* 25, no. 101 (2016): 777–91.

28. As Jon Elster, *Nuts and Bolts for the Social Sciences* (Cambridge: Cambridge University Press, 1989), 26, notes, the desire to prevent dismal outcomes by forgoing potential, but risky, benefits is an age-old, rational, strategic response to profound uncertainty: "When choosing among crops, farmers have to consider the likelihood of early frost in the fall, of too little rain in the spring and of too much in the summer. Often they hedge their bets, by choosing a crop that leaves them reasonably well off regardless of weather." This mode of thinking has been adopted and utilized in financial circles too. Like the farmer choosing crops, hedging strategies were developed by risk-aversive investors to ensure a reasonable return on investments regardless of volatile market fluctuations. See Richard A. Brealey and Stewart C. Myers, *Financing and Risk Management* (New York: McGraw-Hill, 2003); Darrell Duffie, *Futures Markets* (Englewood Cliffs, NJ: Prentice Hall, 1989); and James Dow, "Arbitrage, Hedging and Financial Innovation," *Review of Financial Studies* 11, no. 4 (1998): 739–55.

29. Randall L. Schweller, "Managing the Rise of Great Powers, History and Theory," in *Engaging China: The Management of an Emerging Power*, ed. Alastair Iain Johnston and Rob-

approach. As Schweller points out in chapter 1 of the present volume, the debate over whether countries in East Asia will bandwagon with or balance against China is somewhat miscast. They are likely to do both and hedge by developing strategies that combine combative and cooperative elements.

By asking what makes states uncertain in international politics and examining three levels of analysis—system, state, and individual—we can identify the conditions that favor hedging.[30] Causes at the system (anarchy, polarity, and geopolitics), state, and individual level effect uncertainty and explain states' hedging behavior.[31] The emphasis in this chapter is on the role of polarity and how shifting distribution of capabilities, together with geopolitical factors, shapes uncertainty and conditions states' behavior.[32] It is contended that there is high uncertainty under unipolarity, low uncertainty under bipolarity, and medium uncertainty under multipolarity. States are therefore more likely to pursue hedging strategies under unipolarity, least likely under bipolarity, and somewhere in between under conditions of multipolarity.

States have been certain about U.S. primacy in the post–Cold War era but there has been high uncertainty about the strategic choices that states should pursue in an unprecedented unipolar system. Thus, hedging has been a common strategy pursued by states.[33] The power gap in what Barry Buzan has

---

ert S. Ross (London: Routledge, 1999), 1–31. I have discussed the link between Schweller's argument and hedging in Tunsjø, *US Taiwan Policy*, 108, 112–13. See also Yuen Foong Khong, "Coping with Strategic Uncertainty: The Role of Institutions and Soft Balancing in Southeast Asia's Post–Cold War Strategy," in *Rethinking Security in East Asia: Identity, Power and Efficiency*, ed. Allen Carlson, Peter J. Katzenstein, and J. J. Suh (Stanford, CA: Stanford University Press, 2004), 172–208; David M. Edelstein, "Managing Uncertainty: Beliefs about Intentions and the Rise of Great Powers," *Security Studies* 12, no. 1 (2002): 1–40; and Brian C. Rathbun, "Uncertain about Uncertainty: Understanding the Multiple Meanings of a Crucial Concept in International Relations Theory," *International Studies Quarterly* 51, no. 3 (2007): 533–57.

30. Kenneth N. Waltz, *Man, the State and War* (New York: Columbia University Press, 1959). We can also add the level of regional analysis. See Barry Buzan, "The Level of Analysis Problem in International Relations Reconsidered," in *International Relations Theory Today*, ed. Ken Booth and Steve Smith (Cambridge: Polity, 1995), 198–216.

31. For a start, see Randall L. Schweller, this volume, chap. 1.

32. Schweller (chap. 1), Wang (chap. 4), and Chung-in Moon (chap. 7) in this volume point to some of the state and individual conditions that compel states toward hedging.

33. For Southeast Asia, see Evelyn Goh, "Southeast Asian Strategies toward the Great Powers: Still Hedging after All These Years?" *ASAN Forum*, February 22, 2016, http://www .theasanforum.org/southeast-asian-strategies-toward-the-great-powers-still-hedging-after -all-these-years/; Jae Ho Chung, "East Asia Responds to the Rise of China: Patterns and Variations," *Pacific Affairs* 82, no. 4 (2009–10): 657–75; Cheng-Chwee Kuik, "Malaysia between the United States and China: What Do Weak States Hedge Against?" *Asian Politics and Policy* 8, no. 1 (2016): 144–77; Ann Marie Murphy, "Beyond Balancing and Bandwagoning: Thailand's Response to China's Rise," *Asian Security* 6 (2010): 1–27; and Renato Cruz De Castro, "The US-Philippine Alliance: An Evolving Hedge against an Emerging China Challenge," *Contemporary Southeast Asia* 31 (2009): 399–423. For China, see Wang Dong, this

described as a "1 + X" system has been too large for any great power to balance against preponderant U.S. power.[34] Instead, the unipolar power distribution has fostered hedging. The Pacific and the Atlantic Oceans have divided the unipole from potential contending great powers. In contrast to the past, when great power nations shared a land border or superpowers had large armies directly confronting each other on the European continent, U.S. primacy has not been perceived as equally threatening. Less-threatened states are more compelled to hedge. "The stopping power of water" has constrained the United States from maximizing its power into global hegemony, and the great powers have been too weak to contest for regional hegemony.[35]

Conventional balancing and bandwagoning strategies are too drastic for most states as long as the power distribution unambiguously favors the unipole. States prefer in this situation to manage uncertainty through hedging. They aim not to eliminate strategic vulnerability but to reduce it in light of uncertainty and potential future developments. Even the unipole, uncertain about which states will become peer competitors, chooses to hedge until potential rivals become more threatening or substantially increase their share of the distribution of capabilities within the international system.

In sum, structural conditions of unipolarity and high uncertainty have promoted hedging against risks instead of balancing against threat or states' maximizing power or bandwagoning for profit. Balance of power or threat theory should largely be reserved to explain situations in which states com-

---

volume, chap. 4; Foot, "Chinese Strategies"; and Goldstein, *Rising to the Challenge*, 11, 38–40. For Japan, see Eric Heginbotham and Richard J. Samuels, "Japan's Dual Hedge," *Foreign Affairs* 81, no. 5 (2002): 110–21; and Yasuhiro Matsuda, "Engagement and Hedging: Japan's Strategy toward China," *SAIS Review of International Affairs* 30, no. 2 (2012): 109–19; For South Korea, see Sukhee Han, "From Engagement to Hedging: South Korea's New China Policy," *Korean Journal of Defence Analysis* 20, no. 4 (2008): 335–51. For U.S.-China relations, see Evan S. Medeiros, "Strategic Hedging and the Future of Asia-Pacific Stability," *Washington Quarterly* 29, no. 1 (2006): 145–67. For European security, see Robert J. Art, "Europe Hedges Its Security Bets," in *Balance of Power: Theory and Practice in the 21st Century*, ed. T. V. Paul, James J. Wirtz, and Michel Fortmann (Stanford, CA: Stanford University Press, 2004), 179–213; and Asle Toje, "The EU Security Strategy Revisited: Europe Hedging Its Bets," *European Foreign Affairs Review* 15 (2010): 171–90. For Russia, see William Wohlforth, "Revisiting Balance of Power Theory in Eurasia," in *Balance of Power: Theory and Practice in the 21st Century*, ed. T. V. Paul, James J. Wirtz, and Michel Fortmann (Stanford, CA: Stanford University Press, 2004), 214–38. For the Arab world, see Benjamin Miller, "The International System and Regional Balance in the Middle East," in *Balance of Power: Theory and Practice in the 21st Century*, ed. T. V. Paul, James J. Wirtz, and Michel Fortmann (Stanford, CA: Stanford University Press, 2004), 239–66.

34. Barry Buzan, *The United States and the Great Powers: World Politics in the Twenty-First Century* (Cambridge: Polity, 2004), 67; Stephen G. Brooks and William C. Wohlforth, "The Rise and Fall of Great Powers in the Twenty-first Century: China's Rise and the Fate of America's Global Position," *International Security* 40, no. 3 (2016): 7–53.

35. John J. Mearsheimer, *The Tragedy of Great Power Politics* (New York: Norton, 2001).

mit themselves to confrontational strategies and balancing or containing a perceived threat or powerful rival. Conversely, hedging emphasizes the reluctance of superpowers, great powers, and secondary states to define other states as enemies or friends (a core characteristic of U.S.-China relations in the unipolar post–Cold War era) and instead develop a mixture of conciliatory and confrontational policies in order to remain reasonably well off and manage the risk of an uncertain future.

Part 2: Unipolar Post–Cold War Hedging through 2009

This section seeks to demonstrate that the post–Cold War strategies of the United States and China, rather than conforming to the expectations of balance of power or threat theory, can be better explained by the hedging framework advanced here. Such an approach captures the mixed nature of great power relations since the end of the Cold War, encompassing both the competitive and the cooperative aspects of their interaction.

HEDGING ON THE PART OF THE UNITED STATES

Among the most prominent users of the term *hedging* in the post–Cold War era has been the U.S. government; during the Bush administration it became part of officially stated policy toward China.[36] The official strategy documents published by the Obama administration, such as the *Quadrennial Defense Review Report* for 2010 and 2014, did not explicitly refer to U.S.-China policy as one of hedging, but there was evidence to suggest that the administration sought to strike a balance between cooperation and confrontation, or what Vice President Joe Biden has referred to as "cooperate and compete simultaneously" regarding China.[37] Policymakers in the Obama administration, such as James Steinberger, former deputy secretary of state; Jaffrey A. Bader, former special assistant to the president and senior director for East Asian affairs at the National Security Council (NSC); and Evan Medeiros, former special assistant to the president and senior director for

36. White House, *National Security Strategy 2006*, 41–42; U.S. Department of Defense, *National Defense Strategy 2008*, 10; U.S. Department of Defense, *Quadrennial Defense Review Report 2006*.

37. U.S. Department of Defense, *Quadrennial Defense Review Report, February 2010* (Washington, DC: U.S. Department of Defense, 2010, http://www.defense.gov/Portals/1/features/defenseReviews/QDR/QDR_as_of_29JAN10_1600.pdf; U.S. Department of Defense, *Quadrennial Defense Review 2014* (Washington, DC: U.S. Department of Defense, 2014), http://archive.defense.gov/pubs/2014_Quadrennial_Defense_Review.pdf; Joseph Biden, "Remarks by Vice-President Joe Biden to the Munich Security Conference, Hotel Bayerischer Hof Munich, Germany," February 2, 2013, http://www.whitehouse.gov/the-press-office/2013/02/02/remarks-vice-president-joe-biden-munich-security-conference-hotel-bayeri.

East Asian affairs at the NSC, have all drawn upon the concept of hedging in their analysis and writings on U.S.–China relations.[38]

U.S.-China policy was clearly driven by a strategic dilemma caused by uncertainty over China's future and what U.S. policy should be. For the United States, China was an uncertain quantity. Was it a status quo or a dissatisfied revisionist state?[39] Was it a looming threat to the United States? How should the United States respond to the rise of China?[40] The United States was worried that a rising China would choose a more confrontational path, but deferred judgment on whether the nation should be considered a threat. Thus, in the post–Cold War era the United States hedged against the risk that China might become a threat in the future.

On the one hand, the United States signaled benign intent. It encouraged China to become a responsible and integrated player in international affairs. It promoted China as a stabilizing stakeholder because it would benefit the international community and U.S. interests. A China more integrated in world affairs would enhance its participation and partnership on matters for the common good, such as increased participation in UN peacekeeping; nuclear nonproliferation efforts (in North Korea and Iran), stabilizing the international financial system, safeguarding important sea lanes of communication (SLOCs) from piracy, preventing terrorist attacks and environmental hazards, and promoting free trade agreements and climate negotiations. From the U.S. perspective, China's efforts in these matters were welcome and productive.

On the other hand, other U.S. signals likely caused alarm in Beijing. In official strategy papers, China was said to have, of all potential peer competitors, "the greatest potential to compete militarily with the United States." Prudence thus led the United States to consider the eventuality that "a major or emerging power could choose a hostile path in the future."[41] The 2010 *Quadrennial Defense Review Report* did not explicitly refer to China, but its emphasis on "developing a new joint air-sea battle concept for defeating adversaries across the range of military operations, including adversaries equipped with sophisticated anti-access and area denial capabilities" showed that the

38. See James Steinberg and Michael E. O'Hanlon, *Strategic Reassurance and Resolve: U.S.-China relations in the Twenty-First Century* (Princeton, NJ: Princeton University Press, 2014); Jaffrey A. Bader and Richard C. Bush III, *Contending with the Rise of China: Build on Three Decades of Progress* (Washington, DC: Brookings Institution, 2008), 5; and Medeiros, "Strategic Hedging."

39. Alastair Iain Johnston, "Is China a Status Quo Power?" *International Security* 27, no. 4 (2003): 5–56.

40. Thomas J. Christensen, "Posing Problems without Catching Up: China's Rise and Challenges for U.S. Security Policy," *International Security* 25, no. 4 (2001): 5–40; Schweller, "Managing the Rise."

41. U.S. Department of Defense, *Quadrennial Defense Review Report 2006*, 29–30; U.S. Department of Defense, *National Defense Strategy 2008*, 10.

United States sent not only benign signals to China.[42] The continuing redeployment of its military forces to East Asia—whereby defense budgets assigned a larger percentage of the U.S. Navy to the Pacific Fleet and allocated funding to increase U.S. aircraft carrier and submarine deployments in East Asian waters and to improve the forward presence of U.S. air power in the region—fueled suspicion and concern in Beijing about U.S. intentions.[43]

Faced with uncertainty about whether China will be a friend or foe, the United States sent mixed signals in preparation for multiple scenarios. It aimed to profit from China's role as a "responsible stakeholder" while remaining vigilant as to "how China will use its power."[44] It developed its capacity to counter Chinese aggression, but by constraining these efforts it hoped to limit the risk of creating heightened alarm, self-fulfilling prophesies, and dissatisfaction on China's part, which could prompt Beijing to attempt to undermine the international order.

Although the U.S. government identified China as the most likely peer competitor and challenger to U.S. supremacy, it did not pursue a full-fledged containment strategy or shift to strong balancing as the rise of a peer competitor would suggest. A more offensive U.S. stance could have given other great powers, such as Russia, stronger incentives to align with China. It might also have precluded cooperation on pressing transnational challenges, such as terrorism, the spread of weapons of mass destruction, and climate change. Remaining aloof sustained benign relations with China, provided opportunities to address lower policy issues, and provided the United States flexibility to maneuver. The United States aimed to reduce the potentially adverse consequences of a benign approach (by distributing resources and consolidating its position in Asia) and the detrimental effects of a confrontational approach (through confidence- and trust-building measures, strategic dialogue, trade, and cooperation). It hedged against the adverse consequences of confrontational measures *and* cooperative incentives.

In sum, during the 1990s and the early years of the new century, the United States worked extensively with China to avoid brinkmanship and crisis, pursuing a mixed strategy that promoted wide-ranging cooperation

42. U.S. Department of Defense, *Quadrennial Defense Review Report 2010*, 31–32.

43. U.S. Department of Defense, *The National Military Strategy of the United States of America 2011: Redefining America's Military Leadership* (Washington, DC: U.S. Department of Defense, 2011), https://www.army.mil/e2/rv5_downloads/info/references/NMS_Feb2011 .pdf; Ronald O'Rourke, *China's Naval Modernization: Implications for U.S. Navy Capabilities— Background and Issues for Congress* (Washington, DC: Congressional Research Service, 2009); Ross, "Bipolarity and Balancing," 280–82.

44. Robert B. Zoellick, "Not Your Average Banker," *National Interest* 95 (2008): 8–14; Robert B. Zoellick, "Whither China? From Membership to Responsibility: Remarks to National Committee on U.S.–China Relations, New York City, September 21, 2005," http://2001-2009 .state.gov/s/d/former/zoellick/rem/53682.htm.

at the same time as it confronted assertive and aggressive Chinese behavior. During this period the United States avoided taking sides in territorial disputes in the South China Sea and the East China Sea, emphasizing a peaceful resolution of conflicts and making clear that U.S. interest was in maintaining freedom of navigation. Washington has collaborated with Beijing in stabilizing the Taiwan issue and isolating Taiwan's former president Chen Shui-bian and the independence movement on the island. In order to improve ties in the post–Cold War era, the United States acknowledged China's sphere of influence on the East Asian mainland. Successive administrations rebuffed Vietnam's desire for more substantial defense ties, and the Bush administration scaled down the U.S. military presence in South Korea.[45] The United States and China have sought cooperation in the Six-Party Talks on the North Korean nuclear issue and in the UN on the Iran nuclear issue.

HEDGING ON THE PART OF CHINA

China's peaceful rise or development strategy has been characterized by a combination of cooperation and confrontation. By pursuing an extensive hedging strategy, the nation created a benign external security environment in the post–Cold War era that facilitated stability and its phenomenal economic growth.[46] China managed to increase its power formidably since 1979, emerging as the dominant power in East Asia without resorting to military force. It has avoided war with its neighbors and the counterbalancing strategies rising powers often face. Chinese leaders have shown a preference for preventing brinkmanship and conflict, limiting risks, and obtaining moderate goals in accordance with an extensive hedging strategy.

Examining China's grand strategy in the post–Cold War era, Avery Goldstein notes that the "precise nature of China's role in the more distant future is not yet clearly defined" and that it will rely on a "strategy of transition" that "entails efforts to develop national capabilities and cultivate international partners, but it also aims to avoid the provocative consequences of the more straightforward hegemonic and balancing strategies." He further notes that China's present grand strategy differs from hegemony, balancing, bandwagoning, or isolationism.[47] Rosemary Foot views China's strategy "as

45. Robert S. Ross, "The Problem with the Pivot: Obama's New Asia Policy Is Unnecessary and Counterproductive," *Foreign Affairs* 91, no. 6 (2012): 70–82.
46. U.S. hedging against China has also facilitated China's peaceful rise and been a major factor in creating a benign security environment in East Asia in the post–Cold War era.
47. Avery Goldstein, "An Emerging China's Emerging Grand Strategy: A Neo-Bismarckian Turn?," in *International Relations Theory and the Asia-Pacific*, ed. G. John Ikenberry and Michael Mastanduno (New York: Columbia University Press, 2003), 60. See also Goldstein, *Rising to the Challenge*, 38–39; and Peter H. Gries, "China Eyes the Hegemon," *Orbis: A Journal of World Affairs* 49 (2005): 401–12.

accommodation with the current U.S.-dominated global order," but "it also contains an important 'hedging' element, or insurance policy, through which China seeks to secure its future."[48]

China's sporadic cooperation with other great powers has not matured into robust strategic alliances against the unipole. China and Russia, the two great powers that arguably are the most obvious candidates to balance U.S. preponderance, seemed very reluctant in the post–Cold War era to form a power-aggregated alliance pitted against the United States.[49] Kenneth N. Waltz argued that systemic imbalance compels "secondary states [to] flock to the weaker side" because it is "the stronger side that threatens them."[50] When it comes to China's relations with Russia, India, and European powers, external forces have not propelled "weaker parties toward one another," as Waltz and the balance of power theory predict.[51] Thus, great power behavior during the last two decades renders balance of power theory incomplete.

Great powers have in the post–Cold War era shown a preference for flexibility in the choice of partners and have therefore strived to preserve as wide a choice as possible. China and other great powers worried that a course of action that seems reasonable one year may tie up resources needed to realize other attractive actions in following years. Such concern with opportunity costs encouraged the great powers to put off difficult strategic decisions. Moreover, if China decided to pursue strong balancing, either through arms buildups or alliance formations, it risked fueling a widespread arms race and becoming trapped in a disadvantageous position. This eventuality was avoided by maintaining an attitude of reserve. China remained uncommitted in order to preserve its options, and it sought to be reasonably well-off irrespective of whether the future international system became unipolar, bipolar, or multipolar, and whether the other great powers become rivals, became allies, or remained neutral.

Ken Booth and Nicholas J. Wheeler have directed attention to the moderating conduct of such intents. The ability to envision how certain initiatives might spark fear in potential adversaries, what they call "security dilemma sensitivity," sometimes tempers attempts by great powers to foment threatening initiatives that may escalate conflicts.[52] Until one great power chooses a clearly one-dimensional, confrontational policy, this international state of relative accord is likely to endure. Although China increased its defense

48. Foot, "Chinese Strategies," 88.

49. Wohlforth, "Revisiting," 220; Bobo Lo, *Axis of Convenience: Moscow, Beijing, and the New Geopolitics* (Washington, DC: Brookings Institution Press, 2008).

50. Waltz, *Theory of International Politics*, 126–27.

51. Ibid., 202.

52. Ken Booth and Nicholas J. Wheeler, *The Security Dilemma: Fear, Cooperation, and Trust in World Politics* (New York: Palgrave Macmillan, 2008), 7.

budget significantly during the last decades, its internal balancing efforts were still negligible compared to the Soviet Union's strong balancing and confrontational posture during the Cold War. Chinese leaders have been unwilling to impoverish their people or undermine domestic progress in order to compete militarily with the United States, and they have been reluctant to pursue an arms race that might undermine regional stability conducive to China's rise. Through this behavior China has shown "security dilemma sensitivity" and understood the risk of being perceived as too powerful.[53]

China's economic development is highly dependent on SLOCs for its trade, and roughly 85 percent of its oil imports are seaborne. Nonetheless, it has been cautious about developing naval power projection capabilities. The long-lasting Chinese debate about building an aircraft carrier illustrates how sensitive the government has been to potential security dilemmas.[54] By contrast, the Soviet Union embarked on an ambitious naval arms race with the United States during the Cold War, and Germany initiated a naval arms race with Great Britain to build dreadnought battleships in the early twentieth century, although neither the Soviet Union nor Germany were not as dependent on seaborne trade or imported resources as China is today.[55]

Even though its absolute and relative power have increased significantly over the last three decades, China has not engaged in external balancing to maximize its strategic positioning—that is, through territorial expansion, by entering alliances, developing overseas military bases, stationing troops in foreign countries, or intervening with military force in unstable states when conflicts erupt in order to back China's preferred government. Discarding predictions of balance of power theory, the nation has been unwilling to let its relationship with other great powers, such as those in Europe or Russia, compromise benign U.S.-China relations. For example, it refrained from overt cooperation with the European states or with Russia when the opportunity arose to frustrate U.S. policy. In 2003, when the United States announced its intention to use force against Iraq, and in the case of UN Security Council deliberations on constraining Iranian acquisition of nuclear weapons, confrontation would seem timely, but China remained aloof.

The Chinese government was careful not to take overly provocative measures in its foreign relations during the 1990s and early years of this century; it pursued measures aimed at avoiding conflict escalation and it peacefully

53. Kenneth N. Waltz, *Realism and International Politics* (London: Routledge, 2008), 56.

54. Andrew S. Erickson and Andrew R. Wilson, "China's Aircraft Carrier Dilemma," *Naval War College Review* 59, no. 4 (2006): 12–45; You Ji, "The Debate over China's Aircraft Carrier Program," *China Brief* 5, no. 4 (2005): 8–10.

55. Paul Kennedy, *The Rise and Fall of the Great Powers: Economic Change and Military Conflict from 1500 to 2000* (London: Unwin Hyman, 1988), 212, 386–87.

solved a large number of its territorial disputes.[56] It was willing to work with the United States on the most important foreign policy and security issues facing China in order to constrain former Taiwan president Chen's efforts to promote formal Taiwanese independence. Rather than aiming to maximize its strategic position, China has proceeded with a sophisticated neighborly policy and moderate military measures to avoid sparking regional security dilemmas.

Although China and the United States have pursued extensive and positive moderate hedging in the unipolar post–Cold War era, developments since 2009 indicate a shift in favor of more confrontational approaches and negative moderate hedging. Goldstein argues that China's strategy is likely to change once it "has risen and circumstances are fundamentally different."[57] A similar assumption would apply to U.S. grand strategy and its response to the rise of China. Thus, what is the linkage between a transition to negative moderate hedging and stronger balancing and a shift in the systemic distribution of capabilities from unipolarity to bipolarity?

Part 3: From Unipolar Hedging to Bipolar Balancing since 2009

China's newfound assertiveness[58] and growing regional hegemonic ambitions, the U.S. pivot to the Asia Pacific region, and increased regional conflict in East Asia suggest that unipolar hedging is being challenged.

GROWING ASSERTIVENESS

As several chapters in this volume point out, since 2009 China has taken a more strident turn on issues that hamper bilateral relations and create friction and tension to the benign East Asian security environment. China asserted its interests in the maritime domain in March 2009 when Chinese fishing vessels harassed a U.S. Navy surveillance ship (USNS *Impeccable*) operating within China's exclusive economic zone in the South China Sea, and a Chinese warship nearly collided with a U.S. Navy guided missile cruiser (USS *Cowpens*) in the South China Sea in December 2013. The People's Liberation Army (PLA) naval vessel asked the *Cowpens* to leave the area. When the *Cowpens* replied that it was in international waters and refused to

---

56. M. Taylor Fravel, *Strong Borders, Secure Nation: Cooperation and Conflict in China's Territorial Disputes* (Princeton, NJ: Princeton University Press, 2008).

57. Goldstein, *Rising to the Challenge*, 38.

58. For a discussion of whether or not China's assertiveness is new, see Øystein Tunsjø, "Global Power Shifts, Geography and Maritime East Asia," in *International Order at Sea: How It Is Challenged. How It Is Maintained*, ed. Jo Inge Bekkevold and Geoffrey Till (London: Palgrave Macmillan, 2016), 41–62.

change course, the PLA vessel took offensive maneuvers that forced the *Cowpens* to take evasive action to avoid collusion.[59] In response to Chinese assertiveness and territorial reclamation in the South China Sea, the United States has emphasized freedom of navigation operations, with the navy destroyer USS *Lassen* transiting within twelve nautical miles of five disputed maritime features near the Spratly Islands in October 2015.[60]

Bilateral relations with Japan degraded after an incident in September 2010, when a Chinese fishing boat was arrested by the Japanese Coast Guard in the waters surrounding the Senkaku Islands and about two dozen Chinese maritime surveillance ships entered Japan's contiguous zone in the seas surrounding the disputed islands. Relations worsened during the continued military stand-off in the waters and airspace surrounding the Senkakus after the Japanese government decided to nationalize the islands in September 2012 and China announced the East China Sea Air Defense Identification Zone (ADIZ) in November 2013.[61]

With China pressing its claims to the disputed islands in the South China Sea, tensions increased in China-Vietnam and China-Philippines relations as well as in China's relationships with a number of Association of Southeast Asian Nations (ASEAN) member states.[62] Events include China's dis-

59. Carl Thayer, "*USS Cowpens* Incident Reveals Strategic Mistrust between U.S. and China," *Diplomat*, December 17, 2013, http://thediplomat.com/2013/12/uss-cowpens -incident-reveals-strategic-mistrust-between-u-s-and-china/.

60. Bonnie S. Glaser and Peter A. Dutton, "The U.S. Navy's Freedom of Navigation Operations Around Subi Reef: Deciphering U.S. Signaling," *National Interest*, November 6, 2015, http://nationalinterest.org/feature/the-us-navy%E2%80%99s-freedom-navigation -operation-around-subi-reef-14272.

61. The US Department of State and Defense denounced the Chinese establishment of an ADIZ in strong terms, stating that the "United States is deeply concerned" and "view[s] this development as a destabilizing attempt to alter the status quo in the region." It was further stressed that the U.S. military "will not in any way" abide by China's ADIZ and the United States reiterated its position that "Article V of the U.S. Japan Mutual Defense Treaty applies to the Senkaku Islands." See John Kerry, "Statement on the East China Sea Air Defense Identification Zone," November 23, 2013, http://www.state.gov/secretary/remarks/2013/11 /218013.htm; Chuck Hagel, "Statement by Secretary of Defense Chuck Hagel on the East China Sea Air Defense Identification Zone," November 23, 2013, http://archive.defense.gov /releases/release.aspx?releaseid=16392; and White House Office of the Press Secretary, "Joint Press Conference with President Obama and Prime Minister Abe of Japan," April 24, 2014, http://www.whitehouse.gov/the-press-office/2014/04/24/joint-press-conference -president-obama-and-prime-minister-abe-japan.

62. Ann Marie Murphy, "The End of Strategic Ambiguity: Indonesia Formally Announces Its Dispute with China in the South China Sea," PacNet 26 (Honolulu: Pacific Forum CSIS, 2014), https://csis-prod.s3.amazonaws.com/s3fs-public/legacy_files/files/publication /Pac1426.pdf; Jane Perlez, "Philippines and China in Dispute over Reef," *New York Times*, March 31, 2014, http://www.nytimes.com/2014/04/01/world/asia/beijing-and-manila-in -dispute-over-reef.html?_r=0; "Beijing Sends Four Oil Rigs to Disputed South China Sea," *Taipei Times*, June 21, 2014, http://www.taipeitimes.com/News/front/archives/2014/06 /21/2003593281; "China Sends Four More Oil Rigs into Waters Claimed by Vietnam," NBC

pute with the Philippines over the Second Thomas Shoal (known as Ayungin in the Philippines and Ren'ai Reef in China) and the seizure of the Scarborough Shoal in 2012; the introduction of new rules to regulate fishing in waters under Hainan's jurisdiction; the upgrading and increased deployment of military capabilities in the Paracel Islands, and the building of artificial islands on reefs in the Spratly Islands that will facilitate military power projection, intelligence, and surveillance. All these policies have caused renewed tension and confrontation with neighboring countries and the United States. As China sees it, the nation has not diverted from its peaceful development and its defensive deterrence strategy but rather reacted to foreign aggression, encirclement, and interference in its domestic affairs. Safeguarding China's sovereignty has always been a core objective for the PLA's navy, and China's position on territorial disputes at sea has not fundamentally changed.[63] China's maritime forces have sought to safeguard the nation's enduring interests and enforce its long-standing interpretation of the law of the sea.[64]

Of equal importance are the confrontational measures taken by the United States to counter China's rise. The United States has dispatched more of its resources and military power to the Asia Pacific region and conducted more and larger naval exercises with regional allies to boost its credibility in countering the rise of China. In 2015 the more modern USS *Ronald Reagan* replaced the USS *George Washington* at the Yokosuka naval base in Japan. The modernized guided missile cruiser USS *Chancellorsville* and the Aegis-capable destroyer USS *Benfold* also arrived in Japan in 2015 to boost the Seventh Fleet.[65] An additional Aegis-capable destroyer will be deployed to

News, June 26, 2014, http://www.nbcnews.com/news/world/china-sends-four-more-oil-rigs-waters-claimed-vietnam-n141376?.

63. Shi Xiaoqin, "The Boundaries and Directions of China's Seapower," in *Twenty-First Century Seapower: Cooperation and Conflict at Sea*, ed. Peter Dutton, Robert S. Ross, and Øystein Tunsjø (London: Routledge, 2012), 65–84; Zhang Tuosheng, "On China's Concept of the International Security Order," in *US-China-EU Relations: Managing the New World Order*, ed. Robert S. Ross, Øystein Tunsjø, and Zhang Tuosheng (London: Routledge, 2010), 26–47.

64. Ren Xiaofeng, "China's Maritime Security Policy Making and Maritime Confidence-Building Measures," in *Twenty-First Century Seapower: Cooperation and Conflict at Sea*, ed. Peter Dutton, Robert S. Ross, and Øystein Tunsjø (London: Routledge, 2012), 197–212; Wu Jilu and Zhang Haiwen, "Freedom of the Seas and the Law of the Sea: A Chinese Perspective," in *Twenty-First Century Seapower: Cooperation and Conflict at Sea*, ed. Peter Dutton, Robert S. Ross, and Øystein Tunsjø (London: Routledge, 2012), 281–97.

65. Tyler Hlavac, "USS Ronald Reagan Heads to Yokosuka to Replace USS *George Washington*," *Stars and Stripes*, August 31, 2015, http://www.stripes.com/news/uss-ronald-reagan-heads-to-yokosuka-to-replace-george-washington-1.365419; Erik Slavin, "Upgraded Destroyer USS Benfold Arrives at New Home in Japan," *Stars and Stripes*, October 19, 2015, http://www.stripes.com/news/pacific/upgraded-destroyer-uss-benfold-arrives-at-new-home-in-japan-1.373937. An Aegis-capable naval vessel has an integrated weapon system of advanced computers, radars, missiles, and command and control system to track and guide weapons to destroy enemy targets.

Japan in 2017, and all three of the new DDG-1000 stealth destroyers will be homeporting with the U.S. Pacific Fleet. An additional nuclear attack submarine has been based in Guam, and a rotational deployment of combat ships in Singapore enhances U.S. operations in the region's littoral waters. This is complemented by forward stationing the most capable air assets, including F-22s, continuous deployment of B-2 and B-52 strategic bombers, additional tilt rotor aircraft for the U.S. Marine Corps and Special Forces, and, in 2017, the first forward stationing of F-35s to Iwakuni, Japan.[66]

In June 2012 the United States and South Korea mounted the largest military exercises since the Korean War, and deferred the transfer of wartime command in South Korea.[67] In July 2016 it was announced that the two countries would deploy the Terminal High Altitude Area Defense System in the ROK. Expanded naval exercises with Japan have emphasized the defense and retaking of disputed islands and reaffirmed the U.S. commitment to the defense of Japan, reinforcing that the bilateral defense treaty covers the disputed Senkaku Islands. The United States has also boosted its military cooperation with India, Indonesia, Malaysia, New Zealand, Pakistan, the Philippines, Singapore, Thailand, and Vietnam,[68] and in May 2016 announced an end to its embargo on sales of lethal arms to Vietnam.

In collaboration with Southeast Asian states, the United States outmaneuvered China diplomatically at the ASEAN Regional Forum meeting in Hanoi in July 2010. It suggested that the South China Sea dispute should be settled peacefully through multilateral negotiations and by establishing a binding code of conduct. Intervening in these legally complex issues was a new and provocative action on the part of the United States, and China reacted in strong terms.[69] Similar diplomatic efforts to isolate China were seen during an ASEAN meeting in December 2011. The willingness of China and the United States to ratchet up the pressure suggests a shift to negative moderate hedging. Both powers posture a stronger confrontational and less cooperative stance in relation to their peer competitor.

Nonetheless, the two nations have not stopped emphasizing their readiness to work together. They have collaborated in imposing new sanctions on North Korea in 2016 after its fourth nuclear test in January and long-range

66. U.S. Department of Defense, *Asia-Pacific Maritime Security Strategy*, July 27, 2015, http://www.defense.gov/Portals/1/Documents/pubs/NDAA%20A-P_Maritime_SecuritY_Strategy-08142015-1300-FINALFORMAT.PDF, 20.

67. The United States assumed operational control of South Korea's military during the Korean War. Peacetime control of South Korean forces was handed back to Seoul in 1994, but the United States is still obligated to command combined American–South Korean forces in the event of war. It has not been decided when the United States will hand back operational command, and with renewed North Korean nuclear and missile threats, it is unlikely to happen in the coming years.

68. Ross, "The Problem with the Pivot," 77–78.

69. Ibid.

missile test in February of that year. And China was a partner in negotiating the Iran nuclear deal in 2015. However, China and the United States have increasingly undermined each other's diplomatic positions, especially in East Asia, with the United States taking sides in maritime disputes and China becoming more assertive in East Asian waters and less amenable on global security issues, such as in Syria. Simultaneously, states have fewer incentives to preserve their options, as capabilities are redistributed toward a bipolar international system that increasingly polarizes East Asia. States in the region find it more difficult to hedge and are instead increasingly compelled to choose between closer ties with China or the United States.

THE RETURN OF BIPOLARITY

Many academics and policymakers have contended that the international system is multipolar or believe the current international system is currently becoming multipolar.[70] Unipolarists do not agree, however, with the claim that unipolarity is ending.[71] Both unipolarists and multipolarists correctly

70. Waltz, "The Emerging Structure"; Waltz, "Evaluating Theories," 915; John J. Mearsheimer, "Back to the Future: Instability in Europe after the Cold War," *International Security* 15, no. 1 (1990): 5–56; Mearsheimer, *Tragedy*; Christopher Layne, "The Unipolar Illusion Revisited: The Coming End of the United States' Unipolar Moment," *International Security* 31, no. 2 (2006): 7–41; Christopher Layne, "This Time It's Real: The End of Unipolarity and the *Pax Americana*," *International Studies Quarterly* 56, no. 1 (2012): 203–13; Fareed Zakaria, *The Post-American World* (New York: Norton, 2008); Barry R. Posen, "Emerging Multipolarity: Why Should We Care?" *Current History* 108, no. 721 (2009): 347–52; Arvind Subramanian, "The Inevitable Superpower: Why China's Dominance Is a Sure Thing," *Foreign Affairs* 90, no. 5 (2011): 66–78; Robert Kagan, *The Return of History and the End of Dreams* (New York: Knopf, 2008); National Intelligence Council, *Global Trends 2030: Alternative Worlds* (Washington, DC: December 2012); Randall L. Schweller, *Maxwell's Demon and the Golden Apple: Global Disorder in the New Millennium* (Baltimore: Johns Hopkins University Press, 2014), 20–21, 50, 52, 54, 55, 64, 83, 91; Donette Murray and David Brown, eds., *Multipolarity in the 21st Century: A New World Order* (London: Routledge, 2012); Barry R. Posen, "From Unipolarity to Multipolarity: Transition in Sight?," in *International Relations Theory and the Consequences of Unipolarity*, ed. G. John Ikenberry, Michael Mastanduno, and William C. Wohlforth (Cambridge: Cambridge University Press, 2011), 317–41. The leaders of Brazil, Russia, India, China and South Africa, known as the BRICS group of emerging economies, often refer to an emerging multipolar world.

71. Brooks and Wohlforth, "The Rise and Fall"; Nuno P. Monteiro, *Theory of Unipolar Politics* (Cambridge: Cambridge University Press, 2014); William C. Wohlforth, "How Not to Evaluate Theories," *International Studies Quarterly* 56, no. 1 (2012): 219–22; Michael Beckley, "China's Century? Why America's Edge Will Endure," *International Security* 36, no. 3 (2011–12): 41–78; William C. Wohlforth, "The Stability of a Unipolar World," *International Security* 24, no. 1 (1999): 5–41; Brooks and Wohlforth, *World Out of Balance*; G. John Ikenberry, Michael Mastanduno, and William C. Wohlforth, "Introduction: Unipolarity, State Behavior, and Systemic Consequences," *World Politics* 61, no. 1 (2009): 1–27; Birthe Hansen, *Unipolarity and World Politics; A Theory and Its Implications* (London: Routledge, 2011). See also G. John Ikenberry, ed., *America Unrivaled: The Future of the Balance of Power* (Ithaca, N.Y.: Cornell University

ask whether China has reached a top ranking, but this debate neglects or underemphasizes three important factors.

First, if we compare and contrast the distribution of capabilities at the origins of the previous bipolar system with today, we find that the distribution is roughly similar. In 1950, the Soviet GDP was about half that of the United States and almost twice that of the third-ranked power, the United Kingdom.[72] According to the International Monetary Fund, in 2015 the U.S. share of the world nominal GDP was roughly 24.4 percent, whereas China's share was 15.5 percent, Japan's was 5.5 percent, Germany's was 4.6 percent, the United Kingdom's was 3.9 percent, France's was 3.2 percent, India's was 2.9 percent, and Russia's was 1.6 percent.[73] This shows that in terms of economic strength the gap between the United States and China (24.4 percent versus 15.5 percent) is less than that between the U.S and the Soviet Union in the 1950 (27 percent versus 13.5 percent) and that the gap is larger between China and the third-ranked power today (15.5 percent versus 5.5 percent) than it was in 1950 (13.5 percent versus 6.5 percent).

In 1950, the second-ranked power had defense expenditures that were three times greater than those of the third-ranked power.[74] The Stockholm International Peace Research Institute (SIPRI) ranked China second in terms of world military spending in 2015, accounting for 13 percent of the world total, and Russia ranked fourth, with a 4 percent share. Therefore, China's share of world military spending is three times that of the third-ranked power.[75] In short, the power gap in economic and military terms between the top-ranked powers in 1950 and the other powers was not much different from the distribution of capabilities today.

Second, China does not need to achieve power parity with the United States before the contemporary international system can be considered bipolar. The Soviet Union never measured up to the United States on all the relevant criteria of state capability during the previous bipolar era. The asymmetric nature of American and Soviet power at the beginning of that system in the late 1940s and early 1950s, and throughout the Cold War, is not much different from the uneven power distribution between the United

Press, 2002); and Ethan B. Kapstein and Michael Mastanduno, eds., *Unipolar Politics: Realism and State Strategies after the Cold War* (New York: Columbia University Press, 1999).

72. Charles Wolf Jr., Gregory Hildenbrandt, Michael Kennedy, Donald Putnam Henry, Katsuaki Terasawa, K. C. Yeh, Benjamin Zycher, Anil Bemezai, and Toshiya Hayashi, *Long-Term Economic and Military Trends, 1950–2010* (Santa Monica: RAND, 1989), 4.

73. International Monetary Fund, "IMF Data Mapper: World Economic Outlook," http://www.imf.org/external/datamapper/index.php.

74. Wolf et al., *Long-Term Economic and Military Trends*, 17.

75. The gap between China and Russia is closer if we use figures from the International Institute for Strategic Studies (IISS); others, such as the U.S. Department of Defense, estimate that China's defense spending is much higher than IISS estimates and more in accordance with the SIPRI figures.

States and China today. The relative increase in China's combined capabilities place it in top ranking with the United States, even if only "barely."[76]

Third, the growing power gap between the second- and third-ranked powers is as important as that between the first and second-ranked powers when it comes to determining the polarity of the international system. This is also recognized by Brooks and Wohlforth, but as prominent advocates of unipolarity they seem unwilling to accept the conclusion that the current enormous power gap between China and any third-ranked power has moved the distribution of capabilities in the international system from unipolarity to bipolarity.[77] It was not the asymmetric power relationship between the United States and the Soviet Union at the start of the previous bipolar system that preoccupied observers when defining the international system of the post–World War II period. Instead, scholars such as Hans J. Morgenthau maintained that the international system had shifted from multipolarity to bipolarity in the aftermath of the Second World War because the United States and the Soviet Union, "in view of their enormous superiority over the power next in rank [Great Britain], deserved to be called superpowers."[78] China's unprecedented rise has now changed the distribution of capabilities. Other great powers do not measure up to China's combined score if we use Waltz's definition to measure the international systemic distribution of capabilities based on their "score on all of the following items: size of population and territory, resource endowment, economic capability, military strength, political stability and competence."[79] The power gap between China and the third-ranked power has become so great that we now can start to think of the international system as bipolar.

POLARITY AND ITS EFFECTS

The systemic power shift provides the most important starting point for explaining the tensions and conflicts in East Asia that have intensified since 2009, when U.S. unipolarity began to wane and U.S.-China bipolarity began to emerge. The shift in the systemic distribution of capabilities and the emergence of a more powerful China challenges the regional "geography of peace." East Asian stability has rested on the United States and China not

76. As Posen, "From Unipolarity to Multipolarity," 321, notes, the "Soviet Union was only barely in the US league for most of the Cold War in terms of economic capacity but we think of the era as a bipolar order, in part because the gap between the Soviet Union and the third-ranked power in the immediate aftermath of World War Two and for much of the Cold War was so great."

77. Brooks and Wohlforth, "The Rise and Fall," 15–16, 53.

78. Hans J. Morgenthau, *Politics among Nations: The Struggle for Power and Peace*, 2nd ed. (New York: Knopf, 1955), 324.

79. Waltz, *Theory of International Politics*, 131.

challenging each other's respective maritime and continental spheres of influence.[80] Enhanced capabilities allow China to assert its interests more forcefully in the maritime domain,[81] and the rise of China and the relative decline of other great powers compel the United States to pivot to the Asia Pacific region and rebalance regarding its only peer competitor.

As China is increasing its share in the distribution of capabilities within the international system and as it becomes more powerful, its neighboring states are developing strategies to enhance their own security. These neighboring states have increased their defense spending and some have sought to establish a counterweight to China through closer ties with the United States, shifting from extensive hedging to negative moderate hedging.[82] Yet this new U.S.-China bipolar system has not contributed to systemic effects similar to those of the previous bipolar system of the late 1940s and early 1950s, which fueled strong balancing in Europe and proxy wars in other regions. Whereas the systemic conditions, anarchy, and the distribution of capabilities between the bipolar systems in the twentieth and twenty-first centuries are roughly similar, structure does not produce similar effects, primarily due to distinct geopolitical conditions.

Different regional geographical characteristics account for distinct patterns of behavior under roughly similar structural conditions. Geopolitics in Europe fueled an arms race and the formation of formal military alliances to deter an existential threat in the early bipolar Cold War years. With few geographical barriers on the European continent there was a strong fear that

80. Robert S. Ross, "The Geography of Peace: East Asia in the Twenty-First Century," *International Security* 23, no. 4 (1999): 81–118; Robert Ross, "China's Naval Nationalism: Sources, Prospects and the U.S. Response," *International Security* 34, no. 2 (2009): 46–81.

81. On the debate about China's assertiveness, see Michael Swaine, "Perceptions of an Assertive China," *China Leadership Monitor* 32 (2010): 1–19; Thomas J. Christensen, "The Advantages of an Assertive China," *Foreign Affairs* 90, no. 2 (2011): 54–67; M. Taylor Fravel, *China's Behavior in Its Territorial Disputes and Assertiveness in the South China Sea* (Washington, DC: Center for Strategic and International Studies, 2011); Michael Yahuda, "China's New Assertiveness in the South China Sea," *Journal of Contemporary China* 22, no. 81 (2013): 446–59; Alastair Iain Johnston, "How New and Assertive Is China's New Assertiveness?" *International Security* 37, no. 4 (2013): 7–48; Øystein Tunsjø, "China's Maritime Security Policy in a Bipolar International System," paper presented at the Stockholm International Peace Research Institute conference, April 18–19, 2013, http://books.sipri.org/files/misc/SIPRI-Hu%20Tunsjo.pdf; Dingding Chen and Xiaoyu Pu, "Correspondence: Debating China's Assertiveness," *International Security* 38, no. 3 (2013–14): 176–80; Alastair Iain Johnston, "Correspondence: Debating China's Assertiveness," *International Security* 38, no. 3 (2013–14): 180–83.

82. Although the SIPRI world military expenditure database shows that military spending in East Asia as a percentage of GDP has declined since the end of the Cold War, the same data show that the share of military spending in the economies of most of China's neighbors since 2000 has remained the same or even more than that of China. Moreover, especially since 2010, the growth rate of year-on-year military spending in countries like Indonesia, the Philippines, and Vietnam has been catching up with or exceeding that of China.

the Red Army would march into West Germany and overrun Western Europe within weeks. While China's PLA is a dominating land power on the East Asian mainland, its contemporary military buildup has not created security dynamics in East Asia similar to those of Soviet military dominance in Europe because water barriers constrain the PLA from expanding into maritime East Asia or potentially invading Japan or the Philippines. "The stopping power of water" limits U.S. and China's power projection capability and makes both states less vulnerable to a first strike.[83] Amphibious invasions have always been difficult, and the current technology trends make maritime East Asia "defense dominant."[84] In contrast to the "European continental system,"[85] homeland invasion and territorial conquest is unlikely among the major regional actors in maritime East Asia.[86]

Geographical conditions, then, postpone strong balancing and security dynamics in contemporary East Asia that would be similar to those developed in Europe at the start of the previous bipolar system.[87] The timing of the shift from one type of hedging to another or away from hedging entirely will differ between regions even though the systemic distribution of capabilities is roughly similar. Waltz did not consider the importance of geography in his theory, according to which geography is a unit-level factor and one dimension of states' combined capabilities when fixed to state boundaries. Geography is also part of broader geopolitics, which operates to influence state behavior from forces outside the state. Geopolitics is not a system factor, contrary to what Waltz emphasized regarding anarchy and the distribution of capabilities. But it has important regional and systemic effects that Waltz has disregarded in order to develop a systemic theory.[88]

Conclusion

G. John Ikenberry, Michael Mastanduno, and William C. Wohlforth have noted that "one of the great theoretical challenges in the study of international relations is to identify the extent to which and various ways in which a unipolar distribution of power influences how states act and generate patterns of conflict and cooperation."[89] The hedging theory put forward in the

---

83. Mearsheimer, *Tragedy*, 44.
84. Jennifer M. Lind, "Correspondence: Spirals, Security, and Stability in East Asia," *International Security* 24, no. 4 (2000): 191.
85. Levy and Thompson, "Balancing."
86. Ross, "The Geography of Peace."
87. Øystein Tunsjø, "The Cold War as a Guide to the Risk of War in East Asia," *Global Asia* 9, no. 3 (2014): 15–19.
88. This calls for a new geostructural realist theory. See Tunsjø, *The Return of Bipolarity*.
89. Ikenberry et al., "Introduction," 25; Walt, "Alliances," 100.

present chapter is intended to address this challenge and theorize the implications of unipolarity and a shift to bipolarity for U.S.-China relations. It offers a supplement to other accounts of great power behavior in a post–Cold War international system of unipolarity and prevailing uncertainty about a transition to a new polarity.

It is possible to deny that the United States, China, and other great powers have strayed from balance of power and strong balancing in the past twenty or so years by taking two decades of cooperation, moderation, and diplomatic courtesy as a subtle way of preparing for a great power confrontation or as anomalous examples of contingent accord unworthy of serious attention. Yet even those subscribing to such an argument would probably appreciate that the strategies displayed by the United States and China since the end of the Cold War contain nuances that do not conform to the predictions of balance of power theory. The hedging theory developed here is one way of coming to terms with these nuances analytically.

Structure constrains and compels but does not determine. Contrary to the belief that structure has universal applicability, it has been contended that roughly similar bipolar systemic distribution of capabilities does not produce similar effects. Put differently, at times, "geography trumps structure."[90] The post–World War II Eurocentric bipolar system produced significant internal and external balancing; the emerging bipolar system concentrated on East Asia has not produced similar effects. The unique geographical conditions of East Asia, its topography, and the importance of the stopping power of water postpones contemporary strong balancing in the region and suggests that preference for negative moderate hedging strategies will be sustained. Yet if China manages to develop more power parity with the United States and continues to pursue its objective of becoming a land and sea power, such developments are likely to compel both nations, as well as other states in East Asia, toward strong confrontation and weak cooperation in the future.[91]

90. Ross, "The Geography of Peace," 82.
91. For increased balancing against regional hegemonic ambitions, see Levy and Thompson, "Balancing"; Mearsheimer, *Tragedy*; Nicholas J. Spykman, *The Geography of the Peace* (New York: Harcourt, Brace, 1944); and Robert S. Ross, "US Grand Strategy, the Rise of China, and US National Security Strategy for East Asia," *Strategic Studies Quarterly*, Summer 2013, 20–40.

Perception, Misperception, and Sensitivity

Chinese Economic Power and Preferences after the 2008 Financial Crisis

Daniel W. Drezner

During the depths of the 2008 financial crisis, there were excellent reasons to believe that the global economic order was in jeopardy.[1] Tectonic shifts in the global distribution of power threatened the foundations of global economic governance—the set of formal and informal rules that regulate the global economy and the collection of authority relationships that promulgate, coordinate, monitor, or enforce said rules.[2] A power transition between the United States and China seemed to be commencing. If nothing else, there was a dramatic shift in perceptions about the relative power of the two nations. The "China model" of economic development seemed to augur a radical break from the neoliberal economic orthodoxy of the post–Cold War era.[3] Furthermore, China seemed to be flexing its economic muscle in heretofore unseen ways, using its capabilities to coerce both small and large states alike. At the same time, China's actions in the Pacific Rim security sphere suggested a willingness to challenge the status quo. These shifts in power and preferences came at a time when the complex economic

---

1. The first half of this chapter is adapted and updated from Daniel W. Drezner, *The System Worked: How the World Stopped another Great Depression* (New York: Oxford University Press, 2014).

2. For a recent archaeology of the term *global governance*, see Thomas Weiss and Rorden Wilkinson, "Rethinking Global Governance? Complexity, Authority, Power, Change," *International Studies Quarterly* 58, no. 1 (2014): 207–15. The overwhelming focus of this literature has been on the noneconomic components of global governance.

3. For a summary, see Matt Ferchen, "Whose China Model Is It Anyway? The Contentious Search for Consensus," *Review of International Political Economy* 20, no. 2 (2013): 390–420.

interdependence of the Pacific Rim had increased. This has drawn uncomfortable historical analogies between East Asia now and Europe in 1914.[4]

This chapter examines the post-2008 trends in the global political economy and the challenges to global economic structure. Within this context it considers whether these fears of rising China's impact on the global economy were and are justified and examines how a stronger China influenced the global economy at the height of the financial crisis. The postcrisis era remains unsettled, but several facts are now manifestly clear. Contrary to expectations, there has been no serious disruption to the global economic order because of the 2008 financial crisis. The United States continued to act in a leadership capacity to minimize the damage caused by the Great Recession. Furthermore, China refrained from being a spoiler and instead acted like a "responsible stakeholder" in preserving and supporting global economic governance. In 2005 then U.S. deputy secretary of state Robert Zoellick defined that term to mean that "[China] recognize that the international system sustains their peaceful prosperity, so they work to sustain that system."[5]

A review of China's postcrisis economic policies shows that, on economic policy, China has used its increasing international economic weight primarily in support of current global economic governance. As a result of this continued stability, regional economic integration in the Pacific Rim has deepened. Moreover, despite its growing leadership in the global economy, and despite some recent initiatives that seem to hedge against the Bretton Woods institutions, China has abstained from pursuing a direct ideational challenge to the Washington Consensus and from destabilizing the global economic order. China's post-2008 use of economic coercion has been exaggerated and has, at best, yielded meager political concessions. Indeed, during the financial crisis China's management of its expanded global economic presence contributed to Chinese economic development, to China's stature in the global economy, and to global economic stability.

Despite these facts, the belief that China represents a challenge to the open global economic order persists. The fault for this lies in part with the current distribution of power; periods of waning unipolarity heighten sensitivity even to rhetorical challenges to the status quo. Another possible explanation is the extrapolation from security conflicts in the Pacific Rim. As the other chapters in this volume suggest, 2008 represented an inflection point for Asia Pacific security. It did not for the global political economy.

4. Margaret MacMillan, *The Rhyme of History: Lessons of the Great War*, December 14, 2013, http://www.brookings.edu/research/essays/2013/rhyme-of-history; Harold James, "Cosmos, Chaos: Finance, Power and Conflict" *International Affairs* 90, no. 1 (2014): 37–57.

5. Robert Zoellick, "Whither China: From Membership to Responsibility?," remarks to the National Committee on U.S.-China Relations, New York City, September 21, 2005, http://2001-2009.state.gov/s/d/former/zoellick/rem/53682.htm.

What follows in this chapter are five sections. The first section elaborates why the post-2008 period was expected to be a precarious moment for the global order. The second section examines how the United States and China maintained the post-2008 global economic order, with a focus on the international and domestic determinants of Chinese policy. The third section discusses the fears about the China model and why they were misplaced. The fourth section considers why misperceptions about Chinese revisionism persisted for so long, and the fifth section summarizes and concludes.

The Threats to Global Order in 2008

Prior to the 2008 economic crisis, identifying the great powers in the global economy as the United States and European Union was straightforward.[6] Even then, however, there was considerable talk about the rise of the economies of Brazil, Russia, India, and China (collectively labeled BRIC) and their effect on global order.[7] Once the subprime mortgage bubble burst, the power of these actors, particularly China, flourished at the same time that the power of United States and the European Union seemed to wane. In early 2009, financier Roger Altman lamented that "there could hardly be more constraining conditions for the United States and Europe" while "[China's] economic and financial power have been strengthened relative to those of the West."[8] Altman's assessment encapsulated the punditry on this question.[9] Similarly, Christopher Layne concluded that "in the Great Recession's aftermath . . . a financially strapped United States increasingly will be unable to be a big time provider of public goods to the international order."[10]

This perceived shift in the distribution of power is revealed in public opinion, elite discourse, and headline facts. Since 2008, the Pew Global Attitudes Survey has included a question asking respondents to identify the world's

6. Daniel W. Drezner, *All Politics Is Global: Explaining International Regulatory Regimes* (Princeton, NJ: Princeton University Press, 2007); Kathleen McNamara, "A Rivalry in the Making? The Euro and International Monetary Power," *Review of International Political Economy* 15, no. 3 (2008): 439–59.

7. Dominic Wilson and Roopa Purushothaman, *Dreaming with BRICs: The Path to 2050*, Goldman Sachs Global Economics Paper no. 99 (New York: Goldman Sachs, 2003); Fareed Zakaria, *The Post-American World* (New York: Norton, 2008); Alan Alexandroff and Andrew Cooper (eds.) *Rising States, Rising Institutions: Challenges for Global Governance* (Washington, DC: Brookings Institution Press, 2010).

8. Roger C. Altman, "The Great Crash, 2008: A Geopolitical Setback for the West," *Foreign Affairs* 88, no. 1 (2009): 2–14, 8, 10.

9. See, for example, Zakaria, *The Post-American World*; and Thomas Friedman and Michael Mandelbaum, *That Used to Be Us: How America Fell Behind in the World It Invented and How We Can Come Back* (New York: Farrar, Straus and Giroux, 2012).

10. Christopher Layne, "This Time It's Real: The End of Unipolarity and the *Pax Americana*," *International Studies Quarterly* 56, no. 1 (2012): 211.

leading economic power.[11] The shift in answers in the five years after the 2008 financial crisis was telling. In 2008, pluralities or majorities in twenty of the twenty-two countries that were surveyed (and ten of the twelve G-20 members surveyed, including Chinese and American respondents) said that the United States was the world's leading economic power. Clear majorities in ten of the twenty-two countries surveyed said the United States, and in no country did a majority of respondents say China. By 2012, however, there had been a wholesale shift in public attitudes. Pluralities or majorities in eleven of the twenty-two countries now said China was the world's leading economic power. Clear majorities in five countries named China; only in Turkey and Mexico did majorities of respondents name the United States. In five of the original G-7 economies, strong majorities or pluralities named China as the world's leading economic power. When the survey results are combined, there is an aggregate swing of twenty points from the United States to China between 2008 and 2013.

Both public rhetoric and private diplomatic discourse suggested that U.S. policymakers shared this view of China's new superpower status with the global public. On the U.S. side, for example, the official assessment of Chinese economic power was reflected in Secretary of State Hillary Rodham Clinton's 2009 conversation with Prime Minister Kevin Rudd of Australia, in which Clinton lamented, "How do you deal toughly with your banker?"[12] Similarly, in 2012, Kenneth Lieberthal and Wang Jisi summarized the worldview of the top Chinese leadership: "The rise of China, with its sheer size and very different political system, value system, culture, and race, must be regarded in the United States as the major challenge to its superpower status."[13]

Headline-making facts seemed to corroborate these perceptions. In 2010 China officially surpassed Japan as the world's second-largest economy, and by 2012 China was the largest trading state in the global economy. According to Arvind Subramanian, by 2011 China already had a larger gross domestic product (GDP) than did the United States.[14] Multilateral economic institutions were somewhat more cautious, but the message was largely the

11. All data in this paragraph come from Pew Research Center, "World's Leading Economic Power: What Country Is the World's Leading Economic Power?," http://www.pewglobal.org/database/indicator/17/.

12. On Clinton's remarks, see Ewen MacAskill, "Hillary Clinton's Question: How Can We Stand Up to Beijing?" *Guardian*, December 4, 2010. See, more generally, Evan Osnos, "China and the State of the Union," *New Yorker*, January 25, 2012, http://www.newyorker.com/NEWS/LETTER-FROM-CHINA/CHINA-AND-THE-STATE-OF-THE-UNION.

13. Kenneth Lieberthal and Wang Jisi, "Understanding Strategic Distrust: The Chinese Side," in *Assessing U.S.-China Strategic Distrust* (Washington, DC: Brookings Institution 2012), 11.

14. Arvind Subramanian, *Eclipse: Living in the Shadow of China's Economic Dominance* (Washington, DC: Peterson Institute for International Economics, 2011).

same. The International Monetary Fund (IMF) projected China to overtake the United States in terms of purchasing power by the year 2016; the World Bank said China had become the largest economy by the end of 2014. The U.S. National Intelligence Council predicted that by 2025 China's power would approximate that of the United States.[15] China had also become the hegemonic actor with respect to official currency reserves. It accumulated close to US$2 trillion hard currency reserves in 2008, easily the world's largest stock; five years later, this figure had swelled to more than US$3.4 trillion.[16] This dwarfed the reserve assets of any other actor, including both the United States and the European Central Bank.[17] Multiple commentators predicted that the renminbi would soon displace the dollar as the reserve currency of choice in the Pacific Rim.[18]

China leveraged these reserves to increase its economic influence vis-à-vis smaller countries.[19] Beijing's use of inducements undeniably increased. The *Financial Times* reported that between mid-2008 and mid-2010, Chinese loans to developing countries and companies exceeded those of the World Bank.[20] Bloomberg reported that in 2010, Chinese lending to Latin America exceeded that of the World Bank, Inter-American Development Bank, and the U.S. Export-Import Bank combined.[21] Beijing strengthened its own forums, such as the Forum on China-Africa Cooperation, to cement economic ties between China and emerging markets. By 2015 China was using its myriad Silk Road initiatives to offer infrastructure spending to its Asian allies.

At the same time, China also increased its use of economic coercion. Beijing attempted to use its holdings of U.S. debt to push for changes in American economic policies.[22] Reports multiplied of Beijing using its financial and economic muscle to punish actors in disputes over security and human rights

15. U.S. National Intelligence Council, *Global Trends 2025: A Transformed World* (Washington, DC: Government Printing Office, 2008).

16. Simon Rabinovitch, "China's Forex Reserves Reach $3.4tn," *Financial Times*, April 11, 2013. These figures likely understate the size of China's reserve assets, because of the PRC's efforts to conceal the magnitude its foreign reserve position.

17. See International Monetary Fund, "Data Template on International Reserves and Foreign Currency Liquidity," http://www.imf.org/external/np/sta/ir/IRProcessWeb/colist.aspx.

18. Barry Eichengreen, *Exorbitant Privilege: The Rise and Fall of the Dollar and the Future of the International Monetary System* (New York: Oxford University Press, 2011); Jonathan Kirshner, "Bringing Them All Back Home? Dollar Diminution and U.S. Power." *Washington Quarterly* 36, no. 3 (2013): 27–45.

19. See Daniel W. Drezner, "Bad Debts: Assessing China's Financial Influence in Great Power Politics," *International Security* 34, no. 1 (2009): 42–43.

20. Geoff Dyer, Jamil Anderlini, and Henny Sender, "China's Lending Hits New Heights," *Financial Times*, January 17, 2011.

21. Bloomberg, "Chinese Loans to Latin America Top World Bank, IDB Combined," February 17, 2012.

22. Drezner, "Bad Debts."

issues; China continues to punish Norway for the awarding of the 2010 Nobel Peace Prize to Liu Xiaobo. Chinese officials reacted to routine U.S. arms sales to Taiwan with extremely hostile rhetoric and threats to sanction U.S. firms. Beijing reported imposed "informal embargoes" of rare earth exports to Japan following the escalation of a territorial dispute in the East China Sea, contributing to Japan's decision to return a Chinese fishing boat captain it was holding as prisoner. Imports of bananas from the Philippines nosedived following heightened tensions over the Scarborough Shoal in the South China Sea.[23] These unannounced instances of economic coercion paralleled widespread reports of Chinese cyberespionage on Western multinationals in an effort to steal valuable intellectual property.[24]

Concerns about the rise in Chinese economic power were matched by concerns about whether China would demand changes to the set of neoliberal Washington Consensus ideas that had been privileged in the global economy for the previous generation. The dominant theme of global economic policy for the three decades prior to 2008 was a retreat of the state from the commanding heights of the economy.[25] At the international level, this embrace of market forces led to a series of policies that pushed toward fewer restrictions on cross-border exchange: freer trade, capital account liberalization, and fewer restrictions on foreign investment. In finance, the efficient market hypothesis concluded that state regulation was essentially unnecessary, since all information about any financial asset was encapsulated in its price.[26] At the most abstract level, the spread of neoliberalism was a strong affirmation of Francis Fukuyama's "end of history" thesis—the idea that no universally viable challenger to liberal capitalist democracy would emerge as an alternative mode of domestic governance.[27]

Even prior to the 2008 financial crisis, Chinese resentment against the U.S.-created international economic order was simmering. The U.S. response to the Asian financial crisis in 1997–98 had already created layers of hostility against the Washington Consensus across the Pacific Rim.[28] The Chinese

23. For more examples, see James Reilly, "China's Unilateral Sanctions," *Washington Quarterly* 35, no. 4 (2012): 121–33.
24. See, for example, Robert McMillan, "Google Attack Part of Widespread Spying Effort," Computerworld, January 13, 2010, http://www.computerworld.com/article/2522519/government-it/google-attack-part-of-widespread-spying-effort.html. For a more in-depth detailing of Chinese cyberespionage, see Mandiant, *APT1: Exposing One of China's Cyber Espionage Units,* https://www.fireeye.com/content/dam/fireeye-www/services/pdfs/mandiant-apt1-report.pdf.
25. Daniel Yergin and Joseph Stanislaw, *The Commanding Heights* (New York: Simon and Schuster, 1997).
26. Justin Fox, *The Myth of the Rational Market* (New York: HarperCollins, 2009); John Quiggin, *Zombie Economics* (Princeton, NJ: Princeton University Press, 2010).
27. Francis Fukuyama, *The End of History and the Last Man* (New York: Free Press, 1992).
28. Miles Kahler, "Asia and the Reform of Global Governance," *Asian Economic Policy Review* 5, no. 2 (2010): 187.

public also resented the U.S.-imposed terms for China's 2001 membership in the World Trade Organization (WTO), viewing them as onerous.[29] U.S. pressure on China to liberalize its financial sector and allow the renminbi to appreciate also generated hurt feelings; a December 2007 survey of Chinese citizens and opinion leaders revealed that a plurality in both sets of respondents believed that the United States was trying to prevent China from becoming a great power.[30] Chinese officials ratcheted up their criticism of the U.S.-led economic order. The Chinese Communist Party (CCP) authorized party critiques of the Washington Consensus,[31] and a senior Chinese banking official publicly blasted the United States for having a "warped conception" of financial regulation. Chinese trade officials accused the United States of engaging in its own form of protectionism via dollar depreciation.[32]

Once the acute phase of the crisis hit, there were excellent reasons to believe that the animating ideas of the Washington Consensus would lose their legitimacy. In 2008, global markets in financial assets, food, and energy were buffeted by a series of shocks, and none of them appeared to function terribly well in response. The great powers responded with greater levels of state intervention in all three sectors. In the United States and United Kingdom, the Great Recession rattled even the most devout of free market enthusiasts. Former U.S. Federal Reserve chairman Alan Greenspan made headlines when he testified before Congress that his faith in the "intellectual edifice" of self-correcting markets had "collapsed."[33] At the 2009 G-20 summit in London, British Prime Minister Gordon Brown flatly declared that "the old Washington Consensus is over."[34] Over the next few years, book after book blasted the intellectual edifice of neoliberalism and the Washington Consensus.[35]

29. Margaret M. Pearson, "The Case of China's Accession to GATT/WTO," in *The Making of Chinese Foreign and Security Policy in the Era of Reform, 1978–2000*, ed. David M. Lampton (Palo Alto, CA: Stanford University Press, 2001), 337–70.

30. Committee of 100, *Hope & Fear: American and Chinese Attitudes toward Each Other*, December 2007, http://survey.committee100.org/2007/EN/2007_C-100_EN_Survey.pdf, 27.

31. See Ferchen, "Whose China Model Is It Anyway?," 402–3.

32. Jamil Anderlini, "Chine Rebukes West's Lack of Regulation," *Financial Times*, May 27, 2008; Edward Wong, "Booming, China Faults U.S. Policy on the Economy," *New York Times*, June 17, 2008.

33. Edmund Andrews, "Greenspan Concedes Error on Regulation," *New York Times*, October 23, 2008.

34. Gordon Brown, quoted in Sarah Babb, "The Washington Consensus as Transnational Policy Paradigm: Its Origins, Trajectory and Likely Successor," *Review of International Political Economy* 20, no. 2 (2013): 285.

35. For a sampling, see Quiggin, *Zombie Economics*; and Menzie Chinn and Jeffry Frieden, *Lost Decades: The Making of America's Debt Crisis and the Long Recovery* (New York: Norton, 2011). For an authoritative review, see Andrew W. Lo, "Reading About the Financial Crisis: A Twenty-One-Book Review," *Journal of Economic Literature* 50, no. 1 (2012): 151–78.

If the financial crisis caused a crisis of capitalist faith in the United States, it appeared to encourage more revisionist thinking in China and elsewhere. The contrast between the successful 2008 Beijing Olympics and persistent U.S. malaise convinced many observers that China's moment to supplant the United States had arrived.[36] China's economic success in the wake of the 2008 financial crisis stood in stark contrast to the stagnation in the advanced industrialized economies. In early 2010, the *New York Times* noted that "as developing countries everywhere look for a recipe for faster growth and greater stability than that offered by the now-tattered 'Washington consensus' of open markets, floating currencies and free elections, there is growing talk about a 'Beijing consensus.'"[37] There were multiple definitions of the Beijing Consensus, but a common denominator was the prominent role of state institutions and state-owned enterprises. In 2006, the Chinese government had declared seven strategic sectors where the state would retain absolute control, signaling a shift away from fostering private enterprise in leading sectors.[38] China's massive 2008 fiscal stimulus focused on infrastructure investments, disproportionately empowering these sectors even more.[39] Beyond these sectors China facilitated the development of a panoply of government investment vehicles, including sovereign wealth funds, national oil companies, and state-run development banks.[40] The goal of all of these structures was to ensure that the state could direct resources toward favored and strategic sectors considered crucial to economic development.

Numerous Western analysts argued that the relative success of state-directed growth among energy and manufacturing exporters augured a rise in "authoritarian capitalism" or "state capitalism."[41] China was clearly the most powerful and most potent of these countries. Stefan Halper argued explicitly that "the terms, the conditions and arrangements, of state-directed

36. See, for example, Peter Beinart, "How the Financial Crisis Has Undermined U.S. Power," *Time*, June 21, 2010, http://content.time.com/time/magazine/article/0,9171,1995884,00 .html.

37. Katrin Beinhold, "As China Rises, Conflict with West Rises Too," *New York Times*, January 26, 2010.

38. The seven sectors were defense, electricity generation and distribution, petroleum and petrochemicals, telecommunications, coal, civil aviation, and waterway transport.

39. Yu Hong, "The Ascendancy of State-Owned Enterprises in China: Development, Controversy and Problems," *Journal of Contemporary China* 23, no. 85 (2014): 161–82. See also Adrian Woolridge, "The Visible Hand: Special Report on State Capitalism," *Economist*, January 21, 2012.

40. Stefan Halper, *The Beijing Consensus* (New York: Basic Books, 2010); Martin Jacques, *When China Rules the World: The End of the Western World and the Birth of a New Global Order* (New York: Penguin, 2009), 227–30.

41. For the most prominent versions of this argument, see Azar Gat, "The Return of the Authoritarian Great Powers." *Foreign Affairs* 86, no. 4 (2007): 59–69; and Ian Bremmer, *The End of the Free Market: Who Wins the War Between States and Corporations?* (New York: Portfolio, 2010).

capitalism give Beijing a distinct edge over Western competitors,"[42] and Martin Jacques noted that "China's success suggests that the Chinese model of the state is destined to exercise a powerful global influence, especially in the developing world, and thereby transform the terms of future economic debate."[43] Even former enthusiasts of neoliberalism, such as Francis Fukuyama and Thomas Friedman, began to wonder if the China model was superior.[44] At a minimum, the demonstration effect of China's phenomenal growth suggested that there were pathways to economic development that deviated from the Washington Consensus—and maybe other developing countries would try to adopt its features.[45]

The interest in a Beijing Consensus mirrored shifts in elite and public attitudes in China that were more hostile toward the United States. As China scholars Andrew Nathan and Andrew Scobell have observed, many Chinese elites viewed economic competition with the United States through a relative gains lens in which "China expects Western powers to resist Chinese competition for resources and higher-value-added markets."[46] Chinese officials publicly scorned the flaws of the Washington Consensus and began to talk privately about the virtues of their own development path. Lieberthal and Wang noted in 2012 that "it is a popular notion among Chinese political elites, including some national leaders, that China's development model provides an alternative to Western democracy and experiences for other developing and political systems are experiencing disorder and chaos. The China model, or Beijing Consensus, features an all-powerful political leadership that effectively manages social and economic affairs."[47] Postcrisis public opinion polls also revealed that an increasing number of Chinese citizens believed that U.S.-led global governance structures were designed to contain Chinese power.[48] According to a Pew Global Attitudes Survey,

42. Halper, *The Beijing Consensus*, 104.

43. Jacques, *When China Rules*, 230. See also Christopher A. McNally, "Sino-Capitalism: China's Reemergence and the International Political Economy." *World Politics* 64, no. 4 (2012): 745.

44. Francis Fukuyama, "US Democracy Has Little to Teach China," *Financial Times*, January 17, 2011; Thomas Friedman, "Our One-Party Democracy," *New York Times*, September 8, 2009. See also Joshua Kurlantzick, *Democracy in Retreat* (New Haven, CT: Yale University Press, 2013); and William R. Cline and John Williamson, *Updated Estimates of Fundamental Equilibrium Exchange Rates*, Policy Brief PB12-23 (Washington, DC: Peterson Institute for International Economics, 2012).

45. Dani Rodrik, *The Globalization Paradox* (New York: Norton, 2011); Kurlantzick, *Democracy in Retreat*, chap. 7.

46. Andrew Nathan and Andrew Scobell, "How China Sees America," *Foreign Affairs* 91, no. 5 (2012): 35.

47. Lieberthal and Wang, "Understanding," 10. See also Kurlantzick, *Democracy in Retreat*, chap. 7.

48. Committee of 100, *US-China Public Perceptions: Opinion Survey 2012*, http://survey .committee100.org/2012/EN/C100_2012Survey.pdf.

there was a demonstrable shift in Chinese public attitudes between 2010 and 2013. Chinese citizen attitudes toward the United States went from a net 21 percent positive attitude to a net 13 percent negative attitude—a considerable swing.[49]

After the collapse of U.S. banking giant Lehman Brothers, both Chinese power and Chinese ideas seemed ascendant. The question was whether rising powers like China would support or spoil the U.S.-created global order. Michael Mastanduno worried, "The collective action problem needed to be overcome to sustain effective cooperation is more formidable. And the United States will have to sit down not just with good friends but also with potential adversaries." Charles Kupchan warned that "emerging powers will want to revise, not consolidate, the international order erected during the West's watch."[50] During the depths of the Great Recession, there were excellent reasons to believe that the open liberal international order faced an existential threat.

Post-2008 Trends in Global Economic Governance

Despite widespread perceptions to the contrary, the United States clearly exercised leadership in the postcrisis global political economy. This was particularly true in the financial realm. As early as 2007, the Federal Reserve's decision to announce currency swaps provided a way for European financial institutions to improve their position. Indeed, in 2008, foreign banks comprised a majority of the top twenty borrowers from the Fed's emergency lending programs.[51] In agreeing to currency swaps in the fall of 2008, the Fed prevented a global liquidity crisis. As one European central banker put it, "In a way, we became the thirteenth Federal Reserve district."[52] After the crisis abated, capital rushed from the United States to the rest of the world,

---

49. In 2010, Chinese attitudes toward the U.S. were 58 percent favorable versus 37 percent unfavorable; in 2013, those numbers shifted to 40 percent and 53 percent, respectively. See Pew Research Center, "Opinion of the United States: Do You Have a Favorable or Unfavorable View of the U.S.?," http://www.pewglobal.org/database/indicator/1/survey/all/response/Unfavorable/.

50. Layne, "This Time It's Real," 211; Michael Mastanduno, "System Maker and Privilege Taker: U.S. Power and the International Political Economy," *World Politics* 61, no. 1 (2009): 152; Charles Kupchan, *No One's World: The West, the Rising Rest, and the Coming Global Turn* (New York: Oxford University Press, 2012), 7.

51. W. Thomas Oatley, Kindred Winecoff, Andrew Pennock, and Sarah Bauerle Danzman, "The Political Economy of Global Finance: A Network Model," *Perspectives on Politics* 11, no. 1 (2013): 135n12.

52. Neil Irwin, *The Alchemists: Three Central Bankers and a World on Fire* (New York: Penguin, 2013), 154.

functioning, in the words of one economist, "as a global insurer."[53] The 2008 Troubled Assets Relief Program, the bailout of American International Group, and the Federal Reserve's facilities did not just stabilize the U.S. financial sector—these funds also found their way into the balance sheets of European financial institutions, helping to prevent a meltdown on that continent as well. In reopening those swaps to the European Central Bank in May 2010, the Fed helped avert a meltdown of European financial markets.[54] Other great powers rapidly discovered that U.S. dollar hegemony bound their interests to the United States on financial issues.

Domestic politics might have prevented a more robust U.S. policy response, but partisan gridlock did not prevent the United States from pursuing a plethora of emergency rescue packages (via the 2008 Troubled Assets Relief Program); expansionary fiscal policy (via the 2009 American Recovery and Reinvestment Act); stress tests of large financial institutions; expansionary monetary policy (via interest rate cuts, three rounds of quantitative easing, and Operation Twist); and financial regulatory reform (via the Dodd-Frank Act). These actions helped to secure multilateral cooperation on macroeconomic policy coordination for two years, as well as the stricter banking standards of the Third Basel Accord.[55] Moreover the United States played a leadership role in negotiating IMF reform, though it was slow to implement it.[56] On financial regulation, the United States exercised leadership using myriad dimensions of its power.

The United States also demonstrated leadership in other issue areas where China was initially reluctant to cooperate. On the question of macroeconomic imbalances, Washington took the lead in pressuring Beijing to allow the renminbi to appreciate and comply with G-20 monitoring. For the first few years of the financial crisis, China kept the renminbi strictly pegged to the dollar at an undervalued rate to ensure its export sector. As pressure mounted to correct global macroeconomic imbalances, China was reluctant to discuss its exchange rate policies to avoid pressure to revalue; indeed, it initially stonewalled the G-20 information-sharing process. Beijing missed a

53. Rey, Hélène. "Dilemma, Not Trilemma: The Global Financial Cycle and Monetary Policy Independence," Research Paper No. w21162, National Bureau of Economic Research, 2015, 19.

54. See Frederic Mishkin, *Over the Cliff: From the Subprime to the Global Financial Crisis*, NBER Working Paper no. 16609 (Cambridge, MA: National Bureau of Economic Research, 2010); Irwin, *The Alchemists*; and Yacine Aït-Sahalia, Yochen Andritsky, Andreas Jobst, Sylwia Nowak, and Natalia Tamirisa, "Market Response to Policy Initiatives during the Global Financial Crisis," *Journal of International Economics* 87, no. 5 (2012): 162–77.

55. Drezner, *The System Worked*, chap. 4.

56. Ted Truman, *The Congress Should Support IMF Governance Reform to Help Stabilize the World Economy*, Policy Brief PB13-7 (Washington, DC: Peterson Institute for International Economics, 2013).

November 2009 deadline to provide information about economic plans going forward. When the government did submit information, it was historical and vaguely worded rather than forward-looking in nature.[57] In response, the United States coordinated a March 2010 letter from the leaders of five countries—itself and Canada, France, Great Britain, and South Korea—to the other G-20 members; the letter specifically raised the issue of exchange rates in relation to reducing trade imbalances and urged all members to accelerate their compliance with G-20 processes.[58] In June 2010, President Barack Obama sent another letter to his G-20 colleagues stressing the importance of "market-determined exchange rates." The United States persisted to coordinate action within the G-20 to maintain pressure on China.[59]

Three days after Obama's letter was sent, and just before the June 2010 G-20 Toronto summit, the People's Bank of China announced that it would "enhance the RMB exchange rate flexibility."[60] The slow appreciation of the renminbi began after U.S.-coordinated pressure. For the next three years, the renminbi nominally appreciated at a rate of 5 percent per year—at an even greater rate if one factors in the differences in national inflation rates. Significant appreciations in the renminbi occurred in advance of G-20 meetings, indicating China's desire to avoid clashes over the currency issue at those summits.[61] By late 2012, the renminbi had hit record highs against the dollar, and China had dramatically curtailed its intervention into exchange rate markets.[62] This contributed to a shrinking of global current account imbalances of more than 30 percent in the half decade following the crisis.[63] Assessing the state of current account imbalances in September 2013, the *Economist* concluded that "the world has rebalanced."[64]

57. Keith Bradsher, "China Uses Rules on Global Trade to Its Advantage," *New York Times*, March 14, 2010.

58. Chris Giles and Alan Beattie, "China Reprimanded by G20 leaders," *Financial Times*, March 30, 2010.

59. Coastas Paris and Kanga Kong, "India, Brazil to Press China on Yuan," *Wall Street Journal*, February 18, 2011.

60. For the PBoC announcement, see Bloomberg, "China Central Bank Statement on Yuan Exchange Rate," http://blogs.wsj.com/chinarealtime/2010/06/19/china-issues-statement-on-yuan-flexibility/.

61. James Rickards, *Currency Wars: The Making of the Next Global Crisis* (New York: Portfolio, 2011): 113.

62. Keith Bradsher, "On China Currency, Hot Topic in Debate, Truth Is Nuanced," *New York Times*, October 17, 2012; Simon Rabinovitch, "Renminbi Hits 19-Year High against the Dollar," *Financial Times*, October 12, 2012; Lingling Wei and Bob Davis, "China's Zhu Changhong Helps Steer Nation's Currency Reserves," *Wall Street Journal*, July 16, 2013.

63. Susan Lund, Toos Daruvala, Richard Dobbs, Philipp Härle, Ju-Hon Kwek, and Ricardo Falcón, *Financial Globalization: Retreat or Reset?* (Washington, DC: McKinsey Global Institute, 2013), 6.

64. "Current-Account Imbalances: Less skewed," *Economist*, September 28, 2013.

Partial though significant Chinese accommodation on this issue high-lighted the second major contributor to functional global governance: the surprising role of China as a key supporter of the status quo. This assertion is counterintuitive given the raft of arguments that a rising Beijing has acted as a revisionist actor in the global political economy.[65] It is true that in some arenas—such as export subsidies or cyberattacks—China has been reluctant to engage with other actors,[66] but on a number of key policy dimensions, Chinese leaders adjusted to China's economic rise with policies that bolstered the power of the existing post–World War II governance structures rather than undermining them.

Evidence of its support can be seen in macroeconomic policy coordination. In 2008 China enacted one of the largest fiscal spending packages as a percentage of GDP among the G-20 economies.[67] It acted out of self-interest in doing so, apprehensive that the Great Recession would cause significant unemployment, but the salutary effect on the global economy was still significant.

On trade matters, China's role as a supporting state becomes manifestly clear. On the one hand, it exploited loopholes in global economic governance to keep its currency undervalued, and in doing so it violated the spirit of the rules of the game.[68] On the other hand, it adhered to the letter of the law in its implementation of trade policy—and, for China, the letter of the law imposes significant constraints.[69] When China entered the WTO in 2001, the accession negotiations put significant pressure on Beijing to raise protectionist barriers. In contrast to other developing economies, for example, China's "bound tariffs"—the highest rate at which tariffs could be set—were fixed at a comparatively low level when it joined the WTO. Similarly, stricter limits were placed on its ability to use nontariff barriers as well.

Despite China's rising power, the hard law of the WTO, along with its myriad bilateral and regional free trade agreements, functioned as a binding constraint on China's trade measures. A World Bank research paper on

65. Halper, *The Beijing Consensus*; Bremmer, *The End of the Free Market*; Henny Sanderson and Michael Forsythe, *China's Superbank: Debt, Oil and Influence—How China Development Bank Is Rewriting the Rules of Finance* (New York: Bloomberg, 2013).

66. On cyberespionage, for example, Chinese officials refused to reciprocate U.S. efforts to show transparency on its cyberstrategy. See Helene Cooper, "Hagel Spars with Chinese over Islands and Security," *New York Times*, April 8, 2014.

67. Eswar Prasad and Isaac Sorkin "Assessing the G-20 Stimulus Plabs: A Deeper Look," (Washington DC: Brookings Institution, 2009). Chinese officials stress this fiscal stimulus as their greatest contribution to stabilizing the global economy after the collapse of Lehman Brothers.

68. Joseph E. Gagnon, *Combating Widespread Currency Manipulation*, Policy Brief PB12-19 (Washington, DC: Peterson Institute for International Economics, 2012). See also Keith Bradsher, "China Uses Rules on Global Trade to Its Advantage," *New York Times*, March 14, 2010.

69. Reuters, "China's Decade in the WTO," November 29, 2011.

post-2008 developing country trade policies largely credited the interdependence of global supply chains as acting as a brake on protectionism—except in China. The authors calculated that China's commitments to the WTO and other preferential trade agreements explained more than 95 percent of the variation in Chinese tariff rate movements since 2008.[70] An analysis of China's use of temporary trade barriers revealed a similar finding: compared to the other developing country members of the G-20, China's use of those measures covers the smallest trade-weighted share of imports—smaller, in fact, than the share covered by U.S. temporary trade barriers.[71] China's compliance rate with adverse WTO rulings was better than that of either the United States or the European Union.[72] As Christopher McNally has noted, "China has adopted largely non-disruptive policies supportive of the rules-based multilateral order. China's economy has been integrated globally by relying on multilateral institutional frameworks, especially the WTO. And so far China has mostly complied with its WTO commitments and avoided any aggressive role in trying to change the nature or rules of the organization."[73]

As the immediacy of the crisis period faded, China helped to create new institutions that had the potential to challenge existing global economic governance. It was one of the founders of the BRICS New Development Bank (NDB) and Contingent Reserve Arrangement, each of which was capitalized at US$100 billion. China also spearheaded the formation of the Asian Infrastructure Investment Bank (AIIB), also capitalized at US$100 billion. Despite U.S. disapproval, numerous allies became founding members of the AIIB. The One Belt, One Road Initiative also created a new form of infrastructure finance that seemed to bypass the Asian Development Bank and the Bretton Woods Institutions.

While these new structures could have been viewed as revisionist, neither their capabilities nor their intentions seemed terribly so. The NDB's total capitalization was less than what the World Bank loaned out in a single year,[74] and the AIIB's capitalization was similarly modest. Furthermore, both insti-

70. Kishore Gawande, Bernard Hoekman, and Yue Cui, *Determinants of Trade Policy Responses to the 2008 Financial Crisis*, Policy Research Working Paper no. 5862 (Washington, DC: World Bank, 2011): 25.

71. Chad Bown, "Import Protection Update: Antidumping, Safeguards, and Temporary Trade Barriers through 2011," August 18, 2012, http://voxeu.org/article/import-protection -update-antidumping-safeguards-and-temporary-trade-barriers-through-2011.

72. Xiaowen Zhang and Xiaoling Li, "The Politics of Compliance with Adverse WTO Dispute Settlement Rulings in China," *Journal of Contemporary China* 23, no. 85 (2014): 143–60.

73. McNally, "Sino-Capitalism," 758. See also He Ling-Ling and Razeen Sappideen, "Reflections on China's WTO Accession Commitments and Their Observance" *Journal of World Trade* 43, no. 4 (2009): 847–71; and Kahler, "Asia and the Reform."

74. Isabel Coleman, "Ten Questions for the New BRICS Bank," *Foreign Policy*, April 9, 2013, http://foreignpolicy.com/2013/04/09/ten-questions-for-the-new-brics-bank/.

tutions recruited veteran staff from international financial institutions, suggesting that their lending practices would conform to existing practices. Indeed, in April 2016 the AIIB announced plans for joint financing with the World Bank and the Asian Development Bank.[75] While these structures may offer an alternative to international financial institutions at some point, their first moves indicated little in the way of revisionist intent.

As other chapters in this volume document, there is little doubt that China acted in a more assertive manner on security and territorial matters in the Pacific Rim. On economic matters, however, China largely refrained from challenging the status quo in global economic governance. It requested and received larger quotas in the IMF and World Bank, as well as a larger voice in other global governance clubs. Still, none of these moves involved a shift in the underlying rules of the game. Most of China's demands were designed to give Beijing a greater voice in existing global governance structures, not to revise the purpose of their missions. When opportunities arose for China to subvert these regimes—for example, when Pakistan sought out Chinese aid as a substitute for IMF loans in the fall of 2008—Beijing abstained from action.[76] For the issue areas where China did have the power to alter global governance rules, as in trade, Beijing adhered to the status quo.

Why Didn't China Challenge Global Economic Governance?

There is no single causal explanation for why China acted like a supporter rather than a spoiler in the global economic order. Even a cursory glance at Chinese preferences and power suggest that there were valid reasons for the nation not to pose a systemic challenge to neoliberalism after 2008. In terms of interest, China had clearly benefited from the existing rules of the global economic game between 1978 and 2008. Even scholars who fear its revisionist aims in world politics acknowledge that Beijing has little incentive to alter rules that have enriched the country greatly.[77]

In terms of power (as will be discussed in the next section), perceptions of Chinese capabilities in the immediate post-2008 era were greatly exaggerated. This is revealed most clearly in assessing Chinese efforts at economic coercion. Most assessments of Chinese cases of economic sanctions have concluded that they have not worked in deterring or altering the behavior of

75. Sam Fleming, "AIIB and World Bank to Work Together on Joint Projects," *Financial Times*, April 13, 2016.

76. Jane Perlez, "Rebuffed by China, Pakistan May Seek I.M.F. Aid," *New York Times*, October 18, 2008.

77. See, for example, Aaron L. Friedberg, *A Contest for Supremacy: China, America, and the Struggle for Mastery in Asia* (New York: Norton, 2011).

target governments.[78] China's fitful efforts to use its reserves to economically pressure the United States yielded few, if any, concessions.[79] Indeed, in 2012 the U.S. Defense Department concluded, "Attempting to use US Treasury securities as a coercive tool would have limited effect and likely would do more harm to China than to the United States. . . . The threat is not credible and the effect would be limited even if carried out."[80] Similarly, while China's use of a rare earth embargo against Japan in 2010 did contribute to Tokyo's acquiescence in that case, it also eroded that policy lever. In response to that embargo, both private- and public-sector actors developed substitute sources of supply. In the four years after the rare earth embargo, prices fell by as much as 60 percent for some rare earths, while China's share of this market fell from 95 percent to 80 percent.[81] Even when dealing with smaller countries, Chinese power has been more limited. Chinese aid to the developing world has declined since 2010, making that year an anomaly. In sub-Saharan Africa, blowback has caused a drying up of Chinese foreign direct investment (FDI).[82]

Power and interest go some way in explaining Chinese behavior, but China's actions also have domestic ideational roots. Its reluctance to challenge the status quo in global economic governance matched its reticence to challenge neoliberal orthodoxy. At the level of ideas, Chinese officials were not keen on proselytizing the Beijing Consensus to other countries. Indeed, both boosters and critics of the consensus noted that Chinese officials refrained from promoting such a discourse.[83] The CCP flatly refused to officially promote any formulation of a Beijing Consensus or China model. Chinese officials and commentators also abstained from espousing a China model of development as the pattern to be copied by other developing countries. As the Ministry of Foreign Affairs' director of policy planning Le Yucheng has

78. Drezner, "Bad Debts"; Reilly, "China's Unilateral Sanctions"; Alastair I. Johnston, "How New and Assertive Is China's New Assertiveness?" *International Security* 37, no. 4 (2013): 7–48.

79. Drezner, "Bad Debts."

80. Tony Capaccio and Daniel Kruger, "China's U.S. Debt Holdings Aren't Threat, Pentagon Says," Bloomberg, http://www.bloomberg.com/news/2012-09-11/china-s-u-s-debt-holdings -aren-t-threat-pentagon-says.html.

81. Joseph Steinberg, "How the Great Rare-Earth Metals Crisis Vanished," *Wall Street Journal*, January 8, 2014; Eugene Gholz and Llewelyn Hughes, "Measuring the Key Concepts in Economic Sanctions Research: Market Structure, Dynamics, and Sanctions Effectiveness," paper presented at the Annual Meeting of the American Political Science Association, San Francisco, September 3–6, 2015.

82. Wayne Arnold and Drew Hinshaw, "China Takes Wary Steps into New Africa Deals," *Wall Street Journal*, May 6, 2014.

83. See, for example, Halper, *The Beijing Consensus*, 127; Jacques, *When China Rules*, 427; Ferchen, "Whose China Model Is It Anyway?"; and Wang Hongying and Erik French, "China's Participation in Global Governance from a Comparative Perspective," *Asia Policy* 15, no. 1 (2013): 98.

stated, "There is no Beijing Consensus."[84] Miles Kahler notes that "China's policy preferences might have created an even more serious challenge to the prevailing consensus at the World Bank and the IMF. During the Great Recession, however, China's policy preferences have hardly deviated from this revised [Washington] consensus."[85] This attitude mirrors a more general reluctance from the Chinese government to offer an alternative pole of economic leadership. David Shambaugh concludes, "China does not lead. . . . It does not shape international diplomacy, drive other nations' policies, forge global consensus, or solve problems."[86] Another assessment comparing China with its fellow BRIC economies concludes that "China has yet to provide many major ideas or set many important norms pertaining to global governance."[87]

Why has China not been more outspoken about its economic model? In part, its traditional foreign policy posture stresses noninterference in other countries' affairs, making Beijing a reluctant proselytizer to the rest of the world. In part, however, there's also been a lack of clarity about exactly what constitutes China's growth model. This is particularly true with respect to anything labeled the Beijing Consensus. As one scholarly assessment has noted, "Whatever one may think about the impact and underpinning logic of the so-called 'Washington Consensus,' it did represent a fairly coherent set of policy proposals and implicit normative values. Few people are making similar arguments about the 'Beijing Consensus.'"[88]

One commonality among proponents of a Beijing Consensus is that they come from outside China. This provides a clue as to why Chinese authorities have been reluctant to proselytize a Beijing Consensus—the biggest boosters of this term are not Chinese. As one Chinese academic explained to me on the margins of an academic conference in 2009, "the Washington Consensus and the Beijing Consensus have one thing in common: they were both invented in Washington."[89] Chinese elites are understandably reluctant to embrace the definition of a model as framed by Westerners.[90] And, with this provenance, Chinese officials have been understandably reluctant to adopt the moniker.[91]

84. Daniel W. Drezner, "The Sounds of Chinese Boilerplate," *Foreign Policy*, June 13, 2011, http://foreignpolicy.com/2011/06/13/the-sounds-of-chinese-boilerplate/.

85. Kahler, "Asia and the Reform," 187–88.

86. David Shambaugh, *China Goes Global: The Partial Power* (New York: Oxford University Press, 2013), 45–46. See also Amitav Acharya, "Can Asia Lead? Power Ambitions and Global Governance in the Twenty-First Century," *International Affairs* 87, no. 4 (2011): 851–69.

87. Wang and French, "China's Participation," 97.

88. Mark Beeson, "Can China Lead?," *Third World Quarterly* 34, no. 2 (2013): 239.

89. Comment made at a conference under Chatham House rules.

90. Scott Kennedy, "The Myth of the Beijing Consensus," *Journal of Contemporary China* 19, no. 65 (2010): 476.

91. A related issue is that Chinese officials are wary of advertising the term because it needlessly roils the United States: "[Chinese officials] are acutely aware of American sensitivity to

To be clear, there *has* been a debate among Chinese elites on the China model of economic growth. Even this debate, however, reveals the failure of Chinese policymakers to reach a consensus on an alternative model to the Washington Consensus. There is considerable disagreement among Chinese commentators over what constitutes the China model. As Tsinghua University's Matt Ferchen observes, "The different ways in which the Beijing Consensus or the China Model are portrayed as alternatives to the Washington Consensus are in themselves part of the battle of ideas."[92] The heterogeneity of ideas suggests one reason why Chinese authorities have not been proclaiming an alternative model: there is not enough of a consensus to propose anything. Scott Kennedy concludes, "The word 'model' implies a coherence and guiding plan that likely does not square with the reality of China's path." Randall Schweller and Xiaoyu Pu concur, noting that "Chinese ideas about alternative world orders remain inchoate and contested within China itself. Accordingly, these visions have not yet gained traction within or beyond China."[93]

There is also considerable debate within China about whether its development has been an unqualified success. Chinese elites have been surprisingly candid in discussing the weaknesses of their own development path. In his 2007 press conference, Chinese prime minister Wen Jiabao stated unequivocally, "There are structural problems in China's economy, which cause unsteady, unbalanced, uncoordinated and unsustainable development." He would echo these remarks in his farewell address as prime minister.[94] Similarly, Wen's successor and then vice premier Li Keqiang noted in 2010 that China's development had created an "irrational economic structure" and that "uncoordinated and unsustainable development is increasingly apparent."[95] Both internal and external observers of China's economy have argued that the post-2006 stage of Chinese development had numerous flaws—including environmental degradation, the misallocation of capital, low levels of personal consumption, and a bloated state sector.[96]

---

any talk suggesting the emergence of a rival power and ideology—and conflict with America could wreck China's economic growth." See "The Beijing Consensus Is to Keep Quiet," *Economist*, May 6, 2010.

92. Ferchen, "Whose China Model Is It Anyway?," 410.

93. Kennedy, "The Myth," 468; Randall Schweller and Xiaoyu Pu, "After Unipolarity: China's Visions of International Order in an Era of U.S. Decline," *International Security* 36, no. 1 (2011): 52.

94. Tania Branigan, "China's Wen Jiabao Signs Off with Growth Warning," *Guardian*, March 5, 2013.

95. Li Keqiang, quoted in Michael Pettis, "China's Troubled Transition to a More Balanced Growth Model," http://newamerica.net/publications/policy/china_s_troubled_transition_to_a_more_balanced_growth_model.

96. For internal critiques, see Yu Yongding, "A Different Road Forward," *China Daily*, December 23, 2010; and Yao Yang, "The End of the Beijing Consensus," February 2, 2010, https://www.foreignaffairs.com/articles/china/2010-02-02/end-beijing-consensus. For ex-

The trajectory of China's debate over the China model does suggest an emerging consensus—but not in a way that will directly challenge neoliberalism. Until 2012, for example, two leading New Left advocates for a Chinese pathway for development focused on the "Chongqing Model" of Communist Party boss Bo Xilai as their exemplar. These analysts praised Bo's housing policies, anticorruption campaigns, and quasi-Maoist sloganeering in Chongqing as the remedies to the worst ills of neoliberalism. In hitching their star to Bo, however, their argument was vulnerable to his downfall. Bo Xilai was arrested in early 2012; he was tried and convicted a year later. Subsequent media reports revealed that his success in Chongqing was predicated on bribery, corruption, extralegal forms of brutal coercion, and quite possibly murder.[97] At a minimum, this made it much harder for advocates of the emerging Chongqing Model to portray their version of the China model as a roaring success.

As New Left advocates lost their luster, other Chinese officials began to ratchet up their criticism of China's development model. Perhaps the biggest signal that the nation was uninterested in articulating an alternative economic model was the *China 2030* project. This was a joint report—the first of its kind—produced by researchers from the World Bank, China's Ministry of Finance, and the Development Research Center of the State Council, a top government think tank.[98] *China 2030* had the official imprimatur of key organs of the Chinese central government, as well as the personal backing of president Xi Jinping and premier Li Keqiang, who took leadership positions in the party and government in 2012–13.[99] With powerful patrons, *China 2030* carried an authority on the pros and cons of China's economic development that other external assessments of the China model had lacked.

The *China 2030* report made clear that whatever the virtues of the China model, they were fading fast. It stressed that unique factors contributed to China's post-1978 economic growth, thereby making it undesirable as a model to be emulated by others.[100] The report went on to observe the

---

ternal critiques, see Stephen Roach, "Manchurian Paradox," *National Interest* 101 (2009): 59–65; and Michael Pettis, *The Great Rebalancing: Trade, Conflict, and the Perilous Road Ahead for the World Economy* (Princeton, NJ: Princeton University Press, 2013).

97. "Chinese Infighting: Secrets of a Succession War," *Financial Times*, March 4, 2012.

98. Development Research Center of the State Council, and the World Bank, *China 2030: Building a Modern, Harmonious, and Creative Society* (Washington, DC: World Bank, 2013).

99. See Robert Zoellick, "World Bank President Zoellick's Opening Remarks at the High-Level Conference on: 'Development for a Modern, Harmonious, and Creative Society: International Experiences and China's Strategic Choices,'" http://www.worldbank.org/en/news/speech/2012/02/27/world-bank-president-zoellick-opening—remarks; and Ambrose Evans Pritchard, "China May Not Overtake America This Century after All," *Daily Telegraph*, May 8, 2013. Li Keqiang, in particular, provided unwavering political support for the project.

100. Development Research Center and World Bank 2013, *China 2030*, 4. See also Kahler, "Asia and the Reform"; and McNally, "Sino-Capitalism," 767n136.

myriad problems facing China over the next two decades: environmental degradation, rising levels of income and asset inequality, a looming demographic crunch, and low rates of personal consumption. It concluded that "it is imperative that China adjusts its development strategy as it embarks on its next phase of economic growth." Most of the proposed adjustments push China's political economy in a direction that more closely resembles the advanced industrial democracies. For example, the report stressed that the government had to retreat from the commanding heights of the economy, and that its "continued dominance in key sectors of the economy, while earlier an advantage, is in the future likely to act as a constraint on productivity improvements, innovation and creativity."[101]

With respect to the nation's approach to the rest of the world, the *China 2030* report concluded, "China's long-term interest lies in global free trade and a stable and efficient international financial and monetary system. Chinese leaders understand that China's rise benefited enormously from entering the WTO and is now an important stakeholder in the existing global trading system. Similarly, they will use China's enhanced capabilities to contribute to stable international financial markets and a well-regulated international monetary system supported by stable currencies and underpinned by sound monetary policies."[102]

As previously noted, China's "fifth generation" of leaders supported the crafting of the *China 2030* report, and since taking office they have attempted to credibly signal their intent to adopt the core components of the report's recommendations. In a major speech outlining his plan for further economic reform, Premier Li stressed the need to "further develop the market's fundamental role in allocating resources." Among his proposals were to significantly scale back the central government's licensing requirements for new businesses, outsource public services to market forces where appropriate, boost intellectual property rights enforcement, and demonstrate greater adherence to the rule of law. Many of these proposals echoed kindred observations and recommendations from the *China 2030* report.[103]

Following Li's speech, the government issued new edicts that buttressed some of these recommendations. These include proposals for the liberalization of interest rates, easing the credit boom, reducing barriers to FDI in China's service sector, and steps toward the full convertibility of China's currency.[104] Chinese authorities also took measures to crack down on its shadow

---

101. Development Research Center and World Bank 2013, *China 2030*, 25.

102. Ibid., 60.

103. Li quoted in David Barboza and Chris Buckley, "China Plans to Reduce State's Role in the Economy," *New York Times*, May 24, 2013.

104. David Barboza and Chris Buckley, "China Plans to Reduce the State's Role in the Economy," *New York Times*, May 24, 2013; "Chinese Govt Says Financial System Must Support Economy," *Bloomberg*, June 19, 2013.

banking system and tighten credit, allowing economic growth to taper off in the short run. The *New York Times* concluded, "China's recent cooling has been engineered by the authorities in Beijing, who are trying to steer the economy from an increasingly outdated growth model toward expansion that is more productive and sustainable."[105] The government's summer 2013 "mini-stimulus," intended to counteract the effects of tightening credit, rewarded private small businesses and households rather than state-owned enterprises.[106] Beijing restarted negotiations with Washington over a bilateral investment treaty, demonstrating an unexpected willingness to liberalize most of its economy to FDI. China also renewed its intent to sign up to the WTO's Government Procurement Agreement.[107]

The most important signal came at the Third Plenum of the Communist Party's Eighteenth National Congress in November 2013. Traditionally devoted to economic matters, this Third Plenum laid the groundwork for further liberalizing the market and constraining the state's role in the economy. The communiqué explicitly stated that the market must play a "decisive role" in the allocation of resources; this was a stronger rhetoric than in previous Third Plenums, which had described the market's role as merely "basic."[108] Concrete policy pledges included a reform of the permit system that constrains labor mobility and an end to the one-child policy. Several additional planks of the plenum's concrete policy document were drawn from the *China 2030* report.[109] Both the tenor of leadership rhetoric and these announced reforms are consistent with the neoliberal economic ideas that still dominate the global economy. They also suggest that China sees itself as merely the latest Pacific Rim country to transition from a more state-led economy to one with a greater emphasis on market forces.[110]

Three years after that Third Plenum, the leadership's rhetorical and policy gestures appear to be more hype than reality. It is likely that China will continue to deviate from free market orthodoxy in practice. Throughout his term as prime minister, Wen Jiabao made similar noises about the need for further economic and political reforms, with little in the way of follow-through. China's ability to alter its growth model to boost domestic

105. Bettina Wassener and Chris Buckley, "China's G.D.P. Growth Slows as Government Changes Gears," *New York Times*, July 14, 2013.

106. Simon Rabinovitch, "China Unveils Measures to Boost Economy," *Financial Times*, July 24, 2013.

107. Geoff Dyer, "Sino-US Investment Deal Sought," *Financial Times*, July 12, 2013.

108. Tom Mitchell and Lucy Hornby, "China's Pledge of Big Reforms Cements Era of Market Forces," *Financial Times*, November 12, 2013; Carlos Tejada, "China Endorses 'Decisive Role' for Markets as Plenum Concludes," *Wall Street Journal*, November 12, 2013.

109. Christian Murck, "The Third Plenum: Prospects for Reform in China," National Bureau of Asian Research, http://www.nbr.org/research/activity.aspx?id=376#.UtBEovRDtw4.

110. Edward Steinfeld, *Playing Our Game: Why China's Rise Doesn't Threaten the West* (New York: Oxford University Press, 2010).

consumption is far from clear.[111] Furthermore, nothing in the Third Plenum documents guarantees that neoliberal economic reforms will necessarily occur. Vows of reform in earlier Third Plenums did not necessarily lead to concrete policy actions, and nothing in the 2013 documents suggests that state-owned companies will be reformed anytime soon.[112] Unless and until Chinese policymaking institutions are recast to permit consumption-friendly lobbies to thrive, substantial policy change is unlikely. Furthermore, the CCP's goal of maintaining political control will likely override any preference for comprehensive economic reform. The new leadership has made clear its intent to maintain a grip on political power.[113] These sentiments are hard to reconcile with a push toward greater economic liberalization.

A lack of clarity about China's future exists, but that is also beside the point. With the nation being the fastest-growing great power in the post-2008 era, skeptics of the Washington Consensus look to China to articulate an alternative pathway. But China's internal splits about the future of its economic model make it impossible for its officials to articulate a coherent replacement to the Washington Consensus. Indeed, China's response has been to reject any notion of a Beijing Consensus. Prime Minister Li insisted in a *Financial Times* op-ed that China "can no longer afford to continue" its existing growth model.[114]

China might not adhere to its stated reform path, but neither is it articulating an alternative pathway. Even if the global financial crisis bruised and battered the Washington Consensus, it did not break it—in part because the most viable proponent for an alternative pathway acted more like a responsible stakeholder of the status quo.

Why Do Fears of Instability Persist?

The previous sections strongly suggest that despite pre-2008 fears and post-2008 perceptions, the global economic order has demonstrated re-

111. Roach, "Manchurian Paradox"; Jonathan Woetzel, Janamitra Devan, Richard Dobbs, Adam Eichner, Stefano Negri, and Micah Rowland, *If You've Got It, Spend It: Unleashing the Chinese Consumer* (New York: McKinsey Global Institute, 2009).

112. On prior Third Plenum promises coming to naught, see Keith Bradsher, "China's Leaders Confront Economic Fissures," *New York Times*, November 6, 2013. On state-owned enterprises, see Bob Davis and Brian Spegele, "State Companies Emerge as Winners Following Top China Meeting," *Wall Street Journal*, November 13, 2013.

113. See, for example, Jamil Anderlini, "How Long Can the Communist Party Survive in China?," *Financial Times*, September 20, 2013; Simon Denyer, "China's Leader, Xi Jinping, Consolidates Power with Crackdowns on Corruption, Internet," *Washington Post*, October 3, 2013; Evan Osnos, "Born Red," *New Yorker*, April 6, 2015, http://www.newyorker.com/magazine/2015/04/06/born-red; David Shambaugh, "The Coming Chinese Crackup," *Wall Street Journal*, March 6, 2015.

114. Li Keqiang, "China Will Stay the Course on Sustainable Growth," *Financial Times*, September 8, 2013.

markable resilience. There has been no appreciable increase in either trade or financial protectionism. The United States continued to exercise leadership during the Great Recession. China, far from acting like a spoiler, acted primarily as a responsible stakeholder to reinforce the preexisting rules of the global economic game. Economic interdependence has, if anything, *increased* after the 2008 financial crisis. Despite these facts, concerns about a Chinese challenge to the existing global economic order, and fears about China's use of economic power, continue to persist. Why? This section will give three possible answers, however speculative, to this question.

The first answer is that periods of fading unipolarity lead to heightened sensitivity of even rhetorical deviations from status quo policies. As Schweller and Pu observe, balancing behavior is considered to be a system-maintaining function when the global distribution of power is multipolar. In a unipolar world, however, balancing behavior is a system-altering strategy. Therefore, the perception shifts: "unipolarity is the only system in which balancing is a revisionist, rather than status quo, policy. . . . Because balancing under unipolarity is a revisionist process, any state intent on restoring system equilibrium will be labeled an aggressor. This reality implies that balancing under unipolarity must be preceded by a delegitimation phase."[115] In this delegitimation phase, any challenger to the unipolar status quo will attempt to discredit the preexisting rules of the game in order to lower the costs to a future balancing strategy.

Because a delegitimation phase is likely to precede any overt balancing, observers will magnify even rhetorical steps away from the status quo. As previously noted, even prior to the 2008 financial crisis there was no shortage of Chinese rhetoric pushing back against a neoliberal world order. After the collapse of Lehman Brothers, it was easy to point to symbolic actions that seemed designed to delegitimate the status quo—even if such actions were largely aimed at domestic rather than international audiences. For example, in March 2009 the head of the People's Bank of China (PBoC) suggested an end to the dollar's status as the world's reserve currency, to be replaced by a "super-sovereign reserve currency."[116] As rhetoric, this was an undeniably revisionist move. In actuality, however, China had neither the resources nor the inclination to end the dollar's status. Other central bankers were aware of the PBoC's constrained influence within the Chinese state.[117] Even China's fellow BRICS partners mostly resisted any further development of this

115. Schweller and Pu, "After Unipolarity," 45–46.
116. For the proposal, see Zhou Xiaochuan, "Reform the International Monetary System," http://www.bis.org/review/r090402c.pdf?frames=0.
117. Irwin, *The Alchemists*, chap. 20.

proposal.[118] The suggestion was symbolic in nature—but precisely because it hinted at radical change, its effect on perceptions was magnified.

Similarly, in the summer of 2013 the CCP leadership published an ideological memo—Document No. 9—that listed seven perils to the party. One of them was free market neoliberalism.[119] According to the document, "Western countries, led by the United States, carry out their Neoliberal agendas under the guise of 'globalization,' visiting catastrophic consequences upon Latin America, the Soviet Union, and Eastern Europe, and have also dragged themselves into the international financial crisis from [which] they have yet to recover. . . . These arguments aim to change our country's basic economic infrastructure and weaken the government's control of the national economy."[120] The intent of this document was clearly domestic, to encourage CCP resistance to Western ideas—and yet, again, such rhetoric can easily be framed as revisionist in character.

Heightened attention to any Chinese criticism of the existing economic order amplifies the effect of such rhetoric far beyond what is originally intended. For example, as the U.S. Congress flailed about in the fall of 2013, debating whether to increase the debt ceiling, a Xinhua News op-ed blasted the United States for acting irresponsibly. The essay rocketed around U.S. foreign policy circles because of its ominous suggestion "to consider building a de-Americanized world."[121] However, many Western commentators misinterpreted the essay as an official statement of government intent. Xinhua only published the essay in English; its ideas did not even permeate Chinese discourse until *after* it garnered attention in the United States.[122] In each of these episodes, the effect of the rhetoric was far more outsized than intended.

The second answer to our question is that, during periods of fading unipolarity, observers also exaggerate the relative decline of the hegemon and the relative rise of everyone else. A closer look at the actual economic capabilities of the United States and China shows that the latter is far weaker than public perceptions would suggest. This is true whether one looks at production or finance. On production, for example, for example, China's exporting prowess becomes quite clear, as the WTO data in figure 3.1 demonstrate.

118. Bruce Jones, *Still Ours to Lead: America, the Rising Powers, and the Myths of the Coming Disorder* (Washington, DC: Brookings Institution Press, 2014).

119. Chris Buckley, "China Takes Aim at Western Ideas," *New York Times*, August 19, 2013.

120. See "Document 9: A ChinaFile Translation: How Much Is a Hardline Party Directive Shaping China's Current Political Climate?," November 8, 2013, http://www.chinafile.com /document-9-chinafile-translation.

121. Liu Chang, "U.S. Fiscal Failure Warrants a De-Americanized World," Xinhua News Agency, October 13, 2013.

122. See Liz Carter, "Journalist's Call for 'de-Americanized World' Provokes Alarm in U.S., Fart Jokes in China," *Foreign Policy*, October 16, 2013, http://foreignpolicy.com/2013 /10/16/journalists-call-for-de-americanized-world-provokes-alarm-in-u-s-fart-jokes-in -china/.

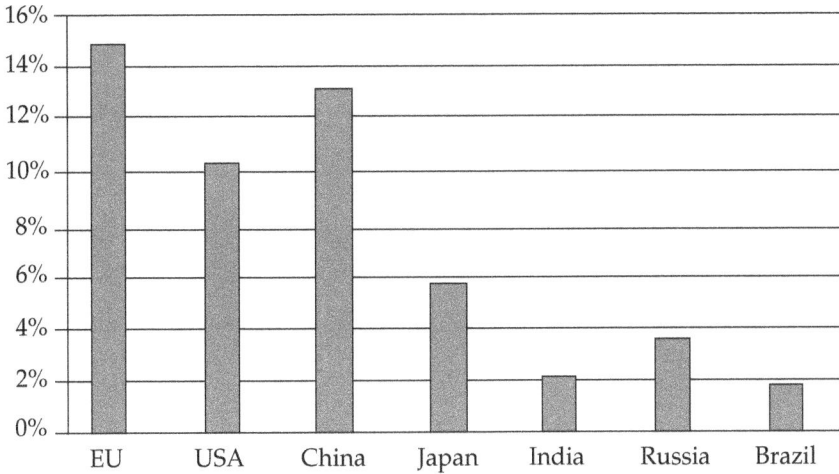

Figure 3.1. Share of global exports, 2011.

China is the world's largest exporter if one disaggregates the European Union, and it has eclipsed the United States as an export powerhouse.

This overstates Chinese trading power in important ways, however. China's gross export statistics overstate its real productive capacity. China's export prowess rests on being the location for the final assembly stage of production. With the global value chains of the twenty-first century, much of the value added in manufactured goods comes from earlier stages of production, which are then imported by China for final assembly. In 2013, the WTO and the Organisation for Economic Development derived estimates for export shares using a value-added calculation; these results can be seen in figure 3.2. They show that in 2009 the European Union remained the world's largest exporter, with 21.8 percent of global exports. The United States was second, responsible for 14.4 percent. China, using value-added calculations, was the third-largest exporter, with 10.1 percent.[123]

Another way that gross exports potentially misrepresent productive capacity is by overlooking the issue of ownership. A large fraction of productive capacity in the European Union, United States, and China is based on foreign direct investment. On the one hand, large FDI inflows represent a source of economic strength. On the other hand, where the profits from production go is also a source of economic power. Sean Starrs has analyzed data on corporate ownership from the Forbes Global 2000 rankings from 2006 and

123. The data in this paragraph come from the Organisation for Economic Development, http://stats.oecd.org/Index.aspx?DataSetCode=TIVA_OECD_WTO. None of the other BRIC economies approach these actors. Japan does somewhat better, but is still responsible for only 6.2 percent of global value-added exports.

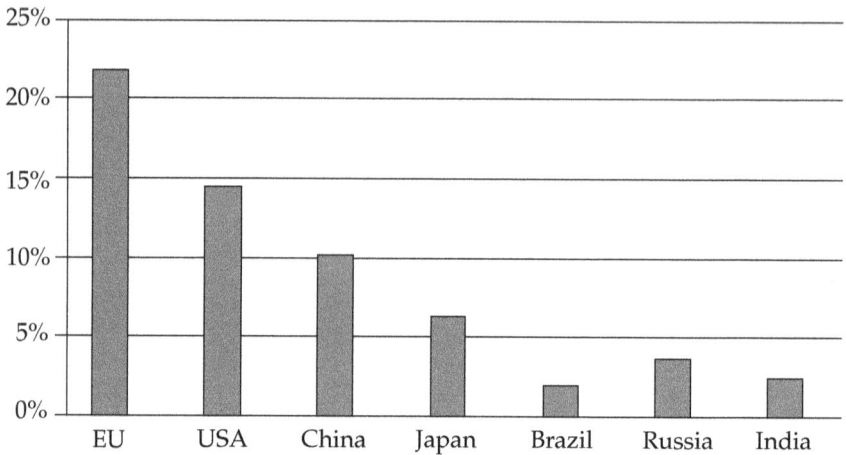

Figure 3.2. Share of global exports with value-added calculation, 2009.

2012 and concluded that "corporations domiciled in the United States continue to dominate by far the largest range of sectors, in particular, those involving advanced technology and knowledge. In fact, since 2008, American dominance has increased in key sectors such as financial services and software, with no serious contenders on the horizon, including China." More than 45 percent of the top five hundred multinational corporations are headquartered in the United States. This might be deceptive, because the cross-national ownership of firms could render corporate nationality less meaningful. Nevertheless, when Starrs analyzed that data, he found that in 2012, Americans possessed 41 percent of all household wealth in the world: "American citizens continue to own the predominant share of the world's wealth—much more so than America's declining share of GDP would suggest."[124] Starrs's findings buttress other research on the distribution of global wealth and corporate control that finds U.S. firms and households at the apex.[125]

A similar story can be told in the area of global finance. Even a glance at the IMF's *Global Financial Stability Report* on the size of capital markets

124. Sean Starrs, "American Economic Power Hasn't Declined—It Globalized! Summoning the Data and Taking Globalization Seriously," *International Studies Quarterly* 57, no. 4 (2013): 818.

125. For firms, see Stefania Vitali, James B. Glattfelder, and Stefano Battiston, "The Network of Global Corporate Control," *PloS ONE* 6, no. 10 (2011), http://dx.doi.org/10.1371/journal.pone.0025995; and Peter Nolan, *Is China Buying the World?* (London: Polity, 2012). For private wealth, see Herman Schwartz, *Subprime Nation: American Power, Global Capital, and the Housing Bubble* (Ithaca, NY: Cornell University Press, 2009); and James Davies, Susanna Sandström, Anthony Shorrocks, and Edward Wolff, "The Level and Distribution of Global Household Wealth," *Economic Journal* 121, no. 551 (2011): 223–54.

shows that the United States maintains market dominance.[126] Indeed, the combined financial markets of all emerging markets combined—including all of the BRIC economies—are still smaller than the U.S. capital markets. Using a network model to chart global financial flows reveals the power of the United States even more clearly. It is the most central actor in the network of global finance, with the United Kingdom a distant second. Indeed, the network centrality of the United States *increased* after 2008. As one recent analysis concluded, "the US is more firmly ensconced at the center of the global financial system than commonly appreciated. . . . [T]he EU's struggles and China's lack of financial development, and extant positive feedback effects interact to keep the US at the center of the global financial system for the foreseeable future."[127]

Despite claims and concerns to the contrary,[128] the Great Recession's effect on the dollar's status has been minimal. Between 2007 and 2010, for example, the dollar's share of official currency reserves declined from 64.1 percent to 61.5 percent. This is still above its share of 56.8 percent in the mid-1990s. The dollar's share of the international banking market increased from 41.9 percent to 43.7 percent during that same time period. As a medium of exchange, the dollar has shifted from being responsible for 85.4 percent of the global foreign exchange market in 2007 to 87.0 percent in 2013.[129] Multiple analyses also confirm that even after the 2008 financial crisis, more countries peg their currency to the dollar than any other currency.[130] The dollar is still a global currency, the euro functions as a regional currency, and no other national currency has attained any significance—including the renminbi, which remains inconvertible.[131] Doug Stokes concludes that "the dollar

126. See, for example, International Monetary Fund, *Global Financial Stability Report*, April 2012, http://www.imf.org/external/pubs/ft/gfsr/2012/01/pdf/text.pdf.

127. Oatley et al., "The Political Economy," 148.

128. For concerns, see Eric Helleiner and Jonathan Kirshner, eds., *The Future of the Dollar* (Ithaca, NY: Cornell University Press, 2009). For claims, see World Bank, *Multipolarity: The New Global Economy* (Washington, DC: World Bank, 2011); and Subramanian, *Eclipse*. For both, see Kirshner, "Bringing Them All Back Home?"

129. These data come from Jeffrey Frankel, "The Dollar and Its Rivals," November 21, 2013, https://www.project-syndicate.org/commentary/jeffrey-frankel-argues-that-the-dollar-s -status-as-the-world-s-top-international-currency-is-not-in-jeopardy?barrier=true. The percentages are out of a possible 200 percent.

130. Benjamin J. Cohen and Tabitha M. Benney, "What Does the International Currency System Really Look Like?," unpublished manuscript, University of California–Santa Barbara, August 2012; Thierry Bracke and Irina Bunda, *Exchange Rate Anchoring: Is There Still a De Facto US Dollar Standard?*, Working Paper Series no. 1353 (Frankfurt: European Central Bank, 2011); Doug Stokes, "Achilles' Deal: Dollar Decline and US Grand Strategy after the Crisis," *Review of International Political Economy* 21, no. 5 (2014): 1071–94.

131. On the difficulties China will have trying to internationalize its currency, see Daniel W. Drezner "Will Currency Follow the Flag?" *International Relations of the Asia-Pacific* 10 (September 2010): 389–414; McNally, "Sino-Capitalism"; and Barry Eichengreen, "Number One Currency, Number One Country?" *World Economy* 36, no. 4 (2013): 363–37. For more

continues to remain the key *global* currency by a considerable margin, with no other currency even close to competing."[132]

Most of the figures cited in the previous paragraphs are easily accessible. They paint a picture of a China that is a great power, but not capable of supplanting the United States as the economic hegemon. Indeed, China's relative weakness and dependence on an open global economy help to explain its behavior as a responsible stakeholder. Why, then, were immediate post-2008 perceptions of Chinese power so at variance with the reality? One explanation is that too many analysts have emphasized the wrong dimensions of economic power—such as hard currency reserves—that are actually quite limited in their utility.

The third answer to the question is that in thinking about the future, even scholars are vulnerable to straight-line extrapolations of recent trends.[133] China's rapid ascent over the previous few decades have caused some to extrapolate the recent past into the future—and then convert those future extrapolations into assessments of current capabilities. As Robert Gilpin has observed, the "reputation for power" is in itself a power resource. Part of China's power comes from the perception of its inexorable rise. Multiple projections have identified China as the economic hegemon by the year 2050.[134] There are excellent reasons to doubt such straight-line extrapolations. Demographic, economic, and political constraints will hamper China's rise over the next few decades.[135] Nevertheless, some commentators seem quite convinced that China's rise is an inexorable process.

There is one fourth, final, and even more speculative answer: China's actions in the security sphere have caused observers to generalize their perceptions of Chinese revisionism across issue areas. It is beyond the scope of this chapter to assess Chinese behavior in the South China Sea and East

---

positive assessments of Chinese efforts to "internationalize" the renminbi, see Subramanian, *Eclipse*; and Kirshner, "Bringing Them All Back Home?"

132. Stokes "Achilles' Deal," emphasis in the original. See also Drezner, "Will Currency Follow the Flag?"; and Cohen and Benney, "What Does the International Currency System Really Look Like?"

133. See Daniel W. Drezner, *Five Known Unknowns about the Next Generation Global Economy.* (Washington, DC: Brookings Institution, 2016).

134. Robert Fogel, "123,000,000,000,000*: *China's estimated economy by the year 2040. Be warned," *Foreign Policy*, January 4, 2010, http://foreignpolicy.com/2010/01/04/123000000000000/; Uri Dadush and Bennett Stancil, *The World Order in 2050* (Washington, DC: Carnegie Endowment for International Peace, 2010), http://carnegieendowment.org/files/World_Order_in_2050.pdf.

135. Dani Rodrik, *The Future of Economic Convergence*, NBER Working Paper no. 17400 (Cambridge, MA: National Bureau of Economic Research, 2011); Barry Eichengreen, Donghyun Park, and Kwanho Shin, *When Fast Growing Economies Slow Down: International Evidence and Implications for China*, NBER Working Paper no. 16919 (Cambridge, MA: National Bureau of Economic Research, 2011); Ruchir Sharma, "Broken BRICS: Why the Rest Stopped Rising," *Foreign Affairs* 91, no. 6 (2012): 2–7.

China Sea; the extent of Chinese revisionism on these issues remains a matter of some contestation. There is a strong consensus, however, that these actions have fostered a perception of increased Chinese assertiveness.[136] If China has been willing to be more assertive in the security sphere—an area where the distribution of power does not yet tilt in Beijing's favor—then it is not surprising that commentators would infer greater assertiveness in the economic sphere as well. Even if China's economic power has been exaggerated, its economic capabilities are relatively more potent vis-à-vis the United States than its military capabilities. For Western observers focusing on capabilities as much as intentions, Chinese assertiveness in global economic governance would be seen as a logical inevitability.

Conclusion

China was the only actor powerful enough and distinct enough from the established great powers to act as a truly revisionist actor in the world of global political economy during the Great Recession. And yet, a rising China did not act in this manner at all. Based on its behavior in the first five years following the 2008 financial crisis, Beijing acted like a responsible stakeholder: it did not advocate abandoning either the open trading system or the open investment regime. This is consistent with the assessment by China scholars about the country's willingness to comply with other global governance mechanisms over time, and its reluctance to articulate a truly revisionist set of policy demands.[137] Iain Johnston provides a concise snapshot of China's postcrisis behavior:

> The pundit and media world thus tended to miss a great deal of ongoing cooperative interaction between the United States and China throughout 2010. Examples include the continued growth of U.S. exports to China during the year . . . [and] a Chinese decision to continue the appreciation of the renminbi prior to the Group of Twenty meeting in Toronto in June 2010. . . .
>
> In addition to these U.S.-specific cooperative actions, throughout 2010 China continued to participate in all of the major multilateral global and regional institutions in which it had been involved for the past couple of decades, including the World Trade Organization, the International Monetary Fund, the United Nations Security Council, the Association of Southeast Asian Nations (ASEAN) Plus 3, the China-ASEAN Free Trade Agreement, UN peacekeeping operations, and antipiracy activities in the Gulf of Aden.

136. See, for example, Johnston, "How New and Assertive Is China's New Assertiveness?"
137. Steinfeld, *Playing Our Game*; Rosemary Foot and Andrew Walter, *China, The United States, and Global Order* (Cambridge: Cambridge University Press, 2011); Shambaugh, *China Goes Global.*

There is no evidence that . . . it began to withdraw from global institutional life or to dramatically challenge the purposes, ideology, or main organizational features of these institutions to a degree that it had not in the past.[138]

Since the start of the Great Recession, China's behavior has reinforced rather than subverted the existing set of global governance rules. China was a supporter, and not a spoiler, of the open global economy.

Why are fears of Chinese revisionist behavior so heightened when their actual behavior has been supportive? I have suggested a three-part explanation. First, in a unipolar world, there is heightened sensitivity to even rhetorical gestures that appear to delegitimate the status quo. While Chinese actions have largely been those of a responsible stakeholder, Chinese rhetoric has been more varied. Second, China's rapid ascent caused observers to overestimate the country's capabilities. China is clearly a great power, but the United States remains a far greater power. Nevertheless, extrapolations of past trajectories have caused some China watchers' expectations to outpace reality. Third, Chinese actions in the security sphere have caused many observers to conclude that Beijing must have revisionist aspirations in the economic realm as well.

This chapter has suggested that there is a high degree of uncertainty and misperception surrounding China's capabilities and preferences in the global political economy. That does not necessarily bode well for the future—even though the liberal economic order has demonstrated remarkable resilience. If enough actors believe that the distribution of power has shifted in a particular direction, then those perceptions can socially construct that reality for a limited period of time. If China is granted the perquisites of hegemonic status, for example, then it will also be expected to assume the responsibilities of that status. Collective perceptions can force countries to either shirk or take on ill-suited obligations—particularly if the perceptions deviate significantly from the material facts of life. This explains some commentators' frustration with the failure of the BRIC economies to shoulder the burden of leadership in global governance structures.[139]

An even deeper question is whether the perceived rise of China threatens the stability of a unipolar global order. The historical evidence suggests that the primary causal mechanism through which unipolarity leads to peace and prosperity is the elimination of uncertainty.[140] When hegemony is uncon-

138. Johnston, "How New and Assertive Is China's New Assertiveness?," 32–33.

139. Stewart Patrick, "Irresponsible Stakeholders?" *Foreign Affairs* 89, no. 6 (2010): 44–53.

140. Robert Gilpin, *War and Change in World Politics* (New York: Cambridge University Press, 1981), 31; Daniel Geller, "Explaining War: Empirical Patterns and Theoretical Mechanisms," in *Handbook of War Studies II*, ed. Manus I. Midlarsky (Ann Arbor: University of Michigan Press, 2000), 438.

tested and acknowledged by all major actors, then secondary states have less of a need to attempt to balance or to engage in status-seeking behavior. Indeed, even scholars who argue for the persistence of unipolarity acknowledge the importance of preeminence across a variety of power metrics. As William Wohlforth notes, "When an actor possesses some attributes of high status but not others, uncertainty and status inconsistency are likely. The more a lower-ranked actor matches the higher-ranked group in some but not all key material dimensions of status, the more likely it is to conceive an interest in contesting its rank and the more likely the higher-ranked state is to resist."[141]

Even though the global economy has bounced back from the 2008 financial crisis, China's perceived rise injected uncertainty into assessing the global distribution of power. Ironically, while China has taken more concrete steps to challenge the Bretton Woods Institutions in recent years, the degree of Western anxiety has abated. The Silk Road Initiatives, the New Development Bank, and the Asian Infrastructure Investment Bank are more tangible examples of nascent Chinese revisionism than anything the country did in the immediate post-2008 period. Nevertheless, with a few notable exceptions,[142] there is less anxiety about Chinese revisionism in 2016 than in 2008. One possible reason is that misperceptions of Chinese power have been reduced. China's growth rate has fallen by half since the 2008 financial crisis. The government's summer 2015 interventions into equity markets were not seen as a policy success. The country faces a severe demographic crunch, environmental degradation, high levels of debt, and significant financial instability. Each of these trends poses problems for its medium-run growth trajectory and political stability.[143] There is newfound pessimism that China will overtake the United States economy anytime soon.[144] China's financial instability, combined with continued U.S. economic growth, finally caused commentators to update their beliefs about each country's future economic capabilities. As perceptions about the distribution of economic power realign more closely with reality, the degree of anxiety about Chinese economic revisionism will wane.

141. William C. Wohlforth, "Unipolarity, Status Competition, and Great Power War," *World Politics* 61, no. 1 (2009): 28–57.

142. Lawrence Summers, "A Global Wake-Up Call for the U.S.?" *Washington Post*, April 5, 2015.

143. Osnos, "Born Red,"; Shambaugh, "The Coming Chinese Crackup"; Miles Kahler, "Conservative Globalizers: Reconsidering the Rise of the Rest," *World Politics Review*, February 2, 2016, http://www.worldpoliticsreview.com/articles/17840/conservative-globalizers-reconsidering-the-rise-of-the-rest.

144. Stephen G. Brooks and William C. Wohlforth, "The Once and Future Superpower," *Foreign Affairs* 95, no. 3 (2016): 91–104.

CHAPTER 4

Two Asias?

China's Rise, Dual Structure, and the Alliance System in East Asia

Wang Dong

The miraculous rise of China in the past three decades has contributed to the titanic shift in and reconfiguration of the regional power order in East Asia. China's breakneck economic and military rise has increasingly posed challenges to U.S. primacy and the U.S.-led alliance system in the region. Particularly, since the alleged Chinese assertiveness and the United States' determined pivot/rebalancing to Asia in the wake of the 2008 global financial crisis, security analysts in the region and beyond have begun wondering whether or not East Asia has been drifting toward polarization. Strategic analysts have taken note of the emergence of "two Asias," or a "dual structure," in which an "Economic Asia" increasingly depends on China for trade, investment and markets and a "Security Asia" looks to the United States for guarantees of security. The problem is that the dynamics of the two Asias or the dual structure has become increasingly "irreconcilable."[1] How does and will China respond to such a dual structure? What are the U.S. stra-

---

1. Evan A. Feigenbaum and Robert A. Manning, "A Tale of Two Asias," *Foreign Policy*, October 31, 2012, http://www.foreignpolicy.com/articles/2012/10/30/a_tale_of_two_asias ?page=full. For the argument about the dual structure, see Qi Huaigao, "Zhongmei zhidu junshi yu dongya liangzhong tixi de jianrong gongcun" [China-U.S. institutional balance of power and the compatible coexistence of two systems in East Asia], *Daidai yatai* 6 (2011): 55–74; Zhou Fangyin, "Zhongguo jueqi, dongya geju bianqian yu dongya zhixu de fazhan fangxiang" [China's rise, changes in East Asian patterns, and the trajectory of East Asian order], *Dangdai yatai* 5 (2012): 4–32. G. John Ikenberry labels it as "dual hierarchies"; see G. John Ikenberry, "Between the Eagle and the Dragon: China, the U.S., and Middle State Grand Strategies in East Asia," paper presented at the 2012 Five University Conference "Toward a New Equilibrium of Regional Order in the Asia-Pacific," Korea University, December 7–8, 2012.

tegic options? How do major regional players respond to the changing dynamics? What impact will the dual structure have on the regional security order? Particularly, will the U.S.-led bilateral alliance system in the region undergo transformation? If so, how is such a transformation to be characterized? And, finally, what will the future trajectories of the two Asias look like?

This chapter attempts to answer these questions. It argues that instead of aiming at pushing the United States out of the Asia Pacific region and constructing a China-dominated order, China has largely pursued a hedging strategy that aims at reducing or minimizing risks, increasing its freedom of action, diversifying its strategic options, and shaping the preferences of the United States. Facing the uncertainties brought about by the rise of China, the United States also employs a hedging strategy toward China. In light of the emergence of a dual structure in East Asia, the U.S.-led hub-and-spoke alliance system is under transformation gearing toward "networkization" (*wangluo hua*) or the emergence of a web of alliances and partnerships that is characterized by enhanced security ties not only between the hub (the United States) and the spokes (U.S. allies and partners), but also between spokes. Both China and the United States have adjusted to China's rise with policies that seek to defend their core security interests while maintaining cooperative relations. To a great extent, regional states, when facing the uncertainties brought about by the rise of China, have also been pursuing hedging strategies. Typically, regional states are reluctant to make a choice between China and the United States, preferring to hedge between Economic Asia and Security Asia. But the dual structure might be difficult to sustain, and the strategic space for hedging might dwindle, as China's capabilities continue to rise, posing increasingly more challenges to the existing regional order. How the dual structure will evolve in the years and decades to come will largely be determined by the trajectory of U.S.-China relations.

In this chapter, I will first examine the characteristics of East Asia's emerging dual structure and determine to what extent a dual structure exists in East Asia. Second, I will look at China's management of its new role in East Asia and its response to the regional dual structure. Third, I will discuss the United States' and other major countries' strategic response to China's rise and its challenge to the regional status quo, particularly the networkization of the U.S.-led alliance system. Finally, I will provide a preliminary assessment of the possible future trajectories of the dual structure.

China's Rise and the Emergence of the Dual Structure in East Asia

Since the end of the Cold War, China's economy, measured in gross domestic product (GDP), has grown from US$424 billion in 1991 to US$10.866

trillion in 2015.[2] By the end of 2015, China's economy had accounted for 51 percent of the total economy of East Asia.[3] Now 59 percent of the trade in East Asia is being conducted within the region.[4] That China has become the powerhouse for regional growth can also be shown in the fact that China now is the biggest trading partner of virtually every country in the region, including the Association of Southeast Asian Nations (ASEAN) economies, Japan, South Korea, and Australia, with total trade volumes reaching US$400.1 billion, US$333.7 billion, US$215.1 billion, and US$122.3 billion, respectively, in 2012.[5]

Between 2004 and 2015, the annual total exports to China by East Asian economies has grown 225 percent, from US$297.2 billion to US$667.4.[6] By comparison, during the same period, East Asian economies' annual exports to the United States had only grown modestly, from US$309.4 billion to US$380 billion.[7] In less than a decade, East Asian economies' exports to China (or China's imports from other East Asian economies) have overtaken those of the United States by over 200 percent. Globally, in 2006 the United States was the largest trading partner in 127 countries and regions, whereas China was the largest in only seventy. By 2011 the global trade landscape had experienced an upside-down shift: China had become the largest trading partner in 124 countries and regions, whereas the United States remained the largest trading partner in only seventy-six.[8] Moreover, according to statistics released by the Society for Worldwide Interbank Financial Telecommunication in April 2015, 31 percent of the trade transactions with greater China in the Asia Pacific were conducted in renminbi (RMB), up from

2. These data are drawn from the World Bank, "World Development Indicators," http://databank.worldbank.org/data/reports.aspx?Code=NY.GDP.MKTP.CD&id=af3ce82b&report_name=Popular_indicators&populartype=series&ispopular=y.

3. This number is calculated by the author using data drawn from the World Bank, "World Development Indicators."

4. The number is calculated by the author using data drawn from UN Comtrade's trade data extraction interface, http://comtrade.un.org/data/.

5. Phoenix New Media, "Deputy Director of the Department of Asian Affairs at the MOCOM Liang Wentao: It Is of Significant Importance to Successfully Host the 10th China-ASEAN Expo," March 29, 2013, http://tech.ifeng.com/telecom/detail_2013_03/29/23680636_0.shtml; Japan External Trade Organization, "Summaries of Data on China-Japan Trade and Investments," http://www.jetro.go.jp/china/data/trade/; Korea International Trade Association, "K-Statistics: All Countries," http://www.kita.org/kStat/byCount_AllCount.do; China Network Television, "China: Australia's Largest Trade Partner," April 9, 2013, http://english.cntv.cn/program/china24/20130409/107022.shtml.

6. This number is calculated by the author using data drawn from UN Comtrade's trade data extraction interface, http://comtrade.un.org/data/. East Asian economies are defined as the following: the ASEAN, Australia, Japan, New Zealand, South Korea, and Taiwan.

7. These data are drawn from the U.S. Department of Commerce, Bureau of Economic Analysis, "International Economic Accounts," http://bea.gov/international/index.htm#trade.

8. Yan Xuetong, *Lishi de guanxing* [The inertia of history] (Beijing: Zhongxin chubanshe, 2013), 10–13.

7 percent in April 2012. The renminbi is the world's fifth largest currency now, accounting for 2.03 percent of total global payments. With the establishment of four new clearing centers (Australia, Malaysia, South Korea, and Thailand) in the region, RMB adoption is expected to increase, further solidifying the important role of RMB within the Asia Pacific and beyond.[9]

To be sure, despite China's increasingly prominent role in regional trade and economic activities, the United States remains one of the primary economic players in East Asia. Measured by direct investment in East Asian economies, China lags far behind the United States. In 2015, U.S. direct investments in the region totaled US$402 billion, dwarfing China's US$118 billion.[10] In other words, despite its increasingly prominent trade ties with regional countries, China's economic clout in the region remains limited, and the region still looks to the United States for investments and technology. The fact that regional countries still regard the United States rather than China as the top economy is also reflected in a Pew Global Attitudes Project survey. According to the poll, which was conducted between March and June 2014, 55 percent of the surveyed Asian countries considered the United States the world's leading economic power, while merely 25 percent in the region would accord such an honor on China.[11]

The economic rise of China has not yet brought about a fundamental change to the regional security order, which is characterized by a U.S.-led hub-and-spoke bilateral alliance system. While China has become the largest trading partner of virtually all countries in East Asia (and the share of trade with the United States is diminishing for nearly every East Asian country's total trade volume),[12] the United States remains the primary security guarantor of the region's maritime countries, buttressed by five formal bilateral military alliances (with Australia, Japan, the Philippines, South Korea, and Thailand) and a number of close security partnerships in the region (including partnerships with Malaysia, Mongolia, and Singapore, among other nations).[13]

9. "RMB Ranks #1 in Asia Pacific for Payments with Greater China," May 27, 2015, https://www.swift.com/insights/press-releases/rmb-ranks-1-in-asia-pacific-for-payments-with-greater-china.

10. These data are drawn from *Zhongguo Shangwu Tongji Nianjian 2013* [China commerce statistics yearbook 2013] (Beijing: Zhongguo shangwu chubanshe, 2012); and the U.S. Department of Commerce, Bureau of Economic Analysis, "Interactive Data," http://www.bea.gov/itable/index.cfm.

11. Pew Research Center, *Global Opposition to U.S. Surveillance and Drones, but Limited Harm to U.S. Image: Many in Asia Wary about Conflict with China*, July 2014, http://www.pewglobal.org/files/2014/07/2014-07-14-Balance-of-Power.pdf, 35.

12. Feigenbaum and Manning, "A Tale of Two Asias."

13. It is worth noting that a number of regional players (i.e., Cambodia, Laos, Myanmar, and North Korea) are out of the U.S. security system. As China's power continues to rise, these players might increasingly fall under the "sphere of influence" of China. Yet except for the ambiguous case of North Korea, China does not have formal alliance relationships or

China has expanded and modernized its maritime capabilities, and its regional power projection capabilities have significantly improved. It can now challenge the security and territorial claims of U.S. allies, and it is developing a deterrent capability vis-à-vis the U.S. Navy. Nonetheless, the Chinese Navy cannot challenge U.S. maritime superiority. Thus, a bifurcation between economic dynamics and security dynamics in the region has emerged, giving rise to what some strategic analysts call two Asias, or a dual structure. As I have shown, Economic Asia is far from being dominated by China; the United States, in many respects, remains the dominant economic player in the region. Meanwhile, although Security Asia is clearly dominated by the United States, China has become a military power in East Asia. In other words, the two Asias or the dual structure remains an emerging feature of the region.

The region's "schizophrenia," marked by East Asia's "looking to China for profit, the U.S. for security," has unsettled strategy analysts.[14] Evan A. Feigenbaum and Robert A. Manning, for example, worry that tensions between the diverging economic and security dynamics might "overwhelm, or even destroy the economic gains that were beginning to pull the region away from its debilitating past."[15]

Tensions between China and the United States increased after 2009 when Washington "pushed back" against perceived Chinese assertiveness. Washington's "pivot" or "rebalancing" to Asia, including moves to bolster its bilateral military alliances with Japan, the Philippines, and South Korea, enhance security ties with Singapore and Vietnam, deploy 2,500 U.S. Marines to Darwin, Australia, and beef up ballistic missile defense system in East Asia, was widely interpreted by the Chinese scholarly and foreign policy community as a thinly veiled attempt to restrain and counterbalance—if not encircle or contain—China. China's establishment of an air defense identification zone in the East China Sea in December 2013 triggered strong opposition and reactions from the United States. In subsequent years, China's efforts at land reclamation in the South China Sea triggered regional concern and strong U.S. reactions—including high-profile freedom of navigation operations conducted by the U.S. Navy within twelve nautical miles of some of the islands that China controlled. In addition, U.S deployment of the Terminal High Altitude Area Defense system in South Korea invited strong Chinese protests and, potentially, retaliation. The increasing

---

robust security ties with these countries. Therefore, despite such complexity, and short of China's actively forging regional alliances, the regional security order can still be characterized as a U.S.-dominated one.

14. Feigenbaum and Manning, "A Tale of Two Asias"; Greg Torode, "Region Looks to China for Profit, U.S. for Security," *South China Morning Post*, November 15, 2010; Zhou, "Zhongguo jueqi, dongya geju bianqian yu dongya zhixu de fazhan fangxiang."

15. Feigenbaum and Manning, "A Tale of Two Asias."

U.S.-China security frictions and competition have contributed to the growth of strategic distrust between the two, intensified the security dilemma in the region, and altogether increased zero-sum-ness in regional security dynamics.[16]

HEDGING STRATEGIES IN THE DUAL STRUCTURE

In response to the shifting regional balance of power and the emerging East Asian dual structure, states throughout the region have adopted hedging strategies. I define *hedging* in international relations as an insurance strategy states adopt when facing uncertainty; such a strategy aims at reducing or minimizing risks brought about by the uncertainties in the system, increasing freedom to maneuver, diversifying strategic options, and shaping the preferences of adversary. It is a portfolio or mixed strategy that consists of both cooperative and competitive strategic instruments ranging from engagement to enmeshment and all the way up to balancing. Any hedging portfolio will be a mixed strategy—in other words, a combination of both cooperative and competitive strategic instruments. A state actor, when pursuing hedging, will use a combination of strategic instruments such as engagement, enmeshment, and balancing, which are distributed along a spectrum. The major determining factor of the modality and intensity of a hedging portfolio is threat perception, which is defined as the initiator's perception of the target's threat to the initiator's own security. As East Asian states' threat perceptions of China rise, the competitive components of their hedging portfolios toward China will increase.[17] Unsure of China's intentions, and reluctant to choose sides between Beijing and Washington, countries in East Asia have increasingly employed hedging strategies toward China and the United States in an attempt to minimize strategic

16. For an account of the increase in strategic distrust between China and the United States, see Kenneth Lieberthal and Wang Jisi, *Addressing U.S.-China Strategic Distrust* (Washington, DC: Brookings Institution, 2012).

17. There is a small but growing literature on hedging in international relations. Despite the fact that hedging has been increasingly discussed by scholars and policymakers, the concept is notorious for lacking a coherent definition, much less a theory. Elsewhere I have tried to develop a theory of hedging that will answer the following questions: Under what conditions will states choose to hedge? What form will this hedging take, and with how much intensity? See Dong Wang, "The Promise and Perils of Hedging Strategy: A Preliminary Theoretical Framework," paper presented at the First Annual Conference of Democracy and Peace in East Asia, Uppsala University, September 16–18, 2011; Project Team headed by Wang Dong, "Zhongguo jueqi yu yatai guojia duichong xingwei yanjiu" [A study on China's rise and the hedging behavior of Asia-Pacific countries], in *Zhanlue zongheng: 2012–2013 yanjiu baogao huibian* [Strategic aspect: Collection of research reports, 2012–2013] (Beijing: Center for International and Strategic Studies, Peking University, 2013), 70–123. See also Øystein Tunsjø, *Security and Profit in China's Energy Security Policy: Hedging against Risk* (New York: Columbia University Press, 2013); and Øystein Tunsjø, this volume, chap. 2.

uncertainties and potential risks brought on by the rise of China and the emergence of a potential dual structure.[18] In fact, one might argue that "looking to China for profit, the U.S. for security" is precisely a typical hedging strategy. By practicing hedging, East Asian countries aim to reduce or minimize potential risks, maximize freedom to maneuver, diversify strategic options, and shape the preferences of China.[19]

China's Grand Strategic Options

Since the early 1990s, China has adopted a strategy coined by former paramount leader Deng Xiaoping—*taoguang yanghui, yousuo zuowei* (keep a low profile, and accomplish something)—as its overall foreign policy guideline. By 2005 China had unveiled a "peaceful rise" (which later was labeled a "peaceful development") strategy. Under the guidance of *taoguang yanghui, yousuo zuowei* and peaceful development strategy, Beijing avoided security competition with the unipolar hegemon, the United States; actively engaged and reassured ASEAN countries through "good neighbor" diplomacy; and successfully created a stable external environment for its economic growth.[20] The nation's emerging grand strategy was labeled a "neo-Bismarckian" by leading U.S. international security scholar Avery Goldstein.[21] Taking advantage of U.S. preoccupation in counterterrorism efforts and the wars in Afghanistan and Iraq, China reassured and "co-opted" the region by forging close economic and trade relations and provision of positive inducements such as economic aids. In November 2002, China and ASEAN kicked off the process of establishing a free trade area. When it went into effect in January 2010, the China-ASEAN Free Trade Area encompassed 1.9 billion

18. For discussions of East Asian countries' hedging strategy, see Wang, "The Promise and Perils of Hedging Strategy"; Wang et al., "Zhongguo jueqi yu yatai guojia duichong xingwei yanjiu"; C. P. Chung, "Southeast Asia-China Relations: Dialectics of 'Hedging' and 'Counter-Hedging,'" *Southeast Asian Affairs*, 2004, 35–43; and Evelyn Goh, *Meeting the China Challenge: The U.S. in Southeast Asian Regional Security Strategies*, Policy Studies 16 (Washington, DC: East-West Center, 2005).

19. Wang Dong, "Assessing U.S.-China Relations: How We Should not Misread China?," *Asan Forum* 2, no. 2 (2014), http://www.theasanforum.org/sino-us-relations-4/.

20. Zhang Yunling and Tang Shiping, "China's Regional Strategy," in *Power Shift: China and Asia's New Dynamics*, ed. David Shambaugh (Berkeley: University of California Press, 2005), 48–70; Zhu Feng, "China's Rise Will Be Peaceful: How Unipolarity Matters," in *China Ascent: Power, Security, and the Future of International Politics*, ed. Robert S. Ross and Zhu Feng (Ithaca, NY: Cornell University Press, 2008), 34–54.

21. Avery Goldstein, "An Emerging China's Emerging Grand Strategy—A Neo-Bismarckian Turn?" in *International Relations Theories and the Asia Pacific*, ed. G. John Ikenberry and Michael Mastanduno (New York: Columbia University Press, 2003), 57–106; Avery Goldstein, *Rising to the Challenge: China's Grand Strategy and International Security* (Stanford, CA: Stanford University Press, 2005).

people, US$6 trillion in GDP and US$4.5 trillion in trade volume.[22] In November 2012 China and fifteen other regional states formally embarked on negotiations for the Regional Comprehensive Economic Partnership marking a key step toward a deeper level of regional economic integration.[23] In September 2013 Chinese premier Li Keqiang called for upgrading the China-ASEAN Free Trade Area and increasing bilateral trade to US$1 trillion and mutual investments to US$160 billion by 2020.[24] In October 2013 China proposed the building of the Asian Infrastructure Investment Bank to increase interconnectivity and economic integration in the region.[25] In political and security arenas, the nation actively supported and participated in ASEAN-centered regional multilateral regimes such as the ASEAN Regional Forum, ASEAN+3, the East Asia Summit, and the ASEAN Defence Ministers Meeting Plus. In 2003, China signed the Treaty of Amity and Cooperation in Southeast Asia with ASEAN, and the two decided to establish the China-ASEAN Strategic Partnership for Peace and Prosperity. In 2011, China and ASEAN held the first defense ministers meeting.[26] During his trip to Southeast Asia in October 2013, Chinese president Xi Jinping called for the building of a more closely knit China-ASEAN "community of common destiny."[27]

Beijing's expansion of its ties with ASEAN is part of its hedging portfolio, which aims to fulfill the following goals: minimizing the risks brought about by U.S. hegemonic behavior through engagement and accommodating U.S. primacy; diversifying its strategic options vis-à-vis the United States and preserving and expanding its freedom to maneuver (e.g., through forging the Shanghai Cooperation Organization and strengthening ties with Russia); and shaping U.S. preferences through engagement and persuasion (both

22. For the data, China Council for the Promotion of International Trade, "Zhongguo-Dongmeng zimaoqu de tedian" [The characteristics of the China-ASEAN Free Trade Area], April 28, 2012, http://www.cafta.org.cn/show.php?contentid=63875.

23. Association of Southeast Asian Nations, "ASEAN Framework for Regional Comprehensive Economic Partnership," http://asean.org/?static_post=asean-framework-for-regional-comprehensive-economic-partnership.

24. Yao Jing and Li Xiaokun, "Premier Calls for Action on Free Trade Area Upgrade," *China Daily*, October 10, 2013, http://www.chinadaily.com.cn/china/2013livisiteastasia/2013-10/10/content_17018957.htm; Ministry of Foreign Affairs of the People's Republic of China, "Li Keqiang: China-ASEAN Have Become the Model of Good-Neighborly Cooperation," September 5, 2013, http://www.fmprc.gov.cn/ce/ceindo/eng/ztbd/5798112rredf/t1073224.htm.

25. Xinhua News Agency, "Xi's Southeast Asia Tour Boosts Ties, Regional Cooperation: Chinese FM," October 8, 2013, http://news.xinhuanet.com/english/china/2013-10/09/c_125496979.htm.

26. Xinhua News Agency, "China-ASEAN Cooperation, 1991–2011," November 11, 2015, http://news.xinhuanet.com/english2010/china/2011-11/15/c_131248640_2.htm.

27. Xinhua News Agency, "China Vows to Build a Community of Common Destiny with ASEAN," Xinhua Net, October 3, 2013, http://news.xinhuanet.com/english/china/2013-10/03/c_132770494.htm.

peaceful and forceful).[28] One might argue that precisely such a hedging strategy has contributed to restrained U.S.–China competition and has led to the emergence of the dual structure in East Asia.[29] One prominent example of hedging is China's active cultivation and promotion of the Shanghai Cooperation Organization (SCO). Established in June 2001, the SCO has over the years evolved into a premier regional security regime that encompasses China, Russia, and Central Asian states. India, Iran, Mongolia, and Pakistan have also acquired observer status since 2004. Through the SCO, China has expanded security ties with Russia and Central Asian states, diversified and secured sources of energy supply, and enhanced cooperation with member states against threats posed by the "three evils" (*sange shili*)—namely, terrorism, separatism, and extremism. Notably, since 2002 China has conducted annual joint counterterrorist military exercises with member states, and the sophistication and scale of the drills continues to grow over time.[30]

With the perceived relative decline of the West and the shift in the balance of power between China and the West since the 2008 global financial crisis, there developed a renewed debate among Chinese analysts as to whether China should adhere to *taoguang yanghui, yousuo zuowei* as a strategic guideline. An increasing number of analysts question whether this philosophy has become outdated given China's newfound power and its much improved status in the world. It is time for China to "reveal the sword" (*liangjian*), as some Chinese security analysts describe it, and demonstrate China's resolve and determination to defend its core interests (*hexin liyi*).[31] At the policy level, subtle changes were made to the *taoguang yanghui, yousuo zuowei* policy. In July 2009, China convened a four-day ambassadorial conference in which the top leadership and senior diplomats reviewed the international situation since the outbreak of the financial crisis and mapped the direction for China's diplomacy in the years ahead.[32] It was also at this

28. Evan S. Medeiros, "Strategic Hedging and the Future of Asia Pacific Stability," *Washington Quarterly* 29, no. 1 (2005–6): 145–67; Rosemary Foot, "Chinese Strategies in a U.S.-Hegemonic Global Order: Accommodating and Hedging," *International Affairs* 82, no. 1 (2006): 74–94.
29. Zhou, "Zhongguo jueqi, dongya geju bianqian yu dongya zhixu de fazhan fangxiang," 11–12.
30. Stephen Aris, *Eurasian Regionalism: The Shanghai Cooperation Organization* (New York: Palgrave Macmillan, 2011); Chen Yurong, "Shanghai Cooperation Organization: A Banner of Multilateral Cooperation," *China International Studies* 2 (2010): 98–108.
31. "Zhuanjia: Zhongguo yao ganyu liangjian, shaoyou luohou jiuhui aida" [Experts: China should have the courage to reveal the sword; China will get beaten up if it lags behind], July 29, 2013, http://mil.huanqiu.com/observation/2013-07/4182321.html.
32. Besides Hu and Wen, seven other standing members of the Politburo—He Guoqiang, Jia Qinglin, Li Changchun, Li Keqiang, Wu Bangguo, Xi Jinping, and Zhou Yongkang—were all present at the conference. Also present at the conference were other senior leaders, including Defense Minster Liang Guanglie. State councilor in charge of foreign affairs Dai

conference that *jixu taoguang yanghui, jiji yousuo zuowei* (continue to keep a low profile, and proactively accomplish something) was proposed as the new guideline for China's foreign policy.[33] In October 2013 President Xi advocated that China should be more proactive (*fengfa youwei*) in pursuing its good-neighbor policy.[34] Since assuming leadership, Xi has repeatedly emphasized that in order to achieve the "China dream" the nation should remain "modest and prudent" and stick to the path of peaceful development.[35] This proactive foreign policy agenda advocated by the new Chinese leadership includes ambitious proposals to build a "Silk Road economic belt" extending through Central Asia, a new "maritime Silk Road" with the ASEAN countries, and the Asian Infrastructure Investment Bank. Such a proactive foreign policy agenda clearly reflects China's emerging shift in its foreign policy in response to its arrival as a global economic power and the dominant regional economic power.[36]

Arguably, the new leadership's proactive foreign policy is also characterized by a more clearly stated determination to defend China's sovereignty and territorial integrity. Such a position was best stated by President Xi at a collective study session of the Politburo in January 2013; while emphasizing the importance of sticking to the overarching strategy of peaceful development, Xi stated that China would never "give up our legitimate rights and benefits," warning that "no foreign country should expect that we would trade out our core interests, nor expect that we would swallow the bitter pill of infringement upon our country's sovereignty, security, and development interests."[37] Nevertheless, the Chinese government also stresses

Binguo also gave a talk, and both Foreign Minister Yang Jiechi and Vice Foreign Minister Wang Guangya presented working papers to the conference. For a detailed report of the conference, see Ministry of Foreign Affairs of the People's Republic of China, "Di shiyici shijie huiyi zaijing zhaokai" [The Eleventh Ambassadorial Conference was held in Beijing], July 20, 2010, http://www.mfa.gov.cn/chn/gxh/xsb/xw/t574427.htm.

33. Ministry of Foreign Affairs officials, interview with the author, Beijing, January 2010.

34. Xinhua News Agency, "Xi Jinping: rang mingyun gongtongti yishi zai zhoubianguojia luodi shenggen" [Xi Jinping: Let the consciousness of a community of common destiny take root in neighboring countries], October 25, 2013, http://news.xinhuanet.com/politics/2013-10/25/c_117878944.htm.

35. Xi Jinping, "Zai di shi'er jie quanguo renmin daibiao dahui diyici huiyi shang de jianghua" [Speech at the First Plenary Session of the Twelfth National People's Congress], March 17, 2013, http://www.gov.cn/ldhd/2013-03/17/content_2356344.htm.

36. Peter Neil, "Maritime Silk Road," *Huffington Post*, October 31, 2013, http://www.huffingtonpost.com/peter-neill/maritime-silk-road_b_4181663.html?utm_hp_ref=world&ir=World.

37. "Xi Jinping zai Zhongzhong zhongyang zhengzhiju disanci jiti xuexi shi qiangdiao genghao tongchou guonei guowai liangge daju, hangshi zou heping fazhan dalu de jichu" [At the third collective study session of the Chinese Communist Party Central Committee Politburo, Xi Jinping emphasized the importance of better coordinating both the domestic and international patterns and laying a solid foundation for taking the path of peaceful

the importance of "strik[ing] a balance between rights protection and stability maintenance," as stated in the white paper on China's military strategy released in May 2015.[38]

China's foreign policy activism naturally raises the question of whether or not China aims to "push the United States out" of the Asia Pacific to form an exclusive, China-dominated regional order. Arguably, the SCO, where China remains the main architect and promoter, is a counterbalance to the United States or, as Tyler Roney puts it, "China's NATO."[39] In 2005 the United States was denied observer status in the SCO. The SCO's 2005 decision to demand a withdrawal of foreign forces from the territories of its member states, and its 2006 decision to accept Iran—Washington's archrival—as an observer caused it to be regarded by many Western analysts as an effort to limit U.S. presence in Central Asia. Yet concern that the SCO could develop into an anti-U.S. coalition is overstated. In fact, China was cautious in downplaying the anti-U.S. rhetoric used by some member states (particularly Iran and Uzbekistan).[40] In responding to a press question in June 2012, Chinese Foreign Ministry spokesperson Liu Weimin explicitly ruled out the possibility that the SCO would "evolve into a political and military bloc."[41] On the positive side, China has responded favorably to U.S. calls for a more active Chinese role in Afghanistan. At the SCO Summit Meeting in May 2013, President Xi sanctioned the idea of aiding the Afghanistan peace process through the SCO platform.[42] Thus the shared China–U.S. interest in securing a stable and peaceful Afghanistan has the potential of drawing the United States (and its NATO allies) and China (and the SCO) closer together rather than driving them apart.

development], January 29, 2013, http://politics.people.com.cn/n/2013/0130/c1001-20367778.html.

38. Information Office of the State Council, "Full Text: China's Military Strategy," http://china.org.cn/china/2015-05/26/content_35661433_3.htm.

39. Tyler Roney, "The Shanghai Cooperation Organization: China's NATO?" *Diplomat*, September 11, 2013, http://thediplomat.com/2013/09/the-shanghai-cooperation-organization-chinas-nato-2/.

40. Andy Yee, "Autocratic Peace and the Shanghai Cooperation Organization," May 11, 2011, http://www.eastasiaforum.org/2011/05/11/autocratic-peace-and-the-shanghai-cooperation-organisation/; Akihiro Iwashita, "The Shanghai Cooperation Organization and Japan: Moving Together to Reshape the Eurasia Community," January 28, 2008, http://www.brookings.edu/research/articles/2008/01/28-asia-iwashita.

41. Xinhua News Agency, "Waijiaobu: Shanghe zuzhi bucunzai yanbian cheng zhengzhi junshi jituan de keng" [Ministry of Foreign Affairs: The SCO will not evolve into a political and military bloc], June 6, 2012, http://news.xinhuanet.com/world/2012-06/06/c_112139596.htm.

42. Xinhua News Agency, "Xi Jinping zai Shanghe zuzhi fenghui fabiao jianghua, tichu 4 dian zhuzhang" [Xi Jinping gives speech at the SCO summit meeting, making 4 propositions], September 13, 2013, http://news.xinhuanet.com/world/2013-09/13/c_117365319.htm.

One measure of whether or not China aims to exclude the United States from the region is Beijing's ties with Moscow. In March 2013 President Xi made his first foreign visit to Russia after assuming the presidency, and in Moscow declared that the China-Russia relationship was "the most important bilateral relationship in the world."[43] Apparently Xi's visit was meant to send a message to the United States and the West that Beijing had "Russia option." Specifically, Beijing and Moscow seek to bolster their influence as a combined geopolitical counterweight to Washington; Beijing is increasingly disturbed by perceived U.S. heavy-handed pivoting/rebalancing in Asia, and Moscow's relations with the United States have been increasingly strained since Vladimir Putin was reelected Russian president in March 2012 and, particularly, in the wake of the crises in Crimea and Ukraine.

Over the years, Russia and China have staged quite a number of joint military drills both bilaterally and within the multilateral framework of the SCO. During his April 2014 trip to Asia, U.S. president Barack Obama publicly declared that the U.S.-Japan Mutual Defense Treaty covers the disputed Diaoyu/Senkaku Islands, and signed a ten-year defense pact with Manila that would allow increased U.S. troop presence in the Philippines—moves regarded by China as infringing on its territorial integrity and strategic interests.[44] Meanwhile, the United States and the European Union ratcheted up sanctions against Moscow as the crisis in Ukraine deepened. Not surprisingly, the day after Obama concluded his Asia trip, China and Russia announced that their navies would stage a large-scale joint naval drill in the East China Sea in late May, involving sixteen vessels from both sides, including missile cruisers, missile destroyers, missile frigates, and submarines.[45] On May 20, Xi and visiting Russian president Putin inspected the participating naval vessels, kicking off a weeklong joint naval exercise.[46] Clearly,

43. Xinhua News Agency, "Xi Jinping shouchang yanjiang cheng Zhong'E guanxi zuihao zuizhongyao" [Xi Jinping's first speech declares China-Russia relations are among the best and the most important bilateral relationships], Ta Kung Pao, March 4, 2013, http://news .takungpao.com/opinion/highlights/2013-03/1508612.html.

44. White House, "U.S.-Japan Joint Statement: The United States and Japan: Shaping the Future of the Asia Pacific and Beyond," April 25, 2014, http://www.whitehouse.gov/the -press-office/2014/04/25/us-japan-joint-statement-united-states-and-japan-shaping-future -asia-pac; Juliet Eilperin, "U.S., Philippines Sign 10-Year Defense Agreement amid Rising Tensions," Washington Post, April 28, 2014, http://www.washingtonpost.com/world/asia _pacific/us-philippines-sign-10-year-defense-agreement-amid-rising-tensions/2014/04/28 /74a605d8-cec6-11e3-b812-0c92213941f4_story.html.

45. Su Yincheng, "Zhong'E haijun jiang juxing haishang lianhe junshi yanxi" [Chinese and Russian navies will hold joint naval exercises], People's Daily, May 14, 2014, http:// military.people.com.cn/n/2014/0514/c1011-25013159.html.

46. Li Bin and Li Zhihui, "Xi Jinping he E'luosi zongtong Pu Jing gongtong chuxi Zhong'E haishang lianhe junshi yanxi kaishi yishi" [Xi Jinping and Russian president Putin

strategic pressures from the United States had drawn Beijing and Moscow closer.

Some Chinese strategic analysts and scholars argue that China should consider forming an alliance with Russia. Seeing the U.S.-led hub-and-spoke alliance system as the cornerstone of the existing regional order, they argue that China should make efforts to forge a competing China-Russia alliance. Yan Xuetong, a prominent realist international relations scholar, is among them. Specifically, Yan believes that a China-Russia alliance would enhance China's security environment to the north and to the west, assuage strategic pressures from the eastern and the southern flanks, and be conducive to the emergence of a bipolar structure in East Asia. Therefore, Yan argues, China should abandon the principle of nonalignment it holds dear and actively seek to forge an alliance with Russia.[47]

Yet despite realist scholars' interest in forming a China-Russia alliance, Beijing and Moscow apparently are not prepared to go down that road. In fact, Putin has publicly brushed aside the possibility of such an alliance, dismissing the alliance system overall as "outdated."[48] Beijing seems to be fully aware of the limits to its bilateral relations with Russia; while calling for deepening the "comprehensive, strategic cooperative partnership" between the two countries so as to contribute to the "international strategic balance" (*guoji zhanlue pingheng*), Beijing has so far settled for the strategy of what Ministry of Foreign Affairs spokesperson Liu calls "forging a partnership without forming an alliance" (*jieban er bu jiemeng*).[49] In the joint statement issued during Putin's visit to China in June 2016, the two presidents again reaffirmed that "the China-Russia relationship is not of the na-

jointly attend the opening ceremony of the China-Russia joint maritime military exercise], May 20, 2014, http://news.xinhuanet.com/politics/2014-05/20/c_1110779705.htm.

47. Deng Yuan, "Yan Xuetong: Zhong'E jiemeng zuiju xianshi yiyi" [Yan Xuetong: Forming a China-Russia alliance is of utter practical meaning], *Guoji xianqu daobao*, March 26, 2013, http://ihl.cankaoxiaoxi.com/2013/0326/183592.shtml; Yan, *Lishi de guanxing*, 193–99.

48. Xinhua News Agency, "Putin Urges Intra-Ukraine Dialogue, Eyes Closer Ties with China," *Shanghai Daily*, April 17, 2014, http://shanghaidaily.com/article/article_xinhua .aspx?id=213333; Alessandra Prentice, "Putin Hails Russia's Relationship with China," *Chicago Tribune*, April 17, 2014, http://articles.chicagotribune.com/2014-04-17/news/sns-rt-us -russia-putin-china-20140417_1_russia-and-china-alexei-anishchuk-lidia-kelly.

49. The phrase was first put forward by Ministry of Foreign Affairs spokesperson Liu Weimin at a press conference in June 2012; see Xinhua News Agency, "Waijiaobu: Shanghe zuzhi bucunzai yanbian cheng zhengzhi junshi jituan de keneng"; Xinhua News Agency, "Nianzhong pendian: 2008 Zhongguo yu daguo guanxi—Zhong'E pian" [Year-end Summary: China's relations with the great powers in 2008—China and Russia], December 10, 2013, http://news.xinhuanet.com/world/2008-12/10/content_10482794.htm; "Zhong'E miyue: bujiemeng, wan lianheng?" [China-Russia honeymoon: Not forging alliance, entertaining partnership?], *Zhongguo xinwen zhoukan*, June 13, 2013, http://insight.inewsweek.cn /topic_detail-608.html.

ture of forging an alliance, nor is it targeting against a third party."[50] In the years to come, the likelihood of Beijing and Moscow forging a formal alliance will remain low; nevertheless, the shared interests in promoting a multipolar world and alleviating strategic pressures from the United States will likely continue to draw the two nations closer together.

In his May 2014 speech at the Conference on Interaction and Confidence Building Measures in Asia (CICA), President Xi unveiled China's "new security concept," stating that "it is for the people of Asia to run the affairs of Asia, solve the problems of Asia and uphold the security of Asia." Pointedly denouncing the Cold War alliance system, Xi also called for the development of a regional security cooperation architecture.[51] Xi's speech was read by some Western analysts as a declaration of China's Monroe Doctrine or otherwise excluding the United States from any Asian security architecture.[52] Such anxiety, however, is overblown. A careful reading of Xi's CICA speech reveals that in fact much of what he said was nothing new or by no means revisionist in nature. China has always been critical of the Cold War mentality and the U.S. alliance system associated with it, and it has always stressed the respect of sovereignty and noninterference in internal affairs.[53] At the core of Xi's new security concept is his call for the realization of common security, comprehensive security, cooperative security, and sustainable security—concepts that have been widely accepted by the international community. Moreover, Xi's call for the establishment of an Asian regional security architecture might be more rhetorical than it is substantive.[54] Apparently China, as the presidency of the CICA for 2014–16, aims to revive the regional forum initiated by Kazakhstan that now encompasses twenty-four member states and twelve observers (including the United States). It is unclear, however, how China would be able to turn the CICA into an effective regional security architecture given the heterogeneity in ideologies, religions, history, and social and economic conditions across the member

50. Ministry of Foreign Affairs of the People's Republic of China, "Zhonghua renmin gongheguo yu Eluosi lianbang lianhe shengming" [The Joint Statement of the People's Republic of China and the Russian Federation], June 28, 2016, http://www.fmprc.gov.cn/web/zyxw/t1375315.shtml.

51. Xi Jinping, "New Asian Security Concept for New Progress in Security Cooperation," keynote speech at the Fourth CICA Summit, May 21, 2014, http://www.fmprc.gov.cn/mfa_eng/topics_665678/yzxhxzyxrcshydscfh/t1159951.shtml.

52. Stephen Hadley, "Asia-Pacific Major Power Relations and Regional Security," remarks at the World Peace Forum, June 21, 2014, Beijing, http://www.wpfforum.org/index.php?m=content&c=index&a=show&catid=95&id=266; Zachery Keck, "China's Growing Hegemonic Bent," *Diplomat*, June 26, 2014, http://thediplomat.com/2014/06/chinas-growing-hegemonic-bent/.

53. Bates Gill, *Rising Star: China's New Security Diplomacy* (Washington, DC: Brookings Institution Press, 2007), 4–5, 27.

54. David Cohen, "'A Clash of Security Concept': China's Efforts to Redefine Security," *China Brief* 14, no. 11 (2014): 2.

states. Excluding the United States from any prospective Asian security architecture would be at odds with the will of most Asian countries. In fact, virtually every country in the region would favor a strong U.S. presence as a counterbalance and hedge against a rising China.[55] Perhaps keenly aware of that, President Xi noted in his keynote speech that "we welcome all parties to play a positive and constructive role in promoting Asia's security and cooperation," implicitly acknowledging that China will not pursue a strategy of excluding the United States.[56] As a matter of fact, China's efforts to revive the CICA can be viewed as part of its hedging portfolio, an effort to enmesh the United States into a region-wide security architecture so as to reduce strategic risks, increase China's freedom of action, and shape U.S. preferences.

Xi's policy reflects a long-term trend in Chinese policy that began at the end of the Cold War, when stabilizing U.S.-China relations become the priority of Beijing's "great power diplomacy" (daguo waijiao). In 1993 Chinese president Jiang Zemin proposed a mantra for U.S.-China relations, namely, "to enhance trust, reduce trouble, develop cooperation and avoid confrontation."[57] Despite getting off to a rough start (i.e., the 2001 EP-3 spy plane incident), U.S.-China bilateral relations deepened during the administration of President George W. Bush. After the 9/11 terrorist attacks, Beijing quickly lent support to Washington's global war on terror, and this greatly increased strategic trust between the two countries. China responded positively to Deputy Secretary of State Robert Zoellick's September 2005 call for China to become a "responsible stakeholder" in the international system.[58] In November of that year, Chinese president Hu Jintao pointed out to visiting President Bush that the China-U.S. relationship carried more and more "global implications" (quanqiu yiyi).[59] By the end of Bush's second

55. Keck, "China's Growing Hegemonic Bent."

56. Xi, "New Asian Security Concept."

57. Zhou Shuchun and Ding Qilin, "Zai jieshou 'Meiguo xinwen yu shijie baogao' zongbianji shi Jiang Zenmin zonglun ZhongMei guanxi deng qida wenti" [While doing an interview with the chief editor of U.S. News and World Report, Jiang Zeming discusses seven issues, including China-U.S. relations], People's Daily, March 9, 1993; U.S. Department of Defense, "Secretary Perry Welcomes Chinese Defense Minister Chi Haotian," December 9, 1996, http://www.defense.gov/Transcripts/Transcript.aspx?TranscriptID=827.

58. Robert Zoellick, "Whither China: From Membership to Responsibility?," remarks to the National Committee on U.S.-China Relations, September 21, 2005, http://www.ncuscr.org/files/2005Gala_RobertZoellick_Whither_China1.pdf; "Zoellick: 'Stakeholder' Concept Offers New Direction," China Daily, January 25, 2006, http://www.chinadaily.com.cn/china/09usofficials/2009-05/22/content_7932826.htm; Bates Gill, Dan Blumenthal, Michael Swaine, and Jessica Tuchman Mathews, "China as a Responsible Stakeholder," June 11, 2007, http://carnegieendowment.org/2007/06/11/china-as-responsible-stakeholder/2kt.

59. Xinhua News Agency, "Zhongmei guanxi yuelaiyue juyou quanqiu yiyi" [China-U.S. relations increasingly have global implications], November 21, 2005, http://news.xinhuanet.com/world/2005-11/21/content_3809831.htm.

term, officials in both countries were able to declare that the bilateral relations were at their best since normalization of relations in 1979.[60]

Both privately and publicly, Chinese leaders acknowledge that the United States is a dominant power in the region—and will remain so, probably for decades to come. In December 2011 Chinese assistant foreign minister Le Yucheng noted in a speech given at the Foreign Affairs University that the United States "has never left the Asia Pacific." Confessing that China "has neither desire nor capability to push the United States out" of the region, Le went on to argue, "The Pacific Ocean is vast enough to accommodate the co-existence and cooperation" between the two great powers.[61] In an interview given to the *Washington Post* in February 2012, then vice president Xi Jinping noted that "the vast Pacific Ocean has ample space for both China and the United States." Xi implicitly acknowledged U.S. primacy in the region when he noted, "We welcome a constructive role by the United States in promoting peace, stability and prosperity in the region." To be sure, Xi balanced his statement, adding, "We also hope that the United States will fully respect and accommodate the major interests and legitimate concerns of Asia-Pacific countries."[62] At the summit meetings with President Obama held at Sunnylands, California, in June 2013, President Xi reiterated his belief that "the vast Pacific Ocean has enough room to accommodate" the development of two major powers.[63] The Chinese comment, sometimes misconstrued by Western analysts as implying a division of sphere of influence in the region, in fact reflects Chinese leaders' conviction that China, as the rising power, does not need to be on a collision course with the United States, the established, dominant power. Rhetoric aside, these statements and remarks show that Chinese leaders are trying to avoid a potential security dilemma between China and the United States, and thus seek a non-zero-sum path forward for U.S.-China relations.[64] The idea of a new type of

60. Australian Broadcast Corporation, "Leigh Sales Speaks to U.S. Secretary of State Condoleezza Rice," May 9, 2007, http://www.abc.net.au/lateline/content/2007/s2025319.htm.

61. Le Yucheng, "The Rapid Development of China's Diplomacy in a Volatile World," Address to the Seminar on China's Diplomacy in 2011 and Its Prospects, December 27, 2011, http://gd.chineseembassy.org/eng/zyxw/t890703.htm.

62. Xi Jinping, "Vice President Xi Jinping's Written Interview with the Washington Post, February 2012," February 12, 2012, http://www.cfr.org/china/vice-president-xi-jinpings-written-interview-washington-post-february-2012/p27390; Ministry of Foreign Affairs of the People's Republic of China, "Xi Jinping Accepts a Written Interview with the Washington Post of the United States," February 13, 2012, http://www.fmprc.gov.cn/eng/zxxx/t904674.htm.

63. Xinhua News Agency, "Xi, Obama Meet for First Summit," June 8, 2013, http://news.xinhuanet.com/english/china/2013-06/08/c_132440860.htm. For an assessment after the summit, see Wang Dong, "The Xi-Obama Moment: A Post-Summit Assessment," October 21, 2013, http://nbr.org/research/activity.aspx?id=367.

64. Wang Dong, "Addressing the U.S.-China Security Dilemma," January 17, 2013, http://carnegieendowment.org/2013/01/17/addressing-u.s.-china-security-dilemma/f2rv.

major country relationship was first proposed by Chinese state councilor Dai Bingguo at the second round of the Strategic and Economic Dialogue in May 2010.[65] During his February 2012 visit to the United States, then Vice President Xi argued that China and the United States should build a "new model of major country relationship" characterized by "mutual understanding and strategic trust," "respecting each other's 'core interests'" through "mutually beneficial cooperation," and "enhancing cooperation and coordination in international affairs and on global issues."[66] During his visit to the United States in September 2015, President Xi advocated the importance of preventing Beijing and Washington from falling into the "Thucydides Trap," and again of building a "new model of major country relationship."[67] The concept of a new model, proposed by Chinese leaders as an intellectual framework for transcending the destiny of great power conflict, offers a more optimistic approach to the dual East Asian structure.[68] Policymakers and scholars in both countries who endeavor to break away from the "old pattern" of great power competition and war bear the traits of idealists. This optimistic approach can encompass a wide range of views. One such view would envision the possibility of shared responsibilities and even shared leadership between the United States and China. This would involve U.S. willingness to cede leadership to China or to accommodate a China that will take more responsibilities and play a greater leadership role in shaping the changing regional order in the years and decades to come, including the joint provision of public goods.[69] Some leading Chinese and

65. Dai Bingguo, "Remarks by State Councilor Dai Bingguo at the Opening Session of the Second Round of The China-US Strategic and Economic Dialogues," May 24, 2010, http://www.fmprc.gov.cn/eng/wjdt/zyjh/t704804.shtml; Dai Bingguo, "Remarks by State Councilor Dai Bingguo at Joint Press Conference of the Second Round of the China-US Strategic and Economic Dialogues," May 27, 2010, http://www.fmprc.gov.cn/eng/wjdt/zyjh/t705280.shtml.

66. Xi Jinping, "Speech by Vice President Xi Jinping at Welcoming Luncheon Hosted by Friendly Organizations in the United States," February 15, 2012, http://www.chinausfocus.com/library/government-resources/chinese-resources/remarks/speech-by-vice-president-xi-jinping-at-welcoming-luncheon-hosted-by-friendly-organizations-in-the-united-states-february-15-2012/.

67. Ministry of Foreign Affairs of the People's Republic of China, "Waijiaobu: Xi Jiping tong Aobama huiwu shi qiangdiao zengqiang Zhong Mei zhanlue huxin, tuidong Zhong Mei xinxing daguo guanxi buduan xiangqian" [Ministry of Foreign Affairs: Xi Jinping, when meeting Obama, emphasizes that China and the U.S. should enhance mutual strategic trust, and continuously promotes the development of the new China-U.S. model of a major-country relationship], September 25, 2015, http://www.mfa.gov.cn/mfa_chn/ziliao_611306/zt_611380/dnzt_611382/xpjdmgjxgsfw_684034/zxxx_684036/t1300385.shtml.

68. Wang, "The Xi-Obama Moment"; Susan Rice, "America's Future in Asia: Remarks as Prepared for Delivery by National Security Advisor Susan E. Rice," November 20, 2013, http://www.whitehouse.gov/the-press-office/2013/11/21/remarks-prepared-delivery-national-security-advisor-susan-e-rice.

69. Terry Cooke, "New Strains in the U.S.-China-Taiwan Triangle," *China Brief* 10, no. 4 (2010): 11–14.

American scholars have mentioned the possibility of "joint patrol" of sea lanes in the future, an idea that has been endorsed by senior former U.S. policymakers such as former U.S. national security adviser Stephen Hadley. Speaking at a forum in Beijing in June 2014, Hadley argued that the United States was "ready to accept a growing Chinese open sea naval capability to defend the sea lanes" and that allowing China to share the responsibility of sea lane protection would be "of significant benefit" to the United States.[70]

U.S. Strategic Responses to China's Rise and the Networkization of the Hub-and-Spoke System

A rising China poses a great challenge to the United States and the regional order. As early as the mid-1990s, Joseph S. Nye, then U.S. assistant secretary of defense, proposed "to integrate, but hedge" as an East Asian security strategy in dealing with the uncertainties brought about by the rise of China. Nye's hedging strategy hinges on two pillars: first, the invigorating and strengthening of the U.S. security alliance with Japan as an insurance against the scenario in which China becomes aggressive; second, engaging and integrating China into the world market to ensure that if "China mellows as it prospers and its ties of interdependence deepens, the world may see a more benign outcome."[71] Nye's idea "to integrate, but hedge" signifies an embryonic form of hedging strategy. It has transcended the debate of U.S. engagement versus containment toward China, and indeed is more balanced and nuanced than the simple dichotomy between engagement and containment.[72]

It was not until the second term of President Bush, however, that the first well-articulated hedging strategy was crafted. In a September 2005 speech, Deputy Secretary of State Zoellick unveiled the concept of transforming the

70. Both Wang Jisi and Susan Shirk have mentioned such a possibility. Wang Jisi, interview with the author, Beijing, February 2012; Susan Shirk, interview with the author, Washington, DC, November 2011. See also Hadley, "Asia-Pacific Major Power Relations and Regional Security."

71. Joseph S. Nye Jr., "The Case for Deep Engagement," *Foreign Affairs* 74 (1995): 90–102; Joseph S. Nye Jr., "International Relations: The Relevance of Theory to Practice," in *The Oxford Handbook of International Relations*, ed. Christian Reus-Smit and Duncan Snidal (New York: Oxford University Press, 2008), 656–57.

72. For the engagement versus containment debate, see Harry Harding, "Neither Friend nor Foe: A China Policy for the Nineties," *Brookings Review* 10, no. 2 (1992): 7–11; David Shambaugh, "Containment or Engagement of China? Calculating Beijing's Responses," *International Security* 72, no. 3 (1993): 22–49; Gerald Segal, "East Asia and the 'Constrainment' of China," *International Security* 20, no. 4 (1996), 107–35; Robert S. Ross, "Beijing as a Conservative Power," *Foreign Affairs* 76, no. 2 (1997): 33–44. See also Michael E. Brown, Owen R. Cote Jr., Sean M. Lynn-Jones, and Steven E. Miller eds., *The Rise of China* (Cambridge, MA: MIT Press, 2000).

rapidly growing China into a responsible stakeholder in the international system.[73] *Responsible stakeholder* quickly became a catchphrase of the Bush administration's policy toward China, and Zoellick himself was even dubbed by both extollers and detractors as the "panda hugger."[74]

What is less known to the public, however, is that Zoellick also played an instrumental role in formulating the Bush administration's hedging strategy toward China. Together with Secretary of Defense Donald H. Rumsfeld, Zoellick was among the key architects of a comprehensive hedge strategy against potential threats posed by the rise of China.[75] In a sense, it is thus perfectly epitomic of U.S. policy that Zoellick was at once both an advocate of the engagement of China and yet hedged by bolstering U.S. strategic and military postures in Asia.

In March 2006 Peter Rodman, the assistant secretary of defense for international affairs, told a congressional commission that a "prudent" hedging strategy was an "essential" part of U.S. national security strategy. Key elements of the U.S. hedging strategy, as top Pentagon officials noted, were aimed at nations with "uncertain futures," China being one of them. Rodman noted that cooperation with emerging powers such as China would, of course, be preferred, but the United States must prepare "for the possibility that others could choose a more hostile path." In responding to the merging military threat from China, the United States should "be ready to deal with it, if the worst case should happen."[76]

Because of its pivotal geostrategic and military importance, the island of Guam has become a key element of the U.S. hedging posture. Strategic bombers deployed on Guam can launch strikes against targets throughout Asia within three hours, giving the base there an unparalleled strategic and military value. As Admiral William J. Fallon, then head of the Pacific Command, noted, Guam would become a "pivot point" for U.S. forces in the Pacific because of the relatively short distance to the Taiwan Strait, the Korean peninsula and Southeast Asia.[77] Under its hedging strategy, the Pentagon made plans for a significant build-up of forces in the Asia Pacific theater, which involved more frequent rotations of B-2 strategic bombers to Guam, gradual shifting of up to 60 percent of the U.S. attack submarine fleet to the

73. Zoellick, "Wither China?"

74. Edward Cody, "U.S. Envoy Engaged in Panda Diplomacy," *Washington Post*, January 26, 2006, http://www.washingtonpost.com/wp-dyn/content/article/2006/01/25/AR20060 12500744.html; John Tkacik, "Revenge of the Panda Hugger," *Weekly Standard*, February 21, 2006, http://www.heritage.org/research/commentary/2006/02/revenge-of-the-panda -hugger.

75. Bill Gertz, "More Muscle, with Eye on China: Covert Strategy Aims to 'Hedge' against Threats Posed in Asia," *Washington Times*, April 20, 2006.

76. Bill Gertz, "Pentagon 'Hedge' Strategy Targets China," *Washington Times*, March 18, 2006.

77. Ibid.

Pacific and the addition of two or up to four strategic missile submarines (thus bringing the ability to deploy up to four aircraft battle groups at once in Asia), and the repositioning ground forces in Guam, Japan, and the western United States.[78]

The Obama administration's pivot/rebalancing to Asia can be conceptualized as a hedging strategy. In light of the perceived increase in Chinese assertiveness, the United States resorted to the competitive strategic instruments in its hedging portfolio, external balancing. After it was first rolled out in November 2011, the "pivot" (the term was quickly replaced by "rebalancing") strategy put an emphasis on strengthening U.S. military alliances with Australia, Japan, the Philippines, and South Korea.[79] To enhance U.S. military presence in the Asia Pacific, in November 2011 the United States began rotating up to 2,500 U.S. Marines to a base in Darwin, Australia.[80] Since the sinking of the South Korean corvette *Cheonan* (presumably by North Korea) in March 2010, the United States strengthened its military alliance with South Korea. In light of the growing tensions between China and Japan in the East China Sea, and China and the Philippines in the South China Sea, the United States bolstered its military alliances with both Tokyo and Manila.

After initially putting too much emphasis on the military and security aspects of the pivot/rebalancing strategy, the Obama administration went on to balance the hedging portfolio by stressing cooperative instruments such as engagement and enmeshment. In fact, during Obama's second term, the administration has taken steps to recalibrate its approach to pivot / rebalancing—one may call it "rebalancing the rebalancing strategy"—by emphasizing that engagement with China would be one of the pillars of U.S. rebalancing to Asia.[81] In a major foreign policy speech delivered at the Asia Society in March 2013, National Security Adviser Thomas Donilon stressed that "building a stable, productive, and constructive relationship with China" would be one of the pillars of U.S. rebalancing strategy.[82] But after a series

78. Ibid.

79. Hillary Clinton, "America's Pacific Century," *Foreign Policy*, October 11, 2011, http://foreignpolicy.com/2011/10/11/americas-pacific-century/; Hillary Rodham Clinton, *Hard Choices: A Memoir* (New York: Simon and Schuster, 2014), 45–46.

80. Caren Bohan and James Grubel, "Obama Boosts U.S. Military in Australia, Reassures China," November 16, 2011, http://www.reuters.com/article/2011/11/16/us-usa-australia-idUSTRE7AF0F220111116.

81. Wang, "Addressing the U.S.-China Security Dilemma." Notably, U.S. policymakers have publicly emphasized the need to "rebalance the rebalancing strategy." See Committee on Foreign Relations of U.S. Senate, *Rebalancing the Rebalance: Resourcing U.S. Diplomatic Strategy in the Asia Pacific Region* (Washington, DC: U.S. Government Printing Office, 2014), http://www.foreign.senate.gov/imo/media/doc/872692.pdf.

82. Thomas Donilon, "The United States and the Asia Pacific in 2013," remarks at the Asia Society, March 11, 2013, http://www.whitehouse.gov/the-press-office/2013/03/11/remarks-tom-donilon-national-security-advisory-president-united-states-a.

of events in the ensuing years, including China's establishment of an Air Defense Identification Zone in the East China Sea, its placement of an oil rig in waters it claims as its own (but Vietnam disputes), and China's rapid land reclamations in the South China Sea, the U.S. threat perception of China increased, causing Washington to enhance the competitive components, such as external balancing, in its hedging portfolio—including signing the ten-year Enhanced Defense Cooperation Agreement with the Philippines and lifting arms sales embargoes on Vietnam.

In addition to strengthening bilateral ties with regional allies and partners, the United States also promoted the networkization of the hub-and-spoke system by bolstering minilateral security cooperation mechanisms, such as trilateral cooperation with Japan and South Korea and with Japan and Australia, as part of a hedging portfolio against the strategic uncertainties brought about by the rise of China and the emerging dual structure in East Asia.[83]

After Lee Myung-bak became South Korea's president in February 2008, the United States took the lead in bolstering trilateral cooperation between itself, Japan, and South Korea. Trilateral consultations are conducted at the bureau level, the vice ministerial level, the ministerial level, and the summit level. The first meeting of the three nations' defense chiefs was held during the Shangri-La Dialogue in June 2009; the trilateral meeting was institutionalized in 2012.[84] In June 2012 the United States, Japan, and South Korea held the first open trilateral joint military exercise.[85] However, trilateral cooperation is hamstrung by historical issues and territorial disputes between Tokyo and Seoul. Since the ultranationalist Shinzo Abe was reelected as Japan's prime minister in January 2013, historical revisionism—denial of war atrocities, including the "comfort woman" issue—has effectively hindered any real progress in the trilateral cooperation, to the chagrin of many U.S. officials and strategic analysts.

In terms of the trilateral consultation mechanism between the United States, Japan, and Australia, vice foreign ministerial–level trilateral meetings began in 2002, and the foreign ministerial–level Trilateral Strategic Dialogue

---

83. For the view that minilateralism is a form of a hedging strategy, see Rory Medcalf, *Squaring the Triangle: An Australian Perspective on Asian Security Minilateralism* (Seattle: National Bureau of Asian Research, 2012), 23–31.

84. Richard L. Armitage and Joseph S. Nye, *The U.S.-Japan Alliance: Getting Asia Right through 2020*, https://csis-prod.s3.amazonaws.com/s3fs-public/legacy_files/files/media/csis/pubs/070216_asia2020.pdf, 8.

85. Xinhua News Agency, "MeiRiHan jiangzai Chaoxian bandao nanbu haiyu juxing lianhe junyan" [The United States, Japan, and South Korea will hold joint military exercise in the sea area south of the Korean Peninsula], June 16, 2012, http://news.xinhuanet.com/mil/2012-06/16/c_123291873.htm.

kicked off in March 2006. In 2007 the first trilateral defense chief meeting and the first trilateral summit were held.[86]

The United States has actively leveraged "minilateral" mechanisms to promote security cooperation in a variety of areas. For instance, on the missile defense issue, in addition to bilateral consultation and agreements, Washington announced in March 2012 that it sought a regional anti-missile system akin to that of the European system through trilateral talks between the United States, Japan, and South Korea and the United States, Japan, and Australia.[87] Washington has also taken the lead in pushing for trilateral joint military drills, and in October 2007 the United States, Japan, and Australia held the first such drill. In July 2011 the three countries again held a trilateral joint military drill in the South China Sea near Brunei.[88]

Another prominent feature of the networkization process is the strengthening of bilateral security ties between some of the key U.S. allies, an exemplary case being that of Australia and Japan. In March 2007 the two nations signed the Joint Declaration on Security Cooperation which established the regular 2+2 talks between their foreign and defense ministers, and in May 2010 they signed an agreement on defense logistics cooperation. In May 2012, the two agreed to share classified information. At the fifth 2+2 talk in June 2014, Canberra and Tokyo decided to facilitate the joint research of submarine technology (which may pave the way for the sale of Japanese submarines to Australia), expand joint military exercises, and support the Abe administration's efforts to lift the ban on the "collective defense right."[89]

The multidimensional aspect of the networkization process of the hub-and-spoke system is also manifested in the fact that the United States has strengthened security cooperation with non-allied partner countries. For instance, against the backdrop of pivot/rebalancing and as Chinese assertiveness has been perceived to rise, the United States has forged increasingly close ties with Vietnam. The *Quadrennial Defense Review Report* for 2010 billed Vietnam as a potential regional partner for the United States, and held that Washington should "develop a new strategic relationship" with Hanoi.[90] In July 2011, U.S. and Vietnamese navies held a series of noncombat joint

86. Sun Ru, "Meiguo yatai tongmeng de wangluohua jiqi qianjing" [The networkization of the U.S. Asia-Pacific Alliance and its prospects], *Guoji wenti yanjiu* 4 (2012): 39–50.

87. Ibid.

88. Xinhua News Agency, "MeiRiHan jiangzai Chaoxian bandao nanbu haiyu juxing lianhe junyan."

89. Australian Department of Foreign Affairs and Trade, "Japan Country Brief," http://dfat.gov.au/geo/japan/japan_brief.html; Associated Press, "Japan, Australia Eye Sub Deal, Closer Defense Ties," June 11, 2014.

90. U.S. Department of Defense, *Quadrennial Defense Review Report February 2010*, http://www.defense.gov/Portals/1/features/defenseReviews/QDR/QDR_as_of_29JAN10_1600.pdf, 59.

training exercises,[91] and in August of that year Washington and Hanoi signed a memorandum of understanding for promoting bilateral defense cooperation—the first such since the United States and Vietnam normalized diplomatic relations in 1995.[92] In June 2012, U.S. secretary of defense Leon Panetta visited Vietnam and became the first U.S. defense chief to set foot on Cam Ranh Bay, a former U.S. naval base, since the end of the Vietnam War. Standing on a U.S. naval cargo ship that was making a port call at Cam Ranh Bay, Panetta stressed the importance of "access for U.S. naval ships into this facility."[93] In fact, since 2010, two U.S. carrier battle groups have visited the port city of Da Nang, and dozens of U.S. naval ships had made port calls to Vietnam since 2009.[94] During a meeting with the visiting Vietnamese president Truong Tan Sang in July 2013, President Obama and his Vietnamese counterpart agreed to form the U.S.-Vietnam Comprehensive Partnership, and agreed that both sides should continue the U.S.-Vietnam Defense Policy Dialogue as well as bilateral political, security, and defense dialogues in an effort to expand defense cooperation.[95] During his state visit to Hanoi in May 2016, Obama announced that the United States would lift its arms sales embargo on Vietnam, signifying the further expansion of defense cooperation between Washington and Hanoi.[96]

The U.S. networkization strategy was perhaps best illuminated in U.S. Secretary of Defense Ashton Carter's speech at the 2016 Shangri-La Dialogue, where he advocated building a "principled security network" in the Asia Pacific region.[97]

Nevertheless, the United States has also tried to balance its hedging portfolio by endeavoring to enmesh China in multilateral institutions and

91. Patrick Parta, "U.S., Vietnam Begin Naval Exercises amid Tension with China," *Wall Street Journal*, July 16, 2011, http://online.wsj.com/news/articles/SB10001424052702304223 80457644741274846574.

92. Xinhua News Agency, "MeiYue zhanhou shouci jianli zhengshi junshi guanxi" [For the first time since theVietnam War, the U.S. and Vietnam establish formal military relationship], August 3, 2011, http://news.xinhuanet.com/world/2011-08/03/c_121780272.htm.

93. Demetri Sevastopulo, "Panetta Makes Symbolic Visit to Vietnam," *Financial Times*, June 3, 2012, http://www.ft.com/cms/s/0/e98dd6d4-ad6f-11e1-bb8e-00144feabdc0.html.

94. Liu Qing, "Meiyue guanxi xinfazhan ji qianjing" [The New Development in and the prospects of U.S.-Vietnam relations], *Guoji wenti yanjiu* 2 (2012): 91.

95. White House, "Joint Statement by President Barack Obama of the United States of America and President Truong Tan Sang of the Socialist Republic of Vietnam," July 25, 2013, http://www.whitehouse.gov/the-press-office/2013/07/25/joint-statement-president -barack-obama-united-states-america-and-preside.

96. Michael Peel and Geoff Dyer, "Obama Lifts 50-Year Arms Sales Embargo on Vietnam," *Financial Times*, May 23, 2016, http://www.ft.com/cms/s/0/225957ca-20cd-11e6 -9dea-6c9f084f551d.html#axzz4EgbBq9Lx.

97. Ashton Carter, "Remarks on 'Asia Pacific's Principled Security Network' at 2016 IISS Shangri-La Dialogue," June 4, 2016, http://www.defense.gov/News/Speeches/Speech -View/Article/791213/remarks-on-asia-pacifics-principled-security-network-at-2016-iiss -shangri-la-di.

regional architectures. Emphasizing the importance of expanding ties with multilateral institutions when pursuing its pivot/rebalancing strategy, the United States has attempted to shape China's preferences and reduce strategic risks through institutional binding and enmeshment. It is therefore no coincidence that U.S. officials have repeatedly urged China to abide by the rules and norms of the existing institutions, including multilateral regimes such as the United Nations Convention of Law of Seas, as Washington perceives Beijing's "assertiveness" in its maritime territorial disputes as the main cause of rising tensions between China and several of its neighboring countries.

Another prominent case of enmeshment is the U.S. invitation to China to participate in the Rim of the Pacific Exercise (RIMPAC), a biennial U.S.-led, multilateral naval exercise involving most Pacific countries and the largest of its kind in the world. The 2014 RIMPAC exercise involved forty-eight vessels, six submarines, and altogether 25,000 naval officers and sailors from twenty-two participating countries. By inviting China to participate in the RIMPAC exercise, U.S. policymakers believe that the best way to engage the Chinese military and shape its preferences is not through exclusion or punishment but by encouraging the Chinese military to cooperate with other forces in the Pacific region. China was invited as an observer for the first time in the 2012 RIMPAC Exercise, and the United States extended a formal invitation to participate in the exercise later in 2012. China's active participation—with the largest participating force comprising four naval vessels, two helicopters, and eleven hundred sailors, and second only to the U.S. force—has been billed as considerable progress in military-to-military relations between China and the United States.[98] Moreover, despite growing U.S.-China friction following China's land reclamation activities and U.S. freedom of navigation operations in the South China Sea, the United States invited China to participate in its 2016 RIMPAC naval exercise.[99]

REGIONAL RESPONSES TO THE RISE OF CHINA

Regional states have similarly pursued a hedging strategy in response to the strategic uncertainties brought about by the emergence of a dual structure. On the one hand, most regional states are generally poised to engage and cooperate with China; on the other hand, as China has developed its maritime capabilities, these other nations have relied on security

98. "In Pacific Drills, Navies Adjust to New Arrival: China," *Wall Street Journal*, July 17, 2014, http://online.wsj.com/articles/in-rimpac-naval-drills-off-hawaii-militaries-adjust-to -new-arrival-china-1405527835.

99. Xinhua News Agency, "Chinese Fleet Leaves Pearl Harbor for RIMPAC Exercise 2016," July 13, 2016, http://news.xinhuanet.com/english/photo/2016-07/13/c_135509952 _2.htm.

alliances or partnerships with the United States should China become an aggressive power.[100] Some regional U.S. allies have actively forged security ties and bolstered security cooperation not only with the United States but also among themselves, thus contributing to the networkization of the hub-and-spoke system.

Japan. In light of the perceived increase in Chinese assertiveness in territorial disputes and potential threats to Japanese security, Tokyo has played a particularly active role in cultivating and enhancing security ties with some U.S. regional allies and partners—especially with Australia, the Philippines, and Vietnam. As noted earlier, Japan has, since 2007, made considerable progress in bolstering its strategic and security ties with Australia. In addition, it has actively courted the Philippines and Vietnam, two ASEAN countries that have maritime territorial disputes with China. In April 2012 Japan decided to provide patrol vessels and communication equipment to Malaysia, the Philippines, and Vietnam. In May 2012 two cutters of the Japanese Maritime Self Defense Forces made their first visit to the Philippines, and Tokyo promised to provide at least ten patrol ships to Manila.[101] In June 2012 Japanese foreign minister Koichiro Gemba visited Manila, and both sides agreed to deepen maritime security cooperation, and in July of that year Japan and the Philippines signed a memorandum on defense cooperation.[102] In August 2012, a Japanese Coast Guard patrol ship held a joint counterpiracy exercise with the Philippines Coast Guard. Afterward, the ship held similar joint counterpiracy exercise with the Vietnamese Coast Guard.[103] In January 2013 Japanese prime minister Abe chose Indonesia, Thailand, and Vietnam—three ASEAN countries that are either U.S. partners or allies—as destinations for his first foreign trip after being reelected. During his meeting with Vietnamese prime minister Nguyen Tan Dung, Abe noted that Tokyo and Hanoi faced "common regional challenges" and vowed to promote bilateral security.[104]

100. Mingjiang Li and Dongmin Lee, "Introduction," in *China and East Asian Strategic Dynamics: The Shaping of a New Regional Order*, ed. Mingjiang Li and Dongmin Lee (Lanham, MD: Lexington, 2011), xi–xii.

101. Michael Green, *Japan Is Back: Unbundling Abe's Grand Strategy* (Sydney: Lowy Institute for International Policy, 2013), http://www.lowyinstitute.org/publications/japan-back-unbundling-abes-grand-strategy.

102. "Philippines, Japan to Enhance Maritime Security Ties," *Philippine Daily Inquirer*, July 9, 2012, http://globalnation.inquirer.net/43508/philippines-japan-to-enhance-maritime-security-ties.

103. Xinhua News Agency, "Riben jiang xianhou yu Feilvbin, Yuenan juxing lianhe junyan" [Japan will hold joint exercises with the Philippines and Vietnam], August 29, 2012, http://news.xinhuanet.com/world/2012-08/29/c_123643244.htm.

104. "Japan, Vietnam to Deepen Security Ties amid China's Growing Assertiveness," *Mainichi Japan*, January 17, 2013.

Amid rising tension between China and Vietnam over maritime territorial disputes in the South China Sea, Japan decided to help Vietnam improve its maritime law enforcement capability. During a meeting in Tokyo with the visiting Vietnamese foreign minister Pham Binh Minh in August 2014, Japanese foreign minister Fumio Kishida announced that Tokyo would provide Hanoi with six used coast guard ships and related equipment valued at US$4.9 million.[105]

Australia. In a 2009 defense white paper, Australia highlighted "strategic hedging" as an insurance strategy against future uncertainties and potential risks brought about by the changing regional strategic and security dynamics.[106] Insofar as the United States continued to be "the world's strongest military power and the most influential strategic actor" in the region for the foreseeable future and believing that the U.S. strategic primacy remained the key to the regional security order, Australia took steps to beef up its alliance relationship with the United States and forge closer security ties with other U.S. allies and partners, and particularly Japan, thus increasing the networkization of the hub-and-spoke system.[107] Among other things, Australia and the United States decided to expand defense cooperation, and Canberra agreed in November 2011 to accommodate up to 2,500 U.S. marines, to be rotationally deployed to Darwin and northern Australia.[108] At the same time, to balance the hedging portfolio, Australia has actively engaged China. In addition to deepening economic and trade ties with Beijing, Canberra has also tried to expand China–Australia defense exchanges and cooperation. In April 2013 Australia and China established a strategic partnership through a "new bilateral architecture," including an annual foreign and strategic dialogue between foreign ministers, an annual strategic and economic dialogue, and working-level discussion between the two militaries.[109] In April 2014 Australian prime minister Tony Ab-

105. Vu Trong Khanh, "Japan Offers Maritime Assistance to Vietnam," *Wall Street Journal,* August 2, 2014.

106. Australian Department of Defence, *Defending Australia in the Asia Pacific Century: Force 2030* (Canberra: Australian Department of Defence, 2009), http://www.defence.gov.au /whitepaper/docs/defence_white_paper_2009.pdf, 33. For advocates of the hedging strategy, see also Gerard Henderson, "A Prudent Approach on China," *Sydney Morning Herald,* May 5, 2009; Rory Medcalf, "Our China Question: Friend or Foe?" *Sydney Morning Herald,* April 28, 2009; and Ross Babbage, "Australia's Strategic Edge in 2030," Kokoda Paper no. 15 (Kingston, Australian Capital Territory, Australia: Kokoda Foundation, 2011).

107. Australian Department of Defence, *Defence White Paper 2013,* http://www.defence .gov.au/whitepaper/2013/docs/WP_2013_web.pdf, 10.

108. Peter Jennings, "U.S. Rebalance to the Asia Pacific: An Australian Perspective," *Asia Policy,*15 (2013), 38.

109. Carlyle A. Thayer, "Gillard Lifts Bilateral Relations to New Level," *Global Times,* April 16, 2013.

bott proposed that Australia and China establish closer military relations, including holding high-level meetings and bilateral and trilateral joint military exercises.[110] Australian strategic analysts and officials believe that facing a changing regional order, Australia does not have to choose between the United States, its key ally, and China, its largest economic and trade partner.[111]

South Korea. Compared to Japan and Australia, because of its close geographic proximity South Korea faces greater uncertainties resulting from the rise of China and the emerging dual structure.

South Korea has over the years adopted a hedging strategy. On the one hand, it has actively strengthened its alliance with the United States and bolstered its security ties with key U.S. regional allies, particularly with Australia. In March 2009 South Korean and Australian leaders declared in a shared statement that they would jointly deal with transnational and non-military threats and increase cooperation in areas such as UN peacekeeping operations. In May 2009 the two nations signed an agreement for sharing military intelligence, elevating both sides' security cooperation. In December 2011 the two countries held their first bilateral defense minister talks and decided to further enhance bilateral defense and security cooperation. In March 2013, South Korea and Australia held the first 2+2 talks of their foreign and defense ministers.[112]

On the other hand, South Korea has balanced its hedging portfolio by actively engaging China not only in economic relations but also in military and security relations. In July 2011 South Korea and China established a high-level dialogue on defense and strategic matters and they reached an agreement to expand military exchanges, increase cooperation in counterpiracy and disaster rescue operations, and maintain peace and stability on the Korean Peninsula.[113] After Park Geun-hye's election as South Korea's president, the two nations elevated their strategic partnership to a new level. In June 2013 President Park made a visit to China that aimed to "cement the foundation of the nations' bilateral ties in the next

110. Philip Wen and Mark Kenny, "Tony Abbott's China Visit Nets Closer Military Ties," *Sydney Morning Herald*, April 13, 2013, http://www.smh.com.au/world/tony-abbotts-china-visit-nets-closer-military-relations-20140412-36jz8.html.

111. Matthew Franklin and Michael Sainsbury, "Julia Gillard's US-China Balancing Act," *Australian*, April 26, 2011; Tom Hyland, "Explainer: Do We Have to Choose between China and the US?," *Sydney Morning Herald*, May 20, 2012.

112. Wang et al., "Zhongguo jueqi yu yatai guojia duichong xingwei yanjiu," 101; Australian Department of Foreign Affairs and Trade, *Republic of Korea Country Brief*, http://www.dfat.gov.au/geo/rok/brief_index.html.

113. Wang et al., "Zhongguo jueqi yu yatai guojia duichong xingwei yanjiu," 102.

five to twenty years."[114] During a May 2014 return visit to South Korea by Chinese president Xi, the two leaders vowed to enrich and deepen the China–South Korea strategic cooperative partnership elevating it to "a higher level."[115]

The ASEAN Countries. Grappling with a regional security dynamics that had become increasingly "more uncertain and complex,"[116] the ASEAN countries have pursued a hedging strategy against the uncertainties brought about by the emergence of the dual structure. On the one hand, ASEAN has been actively engaging China economically, and it has been receptive to China-led initiatives such as the Regional Comprehensive Economic Partnership and the Asian Infrastructure Investment Bank.[117] On the other hand, uncertain of China's intentions but also confident in U.S. maritime superiority, ASEAN countries also "welcome the reaffirmation of the U.S. presence in the region,"[118] believing the U.S. military presence has a "stabilizing effect" on the security in the region.[119] They hope to reduce the risk of hegemonic conflict by enmeshing both China and the United States into Southeast Asia's nexus of economic interdependence and multilateral institutions.[120] The ASEAN countries' hedging strategy is perhaps best

114. Ji Mingkui, "Park Geun-hye's China Visit Brings Hope," June 28, 2013, http://www.china.org.cn/opinion/2013-06/28/content_29258324.htm.

115. Ministry of Foreign Affairs of the People's Republic of China, "Xi Jinping Holds Talks with President Park Geun-hye of ROK and Two Heads of State Agree to Make China and ROK Partners Seeking Common Development, Striving for Regional Peace, Jointly Promoting Asia's Vitalization and Enhancing World Prosperity," July 4, 2014, http://www.fmprc.gov.cn/mfa_eng/topics_665678/xjpzxdhgjxgsfw/t1172038.shtml; Ministry of Foreign Affairs of the People's Republic of China, "Xi Jinping Meets Again with President Park Geun-hye of ROK," July 4, 2014, http://www.fmprc.gov.cn/mfa_eng/topics_665678/xjpzxdhgjxgsfw/t1172437.shtml.

116. Yuen Foong Khong, "Coping with Strategic Uncertainty: The Role of Institutions and Soft Balancing in Southeast Asia's Post-Cold War Strategy," in *Rethinking Security in East Asia: Identity, Power and Efficiency*, ed. J. J. Suh, Peter J. Katzenstein, and Allen Carlson (Stanford, CA: Stanford University Press, 2004), 175–76.

117. Andrew Elek, "The Potential Role of the Asian Infrastructure Investment Bank," February 11, 2014, http://www.eastasiaforum.org/2014/02/11/the-potential-role-of-the-asian-infrastructure-investment-bank/.

118. "Interview: Ng Eng Hen, Singapore Defense Minister," *Defense News*, April 9, 2012, http://www.defensenews.com/article/20120409/DEFREG03/304090002/Interview-Ng-Eng-Hen-Singapore-Defense-Minister.

119. Lally Weymouth, "An Interview with Singapore Prime Minister Lee Hsien Loong," *Washington Post*, March 15, 2013, http://www.washingtonpost.com/opinions/an-interview-with-singapore-prime-minister-lee-hsien-loong/2013/03/15/5ce40cd4-8cae-11e2-9838-d62f083ba93f_story.html.

120. Amitav Acharya, *Seeking Security in the Dragons Shadow: China and Southeast Asia in the Emerging Asian Order,*" Working Paper no. 44, (Singapore: Institute of Defence and Strategic Studies, Nanyang Technological University, 2003), 17–18.

manifested in Singapore prime minister Lee Hsien Loong's statement: they do not want to "have to choose sides" between the United States and China, and would like to "have our cake and eat it [too]."[121] In other words, the ASEAN countries do not regard their improved ties with the United States as mutually exclusive of the expansion of relations with China.[122]

The Future Trajectories of the Two Asias

According to a 2015 Pew Global Attitudes Project survey of forty nations, a median of 48 percent of those surveyed in 2015, up from 41 percent in 2008, believe that China will eventually replace America as the dominant world superpower;[123] clearly, the worldwide expectation that China will sooner or later become a global dominant power is on the rise. A 2014 Pew Global Attitudes Project survey shows that most of China's neighboring countries view its economic growth as beneficial, with majorities in Thailand (75 percent), Bangladesh (70 percent), Malaysia (69 percent), Pakistan (62 percent), South Korea (57 percent), and Indonesia (55 percent) believing that China's growing economy is good for their own country.[124] But the same survey reveals that most Asian countries surveyed—eight out of ten—still regard the United States as their top ally.[125] And half or more of the publics in six of ten nations surveyed think U.S. military presence should be welcomed in Asia.[126] The 2015 Pew Global Attitudes survey also finds that Asian nations are divided on whether or not China will replace (or has replaced) the United States as the world's superpower. Across the ten Asian nations surveyed (excluding China), a median of 36 percent believe that China will replace the United States, whereas 41 percent believe the United States will remain the world superpower.[127]

121. Weymouth, "An Interview with Singapore Prime Minister Lee Hsien Loong."

122. Barry Desker, "The Eagle and the Panda: An Owl's View from Southeast Asia," *Asia Policy* 15 (2013): 27.

123. Richard Wike, Bruce Stokes, and Jacob Poushter, "Global Publics Back U.S. on Fighting ISIS, but Are Critical of Post-9/11 Torture: Asian Nations Mostly Support TPP, Defense Pivot—But Also Value Economic Ties with China," June 23, 2015, http://www.pewglobal.org/2015/06/23/global-publics-back-u-s-on-fighting-isis-but-are-critical-of-post-911-torture/, 26.

124. Pew Research Center, *Global Opposition*, 29.

125. The ten countries are Bangladesh, India, Indonesia, Japan, Malaysia, Pakistan, the Philippines, South Korea, Thailand, and Vietnam. Among the ten, only Malaysia and Pakistan name China as their top ally. See Pew Research Center, *Global Opposition*, 10.

126. The six countries are Philippines (71 percent), Vietnam (71 percent), Japan (58 percent), India (55 percent), Australia (51 percent), and South Korea (50 percent). See Wike, Stokes and Poushter, "Global Publics Back U.S.," 35.

127. The numbers are calculated by the author based on data reported in the 2015 Pew Global Attitudes Project report. See Wike, Stokes and Poushter, "Global Publics Back U.S.," 26.

The regional perceptions revealed in the Pew surveys are indicative of the emergence of a dual structure in the region in which China's economic and military rise has been increasingly transforming the existing regional order. In which direction will the "two Asias" be evolving? Looking forward, we might be able to identify several possible trajectories of the regional order. The suggestions below are by no means definitive; they are preliminary conjectures at best. Nevertheless, I offer them as an intellectual exercise for contemplating the prospects of the evolving regional order.

TIANXIA: A SINO-CENTRIC ORDER

Some scholars have envisioned the possibility of a Sino-centric order. The Chinese philosophy scholar Zhao Tingyang proposes the use of *tianxia* (all under heaven), a Chinese traditional political philosophy concept, to construct a new international order that can address the problems of global governance and transcend the limits of nation states.[128] Zhao's theory of *tianxia* echoes the view of scholars such as David Kang, who argues that—partly due to the memory of China's dominant role in East Asian history—the region will be far more willing to bandwagon and accept a dominant role of China than many would expect.[129] There is, however, little evidence that the region is ready to accept a China-dominated order.[130] Quite the contrary, anxiety and fear of China turning aggressive have prompted regional states to pursue hedging strategies. Unlike the United States, China lacks an ideology or a value system that is appealing to regional states. First, the United States enjoys a soft power advantage over China, and U.S. scientific and technological achievements, ways of doing business, and popular culture are embraced by many. Second, many regional states worry about China's expanding military capabilities and view China's growing military power negatively.[131] Moreover, China's maritime territorial disputes with some regional states have unnerved the region at large, further reducing other states' readiness to accept a dominant Chinese role in the regional order in the foreseeable future.[132]

128. Zhao Tingyang, *Tianxia tixi: shijie zhidu zhexue daolun* [The tianxia system: An introduction to world institutional philosophy] (Nanjing: Jiangsu jiaoyu chubanshe, 2005).

129. David C. Kang, *China Rising: Peace, Power, and Order in East Asia* (New York: Columbia University Press, 2007).

130. For the view that a Sinocentric order is unlikely to emerge in East Asia, see Li and Lee, "Introduction," xii.

131. Pew Research Center, *America's Global Image Remains More Positive than China's*, July 2013, http://www.pewglobal.org/files/2013/07/Pew-Research-Global-Attitudes-Project-Balance-of-Power-Report-FINAL-July-18-2013.pdf, 3, 33.

132. Pew Research Center, *Global Opposition*, 8.

A CHINA-LED ALLIANCE SYSTEM LEADING
TO A BIPOLAR SYSTEM

The formation of a China-led alliance system in East Asia vis-à-vis the U.S.-led bilateral alliance system would lead to a bipolar system in the region, thus giving rise to a divided Asia. If China were to follow the suggestions of scholars of offensive realism, such as Yan Xuetong's proposal for China to actively forge alliances and compete for regional hegemony, it would necessarily greatly increase the security and geopolitical competition between China and the United States. In fact, Yan's analysis is self-confirming, and it fails to make a convincing case for why greater strategic competition between China and the United States would not lead to a costly and perilous new cold war.[133]

Yet even from the Chinese perspective, forging alliances in East Asia might prove to be unrealistic. China's protection of possible client countries whose interests are diametrically opposed to those of the United States might increase China's security competition/conflict of security interests with the United States. For instance, enhanced Chinese security ties with North Korea, or renewal of the China–North Korea treaty, will almost certainly aggravate China's security relations with the United States and, by extension, South Korea. On the other hand, if China refuses to endorse one of North Korea's most cherished goals—the possession of nuclear weapons and recognition as a nuclear power—it is doubtful that North Korea would ever be willing to sacrifice its strategic autonomy and independence in exchange for a Chinese guarantee of security. In other words, it is highly unrealistic if not wishful thinking that China can revive its military alliance with North Korea.

When it comes to the possibility of a China-Russia alliance, something Yan strongly advocates, it is difficult to see conditions emerge for such an alliance—unless the United States increases its strategic pressures on and security threats to Beijing and Moscow to the extent that they feel they have no choice but to engage in a formal alliance. Falling short of that, Beijing and Moscow will continue to pursue a hedging strategy, forming a tactical coalition in groupings such as G-20 or the BRICS countries (Brazil, Russia, India, China and South Africa), but shy away from forging any formal alliance—as they are currently doing. The limit of the potential of a China-Russia alliance is highlighted by the 2008 Russo-Georgian War, and again the crises in Crimea and Ukraine, when China refrained from offering out-

<hr/>

133. For Yan's view that growing strategic competition between China and the United States will not lead to a new cold war, see Yan Xuetong, *Lishi de guanxing*, 34; and Yan Xuetong and Qi Haixia, "Football Game Rather Than Boxing Match: China-U.S. Intensifying Rivalry Does Not Amount to Cold War," *Chinese Journal of International Politics* 5, no. 2 (2012): 105–27.

right support to Russia and deliberately kept an ambivalent attitude.[134] In short, a China-Russia alliance is unlikely to occur given the current geostrategic dynamics.

Moreover, Beijing's ability to attract followers and thus form a China-dominated alliance system in East Asia is greatly hamstrung by the fact that it has been embroiled in a series of territorial disputes in the East China Sea and the South China Sea with a number of regional countries.

In theory, conditions for a China-led alliance system to emerge in East Asia would include a continuous decline in U.S. capabilities (both in economic and military terms) and thus reduced U.S. resolve to shoulder the burden of security guarantee. Such a possibility might not be completely unlikely, but it is a long shot.

Therefore, assuming that the United States remains a dominant power (at least in military terms) in the region for the years and decades to come, the trajectory toward a bipolarity in East Asia would more likely than not be conflict prone, unstable, and filled with perils.

A CLASH OF TITANS

John Mearsheimer has argued that the overriding goal of each great power is to "maximize its share of world power, which means gaining power at the expense of other states," and China, after its power grows, will want to challenge the American hegemony;[135] its ambition to establish its own hegemony in East Asia will inevitably lead to the outbreak of a great power conflict or war between China and the United States—a "clash of titans."[136] Or, equally perilous, the United States, the dominant power, might launch preemptive attacks against the rising power, China, when the former sees itself in an inevitable decline.[137] In both scenarios, a great power war will lead to a new regional order, with either China prevailing, thus leading to a China-dominated regional order with the United States bowing out of East Asia, or the United States prevailing and thus preserving U.S. dominance. Either way, the process is likely to be catastrophic and bloody.

134. "Waijiaobu fayanren Qing Gang jiu Nan'aosaiti diqu chongtu da jizhe wen" [Ministry of Foreign Affairs spokesman Qing Gang's remarks to the press concerning the conflicts in South Ossetia], August 8, 2008, http://www.china.com.cn/policy/txt/2008-08/09/content _16172485.htm; "Allies Let Him Down," *Kommersant*, August 29, 2008, http://kommersant .com/p1017558/SCO_refused_to_support_Russia/.

135. John J. Mearsheimer, *The Tragedy of Great Power Politics* (New York: Norton, 2001), 2, 4.

136. For the debate, see Zbigniew Brzezinski and John J. Mearsheimer, "Clash of the Titans," *Foreign Policy*, January 5, 2005, http://www.foreignpolicy.com/articles/2005/01/05 /clash_of_the_titans.

137. Dale C. Copeland, *The Origins of Major War* (Ithaca, NY: Cornell University Press, 2001).

COEVOLUTION, POWER SHARING, AND SHARED LEADERSHIP

Unlike in the above three scenarios, where the equilibrium of the dual structure collapses and the strategic space for hedging quickly disappears, there is one scenario in which the regional order will evolve in a more benign direction and regional states would not have to choose between China and the United States.

Henry Kissinger observes, "An explicit American project to organize Asia on the basis of containing China or creating a bloc of democratic states for an ideological crusade is unlikely to succeed—in part because China is an indispensable trading partner for most of its neighbors. By the same token, a Chinese attempt to exclude America from Asian economic and security affairs will similarly meet serious resistance from almost all other Asian states, which fear the consequences of a region dominated by a single power."[138] Categorically rejecting the idea of bloc competition between China and the United States, Kissinger proposes "co-evolution" between the two nations that will gradually remove mutual suspicions—Chinese fear of American containment, and American concern with a perceived Chinese threat—and move the two toward building a "Pacific Community."[139] Kissinger's "co-evolution" story means that any future regional order would be based on power sharing between China and the United States, a position strongly advocated by some prominent strategists such as Hugh White. As White convincingly argues, Asia's alternative futures are not American primacy or Chinese dominance. In fact, any attempt by either Beijing or Washington to dominate the region will "lead to sustained and bitter strategic rivalry, imposing huge economic costs and real risk of catastrophic war." Therefore, some form of great power accommodation or power sharing between China and the United States will be necessary for a more peaceful regional order to emerge.[140] It would require that both nations exhibit strategic restraint, be willing to compromise and accommodate each other, and be sensitive to the limits to/boundary of their respective power. It would also entail constant bargaining and rebargaining of the boundary of power between them and, by extension, a prospective regional architecture that is able to accommodate both China and the United States and that is reflective of shared responsibilities and leadership.

A future regional order built on power sharing between China and the United States would tend to be inclusive. Regionwide, open, and inclusive architectures would likely prosper. As such an order gradually emerges, strategic rivalry between regional states would be manageable, and they

---

138. Henry A. Kissinger, *On China* (New York: Penguin, 2011), 526–27.
139. Ibid., 527–28.
140. Hugh White, *The China Choice: Why We Should Share Power* (Oxford: Oxford University Press, 2012), 5–6.

would be under much less pressure to choose sides. As uncertainties about the intentions of China as well as about the future trajectory of the regional order diminished, the regionwide intensity of hedging would decrease over time.

Conclusion

China's historic rise has greatly shaped, is shaping, and will continue to shape the geostrategic landscape of East Asia. One of the most significant consequences of its rise on the regional order is the emergence of so-called two Asias, or a dual structure in the region. The two pillars of American regional hegemony—unrivaled primacy in both economic and military arenas—have undergone dramatic shifts since the end of the Cold War. China's economic rise has given it an increasingly prominent role, and the United States is no longer the sole dominant player in the so-called Economic Asia. Nevertheless, the United States retains a prominent status in Economic Asia. Assuming that the Chinese economy will continue to expand in the years and decades to come, China's economic primacy is likely to continue to increase and to consolidate. It is in the military and security realm that U.S. regional predominance is likely to persist into the foreseeable future. Despite the rapid growth in its capabilities, the Chinese military still lags far behind the U.S. military. In the short to medium term, it is unlikely that China would be able to construct a competing alliance system that rivals the U.S.-led bilateral alliance system in the region. In other words, the United States will retain its dominant position in Security Asia. The adaptation of the regional alliance system to the changing geostrategic dynamics, manifested in the networkization of the U.S.-led hub-and-spoke system, will likely help sustain U.S. primacy in Security Asia. That being said, China's prominence in Security Asia will nevertheless increase as it continues to make considerable investments in military modernization as its economy grows.

So far, regional states, facing uncertainties brought about by the rise of China and the emergence of a dual structure, have adopted a hedging strategy that helps minimize risks, expand freedom to maneuver, diversify strategic options, shape China's preferences, and essentially avoid making a choice between China and the United States. But as China continues to rise both economically and militarily it will become increasingly difficult for regional actors to "look to China for profit, the U.S. for security." In other words, the two Asias might just be unsustainable. Nevertheless, at the end of the day, the evolution of the future regional order will largely be determined by the trajectory of U.S.-China relations. A U.S.-China competition and rivalry for regional dominance is likely to be perilous, and prone to conflict and even war. For a more peaceful future to emerge in East Asia, the United States and China, as an incumbent power and a rising power, respectively, would have to accommodate each other and negotiate and renegotiate the boundaries of their relative power as well as their respective roles in the future regional order. Beijing and Washington would need to learn to share responsibilities and leadership.

II. JAPAN, SOUTH KOREA, AND THE RISE OF CHINA
NATIONAL SECURITY AND NATIONALISM

Protecting the Status Quo

Japan's Response to the Rise of China

Ian Bowers and Bjørn Elias Mikalsen Grønning

China's resurrection as a great power is, in Japan's view, altering the "the balance of power that underpinned the traditional international order."[1] Beijing is leveraging its economic and industrial might to build up its maritime and naval forces. The use of these capabilities to apply pressure on Japan over disputed islands in the East China Sea and its application of coercive measures to impose Beijing's vision of a new maritime order in the South China Sea are seen in Tokyo as proof of a significant Chinese threat and a signs of a sustained challenge to the favorable international status quo.[2]

Japan's response to these altered circumstances indicates that it is becoming the archetypal status quo power, looking to preserve the established international order as a means to maximize its security.[3] By adjusting its defense posture, altering the terms of its alliance with the United States, and increasing its involvement in regional security, Japan

1. Ministry of Foreign Affairs of Japan, *Diplomatic Bluebook 2014* (Tokyo: Ministry of Foreign Affairs of Japan), 2.
2. The usage of the term *status quo* in this chapter draws on Robert Gilpin's definition as highlighted by Alastair Iain Johnston; status quo, so defined, comprises "the distribution of power, the hierarchy of prestige (which, however, tends to be coterminous with the distribution of power for realists), and 'rights and rules that govern or at least influence the interactions among states.'" See Alastair Iain Johnston, "Is China a Status Quo Power?" *International Security* 27, no. 4 (2003): 10; and Robert Gilpin, *War and Change in International Politics* (Cambridge: Cambridge University Press, 1993).
3. Randal Schweller, "Bandwagoning for Profit: Bringing the Revisionist State Back In," *International Security* 19, no. 1 (1994): 104–5.

is attempting to balance against the threat it perceives as stemming from China.[4]

The manner and extent of Japan's balancing behavior toward China is, however, influenced by domestic politics. There is a double-sided element to Japanese national identity: on the one hand, the tradition of pacifism and substantial public opposition acts as a break on significant revisions to Japan's security posture; on the other, nationalism and a desire to "normalize" Japan as a security actor influences policy decisions and has been a significant, if occasional, factor in exacerbating tensions between Tokyo and Beijing.

This chapter will demonstrate that it is China's capabilities and actions in the maritime sphere that ultimately dominate Japan's threat perception and fundamentally inform its defense and foreign policy alterations. Herein we assert that domestic politics currently plays an important but secondary role in ultimately shaping Tokyo's responses and contend that Japan's administrative, legal, and military reforms are aimed at maintaining the status quo at sea within the context of China's threat. We further argue that Japan is engaging with countries with similar interests in the region to hinder China's coercive efforts.

Power Shift, Threat, and the Status Quo at Sea

China's inexorable economic growth has altered both the Asian and global distribution of power. This alteration alone is an insufficient factor to explain Japan's heightened threat perception. China, by translating its economic power into military power and, more importantly, naval and maritime power is challenging the core of Japanese security identity—namely, stability at sea and the secure use of sea lines of communication.

As figure 5.1 demonstrates, China's economic strength has developed at an extraordinary rate. Following the end of the Cold War, Japan's gross domestic product (GDP) was over seven times that of China; in the succeeding years, however, Japan maintained anemic levels of growth averaging less than 1 percent between 1992 and 2014, while China's average growth was over 10 percent for the same time period. Since then China's growth has slowed to between 6 and 7 percent, but it maintains a healthy lead over its East Asian neighbor and has significantly closed the gap with the United States.

This substantial growth in economic capability has provided the leadership in Beijing with the capacity to increase its military spending. While as

---

4. Japan's behavior and the geostrategic conditions in which it finds itself conform to Stephen M. Walt's hypothesis regarding balancing. See Stephan M. Walt, *The Origins of Alliances* (Ithaca, NY: Cornell University Press, 1987), 32–33.

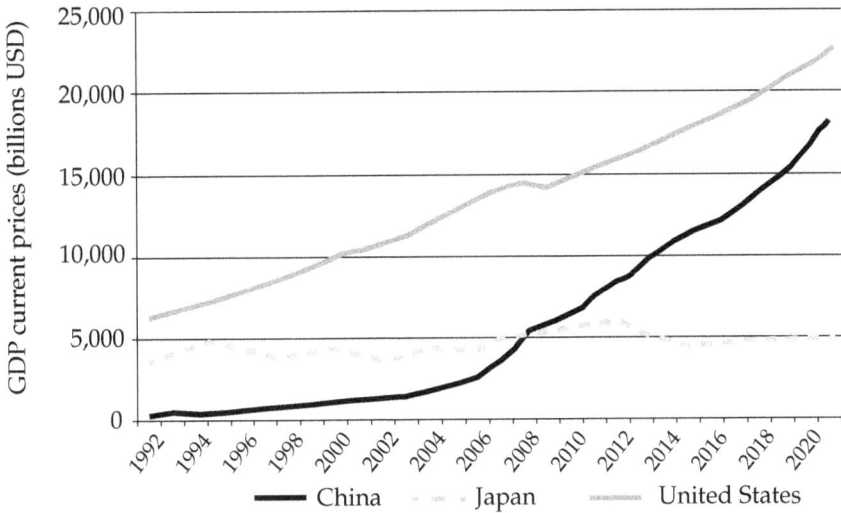

Figure 5.1. GDP of the United States, China, and Japan.
Source: International Monetary Fund, "World Economic Database," April 2016, http://
www.imf.org/external/pubs/ft/weo/2016/01/weodata/index.aspx.

a percentage of GDP defense spending in China has remained consistent at just over 2 percent of GDP, its economic growth has provided for large-scale relative increases in comparative terms. In 1990, China's military spending was estimated by the Stockholm International Peace Research Institute to have been 58 percent less than that of Japan; by 2000 this difference was reduced to 38 percent, and in 2004 China surpassed Japan's spending by just over 3.5 percent. Ten years later, China's total military expenditure was over three times that of Japan.

As figure 5.2 demonstrates, this large year-on-year increase in China's military spending has also brought it closer to the defense expenditure of the United States. In 1990 China's defense spending was 3.5 percent of the United States; in subsequent years the gap has closed. It is important to note, however, that in 2015 U.S. defense expenditure remained on top, being three and a half times greater than that of China. If the percentage rates of change in China and the United States continue, some forecasts suggest that China may surpass the world's superpower in military spending by 2030.[5]

5. Ken Jimbo, "The Rise of China and Japan's Foreign Policy Reorientation," in *China's Power and Asian Security,* ed. Li Mingjiang and Kalyan M. Kemburi (London: Routledge, 2014),253–54. This is based on the assumption that China's leadership will continue to commit to increases in military spending despite periods of potentially lower growth. At the same time, the United States maintains spending of about 3.5 percent of GDP, but it should be noted that at the height of the Cold War the United States was capable of sustained

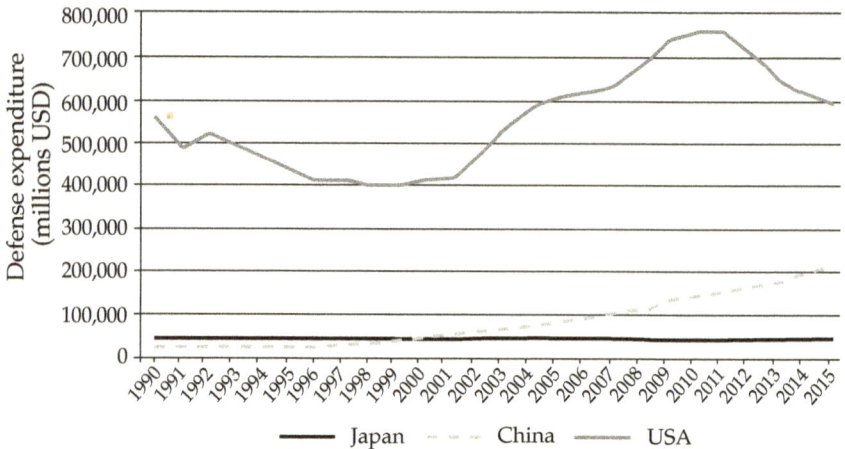

Figure 5.2. Arms expenditure of the United States, China, and Japan (in constant USD, 2014). *Source:* Stockholm International Peace Research Institute, "SIPRI Military Expenditure Database," 1998–2015, http://www.sipri.org/research/armaments/milex/milex_database.

The U.S. role as Japan's only treaty ally would indicate that given the two nations' defense spending, their combined military power would be considerably larger than that of China's. But the global dispersion of U.S. military capabilities dilutes its ability to concentrate its significant military industrial capacity in the Asia Pacific region, despite the continued U.S. strategy of rebalancing.[6] In contrast, China—currently a regional rather than global military power—has home field advantage and maintains the majority of its capabilities in the East Asia region.

THE VULNERABILITY OF THE SEA

Why this shift in regional capabilities matters to Japan lies in the uncertainty that a rising and relatively more powerful China brings. Japan is a maritime state and is therefore vulnerable to disruptions in what is a maritime regional system. Japan's 2013 *National Security Strategy* highlights this

---

military spending of over 7 percent of GDP. See Dinah Walker, *Trends in Military Spending* (New York: Council on Foreign Relations, 2015), http://www.cfr.org/defense-budget/trends -us-military-spending/p28855. As Austin Long argues, the United States could, if need be, increase its military spending with some ease. See Austin Long, "A New Wary Titan: US Defence Policy in an Era of Military Change, Asian Growth and European Austerity," in *Security Strategy and Military Change in the 21st Century: Cross-Regional Perspectives*, ed. Jo Inge Bekkevold, Ian Bowers, and Michael Raska (London: Routledge, 2015), 241–65.

6. With the rebalancing, the U.S. Navy intends to deploy over 60 percent of its platforms to the Asia Pacific theater. Additionally, the most modern platforms will be deployed there.

core determinant of Japanese security posture, stating, "Surrounded by the sea on all sides and blessed with an immense exclusive economic zone and an extensive coastline, Japan as a maritime state has achieved economic growth through maritime trade and development of marine resources, and pursued "Open and Stable Seas."[7] Japan is reliant on the security of its sea lines of communication (SLOCs) and the maintenance of its maritime territory to ensure its economic well-being,[8] as it transports over 99 percent of its imports and exports via the sea.[9] It is also one of the world's largest energy importers, the vast majority of which comes via the sea; all of Japan's crude oil is imported, 93 percent of which comes via the sea (81 percent of that from the Middle East).[10] Imports of goods and energy from the Middle East transit through the SLOCs of the South China Sea which, as M. Taylor Fravel demonstrates in chapter 8 of the present volume, are waterways riven with maritime territorial disputes involving China and other local powers.[11]

Therefore, the safe and secure use of the sea is a national security imperative for Tokyo. During the Cold War, Japan rested both its economic and national well-being on a foundation of U.S.-imposed maritime security supported by substantial indigenous naval and coast guard forces. In the post–Cold War period these two pillars of security remain underpinned by a third: the maintenance and utilization of international norms and the law of the sea.[12] Further, SLOC security moved beyond being a wartime operational concept for the Japanese Maritime Self-Defense Force (JMSDF) and the government of Japan; it became a peacetime operational imperative.[13] As a result, Japan's security interests moved away from areas solely surrounding

7. Ministry of Defense of Japan, *National Security Strategy: December 17, 2013* (Tokyo: Ministry of Defense of Japan, 2013), 2.

8. Ministry of Defense of Japan, *Defense of Japan 2015* (Tokyo: Ministry of Defense of Japan, 2015), 157.

9. Japan Maritime Center, *Key Figures of Japanese Shipping 2013–2014* (Tokyo: Japan Maritime Public Relations Center, 2014), http://www.jpmac.or.jp/img/relation/pdf/epdf-full .pdf, 1.

10. U.S. Energy Information Administration, "Countries: Japan," January 30, 2015, http:// www.eia.gov/beta/international/country.cfm?iso=JPN.

11. U.S. Energy Information Administration, *South China Sea*, February 7, 2013, https:// www.eia.gov/beta/international/analysis_includes/regions_of_interest/South_China_Sea /south_china_sea.pdf.

12. Toshimi Kitazawa "New Dimensions of Security," speech at the 2010 IISS Shangri-La Dialogue, Singapore, June 5, 2010, http://www.iiss.org/en/events/shangri%20la%20dialogue/archive/shangri-la-dialogue-2010-0a26/second-plenary-session-fccd/toshimi -kitazawa-bfe7; Ministry of Defense of Japan, *National Defense Program Guidelines for FY 2014 and Beyond* (Tokyo: Ministry of Defense of Japan, 2013), http://www.mod.go.jp/j/approach /agenda/guideline/2014/pdf/20131217_e2.pdf, 4.

13. Alessio Patalano, "Japan as a Seapower: Strategy, Doctrine and Capabilities under Three Defence Reviews, 1995–2010,' *Journal of Strategic Studies* 37, no. 3 (2014): 417.

Japan to those where its SLOCs transit.[14] This is reflected in official references to the South China Sea and Japan's need for a secure SLOC to the Middle East.[15]

Japan has thus invested considerable economic, diplomatic, and military resources into the maintenance of maritime security along its trade routes.[16] It has undertaken capacity building in Southeast Asia by assisting littoral states with both training and material resources,[17] and it has promoted bilateral and multilateral cooperation on piracy and other maritime security matters. As an example, it proposed the creation of the Regional Cooperation Agreement on Combating Piracy and Armed Robbery against Ships in Asia (ReCAAP). The JMSDF has also deployed in antipiracy operations in the Gulf of Aden, going as far as to establish a permanent self-defense force in Djibouti since 2011.[18] It now relies on a mixture of hard and soft power supported by international law to both promote and maintain stability on the high seas.[19]

CHINA'S CHALLENGE

Taking into account the inherent weakness imposed by geography and the shift in regional capabilities, Japan is particularly sensitive to how China applies its newfound military power and its limited transparency regarding its intentions.[20] Ordinarily the military capacity of what has traditionally been a continental power would not materially affect Japan; but the reduc-

---

14. Council on Security and Defense Capabilities in the New Era, *Japan's Visions for Future Security and Defense Capabilities in the New Era: Toward a Peace Creating Nation* (Tokyo: Council on Security and Defense Capabilities in the New Era, 2010), 12.

15. Ministry of Defense of Japan, *National Security Strategy*, 8.

16. Shigeru Ishiba, "The Republic of Korea's Force Modernization: Its Goals and Future Directions," speech at the 2004 IISS Shangri-La Dialogue, Singapore, https://www.iiss.org/en/events/shangri%20la%20dialogue/archive/shangri-la-dialogue-2004-c269/second-plenary-session-ee74/shigeru-ishiba-1dad.

17. Nguyen Hung Son, "ASEAN-Japan Strategic Partnership in Southeast Asia: Maritime Security and Cooperation," in *Beyond 2015: ASEAN-Japan Strategic Partnership for Democracy, Peace, and Prosperity in Southeast Asia*, ed. Rizal Sukma and Yoshihide Soeya (Tokyo: Japan Center for International Exchange, 2013), 214–27.

18. Ministry of Foreign Affairs of Japan, *Japan's Actions against Piracy off the Coast of Africa*, April 15, 2015, http://www.mofa.go.jp/policy/piracy/ja_somalia_1210.html.

19. This important mix was reflected in Shinzo Abe's 2013 speech to ASEAN, in which he linked the maintenance of law-based governance of the seas with the U.S. rebalancing in Asia. See Shinzo Abe, "The Bounty of the Open Seas: Five New Principles for Japanese Diplomacy," January 18, 2013, http://www.mofa.go.jp/announce/pm/abe/abe_0118e.html.

20. Ministry of Foreign Affairs of Japan, *Diplomatic Bluebook 2009* (Tokyo: Ministry of Foreign Affairs of Japan, 2009), 6; Council on Security and Defense Capabilities in the New Era, *Japan's Visions*, 11. Shinzo Abe, "Japan and NATO: Toward Further Collaboration," speech at the North Atlantic Council, January 12, 2007, http://www.mofa.go.jp/region/europe/pmv0701/nato.html.

tion of threats on China's land borders, combined with its increasingly broad political, economic, and strategic interests, has allowed the communist country to pursue the development of its sea power. This directly impacts Japan's security, something that was first publicly highlighted in the 2005 National Defense Program Guidelines.[21]

China has embarked on a substantial modernization program for both the People's Liberation Army Navy (PLAN) and its civilian maritime agencies. This program centers on creating modern forces capable of defending China's mainland and maritime interests (including operations in a Taiwan scenario) with the eventual objective of sustaining operations and applying Chinese power farther afield. A picture is emerging of a Chinese naval industrial complex increasingly confident of producing quality vessels in relatively large quantities. The Office of Naval Intelligence estimated that in 2014 and 2015, upwards of 120 vessels of various types were either constructed, launched, or commissioned into the PLAN.[22] Projections show that such construction is not currently aimed at increasing the number of vessels afloat but rather the overall quality of platforms deployed.[23] Alongside this significant investment in naval capabilities, a sustained program to modernize civilian maritime law enforcement agencies has been underway. The 2013 consolidation of four such agencies into a single Chinese Coast Guard indicated a desire in Beijing to operate better coordinated civilian maritime operations. As a result, the PLAN has increasingly taken a backseat to its civilian counterparts in enforcing China's maritime claims.[24] China currently operates over 205 maritime law enforcement vessels, including two coast guard vessels of over ten thousand tons each, making them the largest civilian maritime law enforcement vessels in the world.[25]

Chinese investments in counterintervention and anti-access capabilities have caused strategic planners in Japan and the United States to reassess their ability to safely sustain naval operations in Northeast Asia. The ongoing development of the DF-21D ASBM, or carrier killer missile, has garnered particular attention, but China is introducing a host of capabilities aimed at preventing access to its near seas while at the same time increasing capacity to project power within the East Asian maritime

21. Ministry of Defense of Japan, *National Defense Program Guideline, FY 2005–* (Tokyo: Ministry of Defense of Japan, 2004), 2–3.

22. Ibid., 13.

23. Ronald O'Rourke, *China Naval Modernization: Implication for U.S. Navy Capabilities— Background and Issues for Congress* (Washington, DC: Congressional Research Service, 2014), 39–40.

24. U.S. Office of Naval Intelligence, *The PLA Navy: New Capabilities for the 21st Century* (Washington, DC: U.S. Office of Naval Intelligence, 2015), 44–45.

25. Ibid., 45; IHS Fairplay, "China Building New Coast Guard Ships," October 16, 2014, http://www.ihsmaritime360.com/article/15015/china-building-new-coast-guard-ships.

environment.[26] Significant denial assets include modern conventional and nuclear attack submarines, advanced shore- and ship-deployed anti-ship cruise missiles, and increasingly capable aviation platforms. Additionally, with the purchase of the S-400, an advanced surface-to-air missile system, with a reported range of four hundred kilometers, China has the potential ability to impede operations in the airspace over Taiwan or the Diaoyu/Senkaku Islands.[27]

China's actions both in the East China Sea and the South China Sea have for Japan provided evidence of China's unwillingness to play by internationally established rules and a propensity to use coercion and the threat of force (underpinned by its increasingly powerful maritime forces) against weaker nations to secure its objectives. This to some extent confirms Japanese defense planners' fears; as a result, official language has become increasingly strident on this particular point. Japan's 2015 defense white paper states that China's operational trends include "continuous increases in its defense expenditures at a high level, efforts to deny access and deployment as well as prevention of military activities to its surrounding areas by foreign militaries, insufficient transparency concerning its military, rapid expansion of and intensification of activities in the maritime and aerial domains, and attempts to change the status quo by force in maritime areas."[28] Such sentiments are echoed in the 2014 National Defense Program Guidelines and the 2015 *Diplomatic Bluebook*.[29]

China has increased its naval presence in the waters around Japan. Placed within the context of increased pressure on Japan's maritime security, this presence has been perceived as explicitly threatening by the Japanese government.[30] A host of incidents have bolstered Japan's opinion that China is a somewhat reckless actor and is looking to rewrite the international rule book. The 2004 passage of a PLAN submarine through Japanese territorial waters, the 2009 USNS *Impeccable* incident, the 2010 buzzing by PLAN helicopters of Japanese destroyers, and the 2013 reported (but denied by China) "lock-on incident" in which a Chinese Jiangwei-II frigate directed its fire control radar at a JMSDF vessel all fit in within a pattern of behavior that was described by the Japanese government as outside international norms. In reference to the last incident, the Japanese defense minister stated that the

---

26. M. Taylor Fravel and Christopher P. Twomey, "Projecting Strategy: The Myth of Chinese Counter-Intervention," *Washington Quarterly* 37, no. 4 (2014): 173.

27. Paul N. Schwartz, "Russia Announces Sale of S-400 to China," June 30, 2014, http://www.csis.org/blog/russia-announces-sale-s-400-China.

28. Ministry of Defense of Japan, *Defense of Japan 2015*, 157.

29. Ministry of Defense of Japan, *Defense of Japan 2014* (Tokyo: Ministry of Defense of Japan, 2014), 4; Ministry of Foreign Affairs of Japan, *Diplomatic Bluebook 2014*, 4.

30. Bjorn Grønning, "Japan's Shifting Military Priorities: Counterbalancing China's Rise," *Asian Security* 10, no. 1 (2014): 10.

behavior was "highly unusual" and required Japan "to push China very hard to restrain from engaging in such dangerous acts."[31]

Symptomatic of this wider disconnect between China and Japan on matters relating to international norms and laws was China's November 2013 announcement of its Air Defense Identification Zone (ADIZ) over the East China Sea, which overlapped Japanese airspace around the disputed islands. This decision was made without prior regional consultation and provoked widespread condemnation across East Asia and in the United States.[32]

Japan's focus on SLOC security and on reigning in what it perceives as China's provocative side-stepping of international law is further reflected in its reaction to events in the South China Sea.[33] China's pattern of using its newfound maritime strength to enforce its maritime claims and the initiation of a broad program of land reclamation in both the Spratly and Paracel Island chains exposes Japan's SLOCs to potential Chinese influence.[34] At the same time Beijing's actions toward its territorial claims in the Paracel and Spratley Islands highlights its preference to use power rather than diplomacy and reveals, as far as Tokyo is concerned, what mode of behavior to expect from China in other realms of contention such as the East China Sea.

A core concern is the international acceptance of a new status quo in the South China Sea, one that could be replicated in the East China Sea in the future. Japan, however, must be careful in its operational approach to the South China Sea. It has been argued that China perceives the South China Sea as a core strategic location, and Beijing has publicly warned Japan not to interfere in the region.[35] Japanese efforts to maintain Tokyo's

31. Ministry of Defense of Japan, *Defense of Japan 2013*, *Digest, Part 1* (Tokyo: Ministry of Defense of Japan, 2013); Yuka Hayashi, Jeremy Page, and Julian E. Barnes, "Tensions Flare as Japan Says China Threatened Its Forces," *Wall Street Journal*, February 5, 2013, http://www .wsj.com/articles/SB10001424127887324445904578285442601856314.

32. Ministry of Defense of Japan, *Defense of Japan 2014*, *Digest, Chapter 1* (Tokyo: Ministry of Defense of Japan, 2014).

33. In an unprecedented move, the Ministry of Defense of Japan published a summary of China's actions in the South China Sea and its implications for Japanese security. See Ministry of Defense of Japan, *China's Activities in the South China Sea* (Tokyo: Ministry of Defense of Japan, 2015), http://www.mod.go.jp/j/approach/surround/pdf/ch_d-act_20151222e.pdf.

34. China is not the only country to reclaim land on the disputed islands, but its scale in doing so is unprecedented. Andrew S. Erickson, "Lengthening Chinese Airstrips May Pave Wave for South China Sea ADIZ," *National Interest*, April 27, 2015, http://www .nationalinterest.org/blog/lengthening-chinese-airstrips-may-pave-way-south-china-sea -12736; White House, "Remarks by President Obama and Prime Minister Abe of Japan in Joint Press Conference," April 28, 2015, https://www.whitehouse.gov/the-press-office /2015/04/28/remarks-president-obama-and-prime-minister-abe-japan-joint-press-confere.

35. Zachary Keck, "China Warns Japan to Stay Out of South China Sea," *National Interest*, June 12, 2015, http://nationalinterest.org/blog/the-buzz/china-warns-japan-stay-out-south -china-sea-13102; M. Taylor Fravel, "China's Strategy in the South China Sea," *Contemporary*

vision of the international order may result in increased and unnecessary tensions between the countries. An increased operational presence in South China Sea would represent in itself a new departure for Japan's defense policy, thereby altering the East Asian status quo.

The Challenge of China and Domestic Politics

For policymakers in Japan, China's maritime challenge is of paramount concern, explaining why successive Japanese governments have sought to mitigate the Chinese threat. While subordinate to the international context, this process has not been immune to domestic forces in Japan. Observers have called attention to the steady emergence of a "new nationalism" in Japan as reflected, one early scholarly example notes, in "a major shift in the attitudes of the Japanese about their country and its defense."[36] This new nationalism most notably features a reinvigorated enthusiasm for the role, utility, and legitimacy of military policies in Japan's statecraft. It also promotes Japanese preeminence in international affairs, a notion both challenged and fueled by China's power ascendancy.

Such views have become particularly prominent in Japan's political elite with and since the reelection of Shinzo Abe as prime minister in 2012. Abe himself has been a particularly vocal proponent, promoting an expansive security agenda envisioning a Japan that provides an "active contribution to peace," regionally and globally, without constitutional restrictions on Japanese Self-Defense Forces (SDFs) recast as a full-fledged military.[37] Expressing the nationalist vision of global preeminence shortly after his reelection, Abe commented, "Japan is not, and will never be, a Tier-two country. . . . I am back, and so shall Japan be."[38]

Nonetheless, attributing Japan's security reforms solely to the prime minister's nationalist credentials awards them unwarranted credit. Imbued by

Southeast Asia 33, no. 3 (2011): 296. Tim Huxley and Benjamin Schreer argue that China's island building activities are closely linked to their desire to control the SLOC of the South China Sea and defend the approaches to China's nascent underwater deterrent force. See Tim Huxley and Benjamin Schreer, "Standing Up to China," *Survival* 57, no. 6 (2015):130.

36. Eugene A. Matthews, "Japan's New Nationalism," *Foreign Affairs* 82, no. 6 (2003): 74–90.

37. James Przystup and Tatsumi Yuki, "The Foreign Policy of Abe Shinzo: Strategic Vision and Policy Implementation," *Asan Forum*, 3, no. 3 (2015), http://www.theasanforum.org/the-foreign-policy-of-abe-shinzo-strategic-vision-and-policy-implementation/; Kosuke Takahashi, "Shinzo Abe's Nationalist Strategy," *Diplomat*, February 13, 2013, http://thediplomat.com/2014/02/shinzo-abes-nationalist-strategy/.

38. Shinzo Abe, "Japan Is Back," speech to the Center for Strategic and International Studies, February 22, 2013, http://www.mofa.go.jp/announce/pm/abe/us_20130222en.html.

his own idealism, and supported by a political base of young, conservative, and loyal Liberal Democratic Party (LDP) politicians ascending to parliamentary positions on his nationalist coattails,[39] Prime Minister Abe has accelerated and redraped in nationalist colors Japan's long-standing move toward a normal security stature, setting and relentlessly pursuing a particularly progressive national security and foreign policy agenda.

Japan's mainstream public, far from nationalistic in nature, is pushing back, as evidenced by the considerable public opposition mounted to the security legislative package passed by the Japanese parliament in September 2015.[40] After all, Abe, as this commentary notes,[41] was elected despite, rather than because of, his progressive security and foreign policy agenda, and public opinion remains the most forceful opponent to the implementation of its most blatantly nationalistic elements.

Nonetheless, the political potency of this public opposition is diluted by the continued optimism regarding "Abenomics,"[42] the prime minister's economic recovery policy package (despite its at best questionable track record), and a disarrayed political opposition unable thus far to erect a viable alternative to Abe and the LDP-Komeito government coalition.[43]

Nationalism has nonetheless both influenced and on occasion hijacked Tokyo's policy agenda and its relations with China. The 2010 arrest and detention of a Chinese trawler captain, whose vessel had been operating in and around the disputed waters of the Diaoyu/Senkaku Islands, sparked a major diplomatic incident between the two countries. It exposed deep divisions with Japan's ruling elites regarding the appropriate approach to dealing with China and provided a voice to the nationalist elements of Japanese society.

While the arrest of the trawler captain most likely broke a previously held convention of dealing with similar cases quietly and quickly, the actions of the captain in ramming Japanese Coast Guard vessels was seen as deserving

39. Yuka Hayashi, "Japan's Tea Party? Abe's Young Turks Assert Influence," *Wall Street Journal*, February 27, 2014, http://blogs.wsj.com/japanrealtime/2014/02/27/japans-tea-party-abes-young-turks-assert-influence/.

40. Stephen Robert Nagy, "Is Japan Really Tilting to the Right?," http://www.eastasiaforum.org/2015/06/19/is-japan-really-tilting-to-the-right/.

41. Andy Yee, "The Twin Faces of Japanese Nationalism," http://www.eastasiaforum.org/2013/09/25/the-twin-faces-of-japanese-nationalism/.

42. "Japan Enters Recession Again as Abenomics Falters," *Guardian*, November 16, 2015, http://www.theguardian.com/business/2015/nov/16/japan-enters-recession-again-as-abenomics-falters.

43. In March 2016 Japan's largest and third largest opposition parties (the Democratic Party of Japan and the Japan Innovation Party, respectively) joined forces in a bid to challenge Abe and the Liberal Democratic Party in the summer 2016 Upper House elections. Reiji Yoshida, "Introducing Minshin To, Japan's New Main Opposition Force," *Japan Times*, March 14, 2016, http://www.japantimes.co.jp/news/2016/03/14/national/politics-diplomacy/introducing-minshin-to-japans-new-main-opposition-force/#.Vwutr_mLSUk.

a stronger reaction by the Japanese government.[44] The Chinese reaction included the arrest of Japanese citizens in China, violent anti-Japan protests in Chinese cities, the temporary suspension of rare earth exports, and the cancellation of a number of official engagements. The subsequent release of the captain without charge exposed Naoto Kan, the left wing Democratic Party of Japan (DPJ) prime minister, to significant domestic criticism for giving in too easily to Chinese political pressure, ensuring that his successors would be forced to more vociferously oppose future maneuvers supporting Beijing's claim of sovereignty to the islands and their waters.[45] It also brought a sharp debate regarding the future of Japan's responses to Chinese incursions to the forefront of Japanese politics.[46]

Japanese domestic politics played a substantial role in how Japan managed the arrest of the trawler captain; the nationalism it exposed noticeably changed the Japan-China maritime and strategic relationship. In 2012 Tokyo's outspokenly nationalist governor Shintaro Ishihara announced his intention to purchase the privately owned Diaoyu/Senkaku Islands, his reason being that the Tokyo metropolitan government could protect them better than the national government.[47] Fearful that Ishihara would use the islands to promote his nationalist agenda, the centrist DPJ-led government intervened, assuming proprietary rights, effectively nationalizing the islands in what the official narrative describes as "an effort to minimize any negative impact on [Sino-Japanese] relations."[48]

China's reaction was vociferous, as Japan had itself, no matter the reason, altered the status quo. What followed was a substantial surge in Chinese government and private vessels entering the territorial and contiguous zones around the disputed islands to negate what China perceived as a de facto fortification of Japan's claim and a resulting significant increase in sustained tension between the two countries. As reported by Japanese maritime authorities, in 2013, Chinese government vessels entered and operated in the territorial waters of the disputed islands on average fifteen

44. Linus Hagström, "'Power Shift' in East Asia? A Critical Reappraisal of Narratives on the Diaoyu/Senkaku Incident in 2010," *Chinese Journal of International Politics* 5 (2012): 283; Sheila A. Smith, *Intimate Rivals: Japanese Domestic Politics and a Rising China* (New York: Columbia University Press, 2015), 204.

45. Noboru Yamaguchi, "A Japanese Perspective on the Senkaku/Diaoyu Crisis," in *Tensions in the East China Sea: Papers Presented at International Workshop Organised by the Lowy Institute for International Policy, Sydney, June 2013* (Sydney: Lowy Institute for International Policy, 2013), http://www.lowyinstitute.org/files/tensions_in_the_east_china_sea_web.pdf.

46. Sheila A. Smith, "Japan and the East China Sea Dispute," *Orbis* 56, no. 3 (2012): 377–78.

47. Ibid., 379.

48. Ministry of Foreign Affairs of Japan, "Position Paper: Japan-China Relations Surrounding the Situation of the Senkaku Islands," http://www.mofa.go.jp/region/asia-paci/senkaku/position_paper_en.html.

times per month (the number has dropped somewhat since then, averaging seven and eight times respectively for 2014 and 2015).[49] This sequence of events reveals the potency of nationalism in stoking bilateral tensions that are in turn used to promote and indeed legitimize security reform within Japan.

So too do spasmodic tensions occurring as a result of nationalist policies and maneuvers by government officials and parliamentarians perceived by Beijing as symbolic gestures seemingly whitewashing elements of Japan's wartime past. Between 2000 and 2006, visits to the Yasukuni Shrine by then prime minister Junichiro Koizumi saw large anti-Japan protests in China and a significant downturn in diplomatic and social relations between the two countries.[50]

A surge in Yasukuni visits by Japan's political elite,[51] including Prime Minister Abe, sustained controversies over historical revisionism, and Japanese militarization has fueled anti-Japan sentiment in both the Chinese elite and public discourse. It has also caused reduced economic and political cooperation between the two countries. As a result, mechanisms and incentives for alleviating Sino-Japanese tensions have been marginalized or hindered, and disputes over sovereignty and space have become intertwined with issues of national identity and pride.

Domestic politics and issues of identity and nationalism serve to both exacerbate such tensions and to some extent influence the manner of the response. The following sections will address how Japan is reacting to the reality of the Chinese threat, examining its four basic approaches to managing Chinese assertiveness.

Administrative Reform and Grand Strategy

An altered and increasingly challenging strategic environment, in combination with favorable domestic political circumstances, has resulted in a multifaceted Japanese effort to bolster the nation's security posture. The Abe government is attempting to consolidate decision making, loosen constitutional and legislative restrictions, and develop an integrated defense and foreign policy approach.

49. Ministry of Foreign Affairs of Japan, "Trends in Chinese Government and Other Vessels in the Waters Surrounding the Senkaku Islands, and Japan's Response: Records of Intrusions of Chinese Government and Other Vessels into Japan's Territorial Seas," April 7, 2016, http://www.mofa.go.jp/region/page23e_000021.html.

50. Smith, "Japan and the East China Sea Dispute," 371–72.

51. In 2013, 168 Japanese parliamentarians visited the Yasukuni Shrine during the religiously significant spring festival; that number was up from eighty-one in 2012. Hayashi, "Japan's Tea Party?"

The administrative heart of these reforms is a top-down bureaucratic and doctrinal reorganization aimed at creating a coherent and responsive Japanese security and foreign policy. The end of 2013 saw the Abe government establish a National Security Council (NSC) and release Japan's first National Security Strategy (NSS). The former replaces what was an unwieldy security policy- and decision-making mechanism, one that was reportedly riven with internecine conflict and hindered by excessive red tape.[52] In creating the NSC, the Abe government has attempted to rectify these problems through streamlining decision making and consolidating security policy responsibility. It is important to note that Abe attempted to introduce an NSC during his first term in office, in 2007; while that attempt was a failure, it shows in part that the NSC was born not out of an explicit China threat but a desire on the part of Abe and his supporters to normalize Japan's approach to security policy.[53]

Operating within the prime minister's cabinet, the NSC comprises three separate bodies: four-minister meetings, nine-minister meetings, and emergency situation meetings. At its center are the regularly held four-minister meetings, which include the prime minister, the minister of foreign affairs, the minister of defense, and the chief cabinet secretary. These meetings are designed to serve essentially as a "control tower" for national security policy, and they ostensibly replace the full nine-member cabinet meeting, which formed the previous iteration of the government's security council.[54] The first four-minister meeting, in early December 2013, broached a wide range of subjects, including the new Chinese ADIZ and Japan's wider national security strategy.[55] The nine-member cabinet meeting still exists, but is now only required to provide oversight of important decisions made during the four-minister meetings, thereby reducing competing voices in overall policymaking and increasing the prime minister's control over security decisions. The emergency-situation meeting comprises the prime minister, the chief cabinet secretary, and ministers from relevant departments and is designed to reflect how crises in the current security environment can involve a number of actors and potentially require responses from numerous agencies.[56]

52. J. Berkshire Miller, "How Will Japan's New NSC Work?," *Diplomat*, January 29, 2015, http://www.thediplomat.com/2014/01/how-will-japans-new-nsc-work; Yuichi Hosoya, "The Role of Japan's National Security Council," *AJISS Commentary* 199 (2014), http://www.iips.org/en/publications/data/AJISS-Commentary199.pdf.

53. Michael Green and Nicholas Szechenyi, "Shinzo Abe and the New Look of Japanese Leadership," *Harvard Asia Pacific Review* 9, no. 1 (2007), 29–31, 30.

54. Ministry of Defense of Japan, *Defense of Japan 2014*, 126.

55. Kyodo News International, "Japan's NSC Discusses China, North Korea in 1st Meeting," December 4, 2013, http://www.globalpost.com/dispatch/news/kyodo-news-international/131204/japans-nsc-discusses-china-n-korea-1st-meeting.

56. Ministry of Defense of Japan, *Defense of Japan 2014*, 126.

Supporting the NSC is the National Security Secretariat, which is composed of both civilian and uniformed personnel from a number of ministries and is required to formulate and importantly coordinate security policy.[57] It has reportedly succeeded in its goals of streamlining how information and advice is distributed by distilling the numerous voices involved in informing security policy and has quickened the government's response time to national security contingencies such as the disappearance of Air-Asia flight 8501.[58] As it is still a young institution, the NSC's role and position within the government is not yet concrete; it remains to be seen how it will fit and maintain influence within Japan's notoriously conservative bureaucracy at the end of the Abe administration, when its chief patron is no longer in power.

The National Security Strategy is designed to provide a grand strategic approach to Japan's foreign and defense policy, leveraging military, diplomatic, financial, and industrial capabilities to both improve Japan's strategic position and reorient Tokyo's assets toward better combatting the effects of China's rise. It is unique in being the first official grand strategy, but the vision it sets out—that of Japan being a "proactive contributor to peace"—is the most recent incarnation of an idea that has taken hold in Japanese strategic thinking since the end of the Cold War—namely, the buildup of internal military and diplomatic capabilities tied to a strengthened U.S. alliance and greater involvement in international affairs.[59]

The NSS provides official momentum behind these objectives based upon the significant shifts in the balance of power and security environment in East Asia. Based on these factors the NSS outlines six key approaches: (1) strengthening and expanding Japan's capabilities and roles, (2) strengthening the Japan-U.S. alliance, (3) strengthening diplomacy and security cooperation with Japan's partners for peace and stability in the international community, (4) proactive contribution to international efforts for peace and stability of the international community, (5) strengthening cooperation based on universal values to resolve global issues, and (6) strengthening the domestic foundation that supports national security and promoting domestic and global understanding.[60]

Combined, these six goals mix the hard capabilities required to protect Japan's security with the soft power imperatives of increased cooperation with international partners in Asia and beyond to promote the international

57. National Institute for Defense Studies, "Japan: New Development of National Security Policy," in *East Asian Strategic Review 2014* (Tokyo: National Institute for Defense Studies, 2014), 44–46.

58. "National Security Council Gradually Makes Presence Felt in First Year," *Asahi Shimbun*, January 8, 2015, http://www.ajw.asahi.com/article/behind_news/politics/AJ201501080068.

59. National Institute for Defense Studies, "Japan: New Development," 50.

60. Ministry of Defense of Japan, *National Security Strategy*.

norms so highly valued by Tokyo and challenged by Beijing. The success or failure of these initiatives remains unclear, but as will be outlined in the next section, there have been concrete efforts toward their implementation. With the creation of both the NSC and the NSS, Japan has, for the first time, a coherent and independent forum for integrating and enacting foreign and security policy. Only time will tell if these endeavors will become truly effective, but in their formative stages it is a powerful indicator of Tokyo's willingness and perceived need to shake off its passivity and shape the security environment in its own favor.

Internal Capabilities: Guns, Laws, and New Approaches

Prior to the end of the Cold War, Japan's defense posture had been articulated in the 1976 National Defense Program Outline, which had a rhetorically simplistic goal for the SDFs: to have "a full surveillance posture in peacetime and the ability to cope effectively with situations up to the point of limited and small-scale aggression."[61] This goal was not set in stone, however, as it was informed by a sometimes overlooked caveat that it was dependent on the assumption that "the international political structure in this region [Asia]—along with continuing efforts for global stabilization—will not undergo any major changes."[62]

Thus, with the end of the Cold War, the diversification of threat, and low-level volatility in the security environment, the Japanese government issued a new National Defense Program Outline in 1995, which was succeeded by the renamed National Defense Program Guidelines (NDPG) in 2004 and 2010. Each revision was the product of an altered external security environment and Japan's internal political and fiscal situation, and each built upon existing procurement plans and structures utilizing extant equipment alongside the incremental introduction of new capabilities. Therefore, the posture of the SDFs has not been static but has continuously changed, with an increasing focus on flexibility, responsiveness, and modernity but always operating within the constraints imposed by Japan's interpretation of its constitution.[63]

In 2013, alongside the first NSS, a new NDPG was released that reflected the themes set out in the grand strategic document. The 2013 NDPG was unique in that it was no longer the primary articulation of Japan's national security objectives and principles.[64] Nevertheless, it—alongside the system

---

61. Japan Defense Agency, *Defense of Japan 1995* (Tokyo: Japan Defense Agency), 265.
62. Ibid.
63. National Institute for Defense Studies, "Japan: New Development," 55.
64. Ibid., 48.

for defense expenditures laid out in the 2014–18 Mid-Term Defense Program (MTDP)—is the principle guide to the direction and goals of the SDFs.[65]

The standout policy of the 2013 NDPG is the adjustment of the operational and developmental concept of the SDFs from the 2010 Dynamic Defense Force to a Dynamic Joint Defense Force.[66] While similar, the new moniker reflected Tokyo's concern that the 2010 NDPG was inadequate to deal with the increasingly high-pressure security environment and China's potential for continued provocations. The 2013 assessment emphasizes Tokyo's belief that "gray zone" situations (situations that are neither specifically in peacetime nor conflict) first mentioned in the 2010 NDPG, were increasing in their magnitude and seriousness and were more likely to escalate into potential conflict.[67]

In altering its military posture, Japan does, however, face some significant long-term difficulties in maintaining the regional status quo. Supporting its tremendous economic growth, China, with its massive population, large territory, and vast natural resources, is immensely endowed with the socioeconomic ingredients for national power. Starkly in contrast are Japan's rapidly declining population and economy, which—vigorous reform efforts notwithstanding—refuse to maintain any semblance of healthy growth and, relatedly and more critically, its relatively small island territory with inherently poor natural resource endowment.[68] This disparity in domestic power ingredients at Beijing's and Tokyo's disposal implies that China essentially can outspend and outbuild Japan in defense matters. Despite Japan's best efforts, Chinese air and naval superiority may be inevitable over the long run.

Nevertheless, Japan's response does have mitigating factors in its favor. Japan's military expenditures, while on the increase, still hover around 1 percent of GDP, below the level of comparable states; this leaves Tokyo room to increase its expenditures if the circumstances so warrant.[69] As an island nation and a status quo power, Japan is not required to invest in large-scale and expensive power projection assets. Such a defensive posture is aided by

65. Japan's minister of defense Itsunori Onodera describes the NDPG as the "capstone document of Japan's defense policy and strategy." See Itsunori Onodera, "Strengthening Japan's Defense Force," *Asia Pacific Review* 20, no. 2 (2013): 71.

66. Ministry of Defense of Japan, *National Defense Program Guidelines for FY 2014 and Beyond*, 3.

67. Ministry of Defense of Japan, *Defense of Japan 2014*, 144–45.

68. Milton Ezrati, "The Demographic Timebomb Crippling Japan's Economy," *National Interest*, March 25, 2015, http://www.nationalinterest.org/feature/the-demographic-timebomb -crippling-japans-economy-12479. On the socioeconomic ingredients of power, see John J. Mearsheimer, "Structural Realism," in *International Relations Theories: Discipline and Diversity*, ed. Timothy Dunne, Milja Kurki, and Steve Smith (Oxford: Oxford University Press, 2007), 71–89.

69. Lynann Butkiwicz with Nicholas Eberstadt and Richard Katz, *Roundtable: Implications of Japan's Changing Demographics* (Seattle: National Bureau of Asian Research, 2012), http:// www.nbr.org/downloads/pdfs/ETA/ES_Japan_demographics_report.pdf.

the realities of geography and the difficulties that offensive operations over water pose. Additionally, 60 percent of Japan's defense budget is allocated to the Japanese Ground Self-Defense Force (JGSDF), meaning that considerable funding could be made available for more vital air and naval forces—albeit at high domestic political cost.

The 2010 NDPG focused on deterrence through ensuring continuous intelligence, surveillance, and reconnaissance (ISR) backed up the continuous operations of the SDFs; in other words, deterrence through activity. The new guidelines retain the focus on ISR but emphasize cross-service quality and quantity, pre-positioning of forces, and contingency-based planning so that the SDFs have packages of deployment options if escalation in gray zone situations occurs.[70]

Therefore, joint capability-based assessments to meet these needs have focused on force development in four key clusters of capabilities: ISR; maritime and air superiority; rapid transport and response; and joint command, control, communication, and intelligence (C^3I).[71] These areas of development would be used to maintain deterrence and respond to attacks on Japan's sovereignty and challenges to its administrative control over remote islands, two areas where the China threat takes center stage, while also allowing the SDFs to continue existing operations.[72]

Each cluster builds upon existing procurement programs and provides capabilities across operational requirements. Investment in ISR capabilities centers on the procurement and increased deployment of new and modernized fixed-wing and rotary patrol aircraft. Twenty indigenously designed P-1 maritime patrol aircraft were purchased in 2015, and the acquisition of a new E2-D surveillance aircraft is part of the 2016 defense budget.[73] Additionally, the new 603rd Squadron of the Japan Air Self-Defense Force (JASDF), flying E-2C early warning aircraft, was deployed to Naha Air Base in Okinawa, the closest major military air facility to the disputed territories.[74] It supplements the JMSDF's Fifth Fleet air wing, also based at Naha, which operates two

70. Ministry of Defense of Japan, *National Defense Program Guidelines for FY 2014 and Beyond*, 7–8.

71. Ministry of Defense of Japan, *Medium Term Defense Program (FY2014–2018)* (Tokyo: Ministry of Defense of Japan, 2013), 6–12.

72. Other areas of the SDFs' operations include ballistic missile defense (largely aimed at North Korea), the development of cyberoperations and operations in outer space, responding to natural disasters, strengthening intelligence gathering, and the promotion of a stable Asia Pacific and global security environment. See Ministry of Defense of Japan, *Medium Term Defense Program (FY2014–2018)*, 6–16.

73. Ministry of Defense of Japan, *Defense Programs and Budget of Japan—Overview of FY 2015 Budget Bill* (Tokyo: Ministry of Defense of Japan, 2015), 2–3; Ministry of Defense of Japan, *Defense Programs and Budget of Japan Overview of FY 2016 Budget Bill* (Tokyo: Ministry of Defense of Japan, 2015), 34.

74. Ministry of Defense of Japan, *Defense of Japan 2014*, 187.

flights of antisubmarine maritime patrol P-3C Orion aircraft and the SH-60J and SH-60K, maritime patrol helicopters operating JMSDF vessels. The 2015 and 2016 budgets also provide for the modernization of Japan's E-767 airborne early warning and control force and the acquisition of the Global Hawk unmanned aerial vehicle system.[75] These airborne capabilities have been supplemented by the deployment of the 303rd Coastal Observation Unit on Yonaguni Island (adjacent to the Diaoyu/Senkaku Islands), which began operations in early 2016.[76] The 2016 budget also provides for the deployment of a further mobile warning and control radar on Amami Oshima Island.[77]

The notable buildup in maritime forces is aimed at maintaining maritime superiority. While the altered Chinese threat does not require a significant redeployment or change in operational thinking for the JMSDF, it is increasing its platform numbers. As a result, the latest guidelines maintain the 2010 NDPG's commitment to increasing the number of submarines from sixteen to twenty-two through the modernization of existing platforms and new launches.[78] This was initiated in direct response to the rising numbers of modern Chinese submarines and increased maritime activity in southwest Japan, resulting in the need to maintain a larger continual presence at sea. The 2013 NDPG increases the JMSDF's destroyer fleet from forty-eight to fifty-four platforms, including two new Aegis destroyers.[79] In part this allows for greater ballistic missile defense coverage but also provides for the JMSDF to maintain a higher number of ships available for contingencies in Japanese home waters and beyond. Funds have also been provided for research into a new indigenous class of compact multifunctional destroyers and the acquisition of maritime unmanned aerial vehicles.[80]

In terms of air superiority, the JASDF will reinforce the F-15J presence at Naha Air Base by adding an extra squadron, redeployed from Kyushu, thus

75. Ministry of Defense of Japan, *Defense Programs and Budget of Japan: Overview of FY2016 Budget* (Tokyo: Ministry of Defense of Japan, 2015), 3; Ministry of Defense of Japan, *Defense Programs and Budget of Japan: Overview of FY2015 Budget*, (Tokyo: Ministry of Defense of Japan, 2014), 3.

76. Franz-Stefan Gady, "New Radar Facility: Japan Expands Military Presence in East China Sea," *Diplomat*, March 29, 2016, http://thediplomat.com/2016/03/new-radar-facility-japan-expands-military-presence-in-east-china-sea; Ministry of Defense of Japan, *Defense Programs and Budget of Japan: Overview of FY2015 Budget*, 5.

77. Ministry of Defense of Japan, *Defense Programs and Budget of Japan: Overview of FY2016 Budget*, 4.

78. Isao Miyaoka, "Military Change in Japan: National Defense Program Guidelines as a Main Management Tool," in *Security Strategy and Military Change in the 21st Century: Cross-Regional Perspectives*, ed. Jo Inge Bekkevold, Ian Bowers, and Michael Raska (London: Routledge, 2015), 46–47.

79. Ministry of Defense of Japan, *Defense of Japan 2014*, 151.

80. Ministry of Defense of Japan, *Defense Programs and Budget of Japan: Overview of FY2016 Budget*, 3–4.

raising the number of available aircraft to forty;[81] this reinforcement has occurred due to the incredible pressure being placed on the existing squadron
by repeated scrambles to meet Chinese flights in the region.[82] With the future
introduction of the F-35 to the JASDF's order of battle and the modernization of existing platforms, the 2013 NDPG predicts that the number of JASDF
fighter aircraft will increase for the first time since the end of the Cold War,
reflecting the pressure Japan is facing in maintaining the integrity of its airspace.[83]

The continued development of ISR and maritime and air superiority capabilities feeds into Japan's capacity to defend and maintain control over its remote southwestern islands, an ambition first outlined in the 2010 NDPG.[84]
This scenario most likely involves the Diaoyu/Senkaku Islands and some
form of foreign attempt to occupy them. The requirement to deter and respond to this has led to the creation of a dedicated amphibious unit.[85] While
this has been under development since before the 2010 NDPG, more concrete
details are now emerging and the full unit is scheduled to be operational by
2018.[86] Named the Amphibious Rapid Deployment Brigade, it will be approximately three thousand men strong and will be at the heart of the JGSDF's
threefold plan to be more responsive to the security environment in the southwest.[87] This plan includes the creation of rapid response area security units to
respond to contingencies on uninhabited outlying islands.[88] The provision of
two divisions and two brigades with rapid deployment capabilities, and the
creation of the previously mentioned amphibious forces, is ostensibly directed
toward recapturing lost territory.[89] These new units will leverage existing and

81. Isabel Reynolds, "Chasing Chinese Planes 400 Times a Year Is Wearing Out Japan's
Top Guns,' March 5, 2015, http://www.bloomberg.com/news/articles/2015-03-05/chasing
-chinese-planes-400-times-a-year-stretches-Japan-top-guns.

82. In 2014, Japanese planes scrambled 371 times in response to Chinese flights around
their territory, representing a 29 percent increase over the previous year. This pressure has
been exacerbated by Russia's increasingly active air force. The JASDF has responded 369
times to Russian flights in 2014, a 50 percent increase over the previous year. See Robin
Harding, "Japan Scrambles Warplanes More Often Than in Cold War," *Wall Street Journal*,
January 20, 2015, http://www.ft.com/cms/s/0/22ecfab6-a08b-11e4-9aee-00144feab7de
.html#axzz3ZkLliZNN.

83. Ministry of Defense of Japan, *National Defense Program Guidelines for FY 2014 and
Beyond*, 13.

84. Ministry of Defense of Japan, *National Defense Program Guidelines for FY2011 and
Beyond* (Tokyo, Ministry of Defense of Japan, 2010), 13.

85. The JGSDF has received significant input from the United States on the formation of
this unit, conducting combined training with U.S. Marines since 2005. It also now holds
regular bilateral exercises and internal joint exercises on islands in proximity to the Di-
aoyus/Senkakus.

86. Ministry of Defense of Japan, *Defense of Japan 2014*, 190.

87. Ibid., 154.

88. This unit will be based on Amami Oshima.

89. Ministry of Defense of Japan, *Defense of Japan 2015*, 165.

new transport capabilities, including the MV-22 Osprey aircraft (of which seventeen are scheduled for purchase by 2018), new AAV-7 amphibious vehicles, and an increased number of transport helicopters and aircraft. The JGSDF plans to invest in combat vehicles capable of being transported in aircraft, while the JMSDF is upgrading its three Osumi-class tank landing ships and is researching the procurement of a new multipurpose amphibious vessel. The JMSDF's flat-top fleet of two Hyuga-class and two Izumo-class ships, while ostensibly dedicated to antisubmarine operations, could also be utilized to deploy troops using helicopters and the MV-22. The Izumo-class ship also possesses the ability to act as a C³I hub for air and maritime operations.

How sustainable Japan's military developments will be is ultimately a question of what role the government envisions for its SDFs. Maintaining some semblance of the status quo will be difficult due to the realities of the power shift. Yet, in the long term the SDFs could, given the factors mentioned above, negate to some degree the extent and the pace of the power shift, and shield against its harmful implications in retaining the capacity to sustain a credible deterrent to any conventional threat posed by China.

Moreover, given the geostrategic realities of the contemporary power shift in East Asia, Japan's reforms must be understood, first and foremost, within the context of the Japan-U.S. alliance as efforts to assume a greater responsibility for its own defense while allowing the United States to operate more freely, pursuing broader regional security objectives of common interest to the alliance. As will be discussed in greater detail in the next section, Japan's efforts, in other words, take aim at forging a stronger and more robust alliance that operationalizes to a greater extent its power aggregation potential due to an increase in Japanese contributions.[90]

LEGISLATION

The reorientation of the SDFs' operational posture has gone hand in hand with a sustained legislative effort to alter the legal underpinnings of Japan's security policy. In late March 2016, following a tortuous period of bitter political debate and sustained public opposition, two new security laws came into effect. These laws reflect a belief within the Abe government and establishment defense hawks that the security environment requires a broader spectrum for the permissible application of Japan's military power to defend itself and its allies.[91] The result is SDFs with incrementally more freedom

---

90. On the power aggregation potential (gross) versus realized power aggregation (net) of alliances, see Thomas S. Szayna, Daniel Byman, Steven C. Bankes, Derek Eaton, Seth G. Jones, Robert Mullins, Ian O. Lesser, and William Rosenau, *The Emergence of Peer Competitors: A Framework for Analysis* (Santa Monica, CA: RAND, 2001), chap. 2.

91. Sheila A. Smith, "Reinterpreting Japan's Constitution," July 2, 2014, http://www.blogs.cfr.org/asia/2014/07/02/reinterpreting-japans-constitution.

of action, but freedom that remains constrained by the restrictions imposed by Japan's constitution.

Article 9 of the constitution "renounce[s] war as a sovereign right of the nation" and claims that "land, sea, and air forces, as well as other war potential, will never be maintained. The right of belligerency of the state will not be recognized."[92] Crucially, this has been interpreted by successive governments as permitting the creation and operation of the SDFs for the defense of Japan alone while prohibiting Japan's assertion of its right to collective self-defense and the possession or deployment of offensive weaponry.[93] Despite these restrictions, the SDFs' operational parameters have slowly expanded since the end of the Cold War. Indeed, the reconfiguration of Japan's defense posture can be seen in the passing of twenty-one pieces of security legislation between 1992 and 2007, which have, among other things, allowed for the SDFs' participation in peacekeeping operations and increased security cooperation with the United States in relation to ballistic missile defense.[94]

It is therefore important to resist the temptation to view the creation of the new security laws as an isolated event; instead they fit within a pattern of cumulative changes in which Japan's legal understanding of its security posture changes when circumstances demand. The Abe government has loosened but not overcome the restrictions on the use of military power.

The legislation lowers constitutional barriers on the development and application of Japan's military power. It eases the deployment of SDFs in nonwar gray zone situations, allows Japanese forces to protect U.S. forces if they are operating in contribution to the defense of Japan, broadens the circumstances regarding the provision of logistical support, and loosens restrictions on the nature of the SDFs' involvement in UN peacekeeping operations. The legislation also allows Japan to use force in defense of another country under the following provisos: (1) the country is in a close relationship with Japan and as a result its being subject to attack threatens Japan's survival and poses a clear danger to life, liberty, and the pursuit of happiness;[95] (2) there is no other appropriate means available to repel the attack and ensure Japan's survival and protect its people; and (3) the use of force is limited to the minimum extent necessary. Japan has therefore not yet embraced collective self-defense but has instead made it conditional.

---

92. "The Constitution of Japan," http://japan.kantei.go.jp/constitution_and_government _of_japan/constitution_e.html.

93. Miyaoka, "Military Change in Japan," 39.

94. Dennis Hickey and Lilly Kelan Lu, "Japan's Military Modernization: The Chinese Perspective," in *China and Japan at Odds: Deciphering the Perpetual Conflict*, ed. James C. Hsiung (New York: Palgrave Macmillan, 2007), 102.

95. Ministry of Foreign Affairs of Japan, "Cabinet Decision on Development of Seamless Security Legislation to Ensure Japan's Survival and Protect Its People," July 1, 2014, http:// www.mofa.go.jp/fp/nsp/page23e_000273.html.

Nevertheless, the implications for Japanese defense and security policy could be quite substantial given that this interpretation would potentially allow Japan to come to the aid of East Asian neighbors such as the Philippines or (given Japan's close relationship with the United States) U.S. forces if the standing government in Tokyo could convince Japan's elected parliamentarians—whose approval is a prerequisite—that it would be necessary to achieve the aforementioned security objectives. Significant restrictions on Japan's military posture persist. For this reason, as others have noted, "Japan remains an exceptional U.S. ally" and, moreover, it is "far more self-restrained than any other major economic power."[96]

The process to change the security legislation exposed deep divisions in Japan's domestic political landscape between those who sought to retain the core ethos of the Japanese constitution and those who sought to alter it. This dualism in Japanese politics evidently sits alongside the external threat environment in determining the nature and extent of Japan's security normalization.

Opinion polls and large-scale public protests, notably fronted by Students Emergency Action for Liberal Democracy, suggest a substantial public opposition to security reforms,[97] yet a weak and divided political opposition did not possess the muscle to prevent them. Nevertheless, political and popular opposition played a role in watering down some of the Abe government's more ambitious plans.

Abe, along with nationalist members of his party and their backers, have looked beyond merely changing the interpretation of the constitution to rewriting it. Nationalist elements within Japanese society view the U.S.-authored document as an affront to Japanese sovereignty and as imposing a severe and dangerous restraint on Japan's use of its armed forces.[98] Efforts to do so have been repeatedly delayed by sustained public opposition creating an unfavorable political environment.[99] Widespread public mistrust of such changes will continue to make it difficult for Japanese elites to take a highly active role in future regional or global security matters.[100]

96. Jeffrey W. Hornung and Mike M. Mochizuki, "Japan: Still an Exceptional U.S. Ally," *Washington Quarterly*, 39, no. 1 (2016): 110; Adam P. Liff, "Japan's Defense Policy: Abe the Evolutionary," *Washington Quarterly* 38, no. 2 (2015): 89.

97. Linda Sieg, "Japan Public Divided as Laws Easing Limits on Military Take Effect," March 29, 2016, http://www.reuters.com/article/us-japan-defence-idUSKCN0WV053.

98. Jonathan D. Pollack, "Japan's Defense Policy Revision—Where Is Japan Headed?," August 17, 2014, http://www.brookings.edu/research/opinions/2014/08/17-japan-defense-policy-revision-pollack.

99. "Asahi Poll: Majority of Voters Feel no Need to Revise Constitution," *Asahi Shimbun*, March 3, 2016, http://www.asahi.com/ajw/articles/AJ201605030043.html.

100. Robert Dujarric, "Assessing Japan's New Defense Policy Bills," *Diplomat*, June 4, 2015, http://thediplomat.com/2015/06/assessing-japans-new-defense-policy-bills/.

CHAPTER 5

The United States and New Guidelines

The Japan-U.S. alliance dynamic has undergone significant change in response to the rise of China. As the United States has rebalanced in Asia, it has expected greater cooperation and defense proactivity from its regional allies, Japan and South Korea, than the formative terms of their alliances specified. Tokyo, for its part, has sought greater reassurance from the United States for its protection in the event of escalating gray zone situations. Notably, evidence suggests that Japan is now driving its efforts to adjust the alliance rather than solely reacting to U.S. pressure.

In late April 2015, during a state visit to the United States where Prime Minister Abe became the first Japanese leader to address a joint session of Congress, the U.S.-Japan Security Consultative Committee agreed to new Guidelines for Japan-U.S. Defense Cooperation. Two previous sets of guidelines were released in 1976 and 1997; the latter signaled a shift in the boundaries of Japanese defense policy, as they were aimed primarily at outlining Japan-U.S. defense cooperation in a Korean Peninsula scenario, highlighting cooperation in situations in areas surrounding Japan.[101]

Two main areas of change are highlighted in the 2015 guidelines. The first is a wider range of operational cooperation and coordination in peacetime areas such as ISR, air and missile defense, maritime security, asset protection, training exercises, and logistical support. While in wartime the SDFs will take primary responsibility for the defense of Japan, U.S. forces "will conduct operations to support and supplement the Self-Defense Forces' operations," which suggests that the United States will provide the offensive capabilities in the event of conflict.[102] The second area falls in line with Tokyo's push to utilize force in response to an armed attack against a country other than Japan. This both meets U.S. expectations for Japan and allows Japan to commit resources to the South China Sea, but follows the constitutional reinterpretation outlined previously.

The guidelines are opaque in their description of many of the modified missions the SDFs could undertake. As an example, the guidelines state that the SDFs and the U.S. armed forces will provide mutual protection of each other's assets, as appropriate, if engaged in activities that contribute to the defense of Japan in a cooperative manner, including during training and exercises.[103]

101. Ministry of Defense of Japan, *The Guidelines for Japan-U.S. Defense Cooperation* (Tokyo: Ministry of Defense of Japan, 2014), http://www.mofa.go.jp/region/n-america/us/security/guideline2.html.

102. U.S. Department of Defense, *The Guidelines for Japan-U.S. Defense Cooperation: April 27, 2015* (Washington, DC: U.S. Department of Defense, 2015), http://archive.defense.gov/pubs/20150427_--_GUIDELINES_FOR_US-JAPAN_DEFENSE_COOPERATION.pdf.

103. Ibid., 6.

As one analyst argues, the meaning of "assets" and "activities in defense of Japan" is subject to wide interpretation. Such imprecision in language could mean that Japan may someday need to defend anything from a U.S. vessel to a U.S. city, while it could if politically appropriate sit out a war involving the United States and North Korea if it was not directly threatened.[104]

This opacity in language can be accounted for by both countries' interests in devising an alliance construct that, while stronger and more robust, allows for flexibility with regard to the nature and extent of joint military ventures in response to regional and global situations. This allows the bilateral relationship to adjust to a rapidly evolving geopolitical and domestic context by successively embedding, at Japan's discretion, further military commitments without undertaking a contentious guideline revision,[105] while at the same time demonstrating the allies' continued strong commitment to the alliance.

This flexible alliance construct also mitigates both governments' concerns that the stronger and more robust nature of the alliance could force them into unwanted action. Tokyo's concerns relate primarily to entanglement in U.S. war-fighting ventures not directly linked to Japanese security, potentially exposing Japan as a proxy target. Washington's concerns relate to unwanted entanglement in Sino-Japanese military hostilities, which could potentially jeopardize its broader regional and global interests.[106] It was reported that during negotiations for the new guidelines Japan wanted specific mention of the defense of the southwestern islands, including the Diaoyus/Senkakus, added to the language.[107] This did not occur; rather, it was inserted into the joint statement that announced the guidelines resulting from the 2+2 talks between the two nations' foreign and defense ministers, and by President Barack Obama during a joint press conference with Prime Minister Abe.[108] The guidelines provide rhetorical and political support for Japan from the

104. See Robert S. Ross, this volume, chap. 8; and Kyle Mizokami, "Inside the New U.S.-Japan Defense Guidelines,' *USNI News*, April 29, 2015, http://www.news.usni.org/2015/04/29/inside-the-new-u-s-japan-defense-guidelines.

105. On this point it should be noted that the release of the guidelines in April 2015 predates Japan's September 2015 passing of security laws legalizing the core joint missions for which it created a procedural framework.

106. As such, the new guidelines seek to answer the dual and opposing risks of abandonment and entrapment. While abandonment has always been considered the greater danger, Japan has traditionally considered entrapment the greater risk. The recent reforms suggest that this calculus is changing in the present geopolitical context, with greater emphasis—U.S. rebalancing efforts notwithstanding—being placed on the risk of abandonment.

107. Grønning, "Japan's Shifting Military Priorities," 8.

108. U.S. Department of State, "Joint Statement of the Security Consultative Committee: A Stronger Alliance for a Dynamic Security Environment," April 27, 2015, http://www.state.gov/r/pa/prs/ps/2015/04/241125.htm; White House, "Remarks by President Obama and Prime Minister Abe." https://www.whitehouse.gov/the-press-office/2015/04/28/remarks-president-obama-and-prime-minister-abe-japan-joint-press-confere.

United States while not formally committing the latter to action in gray zone scenarios.[109]

The guidelines also possibly reflect Washington's desire to control the extent of Japan's defense reforms and the direction they are taking. While the United States has long criticized Japan for not carrying its weight in the relationship, it has at times demonstrated concern about letting Japan off the leash in defense terms, especially at times of heightened tension with China or South Korea. This current initiative very much derives from Tokyo and Abe's desire to put the relationship on more equal terms, something that was first brought up in his 2012 election campaign.[110]

The new guidelines do, however, address specific U.S. complaints about the one-sidedness of the relationship. There is evidence that U.S. commanders are already looking into which potential missions the SDFs could carry out in the wider East Asia region, with the implication that a Japanese presence could be a counterweight to China's superiority over the littoral states of the South China Seas.[111] But Japan's contribution to the alliance is constrained by geostrategic and political realities: the amount of force that Japan could realistically deploy in the South China Sea or elsewhere without jeopardizing homeland defense is limited. While changes in Japan's defense posture mean that it will be better able to respond to China locally and assist U.S. forces, it remains reliant on the United States to ensure that the wider regional maritime status quo is maintained. Additionally, even with the legislative change, the Japanese public would most likely remain suspicious of the SDFs' involvement in U.S. operations.

As the following section will highlight, however, Japan is willing to diplomatically engage with nations in the wider Asian region and utilize limited military assets to bolster such engagement. In doing so, Japan assists the United States in potentially developing a loose coalition of states willing to constrain Chinese coercion.

Winning Friends and Influencing the Strategic Environment

The fourth element of Japan's response to the power shift in East Asia has been to engage with regional and extraregional actors in order to solidify an international consensus against China's perceived revisionist posture. This has marked an increasingly activist and securitized foreign policy and

109. If Japanese islands were attacked, it is most likely the United States would respond, as President Obama has previously stated that they are covered by Article 5 of the defense treaty.

110. Grønning, "Japan's Shifting Military Priorities," 8.

111. Tim Kelly and Nobuhiro Kubo, "U.S. Would Welcome Japan Air Patrols on South China Sea," January 29, 2015, http://www.reuters.com/article/us-japan-southchinasea-idUSKBN0L20HV20150129.

fits within the broad strategy outlined in the 2013 NSS. Japan has adopted a policy of highlighting both democratic and normative commonalities with East Asian countries with which it desires cooperation. As Shinzo Abe stated in a 2014 speech in Singapore, "Last year, I visited all ten ASEAN member countries, and my determination grew with each country I visited. This is because these visits taught me that we share common groundwork regarding our commitment to valuing law, and that we enjoy a consensus in our respect for freedom of navigation and freedom of overflight."[112] In emphasizing these values Japan provides a stark contrast with China's assertive actions in East and Southeast Asia.

Japan is attempting to support ASEAN member states engaged in territorial disputes with China—most notably the Philippines and Vietnam—through both material and diplomatic support while at the same engaging in closer security cooperation with Australia and India.[113] While Japan has previously assisted in security capacity building in Southeast Asia, primarily with the provision in 2006 of six coast guard vessels to Indonesia to combat piracy and develop littoral states' ability to maintain maritime security, the direction of this assistance has changed. Japan is now pursing closer security partnerships with these countries, encouraging dialogues and exchanges, and altering the nature of the aid it provides. Japan sees ASEAN attempts (no matter how disjointed they maybe) to enforce the 2002 Code of Conduct signed by China but never truly implemented, as central to stability in the Southeast Asian maritime sphere.[114]

A key development in highlighting how foreign policy has shifted is Japan's overseas development aid (ODA) policy. In 2014, the Japanese government decided that ODA could be utilized strategically to promote Japan's interests and international peace.[115] In 2015 the restriction on the provision of ODA to foreign militaries was lifted on the provision that such aid would not be used for military or wartime purposes.[116] Therefore, the provision of training and materiel is applicable to navies involved in such activities. Such provision builds upon the 2014 loosening of Japan's previously strict defense export restrictions, which now allow the conditional export of military equipment.[117]

---

112. Shinzo Abe, "Keynote Address to the 2014 IISS Shangri-La Dialogue in Singapore," May 30, 2014, https://www.iiss.org/en/events/shangri%20la%20dialogue/archive/2014-c20c/opening-remarks-and-keynote-address-b0b2/keynote-address-shinzo-abe-a787.

113. Ministry of Foreign Affairs of Japan, *Diplomatic Bluebook 2014*, 14–15.

114. Ministry of Defense of Japan, *National Security Strategy*, 24.

115. Ministry of Foreign Affairs of Japan, "FY 2014 Priority Policy for International Cooperation," http://www.mofa.go.jp/files/000040158.pdf.

116. Ministry of Foreign Affairs of Japan, "Decision on Development Cooperation Charter," February 2015, http://www.mofa.go.jp/files/000067702.pdf.

117. One of the rationales behind loosening defense export restrictions was the acknowledgment that Japan could not look after its interests by itself and that such exports could

A beneficiary of this development has been the Philippines, a U.S. ally that has been involved in increasingly strident maritime territorial disputes with China. In pursuing a defense relationship with the Philippines, Japan does not gain much on the surface in terms of direct security benefits; rather, the relationship solidifies Japan's role in supporting nations involved in disputes with China and assisting the United States in its rebalancing toward Asia, bringing two allies closer together. The Japan–Philippine relationship was upgraded in 2011 to a "strategic partnership"; while this term can be applied to a variety of international relationships with varying degrees of military cooperation, its expressed purpose is to "promote concrete forms of cooperation in a comprehensive manner."[118]

Since this development Japan has repeatedly and publicly backed Manila in its dispute with China and supported efforts on the part of former president Benigno Aquino's government to bring the Spratly Island maritime territorial dispute to an international tribunal.[119] The two governments also signed a 2012 statement of intent on defense cooperation that focused on a number of other security matters including peacekeeping operations, humanitarian assistance and disaster relief, and, notably, maritime security; it also instituted a number of working-level and high-level exchanges. Utilizing ODA, Japan provided a monetary loan to the Philippines to procure ten forty-meter coast guard vessels. While loan approval was initially granted in 2013, the contract was not awarded until April 2015.[120] Japan has also agreed to lease the Philippines up to five unarmed TC-90 aircraft to be used for maritime surveillance; such an agreement highlights the weaknesses of the Philippine military and the formative nature of Japan's military assistance efforts.[121]

The defense relationship was further upgraded in 2015 when the respective defense ministries signed the Memorandum on Defense Cooperation. This further embedded exchanges and meetings into the relationship, with

---

promote international peace and security. See Ministry of Foreign Affairs of Japan, "Three Principles on Transfer of Defense Equipment and Technology," April 1, 2014, http://www .mofa.go.jp/files/000034953.pdf.

118. Prime Minister of Japan, "Japan-Philippines Joint Statement on the Comprehensive Promotion of the 'Strategic Partnership' between Neighboring Countries Connected by Special Bonds of Friendship," September 27, 2011, http://japan.kantei.go.jp/noda/diplomatic /201109/27philippines_e.html.

119. Ministry of Foreign Affairs of Japan, "Japan-Philippines Summit Meeting," June 24, 2014, http://www.mofa.go.jp/s_sa/sea2/ph/page3e_000187.html.

120. Republic of Philippines, Department of Transportation and Communications, "Japanese Firm to Build Ten 40-Meter Vessels for Philippine Coastguard—DOTC," April 20, 2015, http://www.gov.ph/2015/04/20/dotc-japanese-firm-to-build-ten-40-meter-vessels-for -philippine-coast-guard/.

121. Agence France-Presse, "Japan Agrees to Lease Military Aircraft to Philippines," May 3, 2016, https://www.yahoo.com/news/japan-agrees-lease-military-aircraft-philippines-0508 15514.html.

both sides agreeing to regular ministerial and vice-ministerial defense dialogues and the establishment of joint staff talks between their armed forces.[122] The agreement's language highlights the countries' mutual interests. Both ministers shared the view that any disputes should be settled peacefully, without use of force or coercion, in accordance with the basic principles of law. They also reaffirmed the importance of the freedom of navigation and overflight on the high seas.[123]

In May 2015 the JMSDF and the Philippine Navy held their first ever bilateral maritime exercise, which was quickly followed by another one the following month.[124] There has also been discussion between Tokyo and Manila of Japanese acquisition of naval access rights in the Philippines.[125] For Manila, the continuing relationship adds a powerful backer in its relationship with China but, as was noted previously, the extent to which Japan can contribute to any combat scenario in the South China Sea is constrained by the security situation in Japan's home waters. Nevertheless, it highlights Japan's willingness to engage in Southeast Asia, develop security relationships with like-minded countries, and create a quasi-coalition of nations willing to stand up for the status quo in East Asia.

This in part explains Japan's increasingly close and somewhat similar relationship with Vietnam, another ASEAN member with a tense and ongoing dispute with China, as was symbolized by the 2014 conflict over the deployment of a Chinese oil drilling rig in disputed waters. In 2014 the relationship between the two nations was upgraded from a "strategic partnership" to an "extensive strategic partnership for peace and prosperity in Asia." This built upon a series of agreements and meetings, including a memorandum of understanding on defense cooperation that committed the defense communities on both sides to "actively boost and exchange defense cooperation in areas under the international laws and laws, policies and regulations of each country."[126]

Between May 2012 and May 2015, Japan and Vietnam held fifteen high-level defense meetings, and in 2014 Tokyo agreed to provide six law enforcement

122. Ministry of Defense of Japan and Department of National Defense of the Republic of the Philippines, "Joint Press Release," 29 January 2015, http://www.mod.go.jp/j/press/youjin/2015/01/29a_jpr_e.pdf.

123. Ibid.

124. Prashanth Parameswaran, "Philippines to Hold Military Exercises with US, Japan," *Diplomat*, June 19, 2015, http://thediplomat.com/2015/06/philippines-to-hold-military-exercises-with-us-japan/.

125. Al Jazeera, "Philippines May Allow Japan's Military to Use Bases," June 5, 2015, http://www.aljazeera.com/news/2015/06/philippines-japan-military-bases-150605072014102.html.

126. "Vietnam, Japan Boosts Defence Cooperation," *People's Army Newspaper*, October 25, 2011, http://en.qdnd/defence-cooperation/vietnam-japan-boosts-defence-cooperation/164726.html.

vessels to Hanoi for maritime security purposes.[127] While noted analyst Carlyle Thayer has highlighted that these are relatively small and well-used commercial and fishery protection vessels, they symbolized an agenda on Tokyo's part similar to that of the Japan-Philippine relationship.[128] This is increasingly evident in the official language in the agreements between the two countries. The initial 2010 statements on joint partnership did not include mention of maritime security or the South China Sea, but by 2014 they affirmed that "peace and stability at sea were in the common interest of both countries" and later that year Abe condemned China's drilling activities in Vietnamese-claimed waters.[129]

Increased Japanese involvement in the security of ASEAN members involved in South China Sea territorial disputes has gone hand in hand with developing security relations with Australia and India. India is of interest because it has been identified as a rising power and a potential check on the rising influence of China. The NSS highlights India's location and proximity to vital SLOCs in the Indian Ocean and calls for a strengthening of bilateral relations in a broad range of areas, including maritime security, based on the two nations' strategic and global partnership.[130] Given India's ongoing investment in naval capabilities, which in part are reported to be driven by China's rise, securitization of the relations between New Delhi and Tokyo presents the potential for significant strategic benefits in terms of maintaining a geographically expansive and comparatively powerful partnership aimed at sustaining the status quo.[131]

In the case of Australia, the security relationship operates on both a trilateral, U.S.-centered basis and an ever-developing bilateral basis. Japan has long sought to increase its security relationship with Australia, with regular 2+2 defense and foreign ministry meetings established as far back as 2006. Australia is a natural partner for Japan, given their shared alliance with the United States, their shared maritime nature, and a lack of historical animosity between the two nations.

---

127. Ministry of Defense of Japan, *Defense of Japan 2015*, 389.

128. Carl Thayer, "Vietnam's Extensive Strategic Partnership with Japan," *Diplomat*, October 14, 2014, http://thediplomat.com/2014/10/vietnams-extensive-strategic-partnership -with-japan/.

129. Ministry of Foreign Affairs of Japan, *Japan-Viet Nam Joint Statement on the Establishment of the Extensive Strategic Partnership for Peace and Prosperity in Asia* (Tokyo: Ministry of Foreign Affairs of Japan, 2014), http://www.mofa.go.jp/files/00031617.pdf; Carl Thayer, "China's Oil Rig Gambit: South China Sea Game-Changer?," *Diplomat*, May 12, 2014, http:// thediplomat.com/2014/05/chinas-oil-rig-gambit-south-china-sea-game-changer/.

130. Ministry of Defense of Japan, *National Security Strategy*, 24.

131. Ministry of Foreign Affairs of Japan, *Japan-India Joint Statement: Intensifying the Strategic and Global Partnership* (Tokyo: Ministry of Foreign Affairs of Japan, 2014), http://www .mofa.go.jp/files/000025064.pdf.

Australia has set out an ambitious strategy to have greater involvement in Asia Pacific security, and while there is a debate regarding the extent to which Canberra should align against Beijing, it has increased its coopera-tion with the United States.[132] It is a worthy question to ask if Australia would move to assist in defending Japan in the event of increased hostilities with China, but it is a valuable partner in maintaining a loose alliance of demo-cratic nations willing to defend international norms at sea. As *Defense of Ja-pan 2015* states, "Both Japan and Australia are allies of the United States and share not only universal values but also strategic stakes and interests in the security field."[133] At the 2014 Japan-Australia 2+2 meeting, both sides agreed upon strong language regarding the ongoing Asian maritime disputes, clearly referring to China by "reconfirming the recognition that the use of force or coercion to unilaterally change the status quo in the East China Sea and South China Sea will be strongly opposed."[134] Australia's 2016 *Defence White Paper* emphasizes its support of a rules-based global order, further highlighting this mutual strategic concern.[135] The increasing closeness of the relationship was demonstrated in 2014 when Australian prime minister Tony Abbott became the first foreign leader to attend a four-minister meeting of Japan's National Security Council. At that meeting Abe referred to Austra-lia as a "special partner for Japan," while Abbott referred to Japan as Aus-tralia's "best friend in Asia."[136]

Both the Australian and Indian militaries are involved in bilateral and mul-tilateral exercises with the Japanese SDFs. The JMSDF held its first bilateral exercise with Australia in 2009, and with India in 2012, building upon an ongoing series of U.S.-involved trilateral exercises with both countries.[137] In 2015 Japan became a permanent participant in the annual Malabar naval ex-ercise, which originally involved the navies of the United States and India.

---

132. Australia has agreed to host up to 2,500 U.S. Marines at a base in Darwin. There are also reports that the United States will permanently station warships in Australia in the future. See Jason Scott and David Tweed, "U.S. Navy Considers Setting Up Ship Base in Australia," February 10, 2015, http://www.bloomberg.com/news/articles/2015-02-10/u-s -considering-basing-navy-ships-in-australia-greenert-says-i5yxouxp.

133. Ministry of Defense of Japan, *Defense of Japan 2015*, 279.

134. Ministry of Foreign Affairs of Japan, "Fifth Japan-Australia Joint Foreign and Defense Ministerial Consultation (2+2)," http://www.mofa.go.jp/a_o/ocn/au/page3e _000188.html.

135. Australia Department of Defence, *2016 Defence White Paper* (Canberra: Australia Department of Defence, 2016), 70.

136. Prime Minister of Japan, "Special Meeting of the National Security Council (Meeting among Four Ministers)," April 7, 2014, http://japan.kantei.go.jp/96_abe/actions/201404 /07kokka4sp.html.

137. Niharika Mandhana, "Japan to Join U.S.—Military Exercises," *Wall Street Journal*, July 22, 2014, http://www.wsj.com/articles/japan-to-join-u-s-india-military-exercises -1406043468.

The 2015 exercises took place in the Bay of Bengal, and the 2016 exercises were held off Okinawa near the South China Sea.[138]

Conclusion

In attempting to maintain the status quo, Japan is altering long-held internal conditions and regulations governing its defense posture and foreign policy. While taken in isolation such changes may seem minor, cumulatively they represent a substantial response to China's assertive application of newfound capabilities on the seas of East Asia. Such a response is viewed by Japan's elites as essential given the archipelagic nation's strategic vulnerabilities. China's move to the sea strikes at the heart of Japanese security sensibilities.

Efforts to counter China have exposed divisions between external threat and domestic politics as primary drivers of Japan's security policy. Nationalism has certainly played a role in the more recent changes, driving some of Prime Minister Shinzo Abe's legislative and security policies and periodically raising tensions between Beijing and Tokyo. As much as nationalism is a factor, however, domestic politics and popular resistance to security reforms have played a substantial role, acting as a bulwark against moves to fully normalize Japan as a security actor.

Ultimately, while domestic politics has influence, the structural challenge posed by Beijing is the dominant determinant of Japan's response. Since the end of the Cold War, Japan has repeatedly altered its defense posture to respond to changes in the external threat environment. The response to China is no different, as previous governments on both the left and right of the Japanese political divide have sought to build up Japan's defense capabilities.

The effectiveness of the response is challenged by limitations imposed by domestic politics and Japan's inherent weaknesses when compared to China. As a result the alliance with the United States remains the central pillar of Japanese security. Nevertheless, Japan will likely sustain its drive to play a wider role in both domestic and international security. Recent history suggests that is unlikely that the changes it has implemented will be rolled back. If anything, if China's challenge continues unabated further strengthening of Japan's defensive posture and a greater securitization of its foreign policy is likely.

138. Sanjeev Miglani, "U.S. Plans Naval Exercises with India and Japan in Philippine Sea," March 3, 2016, http://www.reuters.com/article/india-usa-military-exercise-idUSKC N0W41UH.

Popular Nationalism and Economic Interests in China's Japan Policy

James Reilly

It seems "a good bet," Randall Schweller notes in chapter 1 of this volume, that as China rises and the East Asian balance of power transforms, "domestic politics will play a significant, if not decisive, role in shaping the patterns of foreign policies and, by extension, the dynamics of East Asian regional security."

This chapter takes Schweller's bet, examining the impact of two domestic factors on China's Japan policy: popular nationalism and economic interests. While both nationalism and economic cooperation are generally ascribed a central role in shaping China's Japan policy, the extent and even the direction of their impact remains hotly disputed. Some scholars argue that popular nationalism has pushed Beijing into a more assertive stance toward Japan, though others suggest that fears of popular nationalism growing out of control have actually moderated China's Japan policy. Economic interests have similarly been hypothesized to exert a warming effect on China's Japan policy, have limited impact, or even exacerbate competition and contention. In an effort to untangle these competing claims, this chapter examines the influence of economic interests and popular nationalism on China's Japan policy over the past decade.

The evidence suggests that while China's anti-Japan nationalism has grown stronger since 2002, as measured by the frequency and scale of popular protests, it has not exceeded state control. The Chinese government retains the capacity to curtail popular protests. Indeed, fears that anti-Japan protests risked eroding domestic stability have encouraged Beijing to seek improved diplomatic relations, most notably following widespread anti-Japan demonstrations in spring 2005. During the post-2010 resurgence in bilateral tensions, the Chinese government once again briefly tolerated sporadic outbursts of anti-Japan nationalism before reining them in. While the government continues to use wartime history for domestic and diplomatic purposes, there is limited evidence that popular nationalism played a central role in driving China's policy during the resurgent dispute over the Diaoyu/Senkaku Islands after 2010.

Efforts at economic cooperation fell victim to the surge in anti-Japan nationalism from 2002 through 2005, as populist anger and strategic tensions undermined commercial interactions and stymied efforts at institutionalizing economic ties. Yet once the economic costs of diplomatic discord emerged, Chinese leaders took steps to calm public emotion and stabilize bilateral relations. From 2006 through 2009, the economic significance of Japan for China's economy encouraged Chinese leaders to pursue new modes of economic cooperation. Yet as China's economic strength has grown, Beijing appears less constrained by commercial interests. Increasingly confident in Japan's deepening economic dependence on China, Chinese leaders have become more willing since 2010 to use economic tools to advance strategic interests. The shift in the economic balance of power, it appears, has eroded previous constraints on Chinese foreign policy toward Japan.

These dynamics are broadly consistent with the classical realist approach applied throughout this volume. The differential growth of power among states alters, in Robert Gilpin's words, a state's incentives to enhance its own interests and security as "the expected benefits exceed the expected costs."[1] Rising Chinese power has clearly shifted Beijing's calculations. China's expanded and more advanced navy and coast guard can now operate with greater effectiveness in disputed waters in the East China Sea, contributing to Beijing's increasingly robust defense of its sovereignty claims there. Similarly, the rise of the Chinese economy has reduced Chinese dependency on Sino-Japanese trade and Japanese investment, encouraging Chinese leaders to use economic levers for political advantage while eroding the pacific effects of economic interdependence.

This chapter begins by briefly examining the conceptual arguments underpinning both factors in China's Japan policy, and then compares their impact across three periods: the surge of animosity from 2002 through 2005, a warming of ties from 2006 to 2009, and the resumption of strategic and diplomatic tensions after 2010. I conclude by suggesting that neither popular nationalism nor economic interests is exerting a consistent or significant impact upon China's territorial disputes in the East China Sea. Chinese leaders have not become captured by populist, anti-Japan sentiments; nor are they overly constrained by economic considerations. Instead, Beijing's security policy appears to be driven more by a strategic pursuit of national security objectives, encouraged by China's rise in relative power.

---

1. Robert Gilpin, *War and Change in World Politics* (Cambridge: Cambridge University Press, 1981), 50.

Debating Popular Nationalism and Economic Interests

Most scholars expect China's rapid military modernization and economic resurgence to cause Beijing to adopt a more expansive set of national interests. As its capacity to protect these interests grows, the argument goes, Beijing will become more assertive.[2] Belligerence is particularly likely toward Japan due to geographical proximity, prevalence of territorial and economic disputes, a contentious past between the two nations, nationalist pressures, and competition over strategic resources.[3] Given China's negative threat perceptions, defensive measures by Japan will likely be seen as signaling aggressive intent, spurring Chinese buildups and exacerbating a security dilemma.[4] Festering history disputes, Yinan He argues, aggravate these realist drivers.[5]

Anti-Japanese popular nationalism in China exacerbates these pressures. Concern with negative public opinion inhibits Chinese leaders from taking actions they believe will be publicly criticized, particularly amid a period of heightened public emotion. A divided or weak Chinese leadership can create cracks in the political opportunity structure, offering an opening for popular nationalist protests to grow. During such surges of populist anger, concessions offered Japan also become more costly for Chinese leaders, rendering cooperation less likely. Chinese nationalists can even insert themselves into the relationship, engaging in actions that stimulate popular emotions or causing an event to which Chinese leaders must react. The scope for public debate shrinks as voices of moderation risk being shouted down by online furor.[6]

The combination of China's growing capabilities, Sino-Japanese strategic distrust, and strong mutual public animosity create a dangerous environment in which even minor incidents can spark a major crisis. Once a standoff emerges, Chinese leaders will be reluctant to take conciliatory steps due to their reputational concerns in Japan and at home among the Chinese people. Institutionalized cooperation is unlikely, particularly over strategic issues or topics that engender strong public emotions. Chinese leaders will be hesitant to build the kinds of institutional structures that might constrain them in future crises, offer relative gains for Japan, or spark criticism for being perceived as too "soft" on Japan. Observing these dynamics, most scholars of

2. John J. Mearsheimer, "The Gathering Storm: China's Challenge to US Power in Asia," *Chinese Journal of International Politics* 3 (2010): 381–96.

3. Kent Calder, "Coping with Energy Insecurity: China's Response in Global Perspective," *East Asia* 23, no. 3 (2006): 49–66.

4. Thomas J. Christensen, "China, the U.S.-Japan Alliance, and the Security Dilemma in East Asia," *International Security* 23, no. 4 (1999): 49–80.

5. Yinan He, "Ripe for Cooperation or Rivalry? Commerce, Realpolitik, and War Memory in Contemporary Sino-Japanese Relations," *Asian Security* 4, no. 2 (2008): 162–97.

6. This argument draws from James Reilly, *Strong Society, Smart State: The Rise of Public Opinion in China's Japan Policy* (New York: Columbia University Press, 2012).

China-Japan relations end up with a persistent and pervasive pessimism, predicting "perpetual conflict" between China and Japan.[7]

A few scholars, however, strike a more optimistic tone. Jessica Weis argues that Chinese leaders often tolerate or even encourage nationalist protests to "tie their hands" and gain negotiating leverage with Tokyo, but are not overly constrained by populist pressures.[8] Erica Strecker Downs and Phillip C. Saunders point out that the Chinese leadership's fears of anti-Japanese nationalism have led Beijing to de-escalate strategic standoffs.[9] Indeed, the emergence of even small-scale nationalist protests presents Chinese leaders with a dangerous dilemma: if they suppress or ignore these protests, leaders could be criticized for being too "soft" on foreign policy, yet tolerating nationalist protests runs the risk that they will snowball into a broader protest movement that could encourage opponents of the regime to join together, foster divisions within the leadership, and encourage alliances between popular movements and defectors from the leadership,—all elements linked with authoritarian downfall in other cases.[10] Nationalist demonstrations may turn quickly from being against Japan to being against the Chinese Communist Party. For this reason, anti-Japan demonstrations are rarely tolerated for any extended period. Instead, Chinese leaders have repeatedly responded to swells in such protests; they seek to calm anti-Japan sentiments by directing public attention elsewhere, and work to build popular support for the diplomatic engagement of Tokyo.[11] Yet even as tensions cool, relations are unlikely to return to the status quo ante. Instead, bilateral ties are likely to be more fragile, with nationalist emotions on a higher pitch, reputational concerns exacerbated, and ties of trust and cooperation eroded. A subsequent crisis is thus made more likely by the previous one.

Just as the effects of popular nationalism on China's Japan policy have remained hotly disputed, so too has the impact of economic interests sparked sharp debates among scholars. While most experts acknowledge that shared economic interests foster pacific tendencies, they generally remain skeptical about the power of trade and investment to transform the relationship. As Michael Yahuda argues, "The significant degree of economic interaction between the two sides does not appear to have produced significant con-

7. James C. Hsiung, ed., *China and Japan at Odds: Deciphering the Perpetual Conflict* (New York: Palgrave Macmillan, 2007).

8. Jessica Chen Weiss, "Authoritarian Signaling, Mass Audiences, and Nationalist Protest in China," *International Organization* 67, no. 1 (2013): 1–35.

9. Erica Strecker Downs and Phillip C. Saunders, "Legitimacy and the Limits of Nationalism: China and the Diaoyu Islands," *International Security* 23, no. 3 (1998–99): 114–46.

10. Guillermo O'Donnell and Philippe C. Schmitter, *Transitions from Authoritarian Rule: Tentative Conclusions about Uncertain Democracies* (Baltimore: Johns Hopkins University Press, 1986), 2–15.

11. James Reilly, "Remember History, Not Hatred: Collective Remembrance of China's War of Resistance to Japan," *Modern Asian Studies* 45, no. 2 (2011): 463–90.

stituencies in either country who have been ready to promote publicly the importance of cultivating good relations with other. . . . Arguably, the economic interdependence acts as a constraint against allowing relations to deteriorate unduly. But so far there is little evidence of these considerations spilling over into other aspects of their relations."[12] Others, however, are more sanguine. Richard Katz notes that "an economic version of mutual deterrence is preserving the uneasy status quo between the two sides" despite the 2013–14 standoff over the Diaoyu/Senkaku Islands.[13] Examining five previous disputes over the islands, Min Gyo Koo finds that, each time, "both Japan and China have found it in their interest to de-escalate conflicts because of concerns over damaging their economic relationship."[14]

Certainly, for Chinese leaders, maintaining the legitimacy of Communist Party rule requires ensuring an external environment conducive to domestic economic growth. Japan is a crucial part of that environment. China's bilateral trade with Japan has soared from US$88 billion in 2001 to over US$330 billion in 2013.[15] Japanese investment flows into China have also risen over the decade, from US$4.3 billion in 2001 to US$7.3 billion by 2012, though flows began to decline sharply after 2013 due to a combination of rising labor costs and shifting production patterns, as well as Japanese investors' concerns over persistent security tensions and anti-Japanese populist emotions in China. Yet Japan has maintained its position as one of the leading foreign investors into China, and before 2013 was often the top annual investor (excluding Hong Kong and offshore round-trip investment havens). Even as Japan's investment into China has slowed, Chinese investment into Japan has risen sharply, climbing from a low base of only US$7.3 million in 2003 to US$149 million in 2011.[16] Japan is also the top or second-largest trade partner for eleven Chinese provinces. The largest bilateral trade flows are with China's most dynamic and wealthy coastal provinces, and for many of these provinces

12. Michael Yahuda, "The Limits of Economic Interdependence: Sino-Japanese Relations," in *New Directions in the Study of China's Foreign Policy*, ed. Alastair Iain Johnston and Robert S. Ross (Stanford, CA: Stanford University Press, 2006), 162–86.

13. Richard Katz, "Mutual Assured Production: Why Trade Will Limit Conflict between China and Japan," *Foreign Affairs* 92, no. 4 (2013): 18–22, 24.

14. Min Gyo Koo, "The Senkaku/Diaoyu Dispute and Sino-Japanese Political-Economic Relations: Cold Politics and Hot Economics?," *Pacific Review* 22, no. 2 (2009): 208. See also M. Taylor Fravel, "Explaining Stability in the Senkaku (Diaoyu) Dispute," in *Getting the Triangle Straight: Managing China-Japan-US Relations*, ed. Gerald L. Curtis, Ryosei Kokubun, and Jisi Wang (Washington, DC: Brookings Institution Press, 2010): 144–64.

15. These figures come from International Monetary Fund, "IMF Data: Access to Macroeconomic and Financial Data," http://data.imf.org/?sk=388DFA60-1D26-4ADE-B505-A05A558D9A42.

16. Chinese Ministry of Commerce Database, http://data.mofcom.gov.cn/channel/includes/list.shtml?channel=dwjjhz&visit=A.

Japan is the largest trading partner (excluding oil-exporting nations and Hong Kong).[17]

As Richard Katz explains, between 60 and 70 percent of the goods that China imports from Japan are the parts and machinery that China uses to make its own exports. China's export-driven economic model relies upon sustaining these trade flows. Katz cites a 2012 International Monetary Fund report that calculated that for every 1 percent of growth in China's global exports its imports from Japan rise by 1.2 percent. "Take away those imports," he concludes, "and China's exports collapse."[18] Yang Xing and Zhu Ni, economists with China Industrial and Commercial Bank, now the world's largest bank, agree that the "possible degree of substitution in China's domestic market" for Japanese inputs "is very low or non-existent. Once a supply shortage appears, the negative impact on the relevant industries' production is tremendous."[19] While substitutions can certainly be found eventually, the costs of reorienting trade relations for many Chinese firms in the short or medium term could be significant.

The moderating effect of such commercial ties on diplomatic and security relations can occur through two mechanisms: first, "when states become reluctant to disrupt or jeopardize the welfare benefits of open economic exchange," and second, "when domestic interest groups with a stake in interdependence constrain the ability of the state to act autonomously."[20] In other words, this argument predicts that Chinese leaders are most likely to moderate their foreign policy when they fear that bilateral tensions will damage economic ties, and/or when they face domestic criticism over the economic costs of strategic tensions.

In sum, sharp scholarly divides persist over both the extent and direction of impact by popular nationalism and economic interests on rising China's Japan policy. Competing claims, each grounded in well-respected theoretical schools of thought, offer divergent predictions for how economic factors and popular nationalism are likely to influence China's foreign and security policy toward Japan. To advance this debate, the following sections examine the influence of both factors from 2002 through 2014, beginning with China's swell of anti-Japanese popular nationalism in 2002.

17. This figures come from China Data Online, "China Yearly Macro-Economics Statistics (Provincial)," http://chinadataonline.org/member/macroyr/.

18. Katz, "Mutual Assured Production."

19. Yang Xing and Zhu Ni, "China-Japan Tensions Do Not Benefit China's Economic Recovery," *Economic Observer*, November 27, 2012, http://www.eeo.com.cn/2012/1127/236626.shtml.

20. He, "Ripe for Cooperation or Rivalry?"

A Surge of Nationalism: 2002–2005

As Chinese president Hu Jintao and premier Wen Jiabao came to power in 2002, they began pursuing closer diplomatic ties with Japan. In September 2002 they celebrated the "Year of Japan" in China with a flurry of public events.[21] The front page of the *People's Daily* on September 29, 2002, captured the spirit, proclaiming in large print, "Happy Birthday to China-Japan Friendship."[22] The Sixteenth Party Congress's final resolution in November 2002 announced a new slogan guiding Chinese foreign policy: "Treat neighbors as friends; treat neighbors as partners" (*yilin weishan; yilin weiban*).[23] China's Japan experts widely agreed that this policy signaled the new leadership's intent to strengthen ties with Japan.[24] Even as Prime Minister Junichiro Koizumi persisted in annual visits to the Yasukuni Shrine, as Ming Wan notes, Chinese leaders responded with "measures that were sufficiently high profile to send a clear message of discontent without compromising interests . . . that have a greater substantial impact on China's long-term economic and political interests."[25]

These mixed objectives were evident in Beijing's reversal on Japanese involvement in China's high-speed rail program.[26] After signs that Japan looked likely to win major railway contracts, nationalist activists quickly embarked upon China's first major online petition campaign.[27] Chinese leaders soon reversed course, excluding Japan from a major contracts. As one Japan expert in Beijing later mused, "This project could have been a major support for China-Japan relations, linking the two countries together. Instead, it became a major problem in the relationship."[28]

Over the next few years, bilateral tensions rapidly mounted. In September 2003 an accidental unearthing of abandoned Japanese chemical weapons in Northeast China that left one person dead and thirty-seven severely

21. Lu Yi, *Zhongri xianghu lijie haiyou douyuan? Guanyu liangguo minzhong xianghu renshi de bijiao yanjiu* [How far away is mutual understanding between China and Japan? A comparative study on the mutual perceptions between the two peoples] (Beijing: Shijie zhishi chubanshe, 2006), 45–9.

22. "Zhu zhongri guanxi shengri kuaili" [Wishing happy birthday to China-Japan relations], *People's Daily*, September 29, 2002.

23. Shi Jiafang, *Zhanhou ZhongRi guanxi: 1945–2003* [Postwar China-Japan relations: 1945–2003] (Beijing: Dangdai chubanshe, 2005), 219.

24. Anonymous, interview with the author, Beijing University, May 15, 2007; Anonymous, interview with the author, Renmin University, August 12, 2007.

25. Ming Wan, *Sino-Japanese Relations: Interaction, Logic, and Transformation* (Stanford, CA: Stanford University Press, 2006), 248.

26. James Reilly, "China's History Activism and Sino-Japanese Relations," *China: An International Journal* 4, no. 2 (2006): 189–216.

27. Peter Hays Gries, "China's 'New Thinking' on Japan," *China Quarterly* 184 (2005): 844.

28. Anonymous, interview with the author, Beijing, August 10, 2007.

injured sparked an online petition campaign that collected over one million signatures in a month, supported by 12,518 websites.[29] Online reports of a sex orgy by Japanese businessmen in southern China on September 18, 2003, a sensitive wartime anniversary, further inflamed popular sentiments. Riots soon broke out in Xi'an in response to a licentious skit by Japanese university students and again after a China-Japan soccer match in Beijing. Even Japanese car advertisements and video games sparked online protests.

These pressures peaked in 2005 with an online petition campaign opposing Japan's efforts to obtain a permanent seat on the UN Security Council. Aided by government tolerance, previous petition campaigns, and a highly mobilized atmosphere, the public response was overwhelming. Within a week, there were over 2.5 million signatures, with public petition-signing events being held in cities across China.[30] After conservative Japanese history textbooks were released on April 5, demonstrations broke out on April 9 in cities throughout China.[31] In Shenzhen, after the city government deployed riot police to restrain striking workers, the *China Labor Bulletin* warned, "The present strike . . . contains echoes of the strikes directed at Japanese enterprises that exploded in the 1920s fuelling nationalist and revolutionary movements. It also evokes the Chinese government's worst fears during the 1989 movement upsurge: that workers might join the protests on the side of students and intellectuals."[32]

During the 2002–5 surge of anti-Japan nationalism, economic interests failed to knit the two countries closer together. Instead activists blocked a major economic initiative and sparked consumer boycotts and wildcat strikes in Japanese factories. Yet Chinese leaders responded by rapidly reversing course, cooling public emotions while expanding economic and diplomatic cooperation over the next few years.

Beijing's Reverse Course: 2006–2009

After the violent Shanghai protests, Chinese officials quickly shifted to a familiar blend of propaganda and crackdowns to halt demonstrations. Foreign Minister Li Zhaoxing warned 3,500 propaganda officials that "the

29. Li Mutong, "Wangluo minzhuzhuyi xiankai zhongguo minzhuzhuyi xin pianzhang" [Internet nationalism opens a new chapter in China's nationalism], September 18, 2003, http://news.sina.com.cn/c/2003-09-18/12061767730.shtml.

30. Peng Lewu, "1000 Wan qianming de quanliucheng" [The complete process of gaining ten million signatures], *Nanfang Zhoumou*, March 31, 2005, http://news.sina.com.cn/c/2005 -03-31/19286254269.shtml.

31. Howard W. French, "China Allows More Protests in Shanghai against Japan," *New York Times*, April 14, 2005.

32. "Striking Shenzhen Workers at Japanese-Owned Wal-Mart Supplier Firm Demand Right to Unionize," http://apjjf.org/-China-Labor-Bulletin-/2105/article.html.

masses . . . must believe in the party and the government's ability to properly handle all issues linked to Sino-Japanese relations." The *People's Daily* urged young people to act "calmly and reasonably" toward Japan, while Shanghai's Communist Party–run *Liberation Daily* denounced the protests as part of an "evil plot" with "ulterior motives" designed to undermine the party. A number of China's leading activists received warnings from Public Security Bureau officials to halt all protest activities. The government also embarked upon a propaganda campaign urging the public to adopt a calm, "rational" approach toward Japan.[33]

The government's crackdown emerged in late 2005 and early 2006, well before Shinzo Abe had replaced Koizumi as prime minister and halted the annual visits to the Yasukuni Shrine. Beijing's shift was thus driven primarily by a concern with the risk that anti-Japan protests undermined domestic stability. Chinese leaders were also worried about the economic costs. In announcing statistics showing a decline in trade and investment with Japan on October 20, 2005, a spokesman for China's National Bureau of Statistics stated, "There is no doubt that if the two countries do not get along it will affect the economic and trade relationship between them . . . I think it is the duty of the politicians to take a strategic point of view to secure a favorable environment for the two countries to promote economic and trade exchanges."[34] When Commerce Minister Bo Xilai met his Japanese counterparts on February 21, 2006, in Beijing, he flatly stated that the political tensions in the relationship were finally beginning to affect their economic relationship. A professor at China Foreign Affairs College warned that China-Japan economic and political relations were now "both cold."[35] Scholars pointed to a slowdown in bilateral trade and investment with Japan, even as China's overall trade and inward foreign direct investment (FDI) continued to grow.[36]

Other signs of an "economic chill" included the decline in Japan's official development assistance (ODA), the absence of large-scale economic projects, tensions over a proposed gas pipeline from Russia to Japan, and Japan's pursuit of bilateral free trade agreements that excluded China. While some journalists criticized Japan for playing an "economic card," trying to use

---

33. This paragraph draws from Reilly, "Remember History."

34. Agence France-Presse, "PRC's Zheng Jingping Says Koizumi Shrine Visit Likely to Hurt Economic Ties," October 20, 2005.

35. Jiang Ruiping, "Zhongri jingji guanxi de kunjing yu chulu" [Difficulties and the route out for China-Japan economic relations], *Riben Xuekan* 1 (2006): 61–70.

36. In the third quarter of 2005, China-Japan trade grew at only 10 percent, a drop of 16 percent from the same quarter in 2004. For the first six months of 2006, the number of new Japanese investments in China declined 8.2 percent from the same period the previous year, with contracted FDI down 0.4 percent from the same period in 2004. At the same time, China's trade with the United States and European Union continued to grow at over 20 percent per year. See Jiang Ruiping, "Zhongri jingji guanxi de kunjing yu chulu," 65.

economic pressures to alter China's foreign policy,[37] the majority of scholars simply worried that China's interests were being damaged.[38] They warned of the political implications of a decline in economic ties and urged the government to strengthen the protection of Japanese businesses' rights and interests in China.[39] In short, the combined pressures of domestic instability and economic costs encouraged Chinese leaders to rein in protests and improve bilateral ties.

Chinese leaders began quietly, reaching out to Abe just days before his selection as prime minister on September 26, 2006. Deputy foreign minister and political heavyweight Dai Bingguo was sent to Japan to deliver a private message directly from President Hu Jintao: if Abe would refrain from visiting Yasukuni, he would be welcomed in China at the earliest possible date. Although Abe refused to publicly state that he would not visit Yasukuni, according to Chinese Foreign Ministry officials, the two reportedly reached an informal agreement on this basis.[40] This tenuous accord quickly set off a remarkable burst of diplomatic activism. After five years without a single visit by top leaders, Japan and China held four leaders' summits in two years.

In welcoming Abe to Beijing in September 2006, Premier Wen Jiabao issued a five-point proposal for improving relations that failed to even mention history issues.[41] In his return visit to Japan in April 2007, Wen gave a landmark speech at the Japanese Diet, the first by a Chinese leader since 1985, in which he insisted, "I have come for friendship and cooperation." He acknowledged Japan's repeated apologies and pledged that "the Chinese people will never forget Japan's support of China during our opening, reform, and modernization."[42] As Wen explained to an audience of Chinese residents in Japan, "This is the most important task since I took office. I did a lot of preparation. Every sentence was written by myself, and I did all the

37. Yang Jun, "Zhongri guanxi: Bawo jingji de guanxi" [China-Japan relations: Seizing economic ties], *Nanfengchuang* 4 (2006): 14–16.
38. See, for example, Feng Zhaokui, "Dui zhongri guanxi 'zhenleng jingri' de zai sikao" [Rethinking "cold politics, hot economics" in China-Japan relations], *Riben Yanjiu* 2 (2006): 2.
39. Zhang Tasheng. "Guanyu 21 shiji zhongri changqi youhao hezuo guanxi de jidian sikao" [Several thoughts regarding long-term cooperation and friendly cooperation in China-Japan relations in the 21st century], in *21 shiji de zhongguo yu riben* [China and Japan in the 21st century], ed. Chen Feng (Beijing: Shijie zhishi chubanshe, 2006), 27–45.
40. This discussion reportedly happened on the sides of the China-Japan strategic dialogue held in Tokyo on September 21, 2009. Anonymous, interview with the author, Beijing, January 12, 2010.
41. "Wen Jiabao yu Anbei Pusan shouxiang huitan jiu weilai zhongri guanxi fazhan tichu wuge yijian" [Wen Jiaobao meets Prime Minister Abe Shinzo, puts forth five suggestions for the future development of Sino-Japanese relations], *Renmin Ribao*, October 9, 2006.
42. "Speech by Premier Wen Jiabao of the State Council of the People's Republic of China at the Japanese Diet," April 13, 2007, http://www.fmprc.gov.cn/mfa_eng/wjb_663304/zzjg_663340/yzs_663350/gjlb_663354/2721_663446/2725_663454/t311544.shtml.

research work myself. Why? Because I feel our nation's development has reached a critical moment. We need to have a peaceful and conducive international environment."[43]

Military-to-military ties were soon restored, and long-delayed ship exchanges finally implemented.[44] Beijing responded calmly to a number of potentially inflammatory actions during this period, including Japan's approvals of conservative textbooks, right-wing activist events, and revisionist statements by Japanese politicians.[45] Following the catastrophic earthquake on May 12, 2008, in Sichuan Province, Japan's rescue teams were the first foreign relief team allowed to enter China since 1949. China's fawning media coverage of the Japanese teams exceeded that of any other foreign relief group.[46] Several months later, China, Japan, and South Korea announced plans for joint disaster response efforts. The plan was put into action following the March 2011 earthquake and tsunami in Japan, when Premier Wen, citing Japan's relief effort in Sichuan, sent a Chinese rescue team to the stricken area.[47]

Agreements on even the most contentious issues become easier during periods of diplomatic détente. In June 2008, for instance, the two sides reached a "principled consensus" on joint development of natural resources in the East China Sea. As James Manicom notes, while this represented only "an agreement on the most basic positions of Tokyo and Beijing . . . political elites overcame largely hostile domestic political environments to achieve the agreement."[48] In 2007–9, environmental cooperation expanded, including joint monitoring of acid rain, dust, and sandstorms and collaboration on energy conservation.[49] Financial cooperation, given new impetus by the global financial crisis, also deepened. In December 2008 China, Japan, and South Korea agreed to expand the scale of their currency swap agreements beyond the initial levels of the Chiang Mai Initiative (CMI). In March 2009 they agreed to pool their CMI swap lines to create a regional emergency

43. Howard W. French, "Letter from China: Wen Reveals Himself as a New Kind of Chinese Leader," *International Herald Tribune*, April 19, 2007, http://www.iht.com/articles/2007/04/19/asia/letter.php.

44. Christian Wirth, "The Nexus between Traditional and Non-Traditional Security Cooperation in Japan-China Relations," PhD diss., Waseda University, 2011, 72–73.

45. Mingde Wang and Maaike Okano-Heijmans, "Overcoming the Past in Sino-Japanese Relations?" *International Spectator: Italian Journal of International Affairs* 46, no. 1 (2011): 136–38.

46. Ibid.

47. James J. Przystup, "Japan-China Relations: Looking for Traction," *Comparative Connections* 13, no. 1 (2011), https://csis-prod.s3.amazonaws.com/s3fs-public/legacy_files/files/publication/1101qjapan_china.pdf.

48. James Manicom, "Sino-Japanese Cooperation in the East China Sea: Limitations and Prospects," *Contemporary Southeast Asia* 30, no. 3 (2008): 471.

49. Wirth, "The Nexus."

funding facility.[50] As Injoo Sohn notes, "In practice, financial co-operation" in East Asia had "advanced further than that in other developing regions."[51]

In sum, Beijing's efforts to build cooperation with Japan while tampering down anti-Japan popular nationalism after 2005 cannot be explained by the "perpetual conflict" approach to the bilateral relationship. Instead, Beijing's concerns with economic costs and domestic instability were crucial elements in encouraging Chinese leaders to work to improve bilateral ties, rein in anti-Japan nationalism, and seek new arenas for cooperation.

Popular Nationalism Rises and Falls Again: 2010–2015

In the post-2010 era, renewed nationalist surges have met a state response similar to previous eras: initial tolerance followed by concerted crackdowns. Beijing has, however, become less constrained by economic concerns than in the past, and instead has begun using economic tools in more assertive fashion. As classical realist theories predict, China's rising relative power appears to have encouraged a more assertive approach to bilateral territorial disputes.

Bilateral relations received a jolt on September 7, 2010, when a Chinese fishing ship operating about twelve kilometers northwest of the Diaoyu/ Senkaku Islands collided with a Japanese patrol vessel that was demanding that the Chinese ship leave the disputed area. Japanese Coast Guard forces eventually boarded the vessel and arrested the captain and fourteen crew members. Chinese officials demanded that Japan immediately and unconditionally release the captain, crew, and vessel.[52] In response to the incident, protests emerged in front of several Japanese consulates around China.[53] Beijing suspended talks on joint gas development in the East China Sea and aviation rights, discouraged tourism to Japan, and canceled several official exchanges.[54] On September 22, Wen threatened further actions, warning, "If Japan acts willfully despite advice to the contrary [by failing to release the captain unconditionally] China will take further actions, and Japan must ac-

---

50. Saori N. Katada, "Seeking a Place for East Asian Regionalism: Challenges and Opportunities under the Global Financial Crisis," *Pacific Review* 24, no. 3 (2011): 273–90.

51. Injoo Sohn, "Toward Normative Fragmentation: An East Asian Financial Architecture in the Post–Global Crisis World," *Review of International Political Economy* 19, no. 4 (2012): 586–608.

52. Linus Hagström, "'Power Shift' in East Asia? A Critical Reappraisal of Narratives on the Diaoyu/Senkaku Islands Incident in 2010," *Chinese Journal of International Politics* 5, no. 3 (2012): 267–97.

53. Erik Beukel, *Popular Nationalism in China and the Sino-Japanese Relationship: The Conflict in the East China Sea*, DIIS Report 01 (Copenhagen: Danish Institute for International Studies, 2011).

54. Hagström, "'Power Shift' in East Asia?"

cept full responsibility for all the severe consequences."[55] Two days later, the captain was released.

During the standoff, there were only small-scale protests in Beijing, Chongqing, Shanghai, and Shenyang on September 18, the anniversary of the onset of Japan's invasion of northeast China in 1931. The protests were initially tolerated, but then quickly restrained by police.[56] Several weeks after the captain's release, reports of planned demonstrations in Tokyo by Japanese right-wing groups sparked another round of protests in China on October 16–17.[57] While the major cities of Beijing, Guangzhou, and Shanghai were largely quiet, boisterous anti-Japan protests erupted in two dozen smaller cities around China, including Chengdu, Deyang, Lanzhou, Mianyang, Wuhan, Xi'an, and Zhengzhou.[58]

Official coverage signaled modest support. The Xinhua News Agency reported that "more than 2,000 college students gathered in downtown Chengdu . . . and more than 7,000 college students marched" in Xi'an.[59] Foreign Ministry spokesperson Ma Zhaoxu expressed support for protesters' "legal, rational expressions of patriotic spirit."[60] Yet Chinese television reporting ignored the demonstrations, as did most domestic media. Xinhua's brief report (in English) failed to mention the demonstrations in many smaller cities, and underreported their scale.[61] Following the protests, a *People's Daily* opinion piece warned that "expressing patriotism irrationally may affect the country's social order, economic growth and peaceful life of its people, and give a chance to those who want to make chaos in China, which faces a complicated international environment."[62]

Despite the party's efforts, a second round of protests erupted again the following weekend in smaller cities around China. At one demonstration in Baoji, in Shaanxi Province, demonstrators unfurled banners calling for a

55. Tania Branigan and Justin McCurry, "China Prime Minister Demands Captain's Release," *Guardian*, September 22, 2010, http://www.theguardian.com/world/2010/sep/22/china-demands-captain-release.

56. Al Jazeera, "China Breaks Up Anti-Japan Protests," September 18, 2010, http://www.aljazeera.com/news/asiapacific/2010/09/201091854749549333.html.

57. Barbara Demick, "Thousands in Chinese Provinces Stage Anti-Japan Protests," *Los Angeles Times*, October 18, 2010.

58. Jeremy Wallace and Jessica Chen Weis, "The Political Economy of Nationalist Protest in China: A Subnational Approach" *China Quarterly* 222 (2015): 403–29.

59. Xinhua News Agency, "Chinese Protest against Japan over Diaoyu Islands Issue," October 16, 2010, http://news.xinhuanet.com/english2010/china/2010-10/16/c_13560499.htm.

60. Ji Beibei, "Anti-Japan Protests Spread across Country," *People's Daily*, October 26, 2010, http://english.peopledaily.com.cn/90001/90776/90882/7177159.html.

61. The protests in Chengdu, for instance, included tens of thousands of people, and were hardly limited to college students. For images, see David Bandurski, "Anti-Japanese Protests in China," October 16, 2010, http://cmp.hku.hk/2010/10/16/8117/.

62. Ji Beibei, "Anti-Japan protests."

multiparty political system and complaining about the high price of real estate.[63] In Lanzhou, protesters regrouped even after being dispersed by riot police, burning Japanese flags and shouting slogans.[64] The crackdown then tightened even further, forestalling any further demonstrations. Zhou Yongkang, director of the party's Public Security Commission, warned in the *People's Daily* that the government would "strengthen propaganda and opinion work to guide the public to voice its patriotic aspirations in a rational and orderly way according to the law, protecting social and political stability."[65]

Over the next few months, Chinese leaders sought once again to cool public anger and stabilize bilateral relations. In May 2011 Premier Wen used his trip to Japan to pledge Chinese support in the wake of the devastating earthquake and tsunami; he promised to promote Chinese tourism to Japan, and indeed, in December 2011, Japan's National Tourism Organization announced that Chinese visitors had increased 35 percent over November 2010, the first increase since March 2011.[66]

The calm barely lasted a few months. On the morning of April 16, 2012, Tokyo governor Ishihara Shintaro informed an audience at the Heritage Foundation in Washington, DC, that his city would soon purchase the three privately owned islets in the Senkaku (Diaoyu) chain from their long-time private owner.[67] By mid-August, anti-Japanese protests broke out across China. Thousands of people took to the streets, and Japanese cars were attacked and Japanese restaurant windows smashed. One banner in Chengdu proclaimed, "Even if China is covered in graves, we must kill all Japanese."[68] On September 10, a week before the sensitive September 18 anniversary of Japan's 1931 invasion, Prime Minister Yoshihiko Noda announced that the central government would purchase and thus "nationalize" the three islets. Once again, protests erupted across China. Japanese businesses were ransacked, cars smashed, windows broken, and restaurants set on fire. Thousands of people demonstrated in front of Japanese diplomatic missions. A People's Republic of China–affiliated Hong Kong

63. Peter Ford, "Beijing Now Worried Anti-Japan Protests Could Backfire," *Christian Science Monitor*, October 26, 2010, http://www.csmonitor.com/World/Asia-Pacific/2010/1026/Beijing-now-worried-anti-Japan-protests-could-backfire.

64. Maxim Duncan, "China Breaks Up Anti-Japan Protests," October 24, 2010 http://www.reuters.com/article/2010/10/24/us-china-japan-idUSTRE69N0C320101024.

65. Ford, "Beijing Now Worried."

66. James J. Przystup, "Japan-China Relations: Another New Start," *Comparative Connections* 13, no. 3 (2012), https://csis-prod.s3.amazonaws.com/s3fs-public/legacy_files/files/publication/1103qjapan_china.pdf.

67. BBC News, "Tokyo to Buy Disputed Islands, Says Governor Ishihara," April 17, 2012, http://www.bbc.co.uk/news/world-asia-17747934.

68. Julian Ryall and Malcolm Moore, "Anti-Japan Protests Erupt in China following Island Demonstration," *Telegraph*, August 19, 2012.

newspaper insisted that "the Japanese government must directly face the voice of the Chinese people."[69] On September 10, Premier Wen assured an audience at China's Foreign Affairs University that China would "never yield an inch" of the islands.[70]

The protests soon began to spiral out of control. Several protesters in Beijing carried signs saying, "Diaoyu belongs to China; Bo belongs to the people," a reference to Bo Xilai. A few placards bore portraits of Mao Zedong as an implicit criticism of the current leadership as inadequately nationalistic. A protester in Shenzhen was even heard on television shouting, "Down with Communism!"[71] Violence also began to spread.[72] The most chilling incident was on September 15, when a Xi'an man driving with his wife in a Japanese car was attacked by a mob in the midst of an anti-Japan protest; he was hit in the head repeatedly with an iron bar.[73] A bystander captured the violence in a video that rapidly spread across the Chinese Internet, sparking widespread condemnation.[74]

A survey of Chinese and Japanese public opinion conducted in June–July 2013 found that public attitudes had reached a new low, with 93 percent of Chinese respondents reporting a negative opinion of Japan. These annual survey data, recorded since 2005, reflect the undulating public emotions described above. Chinese respondents with favorable opinions of Japan improved, from 11 percent in 2005 to 38 percent by 2010, before declining over the next three years, reaching a new low of only 8 percent in 2013. Unfavorable opinions of Japan follow a similar pattern, with the lowest percentage in 2007 before climbing to a new peak of 92.8 percent in 2013. Over half of all Chinese respondents saw the relationship as negative in 2005, a figure that dropped to 11 percent in 2008 before rising to a new peak of 90 percent in 2012. Conversely, those who described the relationship as positive rose from

69. "Riben zhengfu bixu zhengshi zhongguo minjian hushing" [Japanese government must directly face the voice of the Chinese people], *Dakung Pao*, September 18, 2012, http://www.takungpao.com/paper/content/2012-09/25/content_1157935.htm.

70. Raymond Li, "Papers Go Ballistic over Diaoyu Dispute with Japan," *South China Morning Post*, September 16, 2012, http://www.scmp.com/comment/insight-opinion/article/1037887/papers-go-ballisticover-diaoyu-dispute-japan.

71. Jane Perlez, "China Alters Its Strategy in Diplomatic Crisis with Japan," *New York Times*, September 28, 2012.

72. "Chinese Ships Leave Disputed Waters Near Diaoyu Islands," *South China Morning Post*, September 14, 2012, http://www.scmp.com/news/china/article/1036502/six-mainland-ships-sail-island-waters-says-japans-coast-guard.

73. Amy Qin and Edward Wong, "Smashed Skull Serves as Grim Symbol of Seething Patriotism," *New York Times*, October 10, 2012, http://www.nytimes.com/2012/10/11/world/asia/xian-beating-becomes-symbol-of-nationalism-gone-awry.html?_r=0.

74. Xie Yuhang, "Meiti fansi xian fanri youxing, shimin he jingcha shangxian zhinen" [Media reflect on the anti-Japan protests in Xi'an: Tender sides of citizens and police come to the fore], *Zhongguo qingnian bao*, October 12, 2012, http://www.chinanews.com/gn/2012/10-12/4243309.shtml.

10 percent in 2005 to a peak of 72 percent in 2010 before falling to a new low of 6 percent by 2013.[75]

For Stephanie Kleine-Ahlbrandt, the 2012 protests revealed "Beijing's eroding control over the ebb and flow of nationalist sentiment," which "significantly restricts China's future options to dial down the situation."[76] "China today is not the China of 2005 or 2010, when relations between the two countries also soured," notes J. Michael Cole. "The belief that nationalistic fervor—a useful instrument for politicians to rally various constituents around the flag in times of domestic discontent—always will be manageable and that precedent provides the assurance of similar outcomes in the future is a recipe for disaster."[77]

And yet, as the sensitive September 18 anniversary approached, official media once again called for "levelheadedness" and urged "sensible patriotism."[78] On September 17, the State Council sent out an emergency directive demanding that local governments maintain order.[79] In response, municipal authorities held coordination meetings, ordering local officials not to "participate in, encourage, or publicize" anti-Japan protests, and to instruct residents to "legally and rationally express their patriotic spirit."[80] On the afternoon of September 17, Shenzhen mobile phone users received a text message urging them to "please express their patriotic fervor rationally, and abstain from illegal or criminal behavior."' As of September 19, the following phrases were being blocked on the Chinese Internet: "anti-Japan (*fanri*), smash car (*zache*), protest (*kangyi*), demonstrate (*youxing*), assembly (*jihui*), and demonstration (*shiwei*).' "[81] The same day, Beijing public safety authorities sent out a mass text message instructing citizens not to go to the embassy area for anti-Japan rallies and to cooperate to ensure order in traf-

75. Genron NPO and *China Daily*, *The 9th Japan-China Public Opinion Poll*, August 12, 2013, http://www.genron-npo.net/en/opinion_polls/archives/5260.html.

76. Stephanie Kleine-Ahlbrandt, "Dangerous Waters: Why China's Dispute with Japan Is More Dangerous Than You Think," *Foreign Policy*, September 17, 2012, http://www.foreignpolicy.com/articles/2012/09/17/dangerous_waters.

77. J. Michael Cole, "China and Japan Turn the Screw over Island Dispute," *China Brief* 12, no. 18 (2012), http://www.jamestown.org/programs/chinabrief/single/?tx_ttnews%5Btt_news%5D=39868&cHash=8b4001d9bcec906eef0710860c2b2d1b.

78. William Wan, "Chinese Government Both Encourages and Reins In Anti-Japan Protests, Analysts Say," *Washington Post*, September 17, 2012, http://www.washingtonpost.com/world/chinese-government-both-encourages-and-reins-in-anti-japan-protests-analysts-say/2012/09/17/53144ff0-00d8-11e2-b260-32f4a8db9b7e_story.html.

79. Xi'an Administration of Work Safety, "Shi anjianju renzhen chuanda shangji wenjian jingshen, qieshi weihuhao dangqian shehui anquan wending gongzuo" [City bureau of work administration earnestly promotes the spirit of the higher-levels' work document on thoroughly protecting current social safety and stability], September 18, 2012, http://www.xasafety.gov.cn/newsshow.asp?cid=35&iid=2403.

80. Ibid.

81. "Sensitive Words: Anti-Japan Protests (2)," *China Digital Times*, September 19, 2012, http://chinadigitaltimes.net/2012/09/sensitive-words-anti-japan-protests-2/.

fic and society.[82] On September 18 the *Global Times* warned, "Protests should not turn to the dark side." One article insisted that "the Chinese government should constrain violent protests through the use of the law"; another posited that "we can find other ways to vent our patriotism, such as offering advice or parades. But destroying others' property is absolutely unacceptable."[83] Just as in 2005 and 2010, these concerted efforts effectively curtailed subsequent public protests.

The most telling example of Beijing's eroding tolerance for anti-Japan nationalist demonstrations was the absence of public protests in China following Prime Minister Abe's controversial visit to the Yasukuni Shrine on December 26, 2013. Predictably, Chinese officials responded to Abe's visit with sharp criticism. Foreign Ministry spokesman Qin Gang recorded China's "strong protest and strident condemnation," describing the visit as "a major new political obstacle."[84] State Councilor Yang Jiechi urged Abe to "mend his ways" by "taking concrete measures to remove its egregious impacts."[85] Yet Beijing's response was modest, and echoed concerns raised in New York, Washington, and around Asia. UN secretary general Ban Ki-moon issued a statement denoting the "need to be sensitive to the feelings of others, especially memory of victims," adding that "leaders bear special responsibility in that regard."[86] Even the U.S. embassy in Tokyo expressed its "disappointment" with Abe's visit as "an action that will exacerbate tensions with its neighbors."[87]

Following the visit, Japanese diplomats and businesses in China braced themselves for another explosion of demonstrations, as protests erupted in front of Japanese diplomatic offices in Chicago, Hong Kong, Seoul, and Taiwan.[88] Surprisingly, the streets in front of Japan's embassy and consulates in China remained quiet, cordoned off by police.[89] "We planned to give petition letters to the Japanese embassy in Beijing and consulate in Shanghai," explained Li Yiqiang, a longtime activist. "But we were blocked by police on the way."[90] China's domestic media also downplayed Abe's visit, while

82. "China Tells Citizens Not to Hold Anti-Japan Protests," *Mainichi News*, September 19, 2012, http://mainichi.jp/english/english/newsselect/news/20120919p2g00m0dm067000c.html.
83. "Protests Should Not Turn to the Dark Side," *Global Times*, September 18, 2012, http://www.globaltimes.cn/NEWS/tabid/99/ID/733745/733745.aspx.
84. Xinhua News Agency, "China Scathing of Abe's Yasukuni Visit," December 26, 2013.
85. "Senior China Official Slams Abe's Yasukuni Visit," *Jiji Press*, December 28, 2013.
86. "UN Chief Voices Regret over Abe's Yasukuni Visit," *IANS English*, December 28, 2013.
87. Anthony Rowley, "Abe's Yasukuni Shrine Visit Whips Up Storm: China, S. Korea Riled; Even America Shows Disappointment," *Business Times*, December 27, 2013.
88. "Japanese Firms in China Fearful after Abe's Yasukuni Visit," *Jiji Press*, December 26, 2013.
89. "See You at Yasukuni: Japan's Shrine and Regional Tensions," *Economist*, December 27, 2013.
90. Teddy Ng and Kwong Man-ki, "Beijing Holds Fire after Abe's Visit to War Shrine," *South China Morning Post*, December 28, 2013.

Weibo messages calling for anti-Japan protests were removed from the Chinese Internet. The normally strident *Global Times* calmly noted, "Challenges from Japan will definitely be a thorn in China's flesh. But Chinese people should open their mind and focus their attention on more important issues."[91]

Once again Beijing's constraints managed to curtail public protests and redirect public attention, reducing the danger of demonstrations growing out of control while retaining Chinese leaders' autonomy in implementing policy toward Japan. While successful in reining in street demonstrations, Beijing continued to use commemorations of the wartime past in strategic fashion. Several weeks after Abe's visit to the Yasukuni Shrine, Chinese leaders announced two new national holidays commemorating their wartime victory over Japan and the Nanjing Massacre of 1937, unveiling a new memorial to Ahn Jung-geun, a Korean resistance fighter executed by Japanese soldiers.[92] In sum, Beijing responded to Japan's 2012 nationalization of the Diaoyu/Senkaku Islands in similar fashion to previous surges of anti-Japan nationalist anger: initial tolerance of demonstrations accompanied by strong diplomatic rhetoric. Yet once protests risked spiraling out of control and undermining domestic stability, Chinese leaders clamped down through a combination of legal restraints and propaganda controls, curtailing public demonstrations and redirecting public attention.

Even as Chinese leaders effectively curtailed anti-Japan public demonstrations, they ramped up military pressure on Japan. Following the 2012 nationalization announcement, Chinese Coast Guard vessels began to regularly traverse the disputed waters around the Diaoyu/Senkaku Islands. Several Chinese experts argued privately that the incursions were part of a diplomatic campaign seeking to pressure the Abe government to offer a compromise in the wake of the nationalization announcement by openly acknowledging, for the first time, that sovereignty of the islands was "disputed."[93] As Tokyo refused to shift its long-standing position, Beijing increased the tempo of its maritime activities in the region. According to the Japanese government, in the year after nationalization a total of 216 Chinese Coast Guard ships entered Japan's territorial waters. From 2013 to 2014, the number declined to 101. Intrusions into Japan's territorial waters averaged approximately five times per month in 2012–13, but declined to 2.8 times per month in 2013–14.[94] From September 2014 to August 2015, Japanese officials recorded a

91. "BBC Monitoring Quotes from China, Taiwan Press," *Global Times*, January 2, 2014.

92. Kian Beng Kor, "China, Japan Spar over Korean National Hero," *Straits Times*, January 21, 2014.

93. Anonymous, interviews with the author, Beijing, November 2014.

94. James J. Przystup, "Japan-China Relations: A Handshake at the Summit," *Comparative Connections* 16, no. 3 (2015), https://csis-prod.s3.amazonaws.com/s3fs-public/legacy_files /files/publication/1403qjapan_china.pdf. For further indicators of a decline in Chinese incursions after October 2013, see M. Taylor Fravel and Alastair Iain Johnston, "Chinese Sig-

total of 708 Chinese government ships operating in Japan's contiguous zone for a total of 233 days. Scrambles by Japanese Air Self-Defense Force planes in response to Chinese aircraft incursions also increased modestly, from 103 in July–September 2014 to 114 over the same period in 2015.[95] Clearly, Chinese leaders were signaling their determination to visibly contest Japan's sovereignty claims through ship and plane incursions into disputed territories—a policy that had the predictable effect of stiffening Japanese resolve and spurring Abe's efforts to bolster Japan's security posture and its military ties throughout the region, as described by Ian Bowers and Bjørn Elias Mikalsen Grønning in chapter 5 of this volume.

Even as normal diplomatic ties were largely restored following the November 10, 2014, meeting between Japanese prime minister Shinzo Abe and Chinese president Xi Jinping in Beijing, Chinese ships and planes continued to challenge Japan's territorial claims in the East China Sea. While it remains plausible that popular nationalism in China was an indirect driver of this policy, the disconnect between the decline in public protests at the same time that Beijing was expanding its ship and plane incursions into the disputed territories undermines the credibility of such claims. Instead, a more likely direct driver of China's policy shift was Beijing's strong reaction to the Abe government's nationalization decision and China's failure to secure a diplomatic quid pro quo following nationalization. More broadly, it is certainly plausible that, as Gilpin would predict, China's overall rise in relative power encouraged policymakers to adopt and sustain a more assertive stance toward maritime disputes in the East China Sea. A similar pattern, also consistent with classical realism, is evident in Beijing's strategic use of economic leverage toward Japan.

Flexing China's Economic Muscles

Chinese leaders have reason to believe that their economic leverage over Japan has increased substantially over the past decade. China's trade dependence upon Japan declined from a peak of 8.7 percent in 2004 to only 4 percent in 2012. Meanwhile, Japan's trade dependence upon China rose from 3 percent in 2003 to 5.6 percent in 2012.[96] If China reorients its domestic

---

naling in the East China Sea," *Washington Post*, April 12, 2014, http://www.washingtonpost.com/blogs/monkey-cage/wp/2014/04/12/chinese-signaling-in-the-east-china-sea/.

95. James J. Przystup, "Japan-China Relations: Moving in the Right Direction," *Comparative Connections* 17, no. 3 (2016), https://csis-prod.s3.amazonaws.com/s3fs-public/legacy_files/files/publication/1503qjapan_china.pdf.

96. These figures come from International Monetary Fund, "IMF Data: Access to Macroeconomic and Financial Data," http://data.imf.org/?sk=388DFA60-1D26-4ADE-B505-A05A558D9A42.

economy toward greater consumer demand and higher-value production, its dependence upon Japan will continue to slide. As Junhua Wu points out, in 2012 Japanese investment actually rose 18 percent, despite a 3.7 percent decline in overall foreign investment into China, which may have encouraged Chinese strategists to dismiss the risk of heightened strategic tensions bringing economic costs. Furthermore, Wu adds, Japanese firms are increasingly dependent upon their China-based profits. In 2010, for instance, Chinese-based subsidiaries of Japanese transportation equipment firms generated 35 percent of all profits in the sector. Finally, China's exports to Japan have shifted from low-value-added (such as garment manufacturing) to high-value-added products such as computers, communication equipment, audiovisual equipment, and metal products. The "psychological impact of these economic achievements," Wu concludes, may "deepen Chinese self-confidence and nationalism."[97]

An early signal of Beijing deploying its economic leverage emerged during the 2010 standoff over the fishing boat captain's detainment. On September 21, 2010, Japanese companies reported to Tokyo that Chinese customs officials were blocking all shipments of rare earth elements (REE) to Japan. The captain was released three days later, but the shipments were still reported blocked. Following a meeting between Japanese prime minister Naoto Kan and Chinese president Hu Jintao, Chinese officials reportedly assured Trade Minister Akihiro Okato that rare earth exports to Japan would be accelerated. On November 20, the Japanese government released a survey of Japanese companies reporting that REE shipments had largely returned to normal.[98] Throughout the standoff, Chinese officials repeatedly denied using rare earth restrictions as "an instrument for bargaining" with Japan.[99] Some reporting confused Japanese complaints with Beijing's tightened export controls over REE—announced publicly in July 2010.[100] Other Chinese experts suggested that central leaders informally ordered local customs officials to reduce the amount of REE released to Japan.[101] As Linus

97. Junhua Wu, "Economics of the Territorial Disputes," in *Clash of National Identities: China, Japan, and the East China Sea Territorial Dispute*, ed. Tatsushi Arai, Shihoko Goto, and Zheng Wang (Washington, DC: Woodrow Wilson International Center for Scholars, 2013), 73.

98. Keith Bradsher, "China Still Bans Minerals for Japan, Reports Say," *New York Times*, November 10, 2010, http://topics.nytimes.com/top/reference/timestopics/people/b/keith_bradsher/index.html?inline=nyt-per.

99. John W. Miller, "Protectionism Hurts Effort to Pressure China: West's Record of Measures against Beijing Stands in Way of Campaign for Looser Restrictions on Rare-Earth Exports," *Wall Street Journal*, November 9, 2010, http://www.wsj.com/articles/SB10001424052748704737504575602472986073564.

100. Jianjan Tu, "An Economic Assessment of China's Rare Earth Policy," *China Brief* 10, no. 22 (2010), http://www.jamestown.org/programs/chinabrief/single/?tx_ttnews%5Btt_news%5D=37141&cHash=a2f6f8c0ab.

101. Anonymous, interviews with the author, Beijing, January 2012.

Hagström concludes, "The rare earths issue was undoubtedly connected with the Diaoyu/Senkaku Islands incident in 2010, but . . . it is highly uncertain whether it was Beijing, journalists, or some other entity that construed the linkage in the first place."[102] While reliable evidence of the rare earths' embargo remains scanty, economists' analysis of the "event widow" from September 7 to October 29, 2010, finds a "large and significant impact of China exposure" for Japanese firms. Raymond Fisman, Yasushi Hamao, and Yongxiang Wang conclude that Japanese "companies operating in industries [in China] dominated by state-owned enterprises (SOEs) are more sensitive to Sino-Japanese tensions."[103] In other words, China's SOEs exact economic costs from their Japanese counterparts amid political tensions.

Consumer boycotts, another lever of China's economic pressure, were on display during the 2012 protests against Japan's nationalization decision. Chinese consumers declined to buy Japanese-branded consumer goods, particularly electronics and cars, and began canceling visits to Japan. Unlike the 2005 campaign, the 2012 effort was largely on the level of the individual rather than collective. As one blogger put it, "the boycott of Japanese goods begins with me."[104] In an echo of the 1930s, other Netizens urged the government to do more; as one put it, "If we only rely upon several slogan-shouting young people to boycott Japanese goods, this will never fundamentally challenge Japan, and will do no damage to Japan's economy. Therefore I believe the [Chinese] government should take the lead in boycotting Japanese goods."[105]

As in 2005, some Chinese scholars criticized the boycott as "irrational," pointing out that the actions also harmed China's own economy.[106] Yet this time, more experts offered support. Zhou Yongsheng urged Chinese consumers to "use the market economy as a tool" to advance Chinese interests.[107] Others called for the boycott to target companies that support

102. Hagström, "'Power Shift' in East Asia?," 283. Hagström further argues (persuasively) that there is no evidence that China's detention on September 20 of four Japanese citizens for trespassing into a restricted military zone was orchestrated to serve as retaliation toward Japan.

103. Raymond Fisman, Yasushi Hamao, and Yongxiang Wang, "Nationalism and Economic Exchange: Evidence from Shocks to Sino-Japanese Relations," *Review of Financial Studies* 27, no. 9 (2014): 2628.

104. "Congwo zuoqi dizhi rihuo aiwo zhonghua" [Boycott Japanese goods, love our China, it begins with me], http://forum.home.news.cn/thread/103614758/1.html.

105. See "2012 Cong dizhi rihuo shuoqi" [2012 Starting to speak from the boycott of Japanese products], September 15, 2012, http://www.tianya.cn/publicforum/content/free/1/2768249.shtml.

106. Gao Mei, "'Dizhi rihuo' bing bushi lixing de zuofa" ["Boycott Japanese goods" is definitely not a rational action], *Xinjingbao*, September 14, 2012, http://finance.people.com.cn/n/2012/0914/c1004-19005598.html.

107. "Dizhi rihuo jiaodong dongya shushinian" [Boycott Japanese goods, agitate East Asia for a decade], Renmin Wang, September 18, 2012, http://news.163.com/12/0918/15/8BMNF9GP00014JB6.html.

Japanese right-wing groups.[108] Feng Wei insisted that China should use economic measures to "push Japan back to the negotiating table."[109] More explicitly, Jin Baisong, a researcher from a Ministry of Commerce think tank, noted, "It's clear that China can deal a heavy blow to the Japanese economy without hurting itself too much by resorting to sanctions." He explained,

> China should work out a comprehensive plan which should include imposition of sanctions and taking precautionary measures against any Japanese retaliation. China should also have several rounds of policies ready to undermine the Japanese economy at the least cost of Chinese enterprises. Furthermore, in case Chinese enterprises suffer because of the sanctions, the Chinese government should be prepared to compensate them. And once China imposes sanctions on Japan, the government should ensure that all enterprises in the country, domestic and foreign, obey the rules.[110]

Unlike its ambivalence toward the 2005 consumer boycott, this time the Chinese government not only implicitly supported the boycott but also added its own economic weight. On September 13, commerce vice minister Jiang Weizeng defended "Chinese consumers' right . . . to take action to demonstrate their stance in response to Japan's infringement upon China's territorial sovereignty."[111] Even as he called for calm in the streets on September 19, Commerce Ministry spokesman Shen Danyang reiterated the government's support for "rational patriotic activities"—presumably including consumer boycotts.[112] Customs authorities began tightening their inspections of seaborne imports from Japan and delayed their approvals of working visas for Japanese employees in China.[113] Japanese firms were asked to withdraw from an international trade fair in Chengdu, and Chinese tourism officials officially discouraged Chinese tourists from visiting Japan.[114] Most notably, most major Chinese banks and top financial officials withdrew

108. "Dizhi rihuo yidan mangmu rongyi zishang" [Boycott Japanese goods—one day of blindness and it's easy to injure oneself], *Global Times*, August 2012, http://money.163.com /12/0822/14/89H3QJ4A00253B0H.html.

109. Wang Chenyan, "Japan Anniversary Events Postponed," *China Daily*, September 24, 2012, http://www.chinadaily.com.cn/china/2012-09/24/content_15776399.htm.

110. Jin Baisong, "Consider Sanctions on Japan," *China Daily*, September 17, 2012, http:// www.chinadaily.com.cn/opinion/2012-09/17/content_15761435.htm.

111. Bai Tiantian, "Diaoyu Spat to Impact Trade Ties: Official," *Global Times*, September 14, 2012, http://www.globaltimes.cn/content/733140.shtml.

112. "China Tells Citizens Not to Hold Anti-Japan Protests."

113. "China Tightens Inspections on Japanese Imports," *Daily Yomuri*, September 22, 2012, http://www.yomiuri.co.jp/dy/national/T120921004211.htm.

114. "Japanese Businesses Booted from Major China Trade Fair," *Japan Times*, September 27, 2012.

from the annual World Bank/International Monetary Fund meetings held in Tokyo on October 12–14.[115]

Japanese companies soon began to feel the economic effects. During the protests, most Japanese manufacturers in China closed their factories.[116] While it soon resumed operations, All Nippon Airways announced that 43,000 seats had been canceled for flights from September through the end of November, the majority from China to Japan. Xinhua reported that over 100,000 Chinese citizens had canceled trips to China, and that tour groups to Japan had plunged by 40 percent.[117] By early October, Honda, Nissan, and Toyota—Japan's top three carmakers—had cut their China production in half, while South Korean brands Hyundai and Kia experienced record sales.[118] Japan's investment in China fell 32 percent in October 2012 compared to a year earlier.[119] Due largely to the tensions with China, J.P. Morgan downgraded its projections for Japan's economy for the final quarter of 2012 to shrinkage of 0.8 percent.[120]

A more confident and assertive use of consumer boycotts and trade sanctions, encouraged by China's rising economic power, is certainly consistent with the classical realist expectations. In February 2014 Beijing unveiled a new tool of economic pressure—seizing Japanese assets as compensation for wartime losses. In 2010 a Chinese court had awarded Chinese plaintiffs US$28 million in compensation from Mitsui OSK Lines for two ships commandeered by the Japanese military in 1936. After out-of-court negotiations stagnated, the Chinese court issued and then executed China's first-ever seizure order, impounding a Mitsui ship then docked in Zhejiang Province in February 2014. The ship was released only after Mitsui paid some US$40 million in compensation. Although Chinese officials dismissed the incident as a "common commercial dispute," Japan's chief cabinet secretary warned that the seizure would have "a chilling effect" on Japanese companies in China.[121]

Albert Hirschman's classic study explores a variety of techniques through which a rising economic power can utilize a smaller state's economic

115. Phred Dvorak, Atsuko Fukase, and Dinny McMahon, "China Banks Pull Out of Meetings in Japan," *Wall Street Journal*, October 2, 2012, http://www.wsj.com/articles/SB10000872396390444004704578032193431362834.

116. J. Michael Cole, "China and Japan Turn the Screw over Island Dispute," *China Brief* 12, no. 18 (2012), http://www.jamestown.org/single/?tx_ttnews%5Btt_news%5D=39868&no_cache=1.

117. Associated Press, "Island Standoff Hits Japan Business," October 9, 2012, http://bigstory.ap.org/article/news-summary-island-standoff-hits-japan-business.

118. Kwan Weng, "Japan Car Giants 'to Halve China Output,'" *Straits Times*, October 9, 2012; "Toyota Eyes Drastic Cuts in China Production," *Japan Times*, October 5, 2012.

119. "Japan's Investment in China Down 32%," *Kyodo*, November 21, 2012.

120. Associated Press, "Island standoff."

121. Nathan Vanderklippe, "Beneath the Rhetoric, Thaw Grows in China-Japan Relations," *Globe and Mail*, April 22, 2014; James Chessell, "Ship Impounded in China-Japan Dispute Loaded with BHP Ore," *Sydney Morning Herald*, April 26, 2014.

dependence for strategic purposes. One of the most potent techniques is by encouraging a "commercial fifth column" within the target country to promote accommodation with the rising great power.[122] Chinese leaders have added this arrow to their quiver, encouraging Japanese business groups to pressure the Abe government to offer compromises in the territorial dispute. As Liu Junhong, a leading Japan expert, explained in September 2013, Japanese firms risked loosing market share in China to their Western competitors. "The most urgent and utmost thing," Liu noted, "is whether this sense of crisis could result in political pressure on the Abe administration and help improve Sino-Japan relations."[123] Hiroaki Kuwajima, a leading Japanese businessman, admitted that "the commitment of Japan's business leaders to China is far stronger than that of Japan's political leaders."[124]

Tang Jiaxuan, a former foreign minister, took the lead in implementing Beijing's strategy. As president of the China-Japan Friendship Association, Tang in early 2013 began a series of meetings with Keidanren, Japan's leading business association, in which he urged Japanese firms to pressure the Abe administration to revise its policies on the islands dispute.[125] Foreign Minister Wang Yi reiterated the message in a January 2013 interview with the *Financial Times*: "If friends in the Japanese business circle are truly worried and do not want the decline to continue, they should step forward and speak their mind, in an effort to stop behaviors that undermine the relations and trust between China and Japan or even turn back the wheel of history. This is what is really needed to fundamentally preserve the cooperation between our two countries."[126]

Yet even as Beijing ramped up the economic pressure, the costs of its strategy began to emerge, sparking considerable concern among Chinese officials and experts. Over the first nine months of 2013, Japan's direct investment to China fell by 37 percent, while Japan's investment in Associa-

122. Albert O. Hirschman, *National Power and the Structure of Foreign Trade* (Berkeley: University of California Press, 1980), 16–31.

123. Xinhua News Agency, "Diaoyu Islands Issue Chills Sino-Japan Economic Ties," September 26, 2013, http://www.shanghaidaily.com/Opinion/chinese-perspectives/Diaoyu-Islands-issue-chills-SinoJapan-economic-ties/shdaily.shtml.

124. Hiroaki Kuwajima, "Keeping Politics Out of the Japan-China Economic Relationship," http://carnegietsinghua.org/2014/02/28/keeping-politics-out-of-japan-china-economic-relationship/h243.

125. Xinhua News Agency, "China Welcomes Japanese People to Improve Bilateral Ties," April 30, 2014; see also "Tang Jiaxuan: Recent Travel & Appearances," http://www.chinavitae.com/biography/Tang_Jiaxuan/travel.

126. Lifen Zhang, "Transcript of Interview with Wang Yi," *Financial Times*, January 29, 2014, http://www.ft.com/intl/cms/s/0/c0b29fd8-88e2-11e3-bb5f-00144feab7de.html#axzz35ncg6puH.

tion of Southeast Asian Nations (ASEAN) countries rose 55 percent.[127] Over the first half of 2014, Japanese FDI in China plunged 42 percent, while investment in ASEAN continued to rise. Commerce Ministry spokesman Shen Danyang admitted that bilateral tensions were causing "economic and trade relations to regress and affecting companies' will to cooperate."[128] In January 2015 China's Ministry of Commerce released figures showing that Japanese direct investment in China in 2014 fell 38.8 percent over the previous year to US$4.33 billion, marking the second consecutive year of decline.[129] Chinese scholars soon echoed officials' concerns over these trends. Tsinghua University's Chu Shulong called for strengthening "benign interactions" in the economic and cultural spheres to advance China's "overall and long-term national interests" in economic development.[130]

Reflecting a deepening anxiety over the economic costs of ongoing security tensions, China's economic and regional officials began to seek opportunities for renewed economic cooperation with Japan. On July 29, 2013, Guangdong Province held the first investment fair for Japanese investors since 2010, and then sent a trade delegation to Japan.[131] Japanese companies were invited to major trade shows in Chengdu and Dalian and met economic officials in Beijing.[132] In June 2014 the first China-Japan CEO forum in three years was held in Tokyo.[133] As former ambassador Xu Dunxin explained to a Japanese business delegation, "We hope the communication between high-profile business entrepreneurs will help result in a turnaround of the strained China-Japan relationship."[134] In May 2014, while hosting the first bilateral cabinet-level meeting since December 2013, Minister of Commerce

---

127. Justin McCurry, "Why Will Japan and China Avoid Conflict? They Need Each Other," *Christian Science Monitor*, February 5, 2014, http://www.csmonitor.com/World/Asia-Pacific/2014/0205/Why-will-Japan-and-China-avoid-conflict-They-need-each-other.

128. Agence France-Presse, "Beijing Denies Row to Blame as FDI Down 6.7%," *Taipei Times*, June 18, 2014, http://www.taipeitimes.com/News/biz/archives/2014/06/18/2003593023

129. James J. Przystup, "Japan-China Relations: Gaining Traction," *Comparative Connections* 17, no. 1 (2015), https://csis-prod.s3.amazonaws.com/s3fs-public/legacy_files/files/publication/1501qjapan_china.pdf.

130. Chu Shulong, "Japan's National Strategy and China's Japan Strategy," *Contemporary International Relations* 1 (2014): 13.

131. James J. Przystup, "Japan-China Relations: Going Nowhere Slowly," *Comparative Connections* 15, no. 2 (2013), https://csis-prod.s3.amazonaws.com/s3fs-public/legacy_files/files/publication/1302qjapan_china.pdf.

132. Kuwajima, "Keeping Politics Out."

133. Agence France-Presse, "Ex-China Minister Says Frayed Japan Ties 'Temporary,'" June 5, 2014, http://www.channelnewsasia.com/news/asiapacific/ex-china-minister-says/1137628.html.

134. McCurry, "Why Will Japan and China Avoid Conflict?"

Gao Hucheng acknowledged that the territorial dispute was "hurting normal relations between the two nations" and explained that to improve relations "we are emphasizing economic ties."[135]

In sum, after 2010, Chinese leaders increased their use of economic
pressure on Japan through consumer boycotts, undeclared or partial trade
embargos, and pressuring Japanese business groups to lobby their government. China's sustained economic growth and the concurrent expansion in
Japan's relative economic dependence upon China may well have encouraged Chinese leaders to embark upon this strategy, as classical realism
predicts. Yet the effort not only failed to compel a shift in the Abe administration's stance toward the territorial dispute but also began to hurt China's
own economy by contributing to a decline in Japanese investment in China.
Despite the concerns expressed by Chinese experts and officials, the pacific
effect of economic interests upon China's security policy remained limited.
Even as high-level diplomatic interactions resumed, Beijing maintained its
policy of regular incursions into the disputed territorial zone through 2015.

Conclusion

In chapter 1 of this volume, Randall Schweller insightfully argues that domestic political processes shape how China responds to its own rise in
relative power and to shifts in its external security environment. However,
evidence that popular nationalism has pushed Beijing to adopt a more assertive security policy toward Japan remains lacking. Instead, this chapter
finds that while the frequency and scale of China's anti-Japan protests have
expanded, they have not exceeded state control. Following each outburst of
anti-Japan protests, in 2005, 2010, and 2012, the Chinese government was
able to successfully curtail subsequent demonstrations. Even as Chinese
leaders reined in popular protests after 2012, they adopted and sustained a
more assertive stance toward the disputed island territories. This discontinuity between the two trends undermines claims of a causal linkage.

What of the effects of economic factors? Concerns with economic costs of
bilateral tensions encouraged Beijing's diplomatic engagement from 2006 to
2009, helping to calm diplomatic relations and tamper down security tensions. Yet in the post-2010 disputes, the moderating effects of commercial
interests were less evident. Instead, as classical realism would predict, greater
confidence in China's relative economic power seems to have encouraged
Chinese leaders to apply economic pressure upon Japan while initially dis-

135. Agence France-Presse, "Japan, China Holds First Ministerial Level Meeting since
Abe's Shrine Visit," May 19, 2014, http://www.channelnewsasia.com/news/asiapacific
/japan-china-ministers/1110480.html.

missing the economic costs resulting from sustained security and diplomatic tensions. Since 2013, growing concerns over economic costs may have encouraged Beijing to seek a restoration of normal diplomatic interactions, but they have not curtailed China's security policy. This finding accords with Shi Yinhong's claims of deepening discontinuity between economic and political interests in China's Japan policy.[136]

China's security stance toward Japan appears to be driven neither by popular nationalism nor by economic interests, but instead by shifts in the relative distribution of power, as classical realism would predict. Such trends are exacerbated by Beijing's anxiety over Japan's own security policies. The danger of spiraling tensions fed by security dilemma dynamics remains a grave threat to regional peace and security.[137] This chapter thus finds that the three main realms of China's foreign relations with Japan—popular nationalism, economic cooperation, and security competition—are increasingly independent of each other, each driven by a distinct set of dynamics with limited impact upon the other two realms of policy. This is, ultimately, a mixed blessing. It undermines claims that anti-Japan sentiments are driving Beijing toward a more aggressive security stance, yet offers scant sustenance for liberal hopes that economic self-interest will curtail Chinese assertiveness in the East China Sea.

136. Shi Yinhong, "Right Wing Trends in Japanese Politics and Ways of Thinking About China-Japan Relations and Strategic Questions," *Japan Studies* 2 (2014): 1–14.
137. Christensen, "China, the U.S.-Japan Alliance, and the Security Dilemma," 54.

China's Rise and Security Dynamics on the Korean Peninsula

Chung-in Moon

On a piercing cold day in January 1637, King Injo and his son of the Chosun dynasty knelt three times and bowed nine times to Qing emperor Hong Taiji in Samjondo, near Seoul's Han River. It was the most painful and humiliating moment in Korean history. King Injo and his advisers had made the fatal strategic mistake of pledging loyalty to the declining Ming dynasty while ignoring the newly rising power, the Qing, which Koreans then regarded as northern barbarians inferior to them. The price for the mistake was grave: it triggered Hong Taiji's invasion, which devastated the country, and more than 500,000 Koreans—almost 10 percent of the entire population—were taken to Shenyang, the Manchurian capital, as slaves. The tragedy was an unavoidable outcome of the mismatch between the adherence to *xiangming paiqing* (pro-Ming, anti-Qing) and a shift in power.[1]

China's rise and the prospect for a changing geopolitical outlook in Northeast Asia since 2010 have rekindled an age-old debate on South Korea's strategic positioning.[2] Will China be the Qing dynasty of the twenty-first century? Will the United States turn into a Ming dynasty? Is the bilateral regional order known as the G-2 real or fictional? How has South Korea been adapting to this changing security environment? What should be South Korea's strategic choice, and what kind of regional order would be most beneficial to the future of the Korean Peninsula? This chapter aims at addressing these questions by examining the foreign policy of the govern-

1. Myong-gi Han, *Byungja Horan* [The barbarian war in the year Byungja], vols. 1 and 2 (Seoul: Purun Yoksa, 2013).
2. Seung-dong Han, "Jeongse Opan: Byongjanyon Chamgeuk" [Misjudging the external situation: The tragedy in the year Byungja], *Hangyerai Shinmun*, November 11, 2013.

ments of South Korean presidents Roh Moo-hyun, Lee Myung-bak, and Park Geun-hye.

The first section of the chapter presents an analytical framework with which to understand how China's rise and the changing distribution of power in Northeast Asia and South Korean domestic politics affect South Korea's policy choices. It also examines Korean policy issues generally. The second, third, and fourth sections make a comparative analysis of the security policy alignments of China and the United States in the Roh (2003–8), Lee (2008–12), and Park (2013–present) administrations, respectively, and attempt to account for determinants of variation among them. These sections focus on how domestic politics influence and interact with region-wide trends, especially the rise of China, to produce particular outcomes. The final section elucidates South Korea's future strategic choices in the age of the power transition in Northeast Asia.

Shifting International Structure, Strategic Choice, and Underlying Determinants in South Korea: An Analysis

Located at the crossroads between the Eurasian land mass and the Pacific Ocean, the Korean Peninsula has always been subject to the dynamics of a geopolitical vortex. As Hans Morgenthau has aptly observed, "for more than two thousand years, the fate of Korea has been a function either of the predominance of one nation controlling Korea or of a balance of power between two nations competing for that control."[3] For the largest part of Korean history, China was the hegemonic power prevailing over the peninsula. At critical junctures of power transition among regional actors, however, Korea underwent agonizing moments of pivotal choice. Hegemonic rivalry between the Hou Jin and the Ming in the late fourteenth century, the Ming and Japan in the late sixteenth century, the Ming and Qing in the early seventeenth century, the Qing and Meiji Japan in the 1890s, and Japan and Russia in the early twentieth century forced Korea to make hard choices. The division of the Korean Peninsula in 1945, and the Korean War from 1950 to 1953, were also products of strategic interactions among superpowers during the Cold War. It is in this context that the balance of power determinism has been deeply implanted in the minds of Koreans.

Nevertheless, contemporary discourses on security dynamics in South Korea attempt to refute the balance of power or structural determinism.[4] It

---

3. Hans J. Morgenthau, *Politics among Nations*, 7th ed. (New York: McGraw-Hill, 2006), 189.

4. See Jae Ho Chung, *Between Ally and Partner: Korea-China Relations and the U.S.* (New York: Columbia University Press, 2007), 111–15; David C. Kang, "Between Balancing and Bandwagoning: South Korea's Response to China," *Journal of East Asian Studies* 9 (2009): 1–9;

is argued that although the shifting distribution of power in the region entails profound impacts on South Korea's foreign policy behavior, it does not necessarily determine or dictate policy outcomes. While shifting power configuration at the system level defines a set of opportunities and constraints, domestic political actors perceive and process these opportunities and constraints and turn them into specific policies. Thus, system-level variables are necessary, but insufficient, conditions for the shaping of foreign and national security policy. Domestic political dynamics and leadership choice should be factored in. As neoclassical realists contend, unit-level variables matter.[5] Likewise, China's rise and an emergent pattern of power transition in Northeast Asia do not unilaterally decide South Korea's policy choice. Interaction of international structure and domestic political calculus can produce a wide range of strategic options: bandwagoning, hedging, balancing, strategic ambiguity (per Jae Ho Chung); balancing and accommodation (per Robert S. Ross), bandwagoning, accommodation, hedging, and balancing (per David Kang), twin hedging (per Sukhee Han), and neutrality (per Robert Manning and James J. Przystup).[6] In this chapter I discuss four distinct strategic choices: balancing, bandwagoning, standing alone, and maintaining status quo/hedging.[7]

Balancing refers to a strategy used to cope with strategic uncertainty resulting from power transition.[8] It involves *internal balancing* through the enhancement of military strength as well as *external balancing* through the formation or strengthening of alliances.[9] The weak, it is argued, will bal-

---

Sukhee Han, "From Engagement to Hedging: South Korea's New China Policy," *Korea Journal of Defense Analysis* 20, no. 4 (2008): 335–51; Robert S. Ross, "Balance of Power Politics, the Rise of China: Accommodation and Balancing in East Asia," *Security Studies* 15, no. 3 (2006): 355–95; Joseph M. Grieco, "Theories of International Balancing, The Rise of China, and Political Alignments in the Asia Pacific," presented at the annual convention of the Korean Association of International Studies, Seoul, December 13–14, 2013; and David Hundt, "South Korea Confronts the Rise of China," in *Global Korea: Old and New—Proceedings of the 6th Biennial Conference, Korea Studies Association of Australasia* (Sydney: Korea Studies Association of Australasia, 2009), 1–22.

5. Gideon Rose, "Neo-classical Realism and Theories of Foreign Policy," *World Politics* 51, no. 1 (1998): p.146. See also Randall L. Schweller, chap. 1 in this volume. For an overview of neoclassical realism, see Steven E. Lobell, Norrin M. Ripsman, and Jeffrey W. Taliaferro, eds., *Neoclassical Realism, the States, and Foreign Policy* (Cambridge: Cambridge University Press, 2009).

6. Robert Manning and James J. Przystup, "Asia's Transition Diplomacy: Hedge against Future Shock," *Survival* 41, no. 3 (1999): 54.

7. Jae Ho Chung classifies South Korea as an "active hedger" along with Singapore, Thailand and, to a lesser extent, the Philippines—one that seeks to carve out a balancing act between Washington and Beijing. Jae Ho Chung, "East Asia Responds to the Rise of China: Patterns and Variations," *Pacific Affairs* 82, no. 4 (2009–10): 669.

8. Kenneth N. Waltz, *Theory of International Politics* (Boston: Addison-Wesley, 1979), chap. 6; John J. Mearsheimer, *The Tragedy of Great Power Politics* (New York: Norton, 2001), 156–57.

9. Waltz, *Theory of International Politics*, 168.

ance against the stronger side because such external balancing behavior is induced by the system.[10] John J. Mearsheimer prescribes balancing as the only viable option to South Korea,[11] for a rich China is bound to be aggressive, and South Korea, being a neighboring country, is doomed to become prey. In a similar vein, some scholars fear "Finlandization" of the Korean Peninsula, first with North Korea and then South Korea.[12] This being the case, the best option for South Korea is to strengthen alliance with the United States and to balance the rise of China.[13] Balancing with the United States constitutes the mainstream conservative discourse on strategic positioning in contemporary South Korea.[14]

But in the world of anarchy, the weak can also choose a bandwagoning strategy by joining forces with a more powerful opponent.[15] Under two circumstances, the weak state could undertake such realignment. First, it might become plausible when and if a weak state sees more chance for survival and security by siding with the challenging or revisionist state. Second, anticipated economic profits could make a weak state bandwagon with the challenging state.[16] It should be kept in mind that as long as the United States remains in the region as a hegemonic stabilizer possessing a greater power parity with China, it seems quite inconceivable for South Korea to side with China, at least in the short term. The scenario of a rising China and a declining America could, however, tempt South Korea to consider this option. Protracted U.S. fiscal rigidity, subsequent defense budget cuts, and a weaker American security commitment through the reduction of its forward-deployed forces could facilitate such realignment by not only fostering China's power parity with the United States but also by precipitating South Korean fear of insecurity resulting from a new power vacuum. This bandwagoning strategy may well place South Korea and/or the entire Korean

10. Ibid., 127.

11. John J. Mearsheimer, "The Rise of China and the Fate of South Korea," in *Korean Questions: Balancing Theory and Practice*, ed. Institute of Foreign Affairs and National Security (Seoul: Institute of Foreign Affairs and National Security, 2011), 77.

12. Bok Geo-il, *Hanbandoe Deriun Joonggukui Gerimja* [The shadow of China over the Korean Peninsula] (Seoul: Moonhakgwa Jisungsa, 2009).

13. Stephan Walt, "The Shifting Security Environment in Northeast Asia," in *Korean Questions: Balancing Theory and Practice*, ed. Institute of Foreign Affairs and National Security (Seoul: Institute of Foreign Affairs and National Security, 2011), 9.

14. Park Sae-il, "Gukga jeolryak uiroseo ui hanmi dongmaeng" [The U.S.–South Korea free trade agreement as Korea's national strategy], *Chosun Ilbo*, November 26, 2006; Han Suk-hee, "Yi Myung Bak Jeongbu ui Daijungguk Gwanggye" [The Lee Myung Bak government's China policy], http://www.kifs.org/contents/sub3/issue.php?method=info&sId=2082; Chung Jae-ho, "Jungguk ui Busang, Miguk ui Gyeongjae, Hanguk ui dilemma [The rise of China, The balancing of America, and Korea's dilemma], *Shin Dong-A*, October, 2000, 246–66.

15. Mearsheimer, *The Tragedy of Great Power Politics*, 162–63.

16. Randall L. Schweller, "Bandwagoning for Profit: Bringing the Revisionist State Back In," *International Security* 19, no. 1 (1994): 72–107.

Peninsula under the Chinese sphere of influence with a full realignment toward China, signaling the termination of the South Korea–U.S. alliance.

Standing alone might become another strategic option for the weak; this refers to an independent path toward security and survival by severing ties with great powers or intentionally keeping a distance from them. Two possibilities can be envisaged here. The first is to seek survival and security actively through internal balancing (i.e., military buildup), while severing alliance ties with great powers (i.e., giving up external balancing). The second is to secure survival passively by declaring a status of neutrality. The neutrality option can take other forms, too, such as hiding from threats or keeping a low profile and not taking any side.[17] The advent of a unified Korea and intense superpower contestation between China and the United States could make this option all the more plausible. Having long suffered from great power interventions in the past, South Koreans have a kind of natural proclivity not to trust the great powers and to favor an independent status. Some nationalists even advocate that South Korea and/or a unified Korea should seek a middle power status with nuclear weapons capability.[18] Meanwhile, some liberals propose the status of a permanent neutral state. This idea emerged during the Cold War period and disappeared during the post–Cold War era, but it is resurfacing. Its proponents argue that the Korean division was a product of great power rivalry and that the best way to achieve Korean unification and to maintain peace and stability on the Korean Peninsula after reunification is to declare permanent neutral statehood like that of Austria and Switzerland.[19]

Finally, maintaining the status quo through an incremental tinkering or adjustment to changes in external environment within the existing security and economic framework could be another option. This can be seen as a sort of "mini-max" strategy through a wise and prudent synchronization of alliance with the United States and strategic partnership with China. This option would allow South Korea to minimize economic uncertainty by

17. Paul Schroeder, "Historical Reality vs. Neo-realist Theory," *International Security* 19, no. 1 (1994): 117.

18. Chung Mong-joon, a lawmaker in the governing Saenuri (New Frontier) Party and a former presidential conservative candidate, stated, "The nuclear deterrence can be the only answer. We have to have nuclear capability." See K. J. Kwon, "Under Threat, South Koreans Mull Nuclear Weapons," March 19, 2013, http://www.cnn.com/2013/03/18/world/asia /south-korea-nuclear/; Kim Dae-jung, "S. Korea Needs to Consider Acquiring Nuclear Weapons," *Chosun Ilbo*, July 10, 2012.

19. Park Hu-geon, *Jungriphwa noseon gwa Hanbando ui Mirae* [Korean Neutrality and the Future of Korea] (Seoul: Seonin, 2007); Eam Sang-yun, "Je 2 Gonghwaguk junglibhwa tongil-ron gwa 21segiae junun hamui: Mansfield, Kim Sam-gyu, and Kim Yong-jung jeanui bun-seok" [The idea of Korean unification through neutralization in the 2nd Republic and implications for the 21st century: An analysis of Mansfield, Kim Sam-gyu, and Kim Yong-jung's proposals], *Kukje Jongchi Ronchong* 43, no. 2 (2003): 97–121.

promoting trade and investment relations with China while reducing security risks by adhering to an alliance with the United States, resembling
the hedging under the regional dual structure that Wang Dong outlines
in chapter 4 of this volume. Only minor alignment and realignment within
the existing framework of external arrangements could make such an option
plausible.[20] Thus, for example, Jae Ho Chung advises South Korea not to
"make any specific choice prematurely," but to "enhance the transparency
of the knowns and to maintain strategic ambiguity with regard to the
unknowns."[21] Sukhee Han also prescribes such dualistic maneuvering (what
he calls a "twin hedging diplomacy") as an ideal policy choice.[22] The status
quo option rejects the dichotomous choice of either China or the United
States. As Randall L. Schweller notes in chapter 1 of this volume, the debate
over whether states in the region will bandwagon with or balancing against
China "is somewhat miscast. They will do both." China's rise is not perceived to be a threat, and an alliance with the United States would be primarily because of North Korean threats. Meanwhile, South Koreans see
greater economic opportunities from China's rise.[23] After all, this is a kind of
"double-dipping" strategy. In this line of thinking, a potential or actual conflict between China and the United States is either underestimated or intentionally ignored.

What factors account, then, for South Korea's strategic choice? Distribution of power capabilities between China and the United States is essential
because it shapes overall strategic parameters governing Seoul's policy behavior. South Korea is likely to adopt a pro-American balancing behavior
as long as American supremacy and its security commitment last. But Seoul
would opt for bandwagoning if power parity is in favor of China amid a
waning American security commitment. South Korea or a unified Korea
could seek the "standing alone" option if its security were to be jeopardized
by intense bipolar confrontation between China and the United States. If the
current dual structure of "economy China" and "security United States" persists without any overt conflict between the two, South Korea is prone to
maintain the status quo. While international structure conditions Seoul's
external policy behavior in a critical manner, unit-level variables such as

20. Alignment is a much broader concept that includes alliance. It can happen *against*
actual or potential foes as well as *with* friends, and it can be incremental or radical in rate and
narrow or comprehensive in scope. In the case of South Korea, the pattern of alignment has
blurred the boundary of friend versus foe, being narrow in scope and incremental in rate of
change. See Glenn H. Snyder, *Alliance Politics* (Ithaca, NY: Cornell University Press, 1997),
6–7.

21. Chung, *Between Ally and Partner*, 120. See also Øystein Tunsjø's conceptualization of
hedging in this volume, chap. 2.

22. Sukhee Han, "From Engagement to Hedging: South Korea's New China Policy," *Korean Journal of Defense Analysis*, 20, no. 4 (2008): 347.

23. Kang, "Between Balancing and Bandwagoning," 4.

interests, identity, and domestic politics are also closely intertwined in the policymaking process, ultimately affecting strategic choice.

National interests are of paramount importance. Within structural constraints, South Korea attempts to enhance its security and economic interests. With regards to security North Korea has always been the key factor. Improved inter-Korea relations, the resolution of the North Korean nuclear dilemma through the Six-Party Talks, and weakened or vanished threat from the north would significantly reduce South Korea's reliance on the American alliance by allowing Seoul greater freedom to maneuver. On the other hand, tense military confrontation between the two Koreas, and Beijing's explicit or tacit support of Pyongyang, would drive Seoul to strengthen its alliance with the United States. China's lukewarm attitude on North Korean nuclear weapons could also cause South Korea to look toward balancing with the United States. Practically speaking, the threat from China is indirect and circumventive. China poses a potential threat largely when it lends support to North Korea. Fear of entanglement in China-Japan or China-U.S. conflicts is usually considered a less pronounced threat.

Economic interests are another variable influencing Seoul's policy behavior. As of 2013, China accounts for 28.3 percent of South Korea's total exports, whereas the United States accounts for only 12.1 percent.[24] South Korea has increasingly fallen into a dependency trap with China, delimiting the scope of foreign policy maneuvering.

Identity-related factors can also influence Seoul's foreign policy behavior. Collective memory regarding events in the past, resurgent nationalism, and subsequent public perception can bring about profound impacts on South Korea's strategic behavior.[25] The memory of Japanese colonial domination and subjugation has precipitated chronic anti-Japanese sentiments. Anti-American sentiments, albeit lessened since 2008, may also be resurrected at any time, negatively affecting Seoul's foreign policy toward the United States.[26] China has not been exempt from this nationalist trap. China's Northeast Project and dispute over historical sovereignty regarding the Goguryeo dynasty have ignited fierce anti-Chinese sentiments in

24. Kim, Seung-uk, "Hanmi gyoyokgamsoaedo bugagachi changchul nuleo" [Albeit reduction in ROK-US trade ratio, value addedness rose], *Yonhap News*, April 24, 2014.

25. Chung-in Moon and Seung-won Suh, "Identity Politics, Nationalism, and the Future of Northeast Asian Order," in *The U.S. and Northeast Asia*, ed. G. John Ikenberry and Chung-in Moon (Lanham, MD: Rowman and Littlefield, 2008), 193–230; Dalchoong Kim and Chung-in Moon, eds., *History, Cognition and Peace in East Asia* (Seoul: Yonsei University Press, 1997); Jennifer Lind, *Sorry States: Apologies in International Politics* (Ithaca, NY: Cornell University Press, 2008).

26. See Chung-in Moon, "Between Banmi (Anti-Americanism) and Sungmi (Worship of the United States): Dynamics of Changing U.S. Images in South Korea," in *Korean Attitudes toward the United States*, ed. David I. Steinberg (Armonk, NY: Sharpe, 2005).

South Korea.[27] Likewise, clashes of nationalism can easily factor into the shaping of South Korea's strategic stance.

International structure, interest, and identity are by and large input variables to be perceived and processed by domestic politics and to be ultimately translated into a set of decisions and policies by the political leadership. Domestic politics is an arena in which divergent political forces compete.[28] South Korea is not a monolithic society. Nationalists versus internationalists, pro-American forces versus pro-Chinese forces, and conservatives versus progressives engage in constant political contests, altering overall public mood or national attitude as well as influencing policy outcomes. But it is the executive leadership that is responsible for ultimate decisions, and the beliefs and preference of such leadership offer an indispensable clue to the understanding of foreign policy making in South Korea.

In what follows, I will examine variations in the policy behavior of the Roh Moo-hyun, Lee Myung-bak, and Park Geun-hye governments regarding China and the United States and elucidate their determinants.

The Roh Government and Rhetorical Bandwagoning

The People's Republic of China (PRC) and the Republic of Korea (ROK) fought fiercely during the Korean War (1950–53) after PRC volunteer forces intervened in October 1950 in the name of *kangmei yuanchao*. Nevertheless, on August 24, 1992, South Korea formally established diplomatic relations with China. It was a kind of diplomatic coup, since it was undertaken without having to let North Korea "cross-normalize" with the United States. Since then, ROK-China relations have not been limited to economic, social, human, and cultural exchanges; there has also been rapid progress in politics, security, and military exchanges. The ROK-China relationship was defined as "good-neighbor cooperative relations" when diplomatic ties were first established in 1992. In 1998 Kim Dae-jung and Jiang Zemin agreed to raise the status of the bilateral relationship to "cooperative partnership relations aimed toward the twenty-first century." This relationship was furthered when former Chinese premier Zhu Rongji visited the ROK in 2000

27. Chung-in Moon and Chun-fu Li, "Reactive Nationalism and South Korea's Foreign Policy on China and Japan: A Comparative Analysis," *Pacific Focus* 23, no. 3 (2010): 345–50.

28. See Schweller, this volume, chap. 1; Jack Snyder, *Myth of Empire: Domestic Politics and International Ambition* (Ithaca, NY: Cornell University Press, 1991); Etel Solingen, *Regional Orders at Century's Dawn: Global and Domestic Influence on Grand Strategy* (Princeton, NJ: Princeton University Press, 1998), 18–61; and Edward Azar and Chung-in Moon, "Legitimacy, Integration, and Policy Capacity," in *National Security in the Third World*, ed. Edward Azar and Chung-in Moon (Ashgate, England: Elgar, 1988), 77–101.

and agreed to "wholeheartedly advance the cooperative partnership relations" between the two nations.[29]

From 1992 to 2003, China–South Korea relations improved over time without affecting South Korea's relationship with the United States. Although China was on the rise, it was no match for the United States because the power gap between the two was rather wide, and China did not raise any questions about the ROK-U.S. alliance. Seoul's economic dependence on Beijing was growing, but not dominant. As of 2000, the United States accounted for 20.1 percent of South Korea's total trade, whereas China accounted for only 9.4 percent. Meanwhile, China, which suffered economic setbacks following the Tiananmen Square incident in 1989, actively sought South Korea's investment. China's equidistant policy on Seoul and Pyongyang, as well as its peaceful development and policy attitude of *taoguang yanghui* (keeping a low profile) mitigated Seoul's China threat perception. Moreover, with the exception of the leadership of Kim Young-sam, the governments in Seoul were pursuing an engagement policy with North Korea, preventing conflict of interests with China on North Korean issues. Thus, such ideas as balancing, bandwagoning, and hedging did not exist in South Korea's discourses on foreign policy. Friction over North Korean defectors, the Dalai Lama's visit to the ROK, and trade dispute over garlic imports soured bilateral ties, but engagement, accommodation, and cooperation characterized the overall contour of South Korea's policy stance on China.[30]

THE ROH GOVERNMENT AND SIGNS OF REALIGNMENT

The start of Roh Moo-hyun's presidency in 2003 signaled a major realignment in the ROK's foreign policy. Newly elected president Roh repeatedly emphasized the need to readjust the ROK-U.S. alliance to a more equal and fair relationship.[31] Such realignment was not induced by China, but more by Roh's personal belief and preferences: he was a progressive political leader and had been elected on progressive platforms that emphasized the priority of inter-Korea relations and a peace regime on the Korean Peninsula over

29. See Jae Ho Chung, *Jungkukui busanggwa hanbandoui mirae* [China's rise and the future of the Korean Peninsula] (Seoul: Seoul National University Press, 2011), chaps. 2 and 3. See also Chung, *Between Ally and Partner*; Scott Snyder, *China Rise and the Two Koreas* (Boulder, CO: Rienner, 2009); and Jung-Nam Lee, *Faltering Korea-China Relations with the Emergence of the G2 Era*, EAI Asia Security Initiative Working Paper 26 (Seoul: East Asia Institute, 2012), 1–2.

30. Chung, *Jungkukui Busang*, 263–83.

31. For an overview of this effort, see Presidential Committee on Policy Planning, *Hanmi Dongmeangui Miraejihyanjok Jojeong* [Future-oriented adjustment of the South Korea–U.S. alliance] (Seoul: Office of the President, 2008); Lee Su-hoon, ed., *Jojeonggiui Hanmi Dongmeang* [The South Korea–U.S. alliance in the period of adjustment] (Seoul: Institute of Far Eastern Studies, 2009).

the ROK-U.S. alliance. Although he recognized past American contributions to South Korea's peace and prosperity, he was also extremely critical of excessive psychological dependency on the United States, which he believed had critically undermined the morale, force structure, and combat capability of the South Korean military.[32]

Equally important was pervasive anti-American sentiments caused by the tragic death of two middle school girls who were run over by American tanks during a routine military exercise in summer 2002. The U.S. military's failure to adequately manage the public outcry caused by the girls' death (i.e., a lukewarm apology and negligence in handling the accident) triggered nationwide anti-American candlelight demonstrations, which in turn helped Roh win the presidential election. U.S. president George W. Bush's hard-line policy on North Korea over the nuclear issue was another factor shaping Roh's anti-American stance.[33]

After his official inauguration in February 2003, President Roh began to take some concrete policy measures for alliance readjustment. Above all, he was skeptical of the American doctrine of strategic flexibility and worried about South Korea's possible entrapment. U.S. secretary of defense Donald Rumsfeld undertook a military transformation strategy after the 9/11 attacks that aimed to make American forces lighter and more mobile. Central to the strategy was the doctrine of strategic flexibility, which would facilitate the relocation and mobilization of American forces at home and abroad more easily.[34] U.S. forces in South Korea were no longer considered fixed assets, but were subjected to a more swift inflow and outflow. The self-reliance school in the Roh Moo-hyun government, known as Jajoopa and mostly composed of younger staff members in the political affairs—and social affairs–related sections of the office of the president, alerted President Roh to the danger of entrapment by such development. They argued that crisis escalation across the Taiwan Strait could implicate South Korea in any conflict through the dispatch of its troops, an alliance obligation, and the U.S. utilization of its military bases for war preparation.[35]

Having been persuaded by the Jajoopa, Roh instructed the National Security Council (NSC) in July 2003 to come up with countermeasures regarding

---

32. See Roh's congratulatory speech at the commencement ceremony of the Third Military Academy, March 16, 2007, http://archives.knowhow.or.kr/record/all/view/87739.

33. See Yoichi Funabashi, *The Peninsula Question: A Chronicle of the Second Korean Nuclear Crisis* (Washington, DC: Brookings Institution Press, 2007).

34. U.S. Department of Defense, *Quadrennial Defense Review Report*, September 30, 2001 (Washington, DC: U.S. Department of Defense, 2001), 26; Paul K. Davis, *Military Transformation? Which Transformation, and What Lies Ahead?* (Santa Monica, CA: RAND, 2010), http://www.rand.org/content/dam/rand/pubs/reprints/2010/RAND_RP1413.pdf.

35. For a detailed description of this debate, see Kim Jong-dae, *Roh Moo-hyun, Sidaeui Munteokul Neomda* [Roh Moo-Hyun, he transcended the threshold of the age] (Seoul: Namuui Sup, 2010), chap. 3.

the doctrine of strategic flexibility. Following his instruction, the NSC directed the ROK delegation attending the ROK–U.S. Future of the Alliance Policy Initiative meeting in Washington in February 2005 to address two points: first, the ROK as an ally understood American strategic flexibility in principle, and second, the ROK wanted no part of a regional conflict that it did not desire.[36] In addition, at the commencement ceremony of the South Korean Air Force Academy on March 8, 2005, President Roh stated, "We will not be entangled in any conflict in Northeast Asia without our will and consent. This is a firm principle that cannot be compromised.[37] The United States accommodated Roh, and at a high-level talk held in Washington on January 19, 2006, both countries adopted a memorandum of understanding stating that the ROK respects changes in U.S. world strategy, whereas the United States respects ROK concern over regional and peninsular security. Although the tone of expression was refined, the Bush administration, especially Secretary Rumsfeld, was not happy and even suspicious of Seoul's alliance commitment. As Robert S. Ross points out, Roh's refusal to accommodate U.S. defense planning framed around strategic flexibility aroused such suspicion.[38]

Roh's attitude on strategic flexibility did not imply a realignment of South Korea's alliance policy, but a weakening of its alliance commitment in fear of entrapment in a China-U.S. conflict over the Taiwan Strait. Nevertheless, it could be easily interpreted as a prelude to bandwagoning with China. Roh's proposal on South Korea's role as balancer further heightened U.S. suspicion.[39] At the commencement ceremony of the Korean Military Academy on March 23, 2005, Roh stated, "The ROK will play a balancer role for peace and prosperity on the Korean Peninsula and in Northeast Asia."[40] He also emphasized the importance of independent and self-reliant armed forces in full military command and control in order to play this balancer role. Even before he elaborated upon the details of his concept, the conservative media mounted massive criticism. The *Chosun Ilbo*, a leading conservative daily newspaper, described the balancer role as a fundamental

36. NSC Secretariat, internal memo, January 30, 2005.
37. President Roh Moo-hyun's congratulatory speech at the 53rd commencement ceremony of the Korean Air Force Academy, March 8, 2005, http://archives.knowhow.or.kr/record/all/view/87093.
38. Robert S. Ross, "Balance of Power Politics and the Rise of China: Accommodation and Balancing in East Asia," *Security Studies* 15, no. 3 (2006): 381.
39. Bae Jong-yun, "Dongbuka jiyok jilseo byunhwawa hangukui jeonryakjok seontaek—Dongbuka gyunhyeonjaron ul jungsimuro" [Changes in Northeast Asia's regional order and South Korea's strategic choice—Debates over the "Northeast Asian balancer"], *Gukje Jeangchi Nonchong* 48, no. 3 (2008): 93–118.
40. President Roh Moo-hyun's congratulatory speech at the 59th commencement ceremony of the Korean Air Military Academy, March 11, 2003, http://archives.knowhow.or.kr/record/all/view/85945.

realignment of Seoul's policy from its adherence to the southern axis alliance between Japan, South Korea, and the United States to a new posture in favor of joining the northern axis of China, Russia, and North Korea.[41] The article successfully popularized Roh's balancer concept as a strategic move to change alliance from the United States to China or to bandwagon with China. What complicated the situation was a remark by Li Bin, Chinese ambassador to Seoul: "Although I do not know details about the balancer policy, China lends unreserved support to South Korea."[42]

But it was a grave distortion.[43] Roh's original intent was for South Korea to be ready to play the balancer role in the case of Sino-Japanese conflict after American disengagement from the region.[44] It was a future strategic vision rather than an operational policy for immediate implementation. For Roh the alliance with the United States was seen as temporal and instrumental only as a stepping-stone toward the creation of a multilateral security cooperation regime in Northeast Asia. Thus, the bilateral alliance with the United States should not hinder South Korea's relations with other great powers—especially China. Roh had some sort of soft balancing in mind.[45]

Transfer of wartime operation control of the ROK forces from the United States was another significant measure for alliance readjustment. The ROK and the United States established the Combined Forces Command (CFC) in 1978, the commander of which was also the commander of U.S. Forces Korea and the United Nations Command. At that time, the South Korean government transferred both peacetime and wartime operational control of its forces to the CFC commander as a tactical move through which American forces would automatically intervene in the case of North Korean military invasion. Although President Kim Young-sam recovered peacetime operational control in 1993, wartime command was still left with the United States. President Roh wanted to recover it for three reasons. First was the issue of sovereignty: Roh could not understand an arrangement in which 650,000 South Korean armed troops were under the operational control of a U.S.

---

41. Shin Jeongrok and Kwon Kyungbok, "Nambang 3gak dongmaeng Jaegeomto" [Government reconsiders the southern alliance axi], *Chosun Ilbo*, March 24, 2005.

42. Ryu Jin, "China Supports South Korea's Balancing Role," *Korea Times*, April 7, 2005.

43. For response to the critiques, see Moon Chung-in, "Dongbuka gyunhyongjaui gil" [The pathway to a balancer in Northeast Asia], *NEXT*, June 2005, 2–35; Moon Chung-in, "Dongbuka gyunhyungjaron eoddeohge bolgeokinga" [The idea of Northeast Asian balancer, how to evaluate?], *Chosun Ilbo*, April 24, 2005.

44. Moon Chung-in, "Gyunhyung oigyowa dajaanbohyupryukjilseo guchuk" [Establishing balanced diplomacy and multilateral security cooperation order], *Gukhoibo*, December 2010, 28–31.

45. *Soft balancing* usually refers to nonmilitary, diplomatic balancing. But Roh's soft balancing is much closer to Paul Schroeder's "transcending." See Stephen G. Brooks and Williams Wohlforth, "Hard Times for Soft Balancing," *International Security* 30, no. 1 (2005): 72–108; and Schroeder, "Historical Reality," 117.

commander with only 27,000 U.S. troops of his own. Second, Roh attributed the deformed ROK force structure (an overexpanded army of 550,000 troops, and an understaffed navy and air force, with around 50,000 troops each) to the continuation of U.S. operational control and subsequent practical psychological dependence on the United States. He wanted to correct such an abnormality through the transfer of wartime operational control. Third, Roh was indignant over North Korea, which not only regarded South Korean forces as an American puppet but which also called for direct peace negotiations with the United States while completely ignoring South Korea. He calculated that the transfer of wartime operational control would enhance South Korea's status as well as gain bargaining leverage with North Korea.[46]

The Bush administration agreed to transfer control by the end of 2012. Its rationale was clear: first, the ROK forces had become mature and strong enough, and second, it was natural for the ROK to assume the main combat role while the United States assumed the supporting role; and finally, the transfer would lessen the U.S. defense burden in Korea. Nevertheless, conservative forces in South Korea, especially retired army generals, strongly opposed the move by claiming the transfer would seriously erode alliance cohesion because it was predicated on the dissolution of the CFC and the establishment of two parallel commands by the ROK and the United States. They even argued that the transfer would mean the beginning of the end of the bilateral alliance.

THE LIMITS OF REALIGNMENT AND RHETORICAL BANDWAGONING

Did the Roh government realign toward China at the expense of alliance with the United States? A close examination of its policies discloses that there were no major realignments in the direction of China, but only minor adjustments within the status quo (the ROK-U.S. alliance) framework.[47]

Strategic flexibility was a hot issue in the early period of Roh's tenure, but in later years he did not raise the issue anymore, realizing that the doctrine was not threatening South Korean security, as the Jajoopa claimed. The balancer debate also disappeared as he pledged to maintain the alliance with

46. Chung-in Moon, "Don't Derail Negotiations on Wartime Operational Control," *Korea Times*, August 28, 2006; Yong-sop Han, "Jonjakgwon banhwanae daehan yongu" [A study of transfer of wartime operational control], in *Jojeonggiui Hanmi Dongmeang* [The South Korea–U.S. alliance in the period of adjustment], ed. Lee Su-hoon (Seoul: Institute of Far Eastern Studies, 2009), 155–202.

47. Su-hoon Lee, "Patannan hanmidongmaeng bokwonronjadeulae daehan bipan" [A critique of those who call for the restoration of the broken South Korea–U.S. alliance], in *Jojeonggiui Hanmi Dongmeang* [The South Korea–U.S. alliance in the period of adjustment], ed. Lee Su-hoon (Seoul: Institute of Far Eastern Studies, 2009), 419–46.

the United States. The Bush administration welcomed the return of wartime operation control to South Korea because the ROK's greater role in common defense would relieve defense burden sharing on the part of the United States. The Roh government took a swift and proactive move to consolidate the American military base in Pyongtaek to house forces scattered around South Korea at fifty-two bases. Progressive forces staged intense and violent demonstrations against base consolidation out of fear that the Pyongtaek base could be used as a regional hub for U.S. strategic flexibility.[48] But President Roh defied such opposition from his own support groups, and secured land and implemented base construction methodically. He also kept South Korean troops in Afghanistan and sent three thousand noncombat troops to Iraq at a time when other countries such as the Czech Republic and Spain had begun to withdraw their troops.[49] Roh's decision severely undercut his political capital within progressive circles.

In addition, the Roh government decided to purchase such advanced military equipment as Airborne Warning and Control Systems (AWACs) and Global Hawk unmanned surveillance aircraft from the United States. Shocking and even scandalous was his decision to initiate bilateral Free Trade Agreement (FTA) negotiations with the United States. Toward the end of his tenure, Roh was denounced by his supporters as a pro-American president who had betrayed his own constituents.

In light of these examples, it is clear that what the Roh government engaged in was nothing but rhetorical bandwagoning. It is true that the government cooperated with China in the Six-Party Talks, often contradicting the American policy line, but it was not because of pro-China bandwagoning but due to complementary national interests in settling the North Korean nuclear issue peacefully through dialogue and negotiation. President Roh heightened Beijing's expectation on Seoul's realignment toward China through the balancer idea and a more independent defense posture.[50] But none of these moves were actually materialized. Judged on this, labeling his government as anti-American and pro-Chinese seems quite misleading.

Why did Roh engage in only rhetorical bandwagoning? National interests mattered. He believed that the alliance with the United States was still

48. Wooksik Cheong, "Joongguk gonggyeokkiji, choeakui sinario" [Attack base against China, worst-case scenario], *Hankyoreh* 21, no. 589 (2005), http://h21.hani.co.kr/arti/cover/cover_general/15602.html.

49. Presidential Committee on Policy Planning, *Hanmi Dongmeangui Miraejihyanjok Jojeong*, 44–46.

50. Chung Jae-ho, "Jeonryakjok dongmaenggwa jeonryakjok donbanja saie" [Between strategic ally and strategic partnership], in Chung Jae-ho, ed., *Jongguk, Bulpyonhan Miraega Doil Geotinga*? [China, will it become an uncomfortable future?] (Seoul: Samsung Economic Research Institute, 2011), 256.

vital to South Korean national interests, and also realized that the North Korean nuclear issue—his top priority policy agenda—could not be resolved without American cooperation and support. Moreover, vested interests in the ROK-U.S. alliance were deeply entrenched and powerful. The Dongmaengpa (pro-American alliance school), composed mostly of bureaucrats from the ROK's Ministry of National Defense and Foreign Ministry, as well as Roh's confidants in the NSC, prevailed over progressive forces. American supremacy was not questioned during his reign, and China-U.S. relations during the period were relatively smooth so there was no need for Seoul to choose an either/or situation. Thus, the thesis that Roh was engaged in pro-China bandwagoning was grossly distorted.

The Lee Government, a Clash of National Interests, and Bounded Balancing

During his state visit to China in late May 2008, President Lee Myung-bak elevated the South Korea–China relationship from "full-scale cooperative partnership" to "strategic cooperative partnership."[51] In August of that year Chinese president Hu Jintao made a reciprocal visit to Seoul to push ahead with the strategic cooperative partnership, and both leaders adopted the China-ROK Coalition Statement, which contained the details of the partnership. The fact that both countries agreed to push forth with the partnership indicates that both countries recognized each other as partners and that the discussions were not limited to pending issues regarding only China and the ROK but were open to multilateral and strategic issues regarding medium- and long-term global approaches.[52] But a reality check tells us that China–South Korea bilateral relations severely deteriorated during the Lee government due to his excessive emphasis on the alliance with the United States, divergence of interests in dealing with North Korean nuclear proliferation, and hard-line policies toward North Korea, which strained ROK-China relations. It is no wonder that Lee is known for his pro-American balancing stance.

51. For an overview of China–South Korea relations during the Lee government, see Heungkyu Kim, "Hanjoong Junryakjuk Hyupryukdongbanjagwangye Hyungsunggwa Hanjoonggwangye" [The formation of the Sino-Korean strategic partnership and Sino-Korean relations], in *Gukje munjewa jeonmang* [International issues and prospects], ed. Institute of Foreign Affairs and National Security (Seoul: Institute of Foreign Affairs and National Security, 2008); Wang wei min, "Li ming bo zheng fu de wai jiao xin si wei yu zhong han guan xi" [The Lee Myung-bak government's new diplomatic thinking and China–South Korea relations], *Xian dai guo ji guan xi* 3 (2008): 32–45.

52. "Zhong han lian he sheng ming" [China–South Korea joint statement], May 28, 2008, http://news.xinhuanet.com/newscenter/2008-05/28/content_8271274.htm.

REPAIRING A BROKEN TIE: A TILT TOWARD A VALUE ALLIANCE

During his visit to Beijing in May 2008, PRC Foreign Ministry spokesman Qin Gang, in an unusual break with diplomatic convention, openly criticized the ROK-U.S. alliance as a relic of the past.[53] The Lee government ignored this warning from China, and pursued dramatic strengthening of the alliance, as well as unprecedented trilateral cooperation between Japan, South Korea, and the United States. The ROK-U.S. alliance did tighten considerably. The Lee Myung-bak government publicly participated in ongoing discussions regarding the establishment of a Japan-ROK-U.S. missile defense system. It also joined the Proliferation Security Initiative, toward which China showed unease, while periodically holding drills with the concerned countries. Despite protests from China, the shelling of Yeonpyong Island incited the ROK and the United States to hold a large-scale joint naval exercise in the Yellow Sea to retaliate against North Korea. Why was there such a sudden change from the previous government?

The politics mattered. During the presidential election campaign, Lee ferociously capitalized on Roh's foreign policy—especially Roh's stance on the alliance with the United States and his support for South Korea's balancer role, independent national defense, and equal alliance relations. Lee's election campaign slogan, "I will fix the broken alliance with the United States," carried a powerful message to voters, and he won the presidential election by a landslide. Upon his inauguration, Lee's foreign and national security policy was essentially a negation of the previous approach—what might be called "anything but Roh." He reversed Roh's policies in every direction, and the most representative case was the ROK-U.S. alliance.

Lee was diametrically opposed to his predecessor Roh in value orientation. While appreciating the values of a liberal democracy and a market economy, he strongly advocated a coalition of market democracies similar to former Japanese prime minister Taro Aso's call for the "arc of freedom and prosperity." His idea was almost in line with that of U.S. neoconservatives and the Japanese right wing. Beijing could not easily agree with Seoul's strengthening of cooperation with the U.S. in order to spread "universal values" such as market competition and liberal democracy. Since Beijing had officially claimed its "socialist market economy and democracy," a conflict with the ROK-U.S. alliance was almost inevitable.

Threats from North Korea played an equally crucial role in justifying President Lee's strengthening of the U.S. alliance. Critical of Roh's engagement policy, Lee sought a hard-line policy on North Korea. The shooting death of

53. Michael Ha, "Chinese Official Calls Korea-US Alliance Historical Relic," *Korea Times*, May 28, 2008.

a South Korean female tourist at North Korea's Mount Kumkang in July 2008, North Korea's missile test launch in April 2009, and its second nuclear test in May 2009 not only aggravated inter-Korea relations but also drove the Lee government to undertake a tough stance toward its northern neighbor. The sinking of ROK naval corvette *Cheonan* and the shelling of Yeonpyong Island in 2010 led the South Korean government to lean more heavily on the alliance with the United States. Transfer of wartime operational control to South Korea, which was scheduled for 2012, was delayed to 2015, and ROK-U.S. joint military exercises and training grew in frequency and size. The talk of a "values" alliance took the form of hard-power security alliance cooperation.

China perceived this defensive act on the part of the ROK as counterproductive to peace and stability in Northeast Asia and a threat to China's national security; it even expressed thoughts that South Korea was trying to revive the Cold War structure in Northeast Asia.[54] In fact, South Korea became a linchpin in the U.S rebalancing strategy toward Asia, seen in Beijing as a thinly veiled effort to contain the rise of China and strengthen the alliance system across the Asia Pacific region while excluding the PRC. President Lee actively sought to satisfy U.S. interest in strengthened trilateral security cooperation with Japan, but the South Korean public rejected this development, starting with the controversy over the ROK-Japan intelligence-sharing protocol in the summer of 2012 and erupting into a bilateral crisis over Dokdo Island and the "comfort women" disputes. The United States proved unable to mediate these disputes between its two allies. Until then, the ROK-U.S. alliance had not been considered a primary concern for China. First, ROK-China relations were growing rapidly, and coordination was improving. Second, China considered the ROK-U.S. alliance a marginal element whose goal was to deter North Korea and to assist the Japan-U.S. alliance. But that perception was beginning to change. Beijing remained skeptical and watchful of the strengthening of ROK-U.S. cooperation, and Korean observers in Beijing saw this as a kind of balancing act.[55]

THE NORTH KOREAN NUCLEAR PROBLEM AND DIVERGENT APPROACHES

Divergent approaches to the management of North Korean nuclear proliferation were another dividing factor under Lee's leadership. Traditionally, China had maintained the position of settling North Korea's nuclear issue

54. "Hou tian an jian shi dai kao yan zhong han guan xi" [China–South Korea relations in the post-Cheonan period), http://view.9van.com/index.php/view/political/2010-10-30/257866.html.

55. Sun Pei-song, "Jin bao han mei tong meng shi han guo de wai jiao bai bi" [Strengthening the South Korea–U.S. Alliance is South Korea's diplomatic defect], *Huanqiu Shibao*, August 10, 2008.

through the Six-Party Talks, which adopted the Joint Statement of September 19, 2005 as well as the agreement of February 13, 2007. But the Lee government was skeptical of the utility of the Six-Party Talks. This was clearly pointed out in Lee's election campaign pledge in regard to his plan for North Korea, the so-called Vision 3000 through Denuclearization and Openness, in which he promised to aid North Korea and increase its per capita income to U.S. $3000 in ten years if North Korea shut down its nuclear weapons program and agreed to go for an open economy. The core meaning of this policy was that South Korea must take the reins in denuclearizing North Korea and that there would be no forms of exchange or cooperation until North Korea gives up its nuclear program.[56]

The denuclearization and openness policy failed to produce any effect, however. Rather, North Korea test-fired its missiles on April 5, 2009 and went ahead with its second underground nuclear test on May 25, 2009. A month later Lee attended a summit meeting in Washington in which U.S. president Barack Obama assured him of the U.S. provision of nuclear umbrella to South Korea under the doctrine of "extended deterrence." Lee Myung-bak also proposed a Five-Party Talk that excluded North Korea in order to develop a tough punitive policy against North Korea through close cooperation with the five remaining countries. Yet this idea eventually foundered after being faced with objections from China and Russia. In September of that year President Lee suggested the idea of a "grand bargain" as an alternative during his visit to the UN General Assembly;[57] this aimed at resolving the issue with a package settlement through a more coordinated movement on the part of the remaining five parties. China, Japan, Russia, South Korea, and the United States.

Lee's policies caused friction with China on several levels. Above all, China was critical of Vision 3000, Five-Party Talks, and the "grand bargain," because they placed denuclearizing under the leadership of South Korea. China believed it was not logical for South Korea to take such leadership without any leverage and that it was undesirable for South Korea to oppose China by undercutting the Six-Party Talks. Furthermore, the Chinese government took a negative stance on Lee's tough policy toward implementing sanctions against North Korea. Beijing believed that placing sanctions for the sake of sanctions would not achieve the desired results, and it also

---

56. Korea Ministry of Unification, "Lee Myung-bak Jeongbui Daebuk Jeongchaekun Ireossumnida" [Explaining the Lee Myung-bak government's North Korea policy] (Seoul: Korea Ministry of Unification, 2008); Chung-in Moon, *The Sunshine Policy: In Defense of Engagement as a Path to Peace in Korea* (Soul: Yonsei University Press, 2012), 119–20.

57. Korea Institute for National Unification, *Bukhaek Ilgwal Tagyeol Bangan Chujinbanghyang* [Directions for the grand bargain policy on the North Korean nuclear problem] (Seoul: Korea Institute for National Unification, 2009).

viewed Seoul's hard-line policy as a move to foster the collapse of the North Korean regime and unification through absorption.

China also regarded any efforts to undermine the stability and peace on the Korean Peninsula as inappropriate. Beijing had long wanted a sustained survival of the North Korean regime as a way of materializing a long-term goal of peace and stability on the Korean Peninsula and across Northeast Asia. But the Lee government sought a short-term resolution to its North Korea problem, aiming for the resolution of North Korea's nuclear program through a hard-line policy. In the process, South Korea maintained a close cooperation with the United States and Japan, further irritating China. Divergent interests over the North Korean nuclear issue pushed Seoul to side with Washington, even risking China's opposition.

DISCORD OVER NORTH KOREA: A COLLAPSE SCENARIO AND A CONTINGENCY PLAN

In a sharp contrast to his predecessors, Lee Myung-bak formulated his North Korean policy on the assumption of its "imminent collapse,"[58] reminiscent of the Kim Young-sam period. Both Kim Young-sam and Lee Myung-bak believed that, since North Korea's collapse was imminent, it was wiser to place heavy pressure on that nation and make contingency plans instead of trying to normalize inter-Korea relations. This also dovetailed with the wishful thinking of the Bush administration's hard-liners, whose North Korea policy was based on an "early collapse" scenario. But it was incompatible with China's long-held favoring of the status quo on the Korean Peninsula.

Concept Plan 5029 (CP 5029), which aimed at coping with a military contingency in North Korea, was a major issue in South Korea–China relations. When the United States proposed CP 5029 in 2004, it was primarily on how combined South Korean and U.S. forces could secure and control North Korea's weapons of mass destruction (WMDs) and prevent the outflow of these weapons to third parties in the case of sudden collapse of the Kim Jong-il regime. The focus was initially on WMDs, but it shifted after Lee came to power. CP 5029's objectives went far beyond just controlling North Korea's WMDs and were geared toward using the military strength of the combined forces for the occupation and stabilization of North Korea.[59] China was quite critical of CP 5029 because it believed that a sudden change or the collapse of North Korea would not occur and that ROK-U.S. military intervention into North Korea was not only a violation of interna-

58. Chung-in Moon, *The Sunshine Policy*, chap. 5, 117–47.
59. Bruce W. Bennett and Jennifer Lind, "The Collapse of North Korea: Military Missions and Requirements," *International Security* 36, no. 2 (2011): 84–85.

tional law but could harm the security of China by radically changing the geopolitics of the Korean Peninsula.[60]

South Korea–China bilateral discord escalated in 2010. On March 26 of that year a patrol corvette of the Korean Navy, the PCC-772 *Cheonan*, sank in the Yellow Sea near the coastal waters of Baengnyeong Island. On May 20 the South Korean government's joint civil-military investigation group stated, "The Cheonan sank due to an external, underwater explosion caused by a North Korean torpedo." Strictly speaking, though the explosion of the *Cheonan* was a matter related to inter-Korea relations, it caused an enormous ripple effect on relations between South Korea and China,[61] for Beijing was skeptical of Seoul's findings. The situation worsened when the South Korean government tried to persuade the UN Security Council to adopt a sanction resolution toward North Korea; the resolution was tabled due to China's objection. In the eyes of Seoul, Beijing's protection of North Korea went too far. Public opinion denounced China as a shameless nation ignoring international norms and distorting the truth. The situation further deteriorated in late November 2010, after North Korea shelled Yeonpyong Island, and the United States then dispatched an aircraft carrier to the Yellow Sea despite Beijing's strong protest. Chinese leaders judged that U.S.-ROK cooperation aimed to transform the Yellow Sea into a "Second Taiwan Strait."[62] Consequently, a neo–Cold War environment developed in the region as a triangulation of Japanese, South Korean, and U.S. efforts to restrain China intensified while China made preparations to counter this structure by strengthening cooperation with North Korea and Russia.

THE LEE GOVERNMENT AND BOUNDED BALANCING

The Lee government adopted a quasi-pro-American balancing stance by strengthening the value alliance with the United States, forming a tight coalition with the United States in the Six-Party Talks, and soliciting U.S. support in preparing a contingency plan regarding North Korea. Despite differences over the value alliance, the North Korean nuclear quagmire, and the future of the North Korean regime, President Lee tried to promote bilateral ties with China. His government even claimed that an improved China–South

60. "'Jakgye 5029' Gyuksangronun Gunsajuk Mohumjuui" [Promotion of "Operation Plan 5029" is military adventurism], *Ohmynews*, September 14, 2008.

61. Jong-dae Kim, *Seohaejeonjaeng* [The West Sea war] (Seoul: Medici, 2013), 221–72.

62. Jong-dae Kim, "Mijunggan Seohae Chicken Game Imbak: Seohaeneun 'Je2ui Daemanhaehyop Doineunga'?" [China-U.S. chicken game in the West Sea: Is "the West Sea" going to be a "second Taiwan Strait"?], *D and D Focus*, December 2010, 18–26.

Korea relationship was one of its major diplomatic achievements.[63] Establishment of a strategic cooperative partnership with China; twenty summit meetings; activation of strategic talks between the two governments at the foreign and defense vice ministerial levels; the start of China–South Korea FTA negotiations; a remarkable expansion of trade; and flourishing social, cultural, and tourism exchanges were cited as evidence for robust bilateral ties. In addition, military cooperation, such as exchanges of high-level military personnel, rapidly increased during his administration. And contrary to widespread expectations, the Lee government did not participate in the U.S-Japan missile defense scheme. Thus, in reality, South Korea's pro-American balancing was bounded by the two motives of security cooperation with the United States and economic cooperation with China.

Why was there bounded balancing? His personal preferences notwithstanding, Lee was by and large dictated by the calculus of national interests. Like Roh, he did not perceive China as a threat. His primary threat perception came from North Korea, and he was concerned about China's patronage of that nation. Lee also came to the conclusion that he could not resolve the North Korean nuclear problem without Beijing's cooperation. The same could be said of his preferred vision of unification through absorption. He desperately needed China's support for his own interests, and that is why he could not overtly stand against it. Economic interests also mattered: in 1992, the trade volume between South Korea and China was at US$6.37 billion, but this number reached up to US$207 billion by 2010, surpassing the US$200 billion mark for the first time, and to US$215 billion in 2012. In fact, South Korea's level of dependence on trade with China greatly deepened. By 2012 it was at 24.5 percent, which was the highest level of dependence among all countries. And trade surplus with China reached a record high US$53.5 billion in 2012. The number of personal exchanges between South Korea and China also increased.[64] Such economic and social transactions fundamentally delimited the scope of the Lee government's maneuvering over China. After all, the government was walking on a tightrope, and thus its pro-American balancing posture was structurally bounded.

The Park Geun-hye Government and New Alignment

Park Geun-hye was well aware of the failure of Lee Myung-bak's foreign policy, and she called for realigning South Korea's policy with the United

63. Executive Office of the President, "Lee Myung-bak Jeongbuui kukjeong seonggwa" [The governance performance of Lee Myung-bak's government], *Cheongwadae Jeongchak News* 141 (2013): 36.

64. South Korea Ministry of Foreign Affairs, *Major Statistics on China 2013* (Seoul: South Korea Ministry of Foreign Affairs, 2013).

States and China as well as improving inter-Korea relations through *trust-politik* during her presidential election campaign in 2012.[65] While realizing that the Lee government had tilted toward the United States too much, she openly emphasized the need to harmonize the ROK-U.S. alliance with a strategic partnership with China.

REALIGNING TWO WHEELS: ALLIANCE VERSUS
STRATEGIC PARTNERSHIP

President Park proposed *gyunhyong oigyo* (balanced diplomacy), which was translated as "diplomacy of alignment" in English in what must have been a conscious effort to differentiate Park's policy from Roh's own *gyunhyong oigyo*.[66] What, in this instance, is meant by "alignment"? Park believed that an alliance with the United States and a strategic partnership with China are like two wheels of Korean diplomacy and that the government of Lee Myung-bak had favored the United States at the expense of China, causing a major wheel-alignment problem.[67] Park's new diplomacy aimed at restoring alignment with both the United States and China. Park saw China's value in its ability to shape a new regional order as well as in bringing changes in North Korea regarding denuclearization, openness, and reform.[68]

Under Park, the Foreign Ministry outlined several specific plans to improve South Korea's ties with China. The first was to develop cooperative networks with China in political and security arenas by diversifying and deepening channels of strategic dialogue and communication on diverse levels. The second was to expand mutually beneficial relations by not only promoting solidarity and trust through the strengthening of humanistic connections and the enhancement of public diplomacy but also achieving the target of bilateral trade volume of US$300 billion earlier than the scheduled date. The third was to expand exchanges and cooperation among the local governments of both countries, and the fourth was to develop a new future vision of bilateral development through which the strategic cooperative partnership based on trust could be furthered.[69]

---

65. Park Geun-hye, "A New Kind of Korea: Building Trust between Seoul and Pyongyang," *Foreign Affairs* 90, no. 5 (2011): 14–15.

66. This section draws partly on Chung-in Moon and Seung-chan Boo, "Korean Foreign Policy: Park Geun Hye Looks at China and North Korea," in *Japanese and Korean Politics: Alone and Apart from Each Other*, ed. Takashi Inoguchi (London: Palgrave Macmillan, 2015), 221–48.

67. Presidential Transition Committee, *Je 18 dae Daetongryongzikinsuwuiwonghoe baekseo: Park geun-hye jeongbu, hyimangui saesidaerul wihan silcheongwaje* [The 18th Presidential Transition Committee white paper: Park Geun-hye's government, practical tasks for new ages of hope] (Seoul: Presidential Transition Committee, 2013), 196.

68. Park Geun-hye, " A New Kind of Korea," 17.

69. South Korea Ministry of Foreign Affairs, *Major Statistics on China 2013*.

President Park sought Beijing's help in improving ties with North Korea because she believed China has much leverage. Her government also sought cooperation with China in the pursuit of South Korea's Northeast Asia Peace and Cooperation Initiative, which Foreign Minister Yoon Byung-se has defined as "small but significant interactions in soft cooperative security issues such as environment, disaster relief, nuclear power safety, and counterterrorism so that they turn into habits of cooperation." He believed that "eventually these habits of cooperation can be nurtured into a building of trust that will usher in an era of a peaceful, cooperative, and responsible Northeast Asia."[70] The initiative can be seen as a strategic move to harmonize Seoul's alliance with Washington and its strategic partnership with China. While maintaining a military alliance with the United States, it aimed to shape new relations with China within the framework of multilateral regional cooperation, starting with nontraditional security issues. China's response has been very favorable.[71] As Michael Green has noted, however, the United States was concerned that such a move could weaken the existing alliance system.[72]

Park's state visit to China during June 27–30, 2013, was an enormous success. Presidents Park Geun-hye and Xi Jinping agreed to enhance the strategic partnership between China and South Korea on the basis of trust, increased exchanges at multiple levels and in multiple areas, deepened economic and technological cooperation, joint efforts to reach a free trade agreement, beefed-up cultural exchanges, and enhanced coordination at the United Nations and in other major international mechanisms.[73] The leaders also agreed to work together to denuclearize the Korean Peninsula, and President Xi put a greater emphasis on calling for restarting the long-stalled Six-Party Talks with the aim of ending Pyongyang's nuclear ambitions.[74] In addition, Park was able to get Xi's full endorsement of her Korean Peninsula trust process and the Northeast Asia Peace and Cooperation Initiative.

70. Dinner address by H. E. Yun Byung-se, minister of foreign affairs, Republic of Korea, May 29, 2013, http://www.mofa.go.kr/news/index.jsp?menu=m_20.

71. Xinhua News Agency, "China Views Park's Peace Pact Positively: FM Spokeswoman," http://news.xinhuanet.com/english/china/2013-05/09/c_124689360.htm.

72. Michael J. Green, "Is Park's Regional Peace Pact realistic?" *JoongAng Daily*, May 10, 2013.

73. Xinhua News Agency, "Chinese, ROK Presidents Hold Talks, Pledge All-Round Cooperation," http://news.xinhuanet.com/english/china/2013-06/27/c_132492654.htm.

74. Shin Ji-hong and Park Sungmin, "Park daetongryong Xi juseak 'hanbando bihaekhwa check quotation mark gonddong iik buhap'" [Park and XI agree on common interests in denuclearizing the Korean peninsula], *Yonhap News*, June 27, 2013.

THE NORTH KOREAN QUESTION AND A LATENT CLASH OF INTERESTS

The Park government's China policy was better balanced than Lee's was, but Park and Xi Jinping held different views toward North Korea. During his meeting with Park, Xi clarified China's three strategic objectives regarding North Korea: peace and stability on the Korean Peninsula, denuclearization of the peninsula, and the primacy of dialogue and negotiation. As a report by the International Crisis Group pointed out, the Chinese are concerned that "the collapse of the regime would result in strategic uncertainty, South Korean or U.S. intervention, and that Korean reunification could lead to China sharing a border directly with a U.S. ally. The presence of American troops in such a sensitive region would fundamentally alter China's regional security environment. The prospect worries Chinese conservatives in particular."[75] Such concern is exacerbated by U.S. plans to intervene in North Korea to maintain stability during a major contingency.[76] Bates Gill's observation also deserves our attention: "Beijing's overriding priority on the Korean Peninsula is to prevent political change or economic collapse in North Korea given the potential consequences for China's social and economic stability."[77] Moreover, the continuing strategic value of North Korea, growing economic interconnectedness, and dense party and military networks between the two would make it difficult for China to let North Korea collapse. In fact, Beijing has welcomed Park's *trustpolitik* because it aims at promoting exchange and cooperation as well as trust-building with North Korea. Nevertheless, Park emphasized deterrence and pressure to end North Korean military provocations. While Park sought dialogue between China, South Korea, and the United States to put pressure on North Korea, China has been pushing for the resumption of all forms of dialogue first—namely, the Six–Party Talks, talks between North Korea and the United States, inter-Korea talks and, ultimately, four-party talks between China, North Korea, South Korea, and the United States.

Beijing and Seoul also have different approaches to dealing with the North Korean nuclear problem. The Chinese government has called for a nuclear weapons–free Korean Peninsula by reopening the Six-Party Talks as soon as possible, and it has blamed the United States for dragging its feet and urges Washington to ease conditions by becoming more tolerant

---

75. International Crisis Group, *Shades of Red: China's Debate over North Korea*, Asia Report no. 179 (Brussels: International Crisis Group, 2009), 17.

76. Bruce W. Bennett, *Preparing for the Possibility of a North Korean Collapse* (Santa Monica, CA: RAND, 2013), 7

77. Bates Gill, *China's North Korea Policy: Assessing Interests and Influences*, Special Report 283 (Washington, DC: United States Institute of Peace, 2011), 9.

toward North Korea. After North Korea's third underground nuclear testing, in February 2013, Beijing took a tough stance by actively implementing sanction measures mandated by the UN Security Council. But such a move did not imply a fundamental strategic change. Stephanie Kleine-Ahlbrandt noted that "for all its rhetoric about denuclearization, Beijing is still not willing—nor does it feel able—to implement punitive measures that might push North Korea to relinquish its nuclear weapons. The consensus view in Beijing is that even if it took punitive measures, they would not succeed in forcing North Korea to abandon its nuclear weapons."[78] The nuclear quagmire notwithstanding, keeping the North Korean regime alive might be better suited for Chinese interests.

But the Park government has not been cooperative with Beijing. Like Japan and the United States, South Korea's position has been firm in that it would not attend the Six-Party Talks unless North Korea satisfied some preconditions, such as an immediate and complete halt in long-range missile and nuclear tests, a halt in uranium and plutonium development, and compliance with inspections from the International Atomic Energy Agency. The Japan-ROK-U.S. trilateral summit in the Hague on March 26, 2014, and the ROK-U.S. summit on April 25, 2014, reaffirmed a unified position that unless North Korea shows sincere efforts to freeze its nuclear and missile programs, there would be no return to the Six-Party Talks.[79] After Pyongyang's fourth nuclear test, Beijing joined Seoul in passing UN Security Council Resolution 2770, which imposed tougher sanctions on North Korea. Yet Beijing still favored the settlement of the North Korean nuclear problem through dialogue and negotiations via the immediate resumption of the Six-Party Talks, while Seoul argued that it was the time for sanctions and pressure, not dialogue. China and South Korea seemed ready to enter another round of uneasy relations over the North Korean nuclear issue.

JAPAN, MISSILE DEFENSE, AND THE BURDEN OF ALLIANCE

Another challenge to the Park government emerged from the contradiction between South Korea's alliance with the United States and its strategic partnership with China. The questions of Japan and missile defense (MD) are two representative examples. Close cooperation between Seoul and Washington is vital to the new U.S. "pivot to Asia" strategy, but it is hardly conceivable for Washington to realize a viable rebalancing strategy without robust trilateral cooperation between Japan, South Korea, and the United

78. Stephanie Kleine-Ahlbrandt, "China's North Korea Policy: Backtracking from Sunnylands?," July 2, 2013, http://38north.org/2013/07/skahlbrandt070213/.

79. David Sanger, "U.S. Confronts Consequences of Underestimating North Korean Leader," *New York Times*, April 24, 2014.

States. Nevertheless, Japan–South Korea relations hit bottom under Park's government. Japanese prime minister Shinzo Abe's negative remarks on the history of Japanese aggression and "comfort women," his tribute at the Yasukuni Shrine, and Japan's assertive claim over Dokdo have made Park rather hostile to Japan. Consequently, she refused to have summit talks with Abe and was reluctant to enhance cooperation in intelligence and logistic areas. Moreover, Park's government was critical of Japan's decision to exercise collective self-defense, which would allow the Japanese Self-Defense Forces to come to the aid of an ally during a military crisis,[80] a development that alarmed Washington. American leaders such as President Barack Obama, Vice President Joe Biden, and former defense secretary Chuck Hagel expressed concern over deteriorating relations between Seoul and Tokyo. But Park's stance remained firm, stating that there is a "lack of trust" between South Korea and Japan due to the Abe administration's chauvinism. The deepening rift between America's two "linchpin" allies in Northeast Asia has become a major impediment to Obama's rebalancing strategy.[81]

Meanwhile, Beijing took advantage of worsening ties between Seoul and Tokyo by suggesting joint cooperation in dealing with Abe's nationalistic behavior. The Chinese government made a proactive gesture by establishing a memorial statue of Ahn Jung-geun, an independence fighter who assassinated Ito Hirobumi, Japan's prime minister, in 1909. Xi told Park during the bilateral summit in the Hague on March 26, 2014, that the idea of a memorial statue was his personal initiative.[82] Park reciprocated by returning to China the remains of 437 Chinese soldiers who were killed during the Korean War. The Chinese media and public expressed an unprecedented appreciation for this reciprocal measure.[83]

China had used a common front against Japan to consolidate China's bond with South Korea. Beijing sought closer ties with Seoul to change the geopolitical order in Northeast Asia. What it feared most was a joint front between Japan, South Korea, and the United States. In particular, it opposed a South Korean agreement with Japan to exchange confidential military information or establish a stronger three-way missile defense system

80. Chung-in Moon, "Abe's *Honne*," *Sisa In*, December 4, 2013.
81. The United States has been urging Seoul to conclude the General Security of Military Information Agreement. See U.S. Department of Defense, "Readout of Secretary Hagel's Meeting with the President of the Republic of Korea," http://www.defense.gov/releases/release.aspx?releaseid=16288.
82. Kim Hyungi, "Xi jinping, Park deatngryong himangdaero gwangbokgun pyojiseok got jungong" [As President Park wishes, China will soon start building a monument for Korean independent fighters], *Joongang Ilbo*, March 25, 2014.
83. Yoon Boram, "Jeonjaeng upnun sesanguro . . . , Junggukgun yuhae 437gu indosik" [To the world without war . . . , a handing over ceremony of 437 Chinese soldiers remains], *Yonhap News*, March 28, 2014.

with Japan and the United States.[84] China leaned toward South Korea, while Japan has attempted to push South Korea away from China. Under such circumstances, Washington demanded that Seoul mend ties with Tokyo. In December 2015, despite domestic political opposition, the Park government finally restored political ties with the Abe cabinet, reaching an agreement on the thorny issue of "comfort women." Then, in November 2016, Seoul and Tokyo reached an agreement to exchange military intelligence. China had failed to block South Korean–Japan military cooperation.

The MD issue emerged as another critical issue affecting Seoul's ties with Beijing and Washington. Washington wanted Seoul to join its missile defense system by acquiring the Terminal High Altitude Area Defense (THAAD) system and sharing information with Japan and the United States because the expanded sensor and interceptor coverage of a trilateral command, control, and communication network could enhance MD effectiveness against North Korea by tracking missiles from multiple angles at multiple points in their flight trajectory.[85] General Martin Dempsey, chairman of the U.S. Joint Chief of Staff, underscored the value of joint missile defense by stating, "Sharing information and intelligence is a key part of this equation. And given the threat that North Korean ballistic missiles pose to the Korean Peninsula and the region, the Joint Integrated Missile Defense System becomes more important."[86]

The Chinese government had long been critical of U.S. and allied MD efforts in the region. During his visit to Moscow in March 2013, President Xi issued a joint statement with Russian president Vladimir Putin that called on the international community "to act cautiously" in deploying and cooperating on ballistic missile defense and voiced their opposition to "the unilateral and unchecked buildup of anti-missile capabilities by a country or a group of countries to the detriment of strategic stability and international security."[87] Since then, President Xi and Chinese government officials persistently expressed their opposition to the deployment of THAAD.

South Korea had been hesitant to join the U.S.-led missile defense network. Contrary to media reports, the Defense Ministry has stated that South Korea would not join the United States and that THAAD is not an option for thwarting North Korea's missile threats. A South Korean defense official argued that "considering need, suitability and budget availability, we will

84. Jin Qiangyi, "ROK's Choice Has Manifold Implications," *China Daily*, July 12, 2012.

85. Ian E. Rinehart, Steven A. Hildreth, and Susan V. Lawrence, "Ballistic Missile Defense in the Asia-Pacific Region: Cooperation and Opposition" (Washington, DC: Congressional Research Service, 2013), 17.

86. U.S. Joint Chiefs of Staff, "U.S., South Korean Military Leaders Hold Talks in Seoul," September 30, 2013, http://www.jcs.mil/Media/News/News-Display/Article/571530/us -south-korean-military-leaders-hold-talks-in-seoul/.

87. Rinehart, et al., "Ballistic Missile Defense," 14–15.

not join the U.S. missile defense system, but take our own path."[88] Thus, technical uncertainty and financial burden discouraged the Park government from joining U.S.-led MD efforts. But China's opposition was also taken into account.[89] Richard Weitz aptly describes the South Korean dilemma in the following way: "South Korea finds itself in a difficult situation. On one hand, it must respond to North Korea's missile threats. On the other, it must do so without provoking Pyongyang or Beijing."[90] Nonetheless, on July 9, 2016, Seoul and Washington jointly announced the deployment of the THAAD system in South Korea. A fourth nuclear testing and missile test launching by North Korea infuriated President Park and prompted her to make a decision in favor of deployment in spite of immense opposition from China and progressive forces in South Korea. The Chinese Foreign Ministry immediately issued a statement of "strong discontent and resolute opposition" to the announcement and summoned U.S. and South Korean ambassadors for an official protest. Chinese Foreign Minister Wang Yi, who was visiting Sri Lanka, also stated, "THAAD is beyond South Korean defense needs, and no excuse can justify its deployment decision"; he urged the U.S. and South Korea to "act prudently and not to make a grave mistake."[91]

President Park's strategy had been to make incremental alignment and realignment within the existing framework of status quo while avoiding both balancing and bandwagoning. Whereas unruly North Korean behavior and its pursuit of nuclear weapons had pulled her government back to a pro-American balancing, economic interests and shared identity against Japan had pushed it toward bandwagoning with China. Yet Park's decisions to normalize ties with Japan, exchange military intelligence with Japan, and deploy the THAAD system, revealed that she had tilted toward the United States. It was a sharp reversal of her earlier position that "South Korea will continue to develop a strategic partnership with China to contribute to the peace and development of the region,"[92] which had been a response to Vice President Biden's statement on December 6, 2013: "It's never been a

88. "We Don't Buy Into US MD," *Korea Times*, October 16, 2013.

89. On a critical view of THAAD, see Chung-in Moon, "THAAD Isn't Answer to Seoul's Anxiety," *Global Times*, May 28, 2015.

90. Richard Weitz, "Global Insights: South Korea Must Widen BMD Cooperation to Counter North Korean Threats," *World Politics Review*, April 9, 2013, http://www.worldpoliticsreview.com/articles/12855/global-insights-south-korea-must-widen-bmd-cooperation-to-counter-north-korean-threats.

91. Jin Byungtae and Lee Junsam, "Thaad baechi gyeoljung; Jung Wang Yi 'Eotteon byunmyeongdo mugiryok'" [Thaad decision: Chinese foreign minister Wang Yi says "no excuse can be justified"], *Yonhap News*, July 9, 2016.

92. Sarah Kim, "Park and Biden Are Hand in Hand," *Korea Joongang Daily*, December 7, 2013, koreajoongangdaily.joins.com/news/article/article.aspx?aid=2981672.

good bet to bet against America," Biden said, adding, "America will continue to place its bet on South Korea."[93] Biden was correct.

Conclusion: China-U.S. Rivalry and South Korea's Strategic Choice

South Korea's policy toward China and the United States under three different presidencies unveils an interesting pattern. Each president made constant incremental adjustments in security and economic relations within an existing status quo order; thus, in many cases their election campaign slogans have not been turned into actual policy performance. Alliance ties with the United States are deeply entrenched, and the distribution of power capabilities between China and the United States has not yet shifted enough to replace such ties. North Korea has been playing a delicate supporting role in sustaining the existing order.

President Roh openly sought a more independent policy regarding the United States while calling for a pragmatic balanced diplomacy. His policy left the South Korean people with an impression that he undertook a pro-China bandwagoning policy. But his would-be pro-China policy ended with simply rhetorical bandwagoning: the South Korea–U.S. alliance remained cohesive, but cooperative ties with China were rather limited. Overall power distribution was in favor of the United States, and the majority of South Koreans supported the alliance with America. Convergence of interests over North Korea, especially its attempts at nuclear proliferation, brought Beijing and Seoul closer, but not to the extent that it could profoundly realign existing alliances. More important, the Dongmaengpa (alliance school) ultimately trumped the Jajoopa (self-reliance school) in the decision-making process, altering Roh's initial policy orientation.

President Lee was committed to repairing the "broken" alliance between South Korea and the United States not only because of his personal belief but also because of a clash of interests with China over North Korea. North Korea's second underground nuclear test, the sinking of the corvette *Cheonan*, and the shelling of Yeonpyong Island compelled Lee to rely more on the United States and to become suspicious of China's motives. He also held the view that the United States was far superior to China in power configuration as well as value orientation. Conservative forces and the mass media were firmly behind his pro-American policy stance. Nevertheless, he did not perceive China as a threat and sought friendly relations with it to maximize economic gains and to utilize its influence over North Korea.

---

93. Deutsche Welle, "Biden Defiant over China, North Korea during South Korea Visit," December 6, 2013, http://www.dw.com/en/biden-defiant-over-china-north-korea-during -south-korea-visit/a-17275896.

Thus, his so-called pro-U.S. balancing policy was rather limited, and he maintained a bidirectional diplomacy, with China on the one hand, and the United States on the other, throughout his administration.

President Park initially fell between the two. Her diplomacy of alignment based on *trustpolitik* was rather similar to Roh's "peace and prosperity" policy, in that she had tried to harmonize the South Korea–U.S. alliance with a strategic partnership with China, as well as to find common ground between the alliance and regional multilateral security cooperation.[94] Her foreign policy toward China and the United States can be seen as incremental adaptation to a changing external environment within the status quo order. But her efforts to maintain equidistant policy on Beijing and Washington were seriously challenged by North Korea's provocative behavior. Facing Pyongyang's fourth nuclear testing and missile test-launching in early 2016, she reaffirmed South Korea's balancing strategy, repairing broken ties with Japan while allowing U.S. deployment of the THAAD system in South Korea.

David Kang has observed that "South Korea neither balanced nor bandwagoned but simply accommodated with no fundamental change either way in military stance or alignment posture."[95] His observation is only partly accurate, for there have been constant minor alignments and realignments that go beyond passive accommodation. All three governments under review have pursued the status quo option with incremental adjustment, but the "standing alone" option was never tried. What options, then, is South Korea likely to try in the future? What options are feasible and desirable for its security posture? What factors would facilitate or inhibit such choices? By way of conclusion, let me examine these questions.

A continuation of the status quo would be the most likely scenario. Since diplomatic normalization in 1992, the South Korean government has pursued this strategy, though to varying degrees under different leaderships. Its logic seems obvious: maximizing economic benefits by promoting trade and investment relations with China while reducing security risks by strengthening its alliance with the United States. Under this option, there is no pressing need for South Korea to choose between China and the United States because it is assumed that South Korea can maintain a good relationship with both. This strategy has worked so far. South Korea has enjoyed huge economic benefits from China without undermining its robust alliance with the United States. Can South Korea continue this opportunistic strategy? Stephen Walt says no; he argues, "If Sino-American rivalry heats up—as I believe it will—then Beijing and Washington will press Seoul to

94. Byung-se Yoon, "Park Geun-hye's *Trustpolitik*: A New Framework for South Korea's Foreign Policy," *Global Asia* 8, no. 3 (2013), 8–14.
95. Kang, "Between Balancing and Bandwagoning," 1.

choose sides. Of course, competition between the United States and China might allow South Korea to extract valuable concessions from both, but it also increases the risk of abandonment by Washington, which would leave South Korea at the mercy of its large near-neighbor."[96] The status quo option might work in the short term, but it will face enormous internal and external constraints in the medium to long term.

If hegemonic rivalry between China and the United States intensifies, Seoul might have to choose either balancing or bandwagoning. Several pundits have predicted the dynamics of rapid power transition and associated strategic uncertainty in the coming decade.[97] In addition to intensified China-U.S. hegemonic rivalry, balancing China by siding with the United States would take place under the following conditions: a U.S. edge over China in power distribution and its continuing security commitment; severe deterioration of inter-Korea relations and China's patronage of North Korea; eruption of territorial and identity conflicts between Beijing and Seoul; a diversification of economic dependence on China; and a domestic political environment in which proalliance conservative forces prevail over progressive forces. A recent Pew survey generally supports this perspective: 91 percent of South Korean respondents believe China's growing military power is a bad thing, whereas only 6 percent believe it is a good thing.[98] But as Steve Chan argues, it might be extremely difficult for South Korea to seek the balancing option not only because of economic calculus and dense human networks between Beijing and Seoul but also because of Seoul's prudent self-restraining policy behavior.[99] Ironically, the tyranny of geographic proximity and the vulnerability embedded in economic dependency on China are likely to inhibit unambiguous balancing with the United States.

The bandwagoning option cannot be ruled out in the medium to long term. Power transition in favor of China and actual or potential American disengagement from the Korean Peninsula; improved inter-Korea relations, and eventually Korean unification; deepening economic dependence on China; and China's self-restraining behavior over identity and territorial issues could encourage South Korea or a unified Korea to consider the bandwagoning option. South Koreans have so far shown a mixed attitude on this pro-China option. Table 7.2 presents a collection of surveys on South Korean

96. Walt, "The Shifting Security Environment," 21.

97. See, for example, Aaron Friedberg, *A Contest for Supremacy: China, America, and the Struggle for Mastery in Asia* (New York: Norton, 2011); and Yan Xue-tong, *Lishide Guanxing* [Inertia of History] (Beijing: China CITIC Press, 2013).

98. Pew Research Center, *America's Global Image Remains More Positive than China's: But Many See China Becoming World's Leading Power*, July 18, 2013, http://www.pewglobal.org /2013/07/18/americas-global-image-remains-more-positive-than-chinas/, 33.

99. Steve Chan, *Looking for Balance: China, the United States, and Power Balancing in East Asia* (Stanford, CA: Stanford University Press, 2012), 225–27.

perceptions of China and the United States between 1997 and 2016. Statistics in the table reveal that South Koreans favored China over the United States between 1997 and 2004. This can be attributed largely to the eroding U.S. reputation under President Bush, generally favorable inter-Korea relations, and robust economic ties with China without any security concerns. South Koreans began to tilt toward the United States between 2005 and 2008 primarily because of historical disputes with China over its Northeast Project. Since 2009, South Koreans who favored the United States have outnumbered those who favored China by a wide margin. According to one survey from 2009, only 6 percent of respondents chose China, whereas 68 percent chose the United States; in 2010, the gap widened further. North Korea's provocative behavior, as exhibited through its second nuclear testing, the sinking of the *Cheonan*, the shelling of Yeonpyong Island, and China's lukewarm attitude toward North Korean provocations amid its rising power might have contributed to aggravating China's image in South Korea.

Although favorable perceptions of China have slightly increased since 2012, overall public perception indicates that bandwagoning is a less likely option—at least in the short term. Several other factors could hamper this option. First, the continuation of a divided Korea may prevent Seoul from taking such a position: as long as the threat from North Korea remains unchanged, it will be harder for Seoul to side with Beijing. Second, collective memory of the past (e.g., of numerous Chinese invasions and the old hierarchical order) is likely to make Korea, be it unified or divided, hesitant to bandwagon with China. Finally, some South Koreans might want to delay the process of power transition until China achieves liberal democracy and a full market economy. Thus, despite the fear of retaliation from China, South Korea could join the United States and other countries in checking and balancing China rather than taking its side. What should be kept in mind, however, is that improved inter-Korea relations could drastically change the South Korean perception of China, tempting Seoul to bandwagon with that nation.

South Korea could also seek the "standing alone" option in the medium to long term either in terms of internal balancing with nuclear weapons capability or by maintaining a permanent neutral status. Given past history, in which great powers have decided the destiny of the Korean Peninsula, a strong revival of nationalist sentiments could popularize this option. Additionally, American disengagement from the region; aggressive China's rise; clashes of assertive nationalism and hostile interactions among regional actors; absence of a balancer or honest broker that could mitigate dyadic conflicts; and the advent of a unified Korea could make South Korea consider this option. A nationwide survey conducted in October 2011 implies such a tendency: 62.1 percent of South Korean respondents felt that South Korea should stay neutral in the case of a serious conflict between the United States and China, whereas only 1.7 percent supported siding with China, and

Table 7.1 South Korean views of China and the United States, 1997–2016

Year	Chose China	Chose U.S.
1997[1]*	56	31
1999[2]*	33	22
2000[3]***	53	8
2001[4]**	29	30
2002[5]**	55	37
2003[6]***	48	33
2004[7]***	48	38
2004[8]*	24	53
2005[9]**	38	37
2005[10]**	11	46
2006[11]**	12	50
2006[12]**	56	51
2007[13]*	20	79
2008[14]***	52	30
2008[15]**	8	61
2009[15]**	6	68
2010[16]**	6	71
2011[15]**	5	69
2012[17]**	12	35
2013[18]*	12	21
2014[19]****	25	60
2015[19]****	31	59
2016[19]****	33	60

Notes:
*Question: With which country should South Korea maintain close relations?
**Question: Toward which country do you feel more favorable?
***Question: Which country should South Koreans regard as more important?
****Question: If the United States and China continue their rivalry, with which country should South Korea strengthen ties?
Sources: Jae Ho Chung, *Leadership Changes and South Korea's China Policy* (Washington, DC: Korea Economic Institute, 2012), 14–15. [1]Sejong Institute, *1997 Seyon Report* (Seoul: Dongseo Research, 1997), 11–13; [2]*Dong-A Ilbo*, January 1, 1999; [3]*Dong-A Ilbo*, December 5, 2000; [4]*Dong-A Ilbo*, December 25, 2001; [5]*Chosun Ilbo*, December 22, 2002; [6]*Joong-Ang Ilbo*, February 12, 2003; [7]*Dong-A Ilbo*, May 4, 2004; [8]*Global View 2004* (Chicago: Chicago Council on Foreign Relations, 2004); [9]*Hankyoreshinmun*, March 17, 2005; [10]*Joong-Ang Ilbo*, December 22, 2005; [11]*Joong-Ang Ilbo*, May 18, 2006; [12]*Hangook Ilbo*, August 7 2006; [13]*Christian Science Monitor*, August 13, 2007; [14]*Dong-A Ilbo*, April 1, 2008; [15]*2013 Tongil eusik josabalpyo* [Survey Report on the Consciousness of Unification] (Seoul: Institute for Peace and Unification, Seoul National University, 2011), 58; [16]*Chosun Ilbo*, August 12, 2010: [17]*Dong-A Ilbo*, January 6, 2012; [18]*Munwha Ilbo*, November 1, 2013; [19]Asan Institute for Policy Studies, *South Koreans and Their Neighbors 2016* (Seoul: Asan Institute for Policy Studies, 2016), 27.

35.5 percent of respondents believed that South Korea should support the United States.[100] But this could be the worst choice for security dynamics on the Korean Peninsula, not only because a nuclear Korea would jeopardize rather than enhance its security posture by triggering a nuclear domino effect in the region, but also because its neutral status could enable further foreign interventions.

I would like to return to the questions raised earlier in this chapter. Will China be a Qing dynasty of the twenty-first century? Will the United States turn into a Ming? Which way should South Korea go? Neither Qing nor Ming seems a proper metaphor. China cannot replace the United States, and the two will coexist, alternating between cooperation and conflict. As Henry Kissinger suggests in his book *On China*, if China and the United States adopt a coevolutionary strategy, South Korea can enjoy the benefits of security and prosperity.[101] If they are entangled in protracted and futile confrontation and conflict, Korea, whether divided or unified, will suffer. What South Korea needs at this critical juncture is a foreign policy of prudence (*shenzhong*) and the middle path (*zhongyong*). It should constantly keep in mind the historical lesson of "too much is as bad as too little." The diplomacy of opportunistically "taking sides" can easily backfire. While maintaining the status quo, South Korea should make every effort to improve inter-Korea relations and to enhance domestic consensus and cohesion. It should play a role of integrative, not divisive, force. That is the direction South Korea should head for.

---

100. Asiatic Research Institute and East Asian Institute, *Survey on National Consciousness of Korea and China* (Seoul: Asiatic Research Institute and East Asian Institute, 2011).

101. Henry Kissinger, *On China* (New York: Penguin, 2011).

III. GREAT POWER RELATIONS AND REGIONAL CONFLICT

Threading the Needle

The South China Sea Disputes and U.S.-China Relations

M. Taylor Fravel

In the South China Sea, China and the United States face pointed policy dilemmas.[1] As a rising power with unresolved maritime disputes, China wants to defend and consolidate its claims while simultaneously maintaining good relations with its neighbors and limiting any growth of U.S. influence in the disputes.[2] As the dominant maritime power, the United States wants to maintain the credibility of its commitments to its allies, freedom of navigation, and peaceful dispute resolution without becoming a direct participant in the disputes against China. The challenge for China has been to assert its claims while avoiding the formation of a balancing coalition, while the challenge for the United States has been to defend its commitments without emboldening other claimant states and becoming entrapped in their disputes with China.

More broadly, the challenge for both the United States and China is to maintain regional stability and avoid elevating the role of the South China Sea disputes in an increasingly competitive bilateral relationship. The United States is already involved in two of China's other sovereignty disputes: Taiwan, through the Taiwan Relations Act, and the Diaoyu/Senkaku Islands through Article V of the U.S.-Japan Treaty of Mutual Cooperation and

1. For helpful comments and suggestions, the author thanks Ian Chong, Kacie Miura, Rachel Esplin Odell, Liselotte Odgaard, Robert S. Ross, and Øystein Tunsjø.
2. In this chapter, "South China Sea disputes" refers to disputes over the territorial sovereignty of islands, rocks, and reefs such as the Paracel and Spratly Islands as well as disputes over maritime jurisdiction. On these different kinds of disputes, see M. Taylor Fravel, "China's Strategy in the South China Sea," *Contemporary Southeast Asia* 33, no. 3 (2011): 292–319.

Security. How China and the United States approach the South China Sea matters not just for the outcome of the disputes but for the dynamics and intensity of great power competition in the region. Historically, states clash and go to war over disputed territory more than any other issue, while power transitions exacerbate tensions between the rising power and the dominant one.[3] The intensification of territorial disputes amid a power transition portends a period of heightened danger of great power conflict in the South China Sea.

For the United States and China, balancing the countervailing pressures that they face in the South China Sea is difficult. As Kenneth Waltz has observed, competitors in international politics face "the necessity of balancing between too little and too much strength, between too many failures that strengthen the potential enemy and too many successes that scare him unduly."[4] China's vigorous assertion of maritime claims can threaten its neighbors and push them toward closer relations with the United States. Likewise, U.S. involvement in the South China Sea can threaten China's position in the disputes and can even embolden states facing China, creating strong incentives for Beijing to push back. Missteps by either side in its involvement in the South China Sea could exacerbate the security dilemma, elevating the role of the disputes as a source of friction in U.S.-China relations and fueling a spiral of regional instability.[5] The United States and China need to thread the needle of defending their interests without unduly provoking the other.

Through an examination of how the two nations have managed these pressures, this chapter yields three findings. First, actions by the United States and China have often created incentives for the other state to push back, creating negative spirals. Many of China's actions have threatened other states in these disputes (including a U.S. ally)—many of whom have sought to strengthen their security ties with Washington to balance Beijing. Some U.S. actions—in particular, the rollout of the pivot and the strengthening of the alliance with the Philippines—have threatened China's position in the South China Sea, eliciting strong responses from Beijing. At the same time, largely to limit further U.S. involvement, China has engaged in tactical pauses or the temporary moderation of the pursuit of its claims.

Second, China and the United States have enhanced their positions in the South China Sea. Through wielding its growing maritime capabilities, China

3. John Vasquez and Marie T. Henehan, "Territorial Disputes and the Probability of War, 1816–1992," *Journal of Peace Research* 38, no. 2 (2001): 123–38.

4. Kenneth N. Waltz, *Man, the State, and War: A Theoretical Analysis* (New York: Columbia University Press, 1959), 223.

5. Robert Jervis, "Cooperation under the Security Dilemma," *World Politics* 30, no. 2 (1978): 167–214; Robert Gilpin, *War and Change in World Politics* (New York: Cambridge University Press, 1981).

has been more active than ever before in asserting its claims in the region. Through these actions, its physical position in the disputes has never been stronger. China has unilaterally exploited the natural resources in contested waters, increased the presence of its naval and law enforcement vessels, seized effective control of contested features like Scarborough Shoal, and engaged in unprecedented land reclamation on seven rocks and reefs to construct harbors and airfields that can further bolster its presence. Likewise, the U.S. security posture in Southeast Asia is more robust than at any time since the end of the Cold War, with invigorated alliances, new security partnerships, and greater access for American forces in the region.

Third, actions taken by both sides have helped to shield the broader relationship from tensions and competition in the dispute. In asserting and consolidating its claims, China has taken actions below the threshold of military force and has not attacked land features occupied by other claimants. By doing so, it has avoided the United States' greatest strength in the region—its ability to project air and naval power—and forced Washington to accept Chinese actions or escalate in response. China has also mostly taken actions to deter others from challenging it rather than to compel them to vacate the features they hold or settle on terms favorable to China. Likewise, the United States has not sought to reverse or roll back Chinese gains, such as the seizure of Scarborough Shoal, that would generally require Washington to engage much more directly in the disputes and probably abandon its principle of neutrality over sovereignty. Moreover, each side has tacitly accepted the advances made by the other. The United States has effectively accepted China's consolidation of its presence, including extensive land reclamation. China has effectively accepted a greater security role for the United States in the South China Sea. In this way, a new equilibrium or balance may be forming.

The Years 2008–2011: The United States Enters the Fray, Tensions Subside

In 2008, as tensions grew in the South China Sea, other claimants—especially Vietnam and the Philippines—desired an increased role for the United States to balance China. In response and to prevent further "internationalization," China moderated the pursuit of its claims from mid-2011 until the Scarborough Shoal incident in April 2012.

GROWING TENSIONS

Tension in the South China Sea disputes has increased substantially since around 2008. A key turning point was the May 2009 deadline for states to submit claims to extended continental shelves beyond two hundred nautical miles to the UN's Commission on the Limits of the Continental Shelf

(CLCS).[6] If a territorial or maritime dispute exists, the commission's rules dictate that it "shall not consider and qualify a submission made by any of the States concerned in the dispute."[7] As a result, claimants in the South China Sea had strong incentives to challenge the continental shelf submissions that overlapped with their own claims to territorial sovereignty or maritime jurisdiction. Accordingly, China and the Philippines both objected to Vietnam's submission and to the joint Vietnamese-Malaysian submission, which sparked objections and counterclaims.[8]

Even though the deadline for submissions had been established ten years earlier, its impending arrival in May 2009 significantly increased the competition in the South China Sea disputes. By submitting claims to the commission, relevant states formally expanded their claims to maritime jurisdiction beyond two hundred nautical miles from their coastlines. In its May 2009 note to the CLCS, for example, Vietnam claimed a broadened continental shelf that extended into the central part of the South China Sea. In addition, in the notes submitted to the CLCS, states not only contested each other's claims to maritime jurisdiction but also their claims to territorial sovereignty over the Paracel and Spratly Islands. Finally, China's first diplomatic note contesting Vietnam and Malaysia's submissions reaffirmed its claims to the islands and included a map of the region that depicted the Paracel and Spratly Islands along with the now infamous "nine-dash line."[9] Although the Chinese note did not mention the line, instead affirming China's "indisputable sovereignty over the islands in the South China Sea and the adjacent waters," Vietnam viewed the map as an expansion of China's claims.

In the eyes of other claimants, China's vigorous response to the CLCS submissions reinforced a view in the region that China had become more assertive in pressing its claims. Between 2006 and 2008, tensions had already begun to increase, especially as China responded to what it viewed as challenges from Vietnam. In 2007, Vietnam announced ambitious goals

6. Under UNCLOS, a state can only exercise rights to the continental shelf if the CLCS certifies the claim.

7. UN Commission on the Limits of the Continental Shelf, *Rules of Procedure of the Commission on the Limits of the Continental Shelf* (New York: United Nations, 2008), 22.

8. For a list of all submissions, see UN Commission on the Limits of the Continental Shelf, "Submissions, through the Secretary-General of the United Nations, to the Commission on the Limits of the Continental Shelf, pursuant to article 76, paragraph 8, of the United Nations Convention on the Law of the Sea of 10 December 1982," http://www.un.org/Depts/los/clcs_new/commission_submissions.htm.

9. People's Republic of China, "Note Verbale," UN Commission on the Limits of the Continental Shelf, May 7, 2009, http://www.un.org/Depts/los/clcs_new/submissions_files/mysvnm33_09/chn_2009re_mys_vnm_e.pdf. This map resembled one originally published by the Republic of China in 1947, which had eleven dashes, with two additional dashes extending north into the Gulf of Tonkin.

for its maritime economy, which included a continuation of efforts to develop oil and gas off its coast. China viewed these actions as a threat to its claims, and responded by threatening foreign oil companies investing in Vietnamese offshore exploration blocks (including several American companies).[10] In April 2007, Chinese and Vietnamese government ships clashed while a Chinese vessel sought to conduct a seismic survey in waters near the Paracel Islands.[11] In 2009 alone, China detained over four hundred Vietnamese fishermen who had ventured into the waters around the Paracel Islands, which China controls. In early 2010, several tense standoffs between Chinese and Vietnamese and Chinese and Indonesian government ships occurred in different parts of the South China Sea.[12]

At the same time, the frequency and scope of China's maritime naval activities increased. In 2008, a People's Liberation Army Navy (PLAN) task force conducted a training exercise in which it circumnavigated the South China Sea for the first time. In May 2009, Chinese vessels harassed the USNS *Impeccable*, an unarmed U.S. naval auxiliary, in waters approximately seventy-five miles from Hainan Island, questioning its right to conduct surveillance in the area. In 2010, the PLAN conducted three significant exercises in these waters, involving ships from all three fleets.[13]

THE UNITED STATES GETS INVOLVED

By 2010, the administration of U.S. president Barack Obama decided that growing tensions warranted a response. According to Jeff Bader, then Obama's senior adviser on Asia policy, the situation prompted the decision "that a new, more comprehensive articulation of U.S. policy was called for."[14] During the July 2010 meeting of the Association of Southeast Asian Nations (ASEAN) Regional Forum, the United States persuaded twelve other countries to express concern about the tensions in the South China Sea. Secretary of State Hillary Rodham Clinton also delivered a public statement of the U.S. position, the highest-level U.S. official ever to do so.[15] Clinton affirmed core elements of an earlier 1995 statement, including "a national interest in freedom of navigation," opposition to "the use or threat of force by any claimant," and a commitment to "not taking sides" in the competing territorial

10. Fravel, "China's Strategy in the South China Sea."

11. Scott Bentley, "Vietnam and China: A Dangerous Incident," *Diplomat*, February 12, 2014, http://thediplomat.com/2014/02/vietnam-and-china-a-dangerous-incident/.

12. Fravel, "China's Strategy in the South China Sea."

13. Ibid.

14. Jeffrey A. Bader, *Obama and China's Rise: An Insider's Account of America's Asia Strategy* (Washington, DC: Brookings Institution Press, 2012), 105.

15. U.S. Department of State, "Remarks at Press Availability," July 23, 2010, http://www.state.gov/secretary/20092013clinton/rm/2010/07/145095.htm.

claims. She also introduced new elements of U.S. policy, emphasizing the need to resolve disputes without coercion via a "collaborative diplomatic process" and articulating the position that "legitimate claims to maritime space in the South China Sea should be derived solely from legitimate claims to land features."[16]

The Clinton statement emphasized broadly accepted international principles relevant to maritime disputes. China was not mentioned by name, but several elements were clearly directed against China more than any other claimant. First, the language regarding "legitimate claims" suggested that the United States opposed any claim by China to maritime jurisdiction based on the nine-dash line on Chinese maps. Second, the emphasis on a "collaborative process" implied support for multilateral talks that stood in contrast to China's preference for dealing with each claimant bilaterally. Although the United States did not take a new position on the underlying sovereignty claims, it did take a position on the legitimacy of claims to maritime jurisdiction that states in the region could pursue and the process by which the dispute should be either managed or resolved. With the 2010 statement, the United States demonstrated that it planned to walk a fine line between maintaining neutrality on sovereignty with a greater involvement to help manage growing tensions.

The United States also indicated that it would become involved in another way: by strengthening ties with Vietnam. Since 2008, the two countries had held an annual political, security, and defense dialogue at the assistant secretary of state level. In 2009, a group of high-ranking Vietnamese defense officials boarded a U.S. aircraft carrier for the first time.[17] Later that year, two U.S. warships made port calls in Vietnam. In August 2010, the United States and Vietnam began to hold annual defense policy dialogues, which reflected a deepening of intermilitary relations. Part of these enhanced military relations included the initiation of what the Pentagon terms "naval engagement activities," a series of low-level exchanges and exercises. The inaugural event, held in August 2010, was noteworthy because a group of Vietnamese political and military leaders were flown to the aircraft carrier USS *George Washington* to observe its operations in the South China Sea.[18] In October 2010, while in Vietnam to attend the East Asia Summit, Clinton met with Vietnamese foreign minister Pham Gia Khiem and "reaffirmed our

16. For a review, see M. Taylor Fravel, *U.S. Policy towards the Disputes in the South China Sea since 1995* (Singapore: S. Rajaratnam School of International Studies, Nanyang Technological University, 2014).

17. Steve Owsley, "Vietnamese Ministry of Defense Officials Visit USS John C. Stennis," April 24, 2009, http://www.navy.mil/submit/display.asp?story_id=44660.

18. U.S. Seventh Fleet Public Affairs, "Seventh Fleet Kicks off Vietnam Naval Engagement Activities," August 9, 2010, http://www.navy.mil/submit/display.asp?story_id=55185.

shared interest in working toward a strategic partnership."[19] This phrase implied that relations might be elevated to a whole new level.

U.S. EMBOLDENMENT?

Overall, the evidence suggests that the United States did not embolden other states in the South China Sea disputes before 2010, though its increased involvement in 2010 likely had that effect (especially with the Philippines, as will be discussed in the next section). Brunei, Indonesia, and Malaysia all maintained very low profiles in the disputes before and after the United States changed its involvement in the South China Sea in July 2010. Vietnam was actively asserting its claims as early as 2006, which means that its behavior cannot be attributed to the 2010 Clinton statement. As was explained above, Vietnam's development of its offshore oil and gas fields in the South China Sea sparked a flurry of Chinese démarches between 2006 and 2008. In 2007, a flotilla of Vietnamese ships blocked a Chinese seismic survey vessel from operating in waters north of Triton Island in the Paracels.[20] Likewise, Vietnamese commercial fishing activity appeared to increase around the Paracel Islands in 2008, while Vietnam submitted two claims to the CLCS in 2009: one unilaterally, which encompassed part of the South China Sea south of the Paracel Islands, and one with Malaysia that encompassed part of the area in the Spratly Islands. Similarly, the Philippines had begun to assert its claims before U.S. involvement increased in July 2010, though not as actively as Vietnam. In November 2007, for example, the Philippine legislature began to debate a law on archipelagic baselines, which encompassed the land features Manila claimed in the South China Sea. The final version included Philippine claims to these features but dropped archipelagic baselines.[21]

After Clinton's statement in July 2010, however, Vietnam and the Philippines sought to increase international and especially American involvement. In October 2010, Vietnam began to give much greater international attention to the plight of Vietnamese fishermen who had been detained by China. Even greater publicity occurred after a China Marine Surveillance vessel severed the towed sonar array of a Vietnamese seismic survey vessel operating approximately one hundred nautical miles off the Vietnamese coast, well within Vietnam's exclusive economic zone. By contrast, the Vietnamese press had rarely commented in 2008 and 2009, when China detained hundreds of

19. U.S. Department of State, "Remarks with Vietnamese Foreign Minister Pham Gia Khiem," October 30, 2010, http://www.state.gov/secretary/20092013clinton/rm/2010/10/150189.htm.
20. Bentley, "Vietnam and China."
21. See Michael D. Swaine and M. Taylor Fravel, "China's Assertive Behavior—Part Two: The Maritime Periphery," *China Leadership Monitor* 35 (2011): appendix, 15–16.

Vietnamese fishermen, or in 2007, when China sought to conduct the seismic survey in waters claimed by Vietnam. Likewise, after two China Marine Surveillance vessels shadowed a Philippine survey vessel in 2011, the Philippines began to speak out. Invoking language used by Clinton in 2010, Secretary of Foreign Affairs Albert F. Del Rosario called for a "rules-based approach" toward the disputes under the framework provided by the UN Convention on the Law of the Sea (UNCLOS).[22] In June 2011, in the context of the disputes in the South China Sea, Philippine president Benigno Aquino invoked the role of the United States, stating, "Perhaps the presence of our treaty partner which is the United States of America ensures that all of us will have freedom of navigation, will conform to international law."[23] That summer, the Philippines renamed the South China Sea as the West Philippine Sea.[24]

CHINA MODERATES ITS APPROACH

The potential for even greater U.S. involvement in the dispute attracted China's attention, suggesting that U.S. coercive diplomacy successfully moderated China's policy during this period. In late June 2011, a spokesperson for the Chinese Ministry of Foreign Affairs stated that the South China Sea disputes were "a matter for the directly concerned parties [and] should be resolved through direct negotiation and friendly consultation by them," adding, "We hope the nonparties respect the concerned parties' efforts to settle disputes peacefully through bilateral dialogue."[25] Cui Tiankai, then vice foreign minister, was even more blunt: "The United States is not a claimant state to the dispute. . . . So it is better for the United States to leave the dispute to be sorted out between the claimant states." Cui further issued a warning: "I believe the individual countries are actually playing with fire, and I hope the fire will not be drawn to the United States."[26]

Accordingly, heading into the July 2011 meeting of the ASEAN Regional Forum (ARF), China wanted to prevent the United States from playing an

22. Albert F. Del Rosario, "A Rules-Based Regime in the South China Sea," *Philippine Star*, June 7, 2011.

23. Johanna Paola D. Poblete, "Aquino Welcomes US Support on Maritime Row with China," *Business World Online*, June 15, 2011, http://www.bworldonline.com/content.php?section=Nation&title=Aquino-welcomes-US-support-on-maritime-row-with-China&id=33112.

24. ABS-CBN News, "PH to call South China Sea 'West Philippine Sea,'" June 13, 2011, http://news.abs-cbn.com/nation/06/13/11/ph-call-south-china-sea-'west-philippine-sea'.

25. Ministry of Foreign Affairs of the People's Republic of China, "Foreign Ministry Spokesperson Hua Chunying's Regular Press Conference," June 28, 2011.

26. Edward Wong, "Beijing Warns U.S. about South China Sea Disputes," *New York Times*, June 22, 2011.

increased role and limit discussion of the South China Sea. One day before the meeting, the solution was announced: an agreement between China and ASEAN on implementing guidelines for the 2002 Declaration on the Conduct of Parties in the South China Sea (DOC).[27] The agreement itself was vague and lacked substance, but it reflected a desire by both parties to reduce tensions and to restart a diplomatic process to address tensions. In particular, the signing of the agreement just before the ARF helped to pre-empt discussion of the South China Sea, which supported Beijing's goal of limiting internationalization of the disputes. Despite its vagueness, U.S. diplomats saw the agreement as a sign of progress. As Assistant Secretary of State Kurt Campbell remarked, "We welcome this. It's an important first step . . . I think it has lowered tensions. It has improved atmospherics."[28] In this way, U.S. diplomacy and China's desire to limit further involvement of the United Stated helped to promote limited cooperation with other claimants.

Following the agreement on guiding principles, China adopted a posture toward the South China Sea that was generally much more moderate. China's efforts at moderation included reaffirming Deng Xiaoping's idea of "setting aside disputes and pursuing joint development," reaching an agreement with Vietnam on basic principles for resolving maritime disputes, and creating a ¥3 billion (US$476 million) China-ASEAN Maritime Cooperation Fund. China hosted several workshops on oceanography and freedom of navigation in the South China Sea in December 2011, and also a meeting with senior ASEAN officials to discuss implementing the 2002 DOC in January 2012. Finally, it halted the assertive behaviors that had attracted so much adverse attention between 2009 and 2011. Vessels from the Bureau of Fisheries Administration detained and held only two Vietnamese fishing vessels between late 2010 and March 2012. Patrol ships from the State Oceanographic Administration did not interfere with Vietnamese or Philippine hydrocarbon exploration activities after May 2011.[29] More generally, China did not obstruct other exploration activities, such as ExxonMobil's successful drilling of an exploratory well in Vietnamese waters claimed by China in October 2011.[30]

27. Qin Jize and Cui Haipei, "Guidelines Agreed with ASEAN on Sea Disputes," *China Daily*, July 21, 2011.

28. VOA, News, "Clinton Welcomes South China Sea Guidelines," July 22, 2011, http://www.voanews.com/a/clinton-welcomes-south-china-sea-guidelines-126002064/142592.html.

29. The only exception is an incident in December 2012, when two Chinese fishing vessels severed the towed sonar array of a Vietnamese ship. See Jeremy Page, "Vietnam Accuses Chinese Ships," *Wall Street Journal*, December 3, 2012.

30. This paragraph summarizes M. Taylor Fravel, "All Quiet in the South China Sea: Why China Is Playing Nice (For Now)," *Foreign Affairs*, March 22, 2012.

Mid-2011 to Mid-2012: U.S. Pivot, Philippine Assertiveness, and Chinese Pushback

The reduction in tensions in the South China Sea collapsed when a standoff erupted between China and the Philippines over the control of Scarborough Shoal. The U.S. pivot to Asia likely encouraged the Philippines to assert its own claims even more vigorously than before. As its moderation in 2011 neither assuaged other claimants nor reduced the demand from states in the region for greater U.S. involvement, China had strong incentives to take new actions to consolidate its claims in the first half of 2012, such as seizing control of the shoal and establishing Sansha City.

THE UNITED STATES PIVOTS AMID THE DISPUTES

Looking back, 2011 was a turning point in U.S.-Philippine relations. In January of that year, the United States and the Philippines held for the first time a "bilateral strategic dialogue" involving senior officials from the U.S. State Department. According to Campbell, one purpose of the talks was to discuss how to "increase the Philippines' maritime capacity" to patrol its waters.[31] In May 2011, the United States agreed to sell the Philippines a decommissioned Hamilton-class coast guard cutter, which became the flagship of the fledging Philippine navy, the BRP *Gregorio del Pilar*.

In the fall of 2011, the United States rolled out the pivot to Asia. Secretary of State Clinton fired the opening salvo in an article in *Foreign Policy* in October 2011, followed by President Obama's speech before Australia's parliament in November 2011. Both sets of remarks highlighted the disputes in the South China Sea as a key issue to be addressed in the region. The South China Sea featured even more prominently in President Obama's participation in the Sixth East Asia Summit in early November 2011, which marked the first time that a U.S. president had attended the gathering. In addition, Australia, India, Malaysia, the Philippines, Thailand, and Vietnam raised the issue of the South China Sea directly, while seven more states expressed concern about maritime security, presumably in the South China Sea.[32] In this way the United States encouraged other states to voice their concerns and may have suggested that it would be willing to back these states in their disputes with China.

Amid the early momentum of the pivot, the United States and the Philippines held a high-profile commemoration of the sixtieth anniversary of the alliance. The centerpiece was the signing of the Manila Declaration aboard

31. Agence France-Presse, "US Pledges Help for Philippine Navy," January 27, 2011.
32. Damian Grammaticas, "Obama's Victory over China?," November 21, 2011, http://www.bbc.com/news/world-asia-china-15818863.

the USS *Fitzgerald*, an Arleigh Burke–class destroyer, in Manila Bay. The declaration reaffirmed the 1951 treaty as the basis of the bilateral relationship, referring to cooperation in the area of maritime security, shared interests in freedom of navigation, the peaceful resolution of disputes, and the pursuit of "collaborative, multilateral and diplomatic processes." Secretary of State Clinton offered a strong statement of support that could have been viewed as increasing the U.S. commitment to the Philippines. In a reference to Philippine boxing champion Manny Pacquino, Clinton stated, "Let me say the United States will always be in the corner of the Philippines. We will always stand and fight with you to achieve the future we seek."[33] Moreover, Clinton used the Philippine name for the South China Sea, the "West Philippine Sea," when describing U.S. policy, creating a perception in the region of greater U.S. support for the Philippines. Finally, in January 2012, a second bilateral strategic dialogue was held, further deepening the U.S.-Philippines relationship. It was announced that the United States intended to transfer a second decommissioned Coast Guard cutter to the Philippine Navy.[34]

THE STANDOFF AT SCARBOROUGH SHOAL

In early April 2012 a Philippine naval ship was dispatched to investigate reports of fishing boats inside Scarborough Shoal, a coral reef approximately 135 miles from the Philippines and 543 miles from China. Philippine soldiers searched the boats and discovered that Chinese fishermen were harvesting giant clams and other marine animals in violation of Philippine law. As the Philippines prepared to arrest the fishermen, two China Marine Surveillance vessels arrived to block the sole entrance to the shoal, thus preventing the arrest. A standoff ensued over the next three months, as both China and the Philippines used government ships to contest control of the shoal and adjacent waters.

Given U.S. diplomacy in previous months, Manila may have concluded that it would be backed by the United States if it challenged China or, alternatively, that by challenging China it could further elicit even more direct intervention from the United States. At the same time, China concluded that the United States had emboldened the Philippines. According to a Xinhua commentary written just days after the incident, "a handful of countries in the past two years have sought to use the backing of external forces to behave in excess of what is proper in the South China Sea." Moreover,

33. U.S. Department of State, "Clinton, Philippine Foreign Secretary Joint Press Availability," November 16, 2011, http://iipdigital.usembassy.gov/st/english/texttrans/2011/11/20111116142331su0.4998852.html.

34. U.S. Department of State, "Toward a Deeper Alliance: United States–Philippines Bilateral Cooperation," January 27, 2012, http://www.state.gov/r/pa/prs/ps/2012/01/182689.htm.

"countries surrounding the South China Sea, including the Philippines, have vowed to conform to the DOC, while resorting to outsiders instead of bilateral talks in their efforts to resolve disputes in the region." Finally, the commentary concluded that involvement by "outsiders" was designed "to tilt the regional balance in their favor."[35]

Nevertheless, the United States appears to have tried to restrain the Philippines or at least not encourage it to take stronger actions. During the first U.S.-Philippines 2+2 ministerial meeting of secretaries of defense and foreign affairs at the end of April, the United States did not alter its South China Sea policy in response to the standoff. Instead, Secretary Clinton opened her remarks on the South China Sea by underscoring that "we do not take sides on the competing sovereignty claims to land features in the South China Sea."[36] Likewise, when President Aquino met with President Obama in early May, Obama did not refer to Scarborough Shoal in his public remarks, and restated the U.S. commitment to developing strong international rules and norms governing maritime disputes in the region.[37] In early June, the United States also actively tried to broker an end to the standoff through a mutual disengagement of government ships from the shoal when Vice Foreign Minister Fu Ying met with Campbell.[38] On June 16, with reports of bad weather approaching the area, the Philippines removed its two ships in the waters around the shoal.[39] Although China may have also removed some ships, they had returned a week later, leaving China in control of the shoal.[40]

In the standoff, the United States chose to accept the outcome of China's assertiveness. The attempt to broker a return to the status quo ante failed. Nevertheless, when Chinese ships returned, the United States did not attempt to compel the Chinese ships to leave. China's use of fishing vessels and government ships left the United States with the uncomfortable choice between escalating its involvement in the dispute, and thus potentially tak-

35. Wu Liming, "Commentary: Do Not Deliberately Create Disputes on Issue of South China Sea," April 12, 2012, http://news.xinhuanet.com/english/china/2012-04/12/c_122970436.htm.

36. U.S. Department of State, "Remarks with Secretary of Defense Leon Panetta, Philippines Foreign Secretary Albert del Rosario, and Philippines Defense Secretary Voltaire Gazmin after Their Meeting," April 30, 2012, http://www.state.gov/secretary/20092013clinton/rm/2012/04/188982.htm.

37. White House, "Remarks by President Obama and President Aquino of the Philippines after Bilateral Meeting," June 8, 2012, http://www.whitehouse.gov/the-press-office/2012/06/08/remarks-president-obama-and-president-aquino-philippines-after-bilateral.

38. Geoff Dyer and Demetri Sevastopulo, "US Strategists Face Dilemma over Beijing Claim in South China Sea," *Financial Times*, July 9, 2014.

39. Reuters, "Philippines Pulls Ships from Disputed Shoal Due to Weather," June 16, 2012.

40. ABS-CBN News, "Chinese Ships Seen Anew at Scarborough," June 23, 2012, http://www.abs-cbnnews.com/nation/06/23/12/chinese-ships-seen-anew-scarborough.

ing sides with the Philippines, or a de facto acceptance of China's control of the shoal.

CONTINUED CHINESE ASSERTIVENESS AFTER SCARBOROUGH

After the Scarborough Shoal standoff, China continued to assert its claims in the South China Sea, which threatened the position of other claimants. In mid-June 2012, the State Council announced the elevation of the Sansha administrative office from a county-level unit to a prefectural-level city.[41] The following week, the state-owned Chinese National Offshore Oil Corporation (CNOOC) invited bids from international companies for nine exploration blocks in the middle portion of the South China Sea.[42] A few weeks later, the State Oceanic Administration dispatched four vessels on a training exercise to the middle and southern portion of the sea to demonstrate China's claims.[43] In early July, a fleet of thirty fishing vessels conducted a two-week cruise in the Spratly Islands to fish at Chinese-held reefs.[44] Also in July 2012, China used its influence over Cambodia, then holding the ASEAN chair, to prevent direct references to Scarborough Shoal from being included in an ASEAN joint communiqué. Exercising its power as chair, Cambodia decided that for the first time in forty-five years no communiqué would be issued.[45] China's meddling posed a threat to the unity of ASEAN as a whole. Finally, in July 2012, China established a division-level military garrison in Sansha City, complementing the Paracels maritime garrison under the South Sea Fleet.[46]

China continued to press its claims for several reasons. First, Chinese leaders may have concluded that the moderate approach from mid-2011 had failed to assuage the concerns of all claimants and reduce what Beijing viewed as challenges to its claims. In particular, the Philippines conducted very active and public diplomacy regarding its claims despite China's shift to a more moderate approach, including pushing for proposals that China viewed as harming its claims at the 2011 East Asia Summit, attempting to

---

41. Xinhua News Agency, "China Raises Administrative Status of South China Sea Islands," June 21, 2012.

42. M. Taylor Fravel, "The South China Sea Oil Card," *Diplomat*, June 27, 2012.

43. Xinhua News Agency, "Chinese Patrol Ships Reach Nansha Islands," July 4, 2012.

44. Huang Yiming and Jin Haixing, "Fishing Vessels Set Off for Nansha Islands," *China Daily*, July 13, 2012.

45. Agence France-Presse, "ASEAN Talks Fail over China Dispute," July 13, 2012, http:// www.abs-cbnnews.com/global-filipino/world/07/13/12/southeast-asian-summit-breaks -acrimony; Ian Storey, "China Pushes on the South China Sea, ASEAN Unity Collapses," *China Brief* 12, no. 15 (2012), http://www.jamestown.org/programs/chinabrief/single/?tx _ttnews%5Btt_news%5D=39728&cHash=7bf80ace68960cfc12b6edf8f11556fd.

46. Dennis J. Blasko and M. Taylor Fravel, "Much Ado about the Sansha Garrison," *Diplomat*, August 23, 2012.

persuade ASEAN in April 2012 to negotiate a code of conduct without China, and seeking international support during the standoff at Scarborough Shoal. At the ASEAN ministerial meeting in July 2012, the Philippines sought to include a direct reference to the Scarborough standoff in the joint communiqué, which prompted China's interference.[47]

Second, although China managed to improve ties with Vietnam during this time period, several Vietnamese actions in June 2012 probably strengthened the argument in China for a return to a more assertive approach. These included Vietnam's first patrol of the islands with advanced Su-27 Flanker fighter aircraft flying as low as five hundred meters over disputed features and its National Assembly's passage of a maritime law that affirmed Vietnam's claims over the Paracels and Spratlys.[48] These actions were largely symbolic, but may have nevertheless given China stronger incentives to consolidate its claims. Secretary of Defense Leon Panetta's early June 2012 trip to Vietnam may have also suggested even greater U.S. support for Vietnam, provoking a more assertive approach by Beijing.

Mid-2012 to 2013: U.S. Pushback, Mutual Restraint

Following resistance from the United States and ASEAN after the Scarborough standoff, China and the United States exercised restraint in the South China Sea in 2013. China indicated a renewed interest in holding consultations with ASEAN states while engaging Brunei and Vietnam. The United States refrained from raising the issue as frequently as it had before.

U.S. AND ASEAN PUSHBACK

If the United States had acted to restrain the Philippines during the Scarborough standoff, it altered its policy in August 2012 after ASEAN failed to issue a joint communiqué. In response, the United States issued another policy statement on the South China Sea. Unlike past statements, this one explicitly identified China as escalating tensions. Specifically, it referred to "the use of barriers to deny access" to the shoal that China had erected at the end of June and noted that "China's upgrading of the administrative level of Sansha City and establishment of a new military garrison there covering disputed areas of the South China Sea run counter to collaborative diplomatic efforts to resolve differences and risk further escalating tensions in the

---

47. Manuel Mogato and Stuart Grudgings, "'ASEAN Way' Founders in South China Sea Storm," July 17, 2012, http://www.reuters.com/article/us-asean-china-idUSBRE86G09N20120717.

48. "Vietnam to Conduct Regular Air Patrols over Archipelago," *Thannien News*, June 20, 2012; "Vietnam Passes Law to Protect Sea and Islands," *Thannien News*, June 22, 2012.

region."[49] As a result, the United States appeared to embrace much more active involvement in the dispute, potentially abandoning neutrality by calling out China.

At the same time, China's actions prompted redoubled efforts within ASEAN to reach agreement on a code of conduct. In early July 2012, before the debacle involving the failed joint statement, the ASEAN Senior Officials Meeting Working Group on the Code of Conduct held its seventh meeting. The main result was that ASEAN reached agreement on elements that should be part of a code of conduct to be negotiated with China.[50] After the failure to issue a joint statement in July, Indonesia's foreign minister led an effort to restore unity within ASEAN, which resulted in a six-point statement on the South China Sea.

In November 2012, the South China Sea remained a contentious issue at the East Asia Summit. President Obama reiterated U.S. policy and "encouraged the parties to make progress on a binding code of conduct in the South China Sea to provide a framework to prevent conflict, manage incidents when they occur, and help resolve disputes."[51] Before the summit, China attempted to keep the disputes off the agenda. In October 2012, Vice Foreign Minister Fu Ying chastised ASEAN states for "internationalizing" the dispute by raising the issue with nonclaimant states such as the United States. She also said that other claimants should not engage in multilateral talks, raise the disputes with nonclaimants like the United States, engage in media interviews, or take action at the United Nations.[52] China also suspended efforts to continue dialogue on a code of conduct that had started in the fall of 2011. In November 2012, Fu indicated that a code of conduct could only be discussed if the DOC was fully implemented, meaning if other states exercised "self-restraint" and stopped challenging China.[53]

CHINESE AND U.S. MODERATION

By the spring of 2013, China moved back to a more moderate approach. In early April, China announced that it wanted to restart stalled talks with

49. U.S. Department of State, "South China Sea," August 3, 2012, http://www.state.gov/r/pa/prs/ps/2012/08/196022.htm.

50. Carlyle A. Thayer, "ASEAN'S Code of Conduct in the South China Sea: A Litmus Test for Community-Building?," *Asia-Pacific Journal: Japan Focus* 10, issue 34, no. 4 (2012), http://apjjf.org/2012/10/34/Carlyle-A.-Thayer/3813/article.html.

51. White House, "Fact Sheet: East Asia Summit Outcomes," November 20, 2012, http://www.whitehouse.gov/the-press-office/2012/11/20/fact-sheet-east-asia-summit-outcomes.

52. Greg Torode, "China 'Dictatorial' in Scarborough Shoal Disputes, Says Albert del Rosario," *South China Morning Post*, November 30, 2012.

53. Fu Ying, "Carry Forward the Spirit of the DOC and Promote Peace and Stability," November 2, 2012, http://brisbane.chineseconsulate.org/eng/zgxw/t984572.htm.

ASEAN over a binding code of conduct.[54] The action was most likely taken in response to the Philippines' move to launch an arbitral tribunal under UN-CLOS on China's claims in the South China Sea in January 2013.[55] During the July 2013 ARF meeting, Chinese foreign minister Wang Yi announced that China-ASEAN talks at the senior official and working group levels would be held to discuss how to pursue a code of conduct.[56] Talks held in mid-September produced a road map for further discussions for 2013–14 and the creation of an eminent persons group to discuss the issue.

In addition, China pursued a more balanced approach toward Vietnam. In early June 2013, defense ministries in each country agreed to establish a hotline between their navies.[57] In mid-June, during President Truong Tan Sang's visit to China, Vietnam and China agreed to establish a hotline between their fisheries departments in addition to resuming talks on the demarcation of the mouth of the Tonkin (Beibu) Gulf and pursuing a political settlement in the South China Sea.[58] In October 2013, during Premier Li Keqiang's visit to Vietnam, the two countries agreed to establish a joint working group on maritime development.

China also pursued joint development agreements with Brunei. In April 2013, China and Brunei agreed "to carry out joint exploration and exploitation of maritime oil and gas resources."[59] In October 2013, CNOOC and Brunei's state-owned oil company agreed to set up an oilfield services joint venture.[60]

Finally, China's top leaders signaled the importance of limiting the potential for the disputes to harm ties with these countries. During a meeting on maritime affairs at the end of July 2013, President Xi Jinping indicated that China might pursue a more moderate approach, affirming Deng Xiaoping's guidance for managing offshore island disputes by "setting aside disputes and pursuing joint development" while also underscoring the need to coor-

54. Agence France-Presse, "ASEAN, China to Meet on Maritime Code of Conduct," April 11, 2013.

55. Philippines Department of Foreign Affairs, "Statement: The Secretary of Foreign Affairs on the UNCLOS Arbitral Proceedings against China,", January 22, 2013.

56. Ministry of Foreign Affairs of the People's Republic of China, "Wang Yi Stressed that the South China Sea Issue Should Be Resolved by Parties Directly Concerned through Negotiation," July 2, 2013, http://www.fmprc.gov.cn/eng/zxxx/t1055452.shtml.

57. Pu Zhendong and Zhang Yunbi, "China, Vietnam Set Up Naval Hotline," *China Daily*, June 7, 2013.

58. Xinhua News Agency, "China, Vietnam Agree to Maintain Maritime Dialogues," June 21, 2013.

59. Ministry of Foreign Affairs of the People's Republic of China, "Joint Statement between the People's Republic of China and Brunei Darussalam," April 5, 2013, http://www.fmprc.gov.cn/mfa_eng/wjdt_665385/2649_665393/t1029400.shtml.

60. China National Offshore Oil Company, "CNOOC and Petroleum Brunei Sign Agreement on Setting up Joint Venture," October 14, 2013.

dinate "rights defense" in the maritime domain with the maintenance of stability.[61] In September and October 2013, Xi Jinping and Li Keqiang visited the region before attending a meeting of the Asia-Pacific Economic Cooperation organization (APEC) and the East Asia Summit, respectively. Taken together, they visited half of the members of ASEAN and four of the five claimants in the South China Sea: Brunei, Indonesia, Malaysia, Thailand, and Vietnam. During a speech before Indonesia's parliament, Xi called for China and ASEAN to build a "maritime Silk Road."[62] Finally, in October, China's top leaders held an unprecedented meeting on regional diplomacy, which was attended by all seven members of the Politburo Standing Committee and lasted for two days.[63] The main theme of Xi's speech was the importance of "maintaining a stable external environment," downplaying China's sovereignty disputes and making no reference to maritime affairs.

This second phase of moderation, however, excluded the Philippines. China remained opposed to the arbitration process that Manila began in January 2013 and essentially froze diplomatic relations with the country to persuade it to drop the case. After taking office in March 2013, Wang Yi, China's foreign minister, soon met at least once with each of his counterparts from all ASEAN states except for the Philippines. In May and June 2013, China dispatched government ships to monitor a Philippine outpost on Second Thomas Shoal, at times preventing Philippine efforts to resupply the garrison located there.[64] In August 2013 President Aquino was disinvited from an ASEAN-China trade fair.

U.S. policy cannot account fully for the second period of moderation. The reaction of the ASEAN states after the failure to issue a joint communiqué in July 2012 is equally important. When Brunei assumed the chairmanship in 2013, progress on the code of conduct was high on ASEAN's agenda. The Philippines' decision to pursue arbitration also increased incentives for China to make progress on the negotiations on the code to isolate Manila within ASEAN and limit support for arbitration. Nevertheless, clear support for the code of conduct from the United States, and the potential for many ASEAN states to deepen ties with Washington as tensions in the disputes increased, was also an important factor. After all, a stable external environment is one

61. M. Taylor Fravel, "Xi Jinping's Overlooked Revelation on China's Maritime Disputes," *Diplomat*, August 15, 2013.

62. Wu Jiao and Zhang Yunbi, "Xi in Call for Building of New 'Maritime Silk Road,'" *China Daily*, October 4, 2013.

63. "Xin Jinping zai zhoubian waijiao gongzuo zuotanhui shang fabiao zhongyao jianghua" [Xi Jinping's important remarks at the forum on peripheral diplomacy], *Renmin Ribao*, October 25, 2013.

64. Manuel Mogato, "South China Sea Tension Mounts near Filipino Shipwreck," May 29, 2013, http://www.reuters.com/article/us-philippines-china-idUSBRE94R0YS20130529.

in which other great powers do not have better relations with China's neighbors than China, thus increasing the influence of the great powers near China's borders.

Notably, the United States also lowered its public rhetoric on the dispute. During a major address on Asia policy in March 2013, for example, National Security Adviser Tom Donilon made no mention of the disputes in the South China Sea and offered only a few general references to maritime security.[65] Secretary of State John Kerry made no detailed statement on the South China Sea until July 2013, during a U.S.-ASEAN meeting just before the 2013 meeting of the ARF.[66] Similarly, although the South China Sea was discussed during the "shirt-sleeves" summit at the Sunnylands estate in California between Obama and Xi, it was not mentioned in any of the public statements.

Mid-2013 to 2014: Philippine Challenges, Chinese Pushback, Regional Blowback

Most likely in response to the Philippine decision to pursue arbitration and the tightening of the U.S.-Philippines alliance, China in early 2014 began to build artificial islands atop the seven reefs and rocks it controls in the Spratly Islands. In a surprising move, China also deployed a drilling rig to waters disputed with Vietnam in May 2014. These actions occurred against the backdrop of China's establishment of the Air Defense Identification Zone (ADIZ) in the East China Sea in November 2013, which signaled China's determination to defend its maritime claims, even if such actions risked escalation. China's actions alarmed states in the region and galvanized greater U.S. involvement in the disputes, as well as deeper ties with other claimants—especially Vietnam and the Philippines. China engaged in damage control in the second half of 2014, but continued with land reclamation.

PHILIPPINE CHALLENGES TO CHINA

China's decision to initiate large-scale land reclamation in the Spratly Islands was perhaps the boldest and most consequential action it has taken in the dispute since occupying six features and clashing violently with Vietnam in early 1988. Why China might have chosen to start land reclamation in early 2014 may have been in response to two challenges from the Philippines, which likely hardened a Chinese perception that the disputes would

65. Tom Donilon, "The United States and the Asia-Pacific in 2013," March 13, 2013, http://www.whitehouse.gov/the-press-office/2013/03/11/remarks-tom-donilon-national-security-advisory-president-united-states-a.

66. U.S. Department of State, "Remarks at the U.S.-ASEAN Ministerial Meeting," July 1, 2013.

persist for a very long time and that China would need to consolidate its physical control of contested features it occupied.

The first Philippine action was a decision to pursue arbitration to challenge China's claims. In January 2013, Manila initiated arbitral proceedings under Article 297 of UNCLOS when it submitted a Notification and Statement of Claim to China. The notification questioned the legality of China's nine-dash line and the maritime entitlements from land features held by China, among other complaints. In February 2013, China announced its rejection of the proceedings, noting that they violated the 2002 DOC, and called on the Philippines to pursue bilateral talks.[67] China continued to oppose arbitration throughout the spring of 2013, but failed to prevent the process from moving forward. By the end of June, the president of the International Tribunal for the Law of the Sea had formed a panel of five judges.[68] In July 2013, the tribunal met and began drafting rules of procedure and a timetable for the proceedings. At the end of July, China repeated its opposition in a note verbale to the tribunal, emphasizing "its position that it does not accept the arbitration initiated by the Philippines."[69] Yet at the end of August 2013, the tribunal issued its rules of procedure and called for the submission of memorials by March 30, 2014. In sum, China was unable to prevent an international legal process that threatened to undermine some of its claims in the dispute.

Second, when the tribunal issued its timetable for the proceedings, the United States and the Philippines began talks to widen U.S. access to bases in the Philippines. The focus of the talks would include increasing the rotational presence of U.S. forces in the Philippines—especially air and naval forces. From the Philippine perspective, an enhanced U.S. presence would help to deter China. Manila's goal was "an arrangement that will help the country achieve a minimum credible defense amid territorial threats and boost the modernization plan for the armed forces."[70] The talks progressed rapidly and, after eight rounds, an agreement was signed when President Obama visited Manila in late April 2014. The title, Enhanced Defense Cooperation Agreement (EDCA), reflected the deepening of the alliance and

67. People's Republic of China, *Note Verbale from the Embassy of the People's Republic of China in Manila to the Department of Foreign Affairs of the Republic of the Philippines*, February 19, 2013, https://assets.documentcloud.org/documents/2165478/phl-prc-china-note-verbale.pdf.

68. Tarra Quismundo, "Panel to Hear PH Case vs. China Now Complete," *Philippine Daily Inquirer*, June 26, 2013.

69. Permanent Court of Arbitration, "Award on Jurisdiction and Admissibility," PCA Case no. 2013-19, October 29, 2015, 17.

70. Philippines Department of National Defense, "Philippine Panel Discusses First Round of Talks with US on Increased Rotational Presence," August 15, 2013, http://www.dnd.gov.ph/philippine-panel-discusses-first-round-of-talks-with-us-on-increased-rotational-presence.html.

created a framework for greater U.S. access and presence in the Philippines. Taken together, the tribunal raised the prospect of delegitimating some of China's claims, while the tightening of the alliance and the EDCA negotiations had the potential to strengthen considerably the state using arbitration to challenge China's claims.

THE EAST CHINA SEA ADIZ AND THE HARDENING OF THE U.S. POSITION

China's November 2013 declaration of the East China Sea ADIZ reverberated in the South China Sea. The action heightened U.S. and regional concerns about Chinese intentions by underscoring China's willingness to assert its maritime claims through unilateral actions that risked escalation. It also raised concerns that China might do the same in the South China Sea, as the Chinese Ministry of Defense noted that "China will establish other air defense identification zones at an appropriate time after completing preparations."[71] Just a few weeks after the ADIZ announcement, Hainan Province updated its fishing regulations, and this was viewed as yet another unilateral effort to increase control over disputed areas.[72] Finally, in December, a near collision between the USS *Cowpens* and a Chinese naval escort increased tensions between the United States and China in the waters of the South China Sea.[73]

All these actions put pressure on the United States to respond in order to demonstrate its commitment to regional stability. A State Department spokesperson described the ADIZ as "a highly provocative act by the Chinese to unilaterally change the status quo."[74] The United States said it would not recognize or accept the new ADIZ and called on China not to implement it. Similarly, the United States described Hainan's revised fishing regulations as "provocative and potentially dangerous." From Beijing's perspective, of course, these statements increased U.S. involvement in the disputes, in contrast to the lower profile adopted by Washington beginning in late 2012. In response, a Xinhua commentary criticized the United States for "resorting to the old trick of 'divide and rule'" by stirring up tensions and then stepping in "to pose as 'mediator' or 'judge' in a bid to maximize its own interests."[75]

71. Xinhua News Agency, "China Exclusive: Defense Ministry Spokesman Responds to Air Defense Identification Zone Questions," November 23, 2013.
72. M. Taylor Fravel, "Hainan's New Fishing Rules: A Preliminary Analysis," *Diplomat*, January 10, 2014.
73. Jon Harper, "Chinese Warship Nearly Collided with USS Cowpens," *Stars and Stripes*, December 13, 2013.
74. U.S. Department of State, "Daily Press Briefing," December 3, 2013, http://www.state.gov/r/pa/prs/dpb/2013/12/218257.htm.
75. Wu Liming, "Commentary: Be Alert to U.S. Hidden Agenda in South China Sea," January 10, 2014, http://news.xinhuanet.com/english/indepth/2014-01/10/c_133035521.htm.

The U.S. position further hardened in early February 2014 after reports surfaced indicating that China might establish an ADIZ in the South China Sea. In late January 2014, a senior member of the U.S. National Security Council staff, Evan Medeiros, stated that the United States would oppose China's establishment of an ADIZ in the South China Sea, noting that it would be viewed "as a provocative and destabilizing development that would result in changes in our presence and military posture in the region."[76] The following week, Assistant Secretary of State Daniel Russel stated that China's actions since 2012 had "raised tensions in the region" and reflected "an incremental effort by China to assert control over the area contained in the so-called 'nine-dash line.'"[77] He then stated that "any use of the 'nine-dash line' by China to claim maritime rights not based on claimed land features would be inconsistent with international law." Russel expressed support for the Philippine decision to pursue arbitration with China and described it as an example of solving disputes in a peaceful, noncoercive way, thereby further linking the United States to the Philippines' position in its dispute with China.

Finally, when President Obama visited Asia in April 2014, the United States underscored its resolve to stay involved in China's maritime disputes. In addition to South Korea, Obama visited three countries involved in disputes with China. In Tokyo, he became the first sitting U.S. president to affirm publicly that Article V of the U.S.-Japan Alliance covered the Diaoyu/Senkaku Islands, underscoring the U.S. role in one of China's other maritime disputes. Obama also became the first U.S. president to visit Malaysia in almost fifty years. The joint statement issued with Prime Minister Najib Razak emphasized maritime security cooperation and "the importance of all parties concerned resolving their territorial and maritime disputes through peaceful means, including international arbitration."[78] In the Philippines, in addition to signing the Enhanced Defense Cooperation Agreement, President Obama declared in a speech to U.S. and Philippine forces that "our commitment to defend the Philippines is ironclad."[79]

76. Kyodo News, "U.S. 'Could Change Military Posture' if China Sets Up Second ADIZ," February 1, 2012.

77. Daniel R. Russel, "Maritime Disputes in East Asia," February 5, 2014, http://www.state.gov/p/eap/rls/rm/2014/02/221293.htm.

78. White House, "Joint Statement by President Obama And Prime Minister Najib Of Malaysia," April 27, 2014, https://www.whitehouse.gov/the-press-office/2014/04/27/joint-statement-president-obama-and-prime-minister-najib-malaysia-0.

79. White House, "Remarks by President Obama to Filipino and U.S. Armed Forces at Fort Bonifacio," April 28, 2014, https://www.whitehouse.gov/the-press-office/2014/04/28/remarks-president-obama-filipino-and-us-armed-forces-fort-bonifacio.

CHINA PUSHES BACK

In early 2014, China launched what would become a large-scale effort to build artificial islands atop all seven features it occupied in the Spratly Islands. Land reclamation at Johnson South Reef began in January 2014, followed by Cuarteron and Hughes Reefs in March and Gaven Reef in June. Then, in August, China began a much larger effort to transform Fiery Cross Reef into an airfield and harbor.[80] The start of land reclamation in early 2014 suggests it was most likely a response to the Philippine decision to pursue arbitration and the tightening of the U.S.-Philippines alliance through the EDCA negotiations. The arbitration reflected a direct challenge to China's claims, while an increased rotational troop presence would clearly bolster the U.S. presence in the South China Sea and support the state's challenging China's claims in court. By greatly expanding China's physical presence, the construction of artificial islands reflected China's resolve to defend its claims and consolidate its material position in the Spratlys, regardless of the tribunal's finding.

In addition to its reclamation efforts, in May 2014 China announced that its largest and most advanced drilling rig, the HYSY 981, would drill in waters near the Paracel Islands for two and a half months. Although close to Chinese-controlled Triton Island, the rig was also within the two hundred nautical miles of Vietnam's exclusive economic zone. China dispatched a fleet of coast guard, oil service, and fishing boats to protect the rig, while Vietnamese coast guard and other government ships sought to block the rig's deployment and disrupt its drilling operations. Anti-Chinese protests also erupted in Vietnam. Although planning for the rig's deployment occurred much earlier in 2014, if not before, the final decision to move forward would have occurred amid the tougher position adopted by the United States.[81]

The deployment of HYSY 981 greatly worsened ties between China and Vietnam while also alarming the region more generally, as it occurred just as the region became increasingly aware of the extent of China's land reclamation efforts. The crisis over the rig prompted ASEAN's foreign ministers to issue a rare statement on May 10, 2014, to express "serious concerns over on-going developments in the South China Sea, which have increased tensions in the area."[82] In June, the United States floated the idea of a volun-

80. Office of the Secretary of Defense, *Annual Report to Congress: Military and Security Developments Involving the People's Republic of China 2016*, April 2016, 14–20.

81. Erica S. Downs, "Business and Politics in the South China Sea: Explaining HYSY 981's Foray into Disputed Waters," *China Brief* 14, no. 12 (2014), http://www.jamestown.org/programs/chinabrief/single/?tx_ttnews%5Btt_news%5D=42519&tx_ttnews%5BbackPid%5D=758&no_cache=1.

82. Association of Southeast Asian Nations, "ASEAN Foreign Ministers' Statement on the Current Developments in the South China Sea," May 10, 2014, http://asean.org/asean-foreign-ministers-statement-on-the-current-developments-in-the-south-china-sea/.

tary freeze on provocative activities by claimants in the South China Sea, which it raised again in early August at the ARF. Immediately after the meeting, ASEAN foreign ministers reaffirmed that they "remained seriously concerned over recent developments."[83] A few weeks later, U.S. general Martin Dempsey, chairman of the Joint Chiefs of Staff, became the highest-ranking American military officer to visit Vietnam since the end of the Vietnam War, and maritime cooperation was a key topic during his visit. In October, the United States announced a partial lifting of the arms embargo toward Vietnam that had been in effect since the end of the war.

CHINA PAUSES, PARTIALLY

In response to regional concerns and deepening U.S. involvement in the region, China sought to moderate its position for a third time. This moderation, however, was more limited than previous ones because land reclamation continued apace. The first component was a renewed engagement of Vietnam. In August 2014, after HYSY 981 had moved away from disputed waters, China and Vietnam announced a three-point agreement to lower tensions in the dispute.[84] Senior party leaders visited Vietnam in a bid to improve relations, including Central Military Commission vice chair Fan Changlong and state councilor for foreign affairs Yang Jiechi in October and President Xi Jinping in November. All the visits affirmed the goal of preventing maritime disputes from harming the broader bilateral relationship.[85]

The second component of China's moderation was renewed engagement of the region more generally by highlighting the potential for substantial investment to meet growing infrastructure needs in Asia. At the APEC meeting in November, President Xi announced the creation of the US$40 billion Silk Road Fund, which was formally established in December.[86] Just a few days after Xi's announcement, Premier Li Keqiang announced at the East Asia Summit a planned US$20 billion in loans for infrastructure in Southeast Asia, with half earmarked for ASEAN and the other half to be channeled through the China Development Bank.[87] These efforts complemented

83. Association of Southeast Asian Nations, "Joint Communiqué 47th ASEAN Foreign Ministers' Meeting," August 8, 2014, http://asean.org/joint-communique-47th-asean-foreign-ministers-meeting/.

84. Xinhua News Agency, "China, Vietnam Call Truce on Maritime Tensions," August 27, 2014.

85. Xinhua News Agency, "China Calls for Closer Maritime Cooperation with Vietnam," November 6, 2015.

86. Paul Carsten and Ben Blanchard, "China to Establish $40 Billion Silk Road Infrastructure Fund," November 8, 2014, http://www.reuters.com/article/us-china-diplomacy-idUSKBN0IS0BQ20141108.

87. Xinhua News Agency, "China Pledges over 20-Bln-USD Loans to Boost Southeast Asian Connectivity," November 13, 2014.

China's move to establish the Asian Infrastructure Investment Bank, which twenty-one Asian states had agreed to join in October 2014.

Finally, perhaps to deflect some attention from the South China Sea, China worked with the United States to produce a successful state visit, and President Obama came to Beijing in November 2014. According to announcements made during the visit, the two sides achieved substantial progress, agreeing on voluntary targets to limit greenhouse gases, reciprocal short-term visas, and trade in information technology. In addition, China and the United States signed two nonbinding memoranda of understanding in the area of crisis management. The first concerned the "rules of behavior for aerial and maritime encounters," including an annex for such encounters. The second concerned the notification of major military activities.[88] These two agreements likely reflected the need to prevent accidents amid the growing intensification of the South China Sea disputes.

The Years 2015 to 2016: The United States and China Hunker Down

Despite the November 2014 summit, China and the United States continued to strengthen their positions in the South China Sea in 2015. China broadened the scope and scale of its land reclamation, while the United States deepened its security relationships with other states in the disputes—especially Vietnam and the Philippines.

In early 2015, the main thrust of China's efforts in the South China Sea was to continue with its effort to build and develop artificial islands. In late January, China started to reclaim land at Subi Reef, while in early February China started to reclaim land at Mischief Reef. China transformed these two reefs into China's largest artificial islands in the Spratlys, 5.7 and 4.9 square kilometers in size, respectively, each with a three-thousand-meter runway and a large harbor.[89] The steady progress of China's land reclamation and island development at all seven features was revealed through satellite imagery and frequently reported in the international media. Despite Chinese efforts to explain in April 2015 that the islands would be used largely for civilian purposes, concern about its intentions increased as land reclamation continued.

The United States responded in several ways. First, it issued a series of high-level statements about China's behavior. In February, Russel called on Beijing to stop land reclamation.[90] In April, in response to a question about

---

88. Office of the Secretary of Defense, *Annual Report to Congress*, 110–44.

89. Ibid., 15, 17.

90. Jeremy Page and Julian E. Barnes, "China Expands Island Construction in Disputed South China Sea," *Wall Street Journal*, February 18, 2015.

land reclamation, Secretary of Defense Ashton Carter stated that "we take a strong stand against militarization of those disputes."[91] Also in April, President Obama expressed concerns about China's behavior, noting that "just because the Philippines or Vietnam are not as large as China doesn't mean that they can just be elbowed aside."[92] Moreover, Obama suggested China was "using its sheer size and muscle to force countries into subordinate positions."

Second, the Pentagon began to float the idea of operational challenges near China's islands. In May 2015, the *Wall Street Journal* reported that the Pentagon was considering "flying Navy surveillance aircraft over the islands and sending U.S. naval ships to well within 12 nautical miles of reefs that have been built up and claimed by the Chinese."[93] A few weeks later, in his speech at the Shangri-La Dialogue, Carter suggested such operations were being considered, stating, "There should be no mistake: the United States will fly, sail, and operate wherever international law allows."[94] After a period of debate within the administration between the White House and the Pentagon, Freedom of Navigation operations (FONOPs) targeting Chinese features in the Spratlys and Paracels began in October 2015, with follow-on operations in January and May 2016.

Third, the United States accelerated the deepening of security ties with other countries in the South China Sea disputes. At the Shangri-La Dialogue, Carter also announced the establishment of the Maritime Security Initiative, a US$425 million fund to bolster maritime capacity in the region, particularly for the Philippines, with roughly half of the funds to be dispersed by the end of 2016. Meanwhile, the United States and ASEAN leaders held their first summit meeting in February 2016—pointedly, at the Sunnylands estate where Xi and Obama had met in 2013. At the meeting, Obama called for "a halt to further reclamation, new construction and militarization of disputed areas."[95] In March 2016, the United States and the Philippines announced that U.S. forces would be granted access to five Philippine air bases, two of which are located adjacent to the South China Sea. The first

91. U.S. Department of Defense, "Remarks by Secretary Carter and Nakatani at a Joint Press Conference Press Operations," April 8, 2015, http://www.defense.gov/News/News-Transcripts/Transcript-View/Article/607035.
92. Matt Spetalnick and Ben Blanchard, "Obama Says Concerned China Bullying Others in South China Sea," April 10, 2015, http://www.reuters.com/article/us-usa-obama-china-idUSKBN0N02HT20150410.
93. Adam Entous, Gordon Lubold, and Julian Barnes, "U.S. Military Proposes Challenge to China Sea Claims," *Wall Street Journal*, May 12, 2015.
94. Ashton Carter, "A Regional Security Architecture Where Everyone Rises," May 30, 2015, http://archive.defense.gov/Speeches/Speech.aspx?SpeechID=1945.
95. Jeff Mason and Bruce Wallace, "Obama, ASEAN Discuss South China Sea Tensions, but No Joint Mention of China," February 17, 2016, http://www.reuters.com/article/us-usa-asean-idUSKCN0VP1F7.

deployment of U.S. aircraft to these bases occurred a month later.[96] During Xi's meeting with Obama in Washington in late March, Obama reportedly warned the Chinese president against taking any actions in the South China Sea "involving American treaty obligations to the Philippines."[97] Also in March, the United States and the Philippines began joint patrols in the South China Sea, which reflected the tightening of the alliance. In May 2016 President Obama visited Vietnam, where he announced that the United States had lifted its arms embargo on that nation, symbolizing further improvement in bilateral relations.

During this period, China continued with its land reclamation and island development but avoided undertaking new actions. In late June 2015, China announced that it had halted land reclamation work in the Spratlys and had shifted to the development phase. In September of that year, the United States and China signed two annexes on aerial encounters and crisis management to the 2014 memorandum of understanding. China has also adopted a low-key approach to U.S. FONOPs that challenge China's excessive maritime claims. Although China has opposed them publicly, it has not tried to interfere with the navigation or movement of U.S. vessels. Moreover, U.S. naval commanders report that Chinese vessels have been operating in a professional manner. China's change in tactics, which one report described as "passive assertiveness," likely represents a response to a concern about miscalculation as well as to the increased U.S. focus on the South China Sea disputes from early 2015.[98]

Conclusion

Since 2008, China and the United States have strengthened their positions in the South China Sea. China's physical presence in the sea has never been stronger: it possesses three military-grade airfields in the Spratly Islands and maintains a steady presence of commercial, military, and law enforcement vessels in contested waters. Similarly, the involvement of the United States in Southeast Asian regional security has never been greater: it has strengthened its alliance with the Philippines and its security partnerships with littoral states, giving U.S. forces much greater access to and presence in the region than at any time since the end of the Cold War. By threatening many of its neighbors, China may have deterred them from physically challeng-

96. Trefor Moss, "U.S. Set to Deploy Troops to Philippines in Rebalancing Act," *Wall Street Journal*, March 20, 2015.

97. Jane Perlez and Chris Buckley, "U.S. and China Offer Competing Views on Disputed Sea," *New York Times*, June 7, 2016.

98. Ashley Townsend and Rory Metcalf, *Shifting Waters: China's New Passive Assertiveness in Asian Maritime Security* (Sydney: Lowy Institute for International Policy, 2016).

ing its claims, but it also pushed them to seek support from the United States to balance China. At the same time, although the United States is more involved in the South China Sea than ever before, it has avoided directly challenging China on the question of sovereignty and has not sought to block, much less roll back, China's growing presence. China has also generally avoided using armed force to seize the islands held by other claimants or to attack their naval or coast guard vessels, which would likely spark greater U.S. involvement, especially in a crisis involving the Philippines.

In this way, the United States and China have sought to defend their interests in the region without significantly worsening ties with each other. China has tacitly accepted an enhanced role for the United States in the disputes and in regional security more generally. Likewise, the United States has tacitly accepted a growing Chinese presence throughout the South China Sea. Although the role of these sea disputes has grown, it does not yet dominate U.S-China relations. As a result, the situation remains relatively stable despite the inherent volatility of territorial disputes and power transitions.

Whether both sides can continue to thread the needle is uncertain. Two outcomes are possible. On the one hand, China's completion of extensive land reclamation might paradoxically help to reduce tensions from growing further. China now possesses the largest land masses in the Spratly Islands, and this enables it to significantly enhance its presence in the southern portion of the South China Sea. This in turn greatly enhances China's position in the disputes and limits the ability of other states to weaken its claims. Historically, China has been less likely to use force and more likely to negotiate when it occupies a strong position in a territorial dispute.[99] Moreover, the scope of the blowback from China's assertiveness is now much clearer given the enhanced presence of the United States in the region. Although the United States has not explicitly sided with states opposing China on the question of sovereignty over disputed islands, it has improved diplomatic and military relationships with many of them and has aided them in strengthening their own maritime capabilities. From this perspective, a new equilibrium or balance may be forming in which China has a stronger presence in the South China Sea, while the United States has a much stronger presence in littoral states and the ability to project power into and over the South China Sea.

On the other hand, having created robust infrastructure in the sea, China may want to press forward. Indirectly, this could include efforts to increase control over contested waters by denying access to the commercial, law enforcement, or military vessels of other countries. In the extreme, it could include physically coercing other claimants to vacate the features they

---

99. M. Taylor Fravel, *Strong Borders, Secure Nation: Cooperation and Conflict in China's Territorial Disputes* (Princeton, NJ: Princeton University Press, 2008).

occupy, either by blockading their positions or seizing them with armed force. To date, however, China has avoided such direct actions. The enhanced U.S. presence in the region, along with its commitment to the defense of the Philippines, suggests that such assertive Chinese actions may be less likely so long as the United States maintains its current involvement in the disputes. Earlier U.S. involvement in the South China Sea at times elicited a strong reaction from China. Now, however, because the United States has consolidated its security relationships in the region, China has chosen not to challenge the United States directly.

The United States and China in Northeast Asia

Third-Party Coercion and Alliance Relations

Robert S. Ross

From 2010 to early 2013, there was heightened tension in Northeast Asia and U.S.-China conflict over regional disputes. In 2010, North Korea launched missiles against South Korean civilians on an island under South Korean control, and one of its submarines sank a South Korean naval ship. When the United States strengthened its deterrence posture toward North Korea and employed coercive diplomacy, China supported North Korea and resisted U.S. policy. The tension on the Korean Peninsula continued through 2012, as China maintained close ties with North Korea, and the United States continued to strengthen its deterrent posture.

In 2010 and again in 2012, Japanese government initiatives challenged Chinese sovereignty claims over the disputed Diaoyu/Senkaku Islands. In 2012 China directly challenged Japanese sovereignty claims, sending coast guard ships into the disputed waters in the East China Sea. China had resorted to coercive diplomacy against Japan. But as Sino-Japanese tension increased, the United States signaled its support for Japanese resistance to Chinese diplomacy.

By early 2013 the tension in Northeast Asia had significantly diminished; Chinese leadership had reconsidered its North Korea policy. It significantly distanced China from North Korean provocations and cooperated with the United States in restraining North Korean belligerence. The United States similarly reconsidered its Japan policy, softening its support for Japan in early 2013, implicitly accepting China's new sovereignty initiatives in the East China Sea, and reducing the importance of Sino-Japanese sovereignty disputes in the U.S.-China agenda. These mutual policy adjustments contributed to a "mini-détente" in U.S.-China relations. In June 2013 U.S. president Barack Obama and Chinese president Xi Jinping held a successful summit in California, and there was greater U.S.-China cooperation through the end of 2013.

In 2013 the United States and China had restored regional stability and great power cooperation because each power adjusted its policies in response to the other's coercive policy toward their respective allies. U.S. policy toward North Korea had challenged Chinese security in Northeast Asia and heightened the risk of war on China's northeast border, causing China to rethink the merits of its support for North Korea's security policy. The Sino-Japanese territorial dispute challenged U.S. interests in regional stability and risked U.S. involvement in hostilities with Japan against China over materially insignificant islands, causing the United States to rethink its support for Japanese policy.

Such "third-party coercive diplomacy" was the critical element in both the heightened regional instability from 2010 to 2012 and in the restoration of U.S.-China cooperation in 2013. In the context of heightened regional conflict, U.S. and Chinese coercive diplomacy toward each other's allies created a situation in which relations between the two countries and Northeast Asian security had to get worse before they could get better.

Nonetheless, in early 2014 regional tension reemerged in Northeast Asia, once again challenging U.S.-China cooperation and regional stability, suggesting that third-party coercive diplomacy has become a recurring dynamic in U.S.-China relations and, more generally, in East Asian security affairs.

This chapter examines the dynamics of U.S.-China third-party coercion from 2010 through 2013, from the emergence of heightened tension to the reemergence of stability and the U.S.-China summit. It begins with an examination of the elements coercive diplomacy, the particular dynamics of third-party coercive diplomacy, and the role of third-party coercive diplomacy in the East Asian context. It then examines onset of instability and the role of third-party coercion in the emergence and then the decline of tension in first the Korean Peninsula and then in Sino-Japanese relations. The chapter concludes with a discussion of the recurrence since late 2013 of third-party coercion in U.S.-China relations as China has continued to develop maritime capabilities that enable a more proactive Chinese diplomacy.

Third-Party Coercive Diplomacy and East Asian Security

Coercive diplomacy aims to persuade an opponent to stop what it is doing or to reverse its policy.[1] States use coercive diplomacy when the target state's

---

1. This definition follows Thomas Schelling, although he uses the term "compellence" rather than *coercion*. See Thomas Schelling, *Arms and Influence* (Westport, CT: Greenwood,

policy challenges the status quo and its national interests. In international security affairs, coercive diplomacy frequently relies on the threat of use of force to persuade the target state of the potential disproportionate costs of its current policy objectives and, hence, the necessity to change course. Successful coercive diplomacy depends on the ability of the coercing state to credibly threaten unacceptable costs to the target state.[2]

Throughout the Cold War, coercive diplomacy was a frequent policy choice of both the Soviet Union and the United States, as each sought to resist the other's policy initiatives that undermined its own security interests. Coercive diplomacy has also been a recurring policy strategy in U.S. policy toward adversarial regional states since the end of the Cold War.[3] In the twenty-first century, coercive diplomacy has reemerged in U.S.-China relations in contemporary East Asia. But whereas the United States during the Cold War and in the post–Cold War era has employed coercive diplomacy to directly influence the target state, recent U.S. and Chinese coercive diplomacy is best understood as "third-party coercion."[4]

In third-party coercive diplomacy, the coercing state targets a small-state ally of a great power that is challenging its interests. But the primary purpose of third-party coercive diplomacy is not to change the behavior of the direct target of the coercive policies but rather to coerce the great power—the third party—to ease its support for the challenging behavior of its smaller ally and thus leave the smaller state no choice but to cease its provocations. By increasing tension with the smaller state, third-party coercion threatens the smaller state's great power ally with entrapment in great power hostilities over its ally's particular interests, encouraging the third party great power to restrain its ally.[5]

1976), 69–72. Schelling's definition is nearly identical to Alexander George's definition of coercive diplomacy. See Alexander George, "Coercive Diplomacy: Definition and Characteristics," in *The Limits of Coercive Diplomacy*, ed. Alexander L. George and William E. Simons (Boulder, CO: Westview, 1994), 7.

2. For a comprehensive analysis of the sources of successful coercive diplomacy, see Robert J. Art, "Coercive Diplomacy: What Do We Know?," in *The United States and Coercive Diplomacy*, ed. Robert J. Art and Patrick M. Cronin (Washington, DC: U.S. Institute of Peace, 2003).

3. For Cold War case studies, see Alexander L. George and William E. Simons, eds., *The Limits of Coercive Diplomacy* (Boulder, CO: Westview, 1994); for post–Cold War case studies in U.S. foreign policy, see Robert J. Art and Patrick M. Cronin, eds., *The United States and Coercive Diplomacy* (Washington, DC: U.S. Institute of Peace, 2003).

4. There are other ways to capture this dynamic, including the terms *extended coercion* and *entrapment coercion*; I am grateful to Daniel Drezner for suggesting the term *third-party coercion*. China's political use of force against Taiwan in 1954, 1958, and 1997 may also be understood as third-party coercion insofar as the United States was the target of Chinese coercion. For Chinese targeting of the United States in the 1996 Taiwan Strait confrontation, see Robert S. Ross, "The 1995–96 Taiwan Strait Confrontation: Coercion, Credibility, and Use of Force," *International Security* 25, no. 2 (2000): 87–123.

5. On entrapment in alliance relations, the benchmark study remains Glenn H. Snyder, "The Security Dilemma in Alliance Politics," *World Politics* 36, no. 4 (1984): 461–95.

From 2010 to 2012, U.S. policy toward North Korea entailed U.S. third-party coercion, compelling China to actively oppose North Korea's nuclear weapons program. Similarly, in 2012 Chinese coercive diplomacy against Japan entailed Chinese third-party coercion against the United States, compelling the latter to restrain Japan's challenges to Chinese sovereignty claims over the Diaoyu/Senkaku Islands.

In the context of great power competition and alliance relations, third-party coercive diplomacy can be an effective and also a low-risk instrument to compel great power compromise based on asymmetric interests.[6] The result can often be renewed regional stability based upon a new understanding of the sources of great power cooperation. This dynamic occurred in Northeast Asia in 2013: U.S. coercive diplomacy toward North Korea moderated Chinese policy toward North Korea and its nuclear weapons program, and Chinese maritime policy toward Japan moderated U.S. policy toward Japan's sovereignty claims. The effect was greater U.S.-China cooperation and regional stability throughout the year.

Instability in Northeast Asia, 2010–2012

By late 2012 the situation in Northeast Asia was the worst it had been since the end of the Cold War. The Sino-Japanese maritime dispute in the East China Sea over the Diaoyu/Senkaku Islands, a dispute that had been mostly dormant since World War II, emerged as a source of significant Sino-Japanese tension that affected U.S. alliance commitments to Japan. In early 2013 conflict on the Korean Peninsula also escalated to its highest level since the crisis of 2003, as North Korea resumed nuclear and missile tests.

Tension in Northeast Asia also contributed to diminished U.S.-China cooperation elsewhere. In February 2012 China cooperated with Russia against U.S. policy in Syria. Secretary of State Hillary Rodham Clinton called China's veto of the United Nations Security Council resolution condemning Syria as "despicable."[7] For the first time China also resisted U.S.-sponsored UN sanctions against Iran, compelling the United States in 2012 to impose sanctions outside the UN framework. Following the decision by the United States, European countries, and Japan to sanction Iranian oil exports, China reached a new agreement with Teheran to purchase

---

6. On asymmetric interests in international bargaining, see Glenn H. Snyder and Paul Diesing, *Conflict among Nations: Bargaining, Decision-Making, and System Structure in International Crises* (Princeton, NJ: Princeton University Press, 1977).

7. Steven Lee Myers, "Nations Press Halt in Attacks to Allow Aid to Syrian Cities," *New York Times*, February 24, 2012, http://www.nytimes.com/2012/02/25/world/middleeast/friends-of-syria-gather-in-tunis-to-pressure-assad.html?pagewanted=all&_r=0.

Iranian oil.[8] Then, in June, Chinese imports from Iran increased.[9] From 2010 to 2012 China also offered little assistance to U.S. policy toward North Korea. It expressed minimal interest in convening the Six-Party Talks on nuclear nonproliferation.

The United States and China had avoided crisis escalation and an arms race. Nonetheless, for the first time since the end of the Cold War, great power relations trended toward strategic confrontation.

In early 2010, North Korean policies challenged U.S. and South Korean confidence in both North Korean restraint and Chinese support for nonproliferation and stability on the Korean Peninsula. The United States, unsure of Beijing's commitment to restrain North Korean belligerence, adopted a range of policies that not only strengthened its deterrence of North Korean use of force and nuclear weapons development but also challenged Chinese security in Northeast Asia. Ultimately, U.S. policy persuaded Beijing to change its North Korea policy.

North Korean Provocations and Chinese Passive Diplomacy. In March 2010 a North Korean submarine sunk a South Korean naval ship. There was near universal criticism of North Korea in South Korea and the United States. Nonetheless, in May, as South Korea carried out its investigation into the incident, Chinese leaders withheld any criticism of Pyongyang and welcomed North Korean leader Kim Jong-Il to Beijing. In November the North Korean military shelled Yeonpyeong Island, killing four and injuring nineteen South Korean civilians. Once again, Chinese leaders did not criticize North Korea; rather, they received Choe Thae Bok, secretary of the Workers' Party of North Korea's Central Committee, and Kim Yong-Il, director of the party's international department, in Beijing.[10]

When the United States responded to North Korean policies in July 2010 with a joint U.S.–South Korea naval exercise in international waters in the Yellow Sea, Chinese leaders criticized the United States. General Ma Xiaotian, chief of staff for the People's Liberation Army, said that the Yellow Sea

---

8. Mark Landler, "China Is Excluded from Waivers for Oil Trade with Iran," *New York Times,* June 11, 2012, http://www.nytimes.com/2012/06/12/world/middleeast/china-not-issued-waiver-for-oil-trade-with-iran.html?_r=0.

9. "Iran to Increase Oil Export to China to 500K BPD in 2012," *China Daily*, February 18, 2012, http://bbs.chinadaily.com.cn/thread-732456-1-1.html; Landler, "China Is Excluded."

10. Helene Cooper and Sharon LaFraniere, "U.S. and South Korea Balk at Talks with North," *New York Times*, November 30, 2010, http://www.nytimes.com/2010/12/01/world/asia/01seoul.html?pagewanted=all.

"is very near Chinese territorial waters and we are very much opposed to such an exercise."[11] That same day the Chinese foreign ministry spokesman expressed China's "grave concern" and declared that China was "firmly opposed to foreign military vessels and planes conducting activities in the Yellow Sea ... that undermine China's security interest." A few days later he insisted that China's position was "unequivocal" and that it "resolutely oppose[d] warships and military aircraft from any country conducting activities that affect China's security interest in the Yellow Sea."[12] Chinese nationalist commentators reinforced Chinese policy. For example, in the Communist Party newspaper *People's Daily*, Major General Luo Yuan declared that the U.S. military exercise would pose "a direct security threat to China's heartland" and that China should have a "sense of crisis" and should "prepare for the worst."[13]

U.S. Coercive Diplomacy in the Korean Peninsula. China's North Korea policy and its response to U.S.–South Korea cooperation undermined U.S. efforts to constrain North Korea's nuclear program and its destabilizing diplomacy. The administration of President George W. Bush had reduced U.S. strategic presence on the Korean Peninsula in part because it was increasingly confident about China's willingness to restrain North Korea's nuclear program and its challenge to South Korean security. But if China could no longer be counted on to restrain Pyongyang, the United States would have to reassert its resistance to North Korea and its support for South Korea—with implications for Chinese security in Northeast Asia.

11. Elisabeth Bumiller and Edward Wong, "U.S. and South Korea Plan Naval Drill as a Message," *New York Times*, July 21, 2010, http://query.nytimes.com/gst/fullpage.html?res=9B02E6DA113EF932A15754C0A9669D8B63; "China 'Very Opposed' to US-Korea Yellow Sea Drill," *Sunday Morning Post*, July 4, 2010, Open Source Center (hereafter OSC), doc. no. CPP20100705718012; Liu Bin, "'Explosive Contact': Chinese and US Navies Stand Off in Yellow Sea," *Nanfang Zhoumo*, July 7, 2010, OSC, doc. no. CPP20100709788015.
12. Ministry of Foreign Affairs of the People's Republic of China, "Foreign Ministry Spokesman's News Conference on 8 Jul 2010," July 8, 2010, OSC, doc. no. CPP20100721467004; Ministry of Foreign Affairs of the People's Republic of China, "Foreign Ministry Spokesman's News Conference on 13 Jul 2010," July 13, 2010, OSC, doc. no. CPP20100721467005; Ministry of Foreign Affairs of the People's Republic of China, "Foreign Ministry Spokesman's News Conference on 15 Jul 2010," July 15, 2010, OSC, doc. no. CPP20100715364001.
13. "Huanghai Taoxin jiang Shi Meiguo Zhanlue Shice" [The Yellow Sea challenge will be a U.S. strategic blunder], *Huanqiu Shibao*, July 6, 2010, http://opinion.huanqiu.com/roll/2010-07/906175.html; Liu Yueshan, "People's Liberation Army Major General Luo Yuan Says That US Aircraft Carrier Can Be Used as Live Target," *Wen Wei Po*, July 7, 2010, OSC, doc. no. CPP20100707788008; Liu, "Explosive Contact"; "Why China Opposes US–South Korean Military Exercises in the Yellow Sea," *People's Daily*, July 16, 2010, OSC, doc. no. CPP20100719787007; "Luo Yuan: Mei Hangmu Huanghai Junyan Banjing Neng Fugai Wo Huabei Diqu" [Luo Yuan: U.S. carrier Yellow Sea exercises and surveillance can cover our North China region], *Renmin Wang*, July 13, 2010, http://military.people.com.cn/GB/42969/58519/12133164.html.

In June 2010, following the North Korean sinking of the South Korean ship and Kim Jong-Il's visit to Beijing, the Obama administration had reversed Bush administration policy by deferring from 2012 to 2015 the transfer of wartime operational control of South Korean forces from the United States to South Korea. As the year progressed, the Obama administration increased U.S. military presence in South Korea. Whereas during the Bush administration the scale and number of U.S.–South Korea joint military exercises declined significantly, the Obama administration significantly expanded the size and frequency of these exercises. In 2010 the two militaries carried out their largest exercise ever, and in October of that year they reached three new defense agreements: the Integrated Defense Dialogue, the first joint Counter-Provocation Plan, and the Extended Deterrence Policy Committee.[14]

In 2012 the United States continued to increase its direct pressure on North Korea. In June it led its first joint naval exercise with both Japan and South Korea; the exercise took place in the Yellow Sea. In October the United States authorized South Korea to extend the range of its missiles so that they could reach Pyongyang and Chinese territory,[15] and also reached agreement with South Korea to develop a "tailored bilateral deterrence strategy against North Korean nuclear and WMD [weapons of mass destruction] threats."[16] Moreover, whereas the Bush administration had reduced U.S. troops in South Korea by 40 percent, through 2012 the Obama administration had increased U.S. troop presence in South Korea by nearly 15 percent.

The United States also expanded its cooperation with Japan against North Korea, reaching agreement in September 2012 to increase deployment of its missile defense systems in Japan. Although U.S. missile defense deployments were ostensibly aimed at North Korea, the United States appreciated that the deployments also had implications for Chinese security. Secretary of State Leon Panetta indicated that if China opposed the U.S. missile defense in Northeast Asia, it should cooperate with U.S. efforts to constrain North

14. On the military agreements, see the text of the Joint Communiqué of the 42nd ROK-US Security Consultative Meeting, October 28, 2010, http://www.mofa.go.kr/webmodule /htsboard/template/read/korboardread.jsp?typeID=24&boardid=11695&tableName =TYPE_KORBOARD&seqno=3463; and "Joint Communiqué Between the U.S. and South Korea, Security Consultative Meeting, October 2012," Council on Foreign Relations, October 24, 2012, http://www.cfr.org/south-korea/joint-communique-between-us-south-korea -security-consultative-meeting-october-2012/p29349. For a record of US–South Korean exercises in 2010, see Xinhua News Agency, December 23, 2010, OSC doc. no. CPP20101223968128.

15. Choe Sang-Hun, "U.S. Agrees to Let South Korea Extend Range of Ballistic Missiles," *New York Times*, October 7, 2012, http://www.nytimes.com/2012/10/08/world/asia/us -agrees-to-let-south-korea-extend-missile-range.html; "United States, Republic of Korea and Japanese Naval Exercises Announced," U.S. Department of Defense news release no. 490-12, June 13, 2012, http://www.defense.gov/releases/release.aspx?releaseid=15367.

16. U.S. Department of Defense, "Joint Press Conference with Secretary Panetta and Defense Minister Kim in the Pentagon Briefing Room," October 24, 2012, http://www.defense .gov/transcripts/transcript.aspx?transcriptid=5141.

Korea's nuclear weapons program.[17] The U.S. understood Chinese concerns, and it had directed its coercive diplomacy at Chinese decision making.

China Responds: The Isolation of North Korea. In 2010 China had failed to respond to North Korean provocations. On the contrary, it had stood behind North Korea, even as North Korea sank a South Korean Navy ship and killed South Korean civilians. The United States responded by increasing its military capabilities in South Korea to coerce North Korea to cease its threats against its southern neighbor. But increased U.S. capabilities also challenged Chinese security. Increased U.S. military presence in South Korea and increased U.S.–South Korea cooperation posed a greater risk of hostilities on China's northern border that could lead to Chinese involvement. China faced a greater risk of "entrapment" in a Korean conflict due to North Korea's provocative nuclear weapons program. Moreover, increased U.S. military presence on the Korean Peninsula and in the Yellow Sea, greater U.S.-Japan cooperation on missile defense, and greater naval cooperation between the United States, Japan, and South Korea undermined China's overall security. In Northeast Asia, the United States had made China, not North Korea United States, pay the price for North Korean belligerence. Jeffery Bader, the senior director for Asian affairs on the National Security Council in 2010, recalled that "We . . . wanted to work with the Chinese to restrain North Korea, but we would first have to persuade Beijing that Pyongyang's behavior constituted a threat to Chinese interests."[18]

The United States and China possessed asymmetric interests regarding North Korea's nuclear weapons program. Whereas China simply had no interest in North Korea's possession of nuclear weapons and had long accepted the status quo, the United States had a major interest in preventing North Korea's nuclear proliferation. At stake for the United States were its defense commitments to its South Korean and Japanese allies. In this strategic context, U.S. defense policy toward North Korea and peninsular instability since 2010 had created a Chinese incentive to change its North Korea

---

17. Karen Parrish, "U.S., Japan Begin Coordination on Second Radar Installation," American Forces Press Service, September 17, 2012, http://www.defense.gov/news/newsarticle .aspx?id=117880; Thom Shanker and Ian Johnson, "U.S. Accord with Japan over Missile Defense Draws Criticism in China," *New York Times*, September 17, 2012, http://www.nytimes .com/2012/09/18/world/asia/u-s-and-japan-agree-on-missile-defense-system.html.   See also Thom Shanker, David E. Sanger, Martin Fackler, "U.S. Is Bolstering Missile Defense to Deter North Korea," *New York Times*, March 15, 2013, http://www.nytimes.com/2013/03 /16/world/asia/us-to-bolster-missile-defense-against-north-korea.html?_r=0.

18. For a Chinese commentary on these trends, see Zhu Feng, "Chaoxian He Shiyan, Zhongguo Sheng le Do Da de Qi" [Korea's nuclear test: How much hot air can China make?], *Huanqiu Shibao Wang*, February 16, 2013, http://opinion.huanqiu.com/opinion_world/2013 -02/3643626.html. Bader's remarks are in Jeffrey Bader, *Obama and China's Rise: An Insider's Account of America's Asia Strategy* (Washington, DC: Brookings, 2012), pp. 87–88.

policy and oppose nuclear proliferation. Moreover, since 2010 the United States had established its resolve to risk heightened instability on the Korean Peninsula and on China's perimeter to resist North Korean possession of nuclear weapons. U.S. coercive diplomacy vis-à-vis North Korea thus raised the cost of China's North Korea policy as reflected in China's deteriorated security environment in Northeast Asia, thus compelling Beijing to alter its policy.

In December 2012 North Korea conducted a long-range missile test, and in February 2013 it carried out its third nuclear test. In response to widespread criticism, North Korea leveled escalating threats of war against South Korea and the United States. The United States responded with escalated coercive diplomacy. In late March, Washington and Seoul announced agreement on its new Combined Counter-Provocation Plan, which threatened offensive operations against North Korean "provocations."[19] Later that week North Korea announced that Kim Jung-un had ordered North Korea's missile units to be on "highest alert" in preparation to launch an attack. In April 2013 the United States increased its deployments in South Korea of offensive military capabilities, including B-2 bombers. The rapidly escalating tension on the Korean Peninsula created heightened concern for significant instability and unintentional hostilities.[20]

Although in 2010 China had seemingly backed North Korean provocations and resisted U.S. coercive diplomacy, beginning in late 2012 it shifted course to restrain North Korean belligerence, including the use of unprecedented economic sanctions and diplomatic isolation. In November 2012, as North Korea prepared to conduct its missile test, China sent a delegation to Pyongyang to advise against it. But North Korea ignored Chinese advice.[21] In January, China cooperated with the United States in drafting the 2013 UN Security Council resolution to impose additional sanctions on North Korea.[22] In April, as the tension mounted following North Korea's nuclear test,

19. Kim Eun-jung, "S. Korea, U.S. Sign Combined Operational Plan against N. Korea," Yonhap News Agency, March 24, 2013, http://english.yonhapnews.co.kr/national/2013/03/22/30/0301000000AEN20130322011000315F.HTML.

20. Choe Sang-Hun, "Global Powers Cast Wary Eye as Korean Tension Escalates," New York Times, March 29, 2013, http://www.nytimes.com/2013/03/30/world/asia/kim-jong-un-of-north-korea-orders-missile-readiness.html?pagewanted=all; Thom Shanker and Choe Sang-Hun, "U.S. Runs Practice Sortie in South Korea," New York Times, March 28, 2013, http://www.nytimes.com/2013/03/29/world/asia/us-begins-stealth-bombing-runs-over-south-korea.html?_r=0.

21. David E. Sanger and William J. Broad, "After Rocket Launching, a Call for New Sanctions," New York Times, December 12, 2012, http://www.nytimes.com/2012/12/13/world/asia/north-korea-rocket-launching.html; Choe, "Global Powers Cast Wary Eye."

22. Rick Gladstone, "U.N. Resolution to Aim at North Korean Banks and Diplomats," New York Times, March 5, 2013, http://www.nytimes.com/2013/03/06/world/asia/china-said-to-back-new-sanctions-against-north-korea.html; Robert A. Wampler, "Will Chinese Troops Cross the Yalu?" Foreign Policy, April 11, 2013.

Chinese premier Li Keqiang met with U.S. secretary of state John Kerry in Beijing. Li opposed "troublemaking" on the Korean Peninsula and warned North Korea that "to do that is nothing different from lifting a rock only to drop it on one's own toes."[23] Kerry was pleased with the results of his meetings, noting that the United States and China had been "able . . . to underscore our joint commitment to the denuclearisation of the Korean peninsula in a peaceful manner."[24] Then, in the midst of the tension, Chinese leaders welcomed General Martin Dempsey, chairman of the Joint Chiefs of Staff, to Beijing. In a meeting with Dempsey, General Fang Fenghui, the vice chairman of the Chinese Central Military Commission, directly criticized North Korea's nuclear program.[25] President Xi Jinping declared at the annual Boao Forum in early April, "No one should be allowed to throw a region and even a whole world into chaos for selfish gains."[26]

Chinese diplomacy with South Korea was equally supportive of U.S. policy. In March, Xi wrote a personal letter to recently elected South Korean president Park Geun-hye. He then telephoned Park and suggested an early China–South Korea summit. As the tension escalated in April, China agreed to establish a hotline with South Korea.[27] In April, Wu Dawei, China's special representative for Korean Peninsula affairs, traveled to Seoul and to Washington, where he met with both Secretary of State Kerry and General Dempsey, and Chinese foreign minister Wang Yi welcomed South Korean foreign minister Yun Byung Se to Beijing.[28] In contrast, throughout this period, Beijing had nothing positive to say about North Korea and conducted no public diplomacy with North Korea; it had isolated North Korea in Northeast Asian diplomacy.

China also imposed economic sanctions on North Korea. The Bank of China announced that it had cut off dealings with the Foreign Trade Bank

23. Xinhua News Agency, "Chinese Premier Meets U.S. Secretary of State," April 13, 2013, http://news.xinhuanet.com/english/china/2013-04/13/c_132306244.htm.

24. Song Jung-a and Geoff Dyer, "US and China in N Korea Pledge," *Financial Times*, April 14, 2013, http://www.ft.com/intl/cms/s/0/5712ef16-a377-11e2-8f9c-00144feabdc0 .html#axzz3B3Y8y3AK.

25. Karen Parrish, "Dempsey Urges More Strategic Dialogue between China, U.S.," American Forces Press Service, April 22, 2013, http://www.defense.gov/news/newsarticle .aspx?id=119839.

26. Jane Perlez and Choe Sang-Hun, "China Hints at Limits to North Korea Actions," *New York Times*, April 7, 2013, http://www.nytimes.com/2013/04/08/world/asia/from-china-a -call-to-avoid-chaos-for-selfish-gain.html?pagewanted=all; see also Xinhua News Agency, "Full Text of Xi Jinping's Speech at Opening Ceremony of Boao Forum," April 8, 2013, http:// english.peopledaily.com.cn/90785/8198366.html.

27. Wampler, "Will Chinese Troops Cross the Yalu?"

28. Yonhap News Agency, "Top Diplomats of S. Korea, China to Set Up Hotline Amid N. Korea Tensions," April 24, 2013, http://english.yonhapnews.co.kr/national/2013/04/24 /11/0301000000AEN20130424014700320F.HTML.

of North Korea. The Chinese government also froze some North Korean bank accounts in the Chinese border cities of Dandong and Hunchun, closed a North Korean foreign exchange bank, increased inspections of North Korean exports to China, and reduced oil shipments to North Korea.[29] In June 2013, in a significant policy shift, Beijing agreed to strengthen UN surveillance of North Korean sanctions violations and to impose sanctions on additional North Korean entities. Secretary of State Kerry had specifically urged China to use its economic leverage to constrain North Korean behavior. In September Kerry praised China for publishing the long list of equipment and chemical substances that it had prohibited for export to North Korea—substances that could be used to develop nuclear and chemical weapons.[30]

In 2013 China had essentially sided with South Korea against North Korea. A senior South Korean foreign affairs official observed that China had to avoid the perception in North Korea that it was "siding completely with the South."[31]

Beijing's diplomacy contributed to restored Chinese cooperation with South Korea and the United States. In June 2013, Park met with Xi in Beijing. In the China–South Korea joint statement, the two sides stated that "nuclear weapon development seriously threatens peace and stability in Northeast Asia, including the Korean Peninsula" and affirmed their commitment to carry out the UN sanctions against North Korea and their support for reconvening the Six-Party Talks.[32] In July 2013, following his meeting with Chinese foreign minister Wang, Kerry stated that the United States and China were "absolutely united," that North Korea "must give up its nuclear

29. Lingling Way and Jay Solomon, "China Publicly Cuts Off North Korean Bank," *Wall Street Journal*, May 7, 2013, http://www.wsj.com/articles/SB10001424127887323372504578 468403543236068; William Ide, "China's Exports to North Korea Fall," *Voice of America*, July 30, 2013, http://www.voanews.com/content/china-exports-to-north-korea-fall/1712903 .html; "Inner Sanctum (1): At Secretive Zhongnanhai, Decisions Are Made That Can Change the World," *Asahi Shimbun*, July 29, 2013, http://ajw.asahi.com/article/asia/china/AJ201 307290005.

30. "China Agrees to Bigger U.N. Panel on N.K." *Korea Herald*, June 24, 2013, http://www .koreaherald.com/common_prog/newsprint.php?ud=20130624000445&dt=2; Jane Perlez, "China Bans Items for Export to North Korea, Fearing Their Use in Weapons," *New York Times*, September 24, 2013, http://www.nytimes.com/2013/09/25/world/asia/china-bans -certain-north-korean-exports-for-fear-of-weapons-use.html?_r=0; U.S. Department of State, "Read Out of Secretary of State Kerry's Meeting with Chinese Foreign Minister Wang Yi," http://www.state.gov/r/pa/prs/ps/2013/09/214801.htm.

31. South Korean leaders perceived China as siding with South Korea. See "Tokyo's Actions Push Seoul and Beijing Closer," *JoongAng Daily*, April 26, 2013, http://koreajoongangdaily .joins.com/news/article/article.aspx?aid=2970744.

32. Lim Soo-Ho, "Park Geun-Hye's Northeast Asia Policy: Challenges, Responses and Tasks," *SERI Quarterly*, April 2013, 15–21. The text of the joint statement is at Xinhua News Agency, June 27, 2013, http://news.xinhuanet.com/world/2013-06/27/c_116319763.htm.

weapons," and that China had assured him that it had made "very firm statements and steps" in support of denuclearization.[33]

Since 2013 China has continued to isolate North Korea. Kim Jung-un became the leader of the Korean Workers Party in December 2011, but as of 2016 China's leaders had yet to agree to a visit by Kim to Beijing, and since late 2013, top Chinese leaders have avoided all personal mention of Kim by name. China has also shunned North Korea in multilateral meetings,[34] and in July 2014, Xi visited South Korea; it was the first time that a new Chinese leader had ever visited South Korea before visiting North Korea. Xi reached agreement in Seoul with President Park for the Chinese and South Korean defense ministries to establish a hotline, in part to facilitate cooperation regarding North Korea's nuclear activities.[35]

U.S. coercive diplomacy against North Korea and instability on the Korean Peninsula, as well as U.S. defense deployments elsewhere in Northeast Asia, had brought home to Chinese leaders the high cost of China's near unqualified support for North Korean behavior. Compelled to reconsider the benefits of continued support for North Korea versus the security costs of U.S. coercive diplomacy on the Korean Peninsula, China compromised, changing its North Korea policy to ameliorate U.S. pressure on Chinese security.

INSTABILITY AND CHINESE COERCIVE DIPLOMACY IN SINO-JAPANESE RELATIONS

From 2010 to 2012, Japan adopted new policies toward the Diaoyu/Senkaku Islands in the East China Sea, which are claimed by both China and Japan. Japan's policies challenged the diplomatic status quo that had maintained stability in the East China Sea since World War II, despite the competing sovereignty claims. The United States, rather than restrain Japan, publicly supported Japan against Chinese growing pressure against Japan. Ultimately, however, China's coercive diplomacy against Japan persuaded the United States to amend its Japan policy, contributing to improved U.S.-China cooperation.

33. Karen DeYoung, "Kerry Praises China on North Korea Efforts, But Criticizes Its Action on Snowden," *Washington Post*, July 2, 2013, http://articles.washingtonpost.com/2013 -07-01/world/40303731_1_south-china-sea-north-korea-president-park-geun-hye. See Kerry's press availability at http://www.state.gov/secretary/remarks/2013/07/211397.htm. See also "Chinese FM Calls for Active, Comprehensive Efforts to Build New Type of Great Power Relations between China, U.S.," Xinhua News Agency, http://news.xinhuanet.com /english/china/2013-07/01/c_132502499.htm.

34. "China Has Few Words for Meeting with N. Korea," *Chosun Ilbo*, August 22, 2014, http://English.Chosun.Com/Site/Data/Html_Dir/2014/08/13/2014081301566.html.

35. Jane Perlez and Choe Sang-Hun, "China Hints at Limits to North Korea Actions," *New York Times*, April 7, 2013, http://www.nytimes.com/2013/04/08/world/asia/from -china-a-call-to-avoid-chaos-for-selfish-gain.html?pagewanted=all.

Sino-Japanese Tension and U.S.-Japan Cooperation. In September 2010, Japan detained a Chinese fishing boat captain after his boat had rammed a Japanese Coast Guard ship within the territorial seas of the disputed islands. Within twenty-four hours of the incident, the Chinese assistant foreign minister and vice foreign minister each "summoned" Japanese ambassador Uichiro Niwa to the foreign ministry to demand the release of the crew.[36] Within a week of the incident, the Japanese ambassador had been summoned five times to receive Chinese protests.

After Japan formally arrested the captain, thereby applying Japanese domestic law against a Chinese citizen fishing in Chinese-claimed waters, Foreign Minister Yang Jiechi summoned the Japanese ambassador and demanded that Japan "immediately and unconditionally" release the crew. China imposed sanctions on Japan. It postponed talks on joint development of a contested gas field in the East China Sea and close to Japanese-claimed waters.[37] It suspended bilateral exchanges at and above the provincial and ministerial levels, including a meeting between the premiers at the UN General Assembly in New York. It also halted discussions on the expansion of civil aviation rights and on coal mining, and canceled a Japanese youth group's visit to China and a major initiative for Chinese tourism in Japan. China also sent maritime surveillance ships to "relevant waters to safeguard China's maritime rights and interests" and to "protect fishermen and their boats."[38] After Japan released the video that established that the Chinese

36. "Transcript of Regular News Conference by PRC Foreign Ministry on 7 September 2010," Ministry of Foreign Affairs of the People's Republic of China, September 7, 2010, OSC, doc. no. CPP20100907364001; "Chinese Ambassador to Japan Lodges Solemn Representations to Japan over Detention of Chinese Fishermen and Fishing Boat in Waters off the Diaoyu Islands," Xinhua News Agency, September 8, 2010, OSC, doc. no. CPP20100908071003; "China Demands Japan Release Detained Fishing Boat, Guarantee Crew's Safety," Xinhua News Agency, September 8, 2010, OSC, doc. no. CPP20100908968215.

37. "Transcript of Regular News Conference by PRC Foreign Ministry on 9 September 2010," Ministry of Foreign Affairs of the People's Republic of China, September 9, 2010, OSC, doc. no CPP20100909364001; "China FM Summons Japanese Ambassador over Japan's Seizure of Chinese Fishing Boat," Xinhua News Agency, September 10, 2010, OSC, doc. no. CPP20100910968159; "China Postpones East China Sea Negotiation with Japan After Boat Seizure," Xinhua News Agency, September 10, 2010, OSC, doc. no. CPP20100910968249; "State Councilor Dai Bingguo Summoms Japanese Ambassador to China for an Urgent Meeting on the Japanese Side's Illegal Arrest and Detention of Chinese Fishing Boat in the Waters Near the Diaoyu Islands," Xinhua News Agency, September 11, 2010, OSC, doc. no. CPP201009 11138004; "China Summons Japan Envoy in Wee Hours to Protest over Ship Collision," Kyodo News Agency, September 12, 2010, OSC, doc. no. JPP20100912969003; "Further on PRC Summoning Japan Envoy 5th Time to Demand Tokyo Release Captain," Agence France-Presse, September 15, 2010, in CPP20100915968051.

38. Bao Daozu, "China Warns Japan of Strong Response," *China Daily*, September 20, 2010, OSC, doc. no. CPP20100920968012; "Foreign Ministry Spokeswoman Jiang Yu Hosted a Regular News Conference on 21 September 2010 and Answered the Following Questions," Ministry of Foreign Affairs of the People's Republic of China, September 21, 2010, OSC, doc. no. CPP20100921364001; "China Rejects Japanese Youths' Visit to Shanghai Expo Amid Ten-

boat was responsible for the collision, China's position hardened. Premier Wen Jiabao spoke out for the first time, saying that the disputed islands were China's "sacred territory" and "strongly urge[d] the Japanese side to release the skipper immediately and unconditionally," warning, "If Japan clings to its mistake, China will take further actions." China then arrested four Japanese nationals from the Fujitsu Corporation for allegedly "illegally filming defense targets" in a military zone.[39] The tension only subsided once Japan released the Chinese fisherman and China then released the Japanese businessmen.

In 2010 China may have overreacted to the fishing incident, but it had made clear to both Japan and the United States its firm resistance to any Japanese challenge to the diplomatic and legal status quo in the East China Sea sovereignty dispute. Nonetheless, on July 7, 2012, Japanese prime minister Yoshihiko Noda announced that the Japanese government was considering the purchase of three of the Diaoyu/Senkaku Islands. Its purpose was to block Governor Shintaro Ishihara, acting on behalf of the Tokyo metropolitan government, from purchasing the islands. An outspoken nationalist, Ishihara could have used ownership of the islands to pursue his nationalist agenda and destabilize Sino-Japanese relations.

But Japanese central government purchase would also suggest a Japanese effort to consolidate the nation's sovereignty over the islands. Regardless of Prime Minister Noda's motive, the purchase of the islands would be a challenge to the status quo that could challenge Chinese sovereignty claims and destabilize Sino-Japanese relations. The U.S. State Department understood that prolonged friction over the islands would be harmful to regional stability and it "quietly gave the Japanese government very strong advice" not to purchase the islands. State Department officials wanted to "speak candidly" to both sides to convey "our key themes of cooling tensions and finding a pragmatic solution."[40]

---

sions," Kyodo News Agency, September 20, 2020, OSC, doc. no. JPP20100920969037; "Major Events in Japan-China Maritime Row," Agence France-Presse, September 22, 2010, OSC, JPP20100922969063.

39. "Chinese Premier Urges Japan to Release Chinese Skipper Immediately, Unconditionally," Xinhua News Agency, September 22, 2010, OSC, doc. no. CPP20100922968052; Keith Bradsher, "Amid Tension, China Blocks Vital Exports to Japan," *New York Times*, September 22, 2010, http://www.nytimes.com/2010/09/23/business/global/23rare.html ?scp=3&sq=japan+china+rare+earths&st=nyt; AFP, September 24, 2010, OSC, doc. no. CPP20100924055002.

40. "Clinton Emails Show U.S. Tried to Heal Tokyo-Beijing Rift over Senkakus," *Japan Times*, February 15, 2016, http://www.japantimes.co.jp/news/2016/02/15/national/politics -diplomacy/clinton-emails-show-u-s-tried-heal-tokyo-beijing-rift-senkakus/# .V4VrnvkrKvV; "U.S. Warned Government against Buying Senkaku Islands: Campbell," *Japan Times*, April 13, 2013, http://www.japantimes.co.jp/news/2013/04/10/national/u-s -warned-government-against-buying-senkaku-islands-campbell/#.Un_g0nBwrTp.

Nonetheless, in late August 2012, as the Noda administration considered whether it should purchase the islands, the United States expressed support for Japan as Tokyo risked conflict with China. The State Department explicitly declared that the U.S.-Japan defense treaty committed the United States to aid Japan in the defense of the Diaoyu/Senkaku Islands.[41] On September 11, Prime Minister Noda announced that the Japanese government had purchased the islands. Soon thereafter, as Sino-Japanese tension increased, despite prior U.S. opposition to the purchase, Assistant Secretary of State Kurt Campbell declared, "We do acknowledge clearly" that the disputed territory "falls clearly under Article 5 of the security treaty."[42] In early January 2013, after Chinese ships had begun to frequently operate within the territorial waters of the islands and Sino-Japanese tension increased, the U.S. Air Force began flights of Airborne Warning and Control System (AWACS) aircraft over the disputed islands to provide support to the Japanese Air Force. The AWACS aircraft approached the Sino-Japanese maritime median line, leading the Chinese Air Force to scramble two aircraft, which then approached and tailed the AWACS aircraft. Secretary of State Clinton then reassured Japanese foreign minister Fumio Kishida that the U.S.-Japan treaty covered the Diaoyus/Senkakus, and publicly expressed U.S. opposition to Chinese actions that would "undermine Japanese administration" of the islands.[43] Shinzo Abe, the presumed successor to Noda following an election in early 2013, interpreted the U.S. remarks as "very meaningful in providing deterrence" against China.[44]

Chinese Coercive Diplomacy against U.S.-Japan Cooperation. Japanese policy toward the disputed Diaoyu/Senkaku Islands presented a diplomatic challenge to China's own sovereignty claim and called into question China's resolve to defend its security interests. Chinese president Hu Jintao had personally warned Noda that China could not accept Japanese government purchase of the islands, saying, "Japan must fully recognize the seriousness of the situation. It should not make an error."[45] Japanese and U.S. officials

---

41. U.S. Department of State, "Daily Press Briefing," August 28, 2012, http://www.state.gov/r/pa/prs/dpb/2012/08/196986.htm.

42. "Top U.S. Diplomat Says Treaty with Japan Covers Islets in China Spat," *Asahi Shimbun*, September 21, 2012, http://ajw.asahi.com/article/asia/china/AJ201209210013.

43. "Japan, China Scrambled Fighters during Jan. 19 Radar Action," *Asahi Shimbun*, February 6, 2013, http://ajw.asahi.com/article/asia/china/AJ201302060075; U.S. Department of State, "Remarks with Japanese Foreign Minister Fumio Kishida after Their Meeting," January 18, 2013, http://www.state.gov/secretary/20092013clinton/rm/2013/01/203050.htm.

44. Yuka Hayashi, "Abe Resolves to Take Tough Line on China," *Wall Street Journal*, November 22, 2012, http://www.wsj.com/news/articles/SB1000142412788732435200457813572 1005214696.

45. Jane Perlez, "China Accuses Japan of Stealing after Purchase of Group of Disputed Islands," *New York Times*, September 11, 2012, http://www.nytimes.com/2012/09/12/world

were aware that Chinese officials were "irate" at Japan's plan to purchase the islands.[46]

At stake for China was thus more than simply its territorial interests in the Sino-Japanese dispute. China had reacted strongly to the 2010 Japanese arrest of the Chinese fisherman, and in 2012 it explicitly warned Japan that it opposed nationalization of the islands; the Noda government's purchase of the disputed islands policy challenged Chinese credibility to defend its sovereignty and the legal status quo. Thus, if China did not respond forcefully to Japanese nationalization of the islands, Japanese leaders might conclude that with U.S. support they could continue to challenge Chinese interests with impunity, enjoying immunity to Chinese retaliation through the U.S. deterrent of China provided by the U.S.-Japan alliance. To curtail the trend on U.S.-Japan relations, China aimed to establish its resolve to impose costs on the United States so as to compel Washington to change its Japan policy. China resorted to third-party coercive diplomacy.

After the Japanese government purchased the three islands, China adopted diplomatic and economic coercive diplomacy against Japan. It suspended high-level political meetings with its neighbor to the east, tolerated violent anti-Japan demonstrations in over a hundred cities in China, and imposed economic penalties, slowing the licensing process for exports to Japan. The government added the disputed islands to China's official weather forecasting programs, and announced Chinese maritime baselines around the disputed islands, which posed a legal challenge to Japan's sovereignty claim.[47]

Most important, China employed forceful coercive maritime diplomacy measures against Japan in disputed waters. Following the Japanese government's purchase of the islands, Chinese government maritime surveillance ships began unprecedented regular patrols within the islands' territorial seas. From September 11, 2012, through March 2013, China's maritime

---

/asia/china-accuses-japan-of-stealing-disputed-islands.html; "Inside Look: Japan Tried but Failed to Avert Disaster in China Dispute," *Asahi Shimbun*, September 26, 2012, http://ajw.asahi.com/article/behind_news/politics/AJ201209260067.

46. See the discussion of Secretary of State Clinton's released e-mail regarding Sino-Japanese relations in "U.S. Urged Japan to Consult with China before 2012 Senkakus Purchase," *Japan Times*, January 31, 2016, http://www.japantimes.co.jp/news/2016/01/31/national/u-s-urged-japan-consult-china-2012-senkaku-purchase/#.V4Vvj_krKvV. See also the text of the cable from Assistant Secretary of State Kurt Campbell to Clinton regarding the dispute at https://mobile.twitter.com/W7VOA/status/693766953144422401.

47. Mure Dickie and Kathrin Hille, "Japan Risks China's Wrath over Senkaku," *Financial Times*, September 10, 2012, http://www.ft.com/intl/cms/s/0/babbfa2a-fb2b-11e1-87ae-00144feabdc0.html#axzz3B3Y8y3AK; Bao Daozu, "China Warns Japan of Strong Response," *China Daily*, http://www.chinadaily.com.cn/china/2010-09/20/content_11325545.htm; "Foreign Ministry Spokesman's News Conference on 21 September 2010," Ministry of Foreign Affairs of the People's Republic of China, September 21, 2010, OSC, doc. no. CPP20100921364001; "China Rejects Japanese Youths' Visit"; "Major Events in Japan-China Maritime Row," Agence France-Presse.

surveillance ships had entered the twelve-mile territorial sea of the islands for thirty-five days and the contiguous zone of the islands for 136 days. Chinese patrols of the disputed territorial seas and Japan's up-close surveillance of the Chinese vessels posed the risk of an unintended collision at sea and escalated hostilities. Chinese behavior not only risked a Sino-Japanese collision but also indirectly threatened the United States with U.S. military involvement in Sino-Japanese hostilities in support of Japan.

In December 2012, China stepped up its coercive diplomacy. On December 13, a Chinese State Oceanic Administration aircraft for the first time ventured within the twelve-mile airspace of one of the disputed islands. Twice in January 2013 Chinese military aircraft approached the islands' contiguous airspace. On January 19, Chinese naval ships directed their fire-control radar at Japanese helicopters, and on January 30 the navy directed its fire-control radar at a Japanese destroyer. On February 4, Chinese surveillance ships drove Japanese fishing boats outside the twelve-mile perimeter, challenging Japan's resolve to defend its citizen's fishing rights in the disputed waters.[48] In December 2012 and in early January 2013, the Japanese Ministry of Defense reported that it was considering authorizing its air force to fire warning shots at Chinese aircraft operating within the twelve-mile perimeter. Throughout this period Japanese and Chinese aircraft frequently "scrambled" against each other's aircraft.

Chinese coercive diplomacy vis-à-vis Japan threatened U.S. security. By posing a heightened risk of intentional or unintentional Sino-Japanese hostilities that could involve the United States, Beijing sought to compel Washington to reconsider its encouragement to Japan in the Sino-Japanese dispute and to restrain Japanese challenges to China's sovereignty claim over the islands.

The U.S. Response to Chinese Coercive Diplomacy. The risk of hostilities between China and Japan over seemingly inconsequential islands persuaded the United States to adopt a more restrained Japan policy. As in the North Korea case, there were asymmetric U.S. and Chinese interests and the

---

48. "Diaoyudao Weiquan Xunhang Yi Zhounian Huigu: Zhifa Shixian Lishixing Tupo" [A look back on the first anniversary of Diaoyu Islands safeguard rights patrols: Law enforcement achieves a historic breakthrough], *People's Daily*, September 10, 2013, http:// politics.people.com.cn/n/2013/0910/c1001-22870944.html; Kathrin Hille, "Japan and China Island Tensions Mount," *Financial Times*, January 11, 2013, http://www.ft.com/intl/cms/s /0/79f1321c-5be8-11e2-bf31-00144feab49a.html#axzz2kHMG4tJ6; "Riben Fabu Zhong Ri Haishang Duizhi Qingkuang" [Japan publicizes Sino-Japan standoffs in the sea], *Lianhe Zaobao*, May 13, 2013; Yuka Hayashi, Jeremy Page, and Julian E. Barnes, "Tensions Flare as Japan Says China Threatened Its Forces," *Wall Street Journal*, February 6, 2013, http://www.wsj .com/articles/SB10001424127887324445904578285442601856314; Martin Fackler, "Japan Says China Aimed Military Radar at Ship," *New York Times*, February 5, 2013, http://www.nytimes .com/2013/02/06/world/asia/japan-china-islands-dispute.html?_r=0.

potential for U.S. entrapment in the Sino-Japanese dispute. On the one hand, for China the islands dispute entailed sovereignty and credibility issues central to security (especially after China's reaction to the 2010 islands incident) and domestic politics. But for the United States the islands are inconsequential. They have minimal strategic and economic value; they are too small to support military operations and there are, at best, minimal energy reserves in the vicinity.[49] The islands are important to Japan, as for China, because they entail sovereignty issues and because of Japanese domestic politics. Given greater Chinese interests in the dispute and the risk of entrapment by Japan, the United States responded to Chinese coercive diplomacy against Japan by moderating its support for Tokyo.

During the 2010 Sino-Japanese fishing dispute and following Japan's purchase of the islands on September 11, 2012, the Obama administration had offered Japan outspoken support in its territorial dispute with China. But beginning in early 2013 it adopted a more distant posture in an effort to restrain Japanese policy and de-escalate the conflict.

In January 2013, U.S. officials who had previously supported Japan now called for "cooler heads to prevail" and "made very clear" the U.S. desire "to see cooler heads prevail and the maintenance of peace and stability over all." During Japanese prime minister Abe's visit to Washington in February 2013, rather than support Japan, the White House merely expressed U.S. interest in lowered Sino-Japanese tension. In contrast to prior policy, neither Obama nor his advisers publicly mentioned the U.S.-Japan treaty. Secretary of State Kerry publicly praised Japan for its "restraint," but he did not publicly criticize Chinese policy, suggesting that the United States preferred that Japan accept China's maritime presence in the disputed waters.[50] Similarly, when Secretary Kerry visited Beijing in April 2013, he did not publicly mention the dispute.

In June 2013, Xi Jinping visited the United States to hold over two days of meetings with President Obama. In his public statements during Xi's visit, Obama did not publicly mention the Sino-Japanese territorial dispute, much less express support for Japan. U.S. national security adviser Thomas Do-

49. In September 2012 the U.S. government estimated that there were merely sixty to one hundred million barrels of oil in the vicinity of the islands. See U.S. Energy Information Administration, *East China Sea*, http://www.eia.gov/countries/analysisbriefs/east_china _sea/east_china_sea.pdf. In 2000, the U.S. Department of the Interior ranked the East China Sea basin at 210 among the world's oil and reserves. See T. R. Klett, James W. Schmoker, and Thomas S. Ahlbrandt, *Assessment Hierarchy and Initial Province Ranking*, U.S. Geological Survey Digital Data Series 60, http://energy.cr.usgs.gov/WEcont/chaps/RH.pdf.

50. White House, "Press Briefing on the Visit of Prime Minister Abe of Japan," February 21, 2013, http://www.whitehouse.gov/the-press-office/2013/02/21/press-briefing -visit-prime-minister-abe-japan; U.S. Department of State, "Remarks with Japanese Foreign Minister Fumio Kishida before Their Meeting," http://www.state.gov/secretary/remarks /2013/02/205116.htm.

nilon reported that Obama and Xi discussed the territorial issue "at some length," but that Obama merely restated that the United States did not take a position on sovereignty and urged both Japan and China "to have conversations about this through diplomatic channels." In September 2013, at the United Nations, Kerry underscored to Chinese foreign minister Wang the U.S. concern for developments in the South China Sea, but he did not mention the Sino-Japanese territorial dispute. In contrast, just a year earlier in New York, Secretary of State Clinton had begun her meeting with Foreign Minister Yang with a discussion of the Sino-Japanese dispute.[51]

Chinese coercive diplomacy toward Japan had heightened the risk of Sino-Japanese hostilities and of U.S. entrapment in hostilities due to Japan's defense of its own national interests. The United States responded by sending signals that it would not support heightened Japanese resistance to China's challenge to Japanese sovereignty, that it expected Japan to reconcile itself to the "new status quo" in the East China Sea, and that the Sino-Japanese territorial dispute would not block U.S.-China cooperation. Compared to U.S. policy in 2010 and in the immediate aftermath of the Japanese government's purchase of the islands, from January 2013 on the United States acted to restrain Japan.

Conclusion: Third-Party Coercion and U.S.-China Relations

The tension in U.S.-China relations over North Korea and over the Sino-Japanese territorial dispute in the East China Sea reflected a sharp break from the post–Cold War norm of regional stability. By 2013, however, U.S. and Chinese third-party coercive diplomacy and the resulting mutual policy adjustment had contributed to improved bilateral relations. The new U.S.-China understanding regarding Chinese policy toward North Korea and U.S. policy toward Japan enabled renewed cooperation not only in Northeast Asia but also on bilateral and global issues.

The June 2013 U.S.-China summit in California reflected a shared success in reducing regional tension; President Obama and President Xi spent over two days in a positive atmosphere at the Annenberg Estate discussing a wide range of bilateral, regional, and global issues, and both U.S. and Chinese leaders expressed considerable satisfaction with the results of the summit.

---

51. "Press Briefing by National Security Advisor Tom Donilon," June 8, 2013, http://www.whitehouse.gov/the-press-office/2013/06/09/press-briefing-national-security-advisor-tom-donilon; U.S. Department of State, "Read Out of Secretary of State Kerry's Meeting with Chinese Foreign Minister Wang Yi," http://www.state.gov/r/pa/prs/ps/2013/09/214801.htm; U.S. Department of State, "State Dept. on Clinton's Meeting with China's Foreign Minister," September 27, 2012, http://iipdigital.usembassy.gov/st/english/texttrans/2012/09/20120927136754.html#axzz3AgGsRWtI.

In the aftermath of the California summit, U.S.-China military-to-military diplomacy resumed, developing greater cooperation than at any time since China's repression of the 1989 democracy demonstrations in Tiananmen Square. China and the United States also developed significant environmental cooperation aimed at controlling global warming and made significant progress toward an agreement promoting direct foreign investment. In 2013 there was U.S.-China cooperation over North Korea. After a prolonged period of silence, China resumed its support for convening the Six-Party Talks on nuclear nonproliferation on the Korean Peninsula. China also cooperated with the United States regarding chemical weapons in Syria and Iran's nuclear program. And in Sino-Japanese relations, China reduced the frequency of its surveillance patrols within the territorial seas of the Diaoyu/Senkaku Islands, apparently signaling its appreciation for the shift in U.S. policy and its interest in reducing the tension in the East China Sea.[52]

Third-party coercion enabled China and the United States to pose indirect challenges to each other's security and a risk of entrapment that encouraged each to change its policy toward its respective ally, North Korea or Japan, rather than toward each other. Compared to direct bilateral great power coercive diplomacy, third-party coercion poses less threat to the great powers, thus constraining escalation, and it requires policy change that entails less credibility/face-saving issues than a direct policy retreat, thus facilitating compromise. This was the dynamic in U.S.-China relations from 2010 to early 2013.

The emergence of coercive diplomacy reflects the rise of China. As M. Taylor Fravel shows in chapter 8 of the present volume, China has also been increasingly resistant to challenges to its sovereignty and economic claims in the South China Sea. The rise of China is far from the point at which it can challenge U.S. primacy in maritime East Asia, but China's modernized maritime capabilities give it the ability to be more proactive in East Asia's maritime conflicts. A mere few years prior to the Japanese government's 2012 purchase of the disputed Diaoyus/Senkakus, China would not have been able to sustain a consistent and capable maritime presence in the vicinity of the islands.

China's improving maritime capabilities suggest the likelihood that U.S.-China competition and tension in East Asia will continue to increase, and that China will become even less tolerant of challenges from both the United States and its allies. And the United States will face greater pressure to defend its allies from Chinese maritime pressures and to signal U.S. resolve to contend with the rise of China. In these circumstances, China and the

---

52. See M. Taylor Fravel and Alistair Iain Johnston, "Chinese Signaling in the East China Sea?," *Washington Post*, April 12, 2014, http://www.washingtonpost.com/blogs/monkey-cage/wp/2014/04/12/chinese-signaling-in-the-east-china-sea/.

United States will each resort to third-party coercive diplomacy to compel the other to moderate its support for its allies' challenges to great power interests.

The 2013 U.S.-China mini-détente ended in late 2014 when the two nations engaged in a new round of heightened tension. China's December 2013 abrupt announcement of the Air Defense Identification Zone (ADIZ) for the East China Sea, its near naval incident with the USS *Cowpens* in the South China Sea, and U.S. concern that Beijing might announce an ADIZ for the South China Sea aroused concerns in Washington that Beijing might be underestimating U.S. resolve to defend the regional order and its alliance commitments.[53]

After nearly a year of moderate U.S. diplomacy, in early 2014 White House and State Department officials publicly challenged Chinese maritime policies throughout East Asia, singling out the nation for creating instability and possessing extreme territorial claims; they warned China that should it declare an ADIZ for the South China Sea that could lead to changes in the U.S. Navy's "presence and military posture" in East Asia.[54]

During his April 2014 visit to East Asia, President Obama increased U.S. resistance to Chinese policies and reaffirmed U.S. commitments to Japan and the Philippines. Prior to his visit to Tokyo, and twice while in Tokyo, Obama broke precedent with past policy and personally noted that Washington's position was that the U.S.-Japan defense treaty covered Japanese control over the Diaoyu/Senkaku Islands. The United States also encouraged Japan to develop naval cooperation with the Philippines and Vietnam and to participate in South China Sea naval exercises with U.S. allies.

In January 2014, the United States supported the Philippines' challenge to Chinese sovereignty claims in the South China Sea at the Permanent Court of Arbitration of the Law of the Sea. When President Obama visited Manila in April 2104, the United States announced a new U.S.-Philippines defense agreement for the deployment of U.S. troops and the construction of U.S. facilities on Philippine military bases. In May 2014 in Singapore, Secretary of Defense Chuck Hagel singled out China for destabilizing Southeast Asia

---

53. On the *Cowpens* incident, see Thom Shanker, "Hagel Criticizes Chinese Navy, Citing Near Miss," *New York Times*, December 19, 2013, http://www.nytimes.com/2013/12/20 /world/asia/hagel-criticizes-chinese-navy-citing-near-miss.html?_r=0. On U.S. concern about a Chinese declaration of an ADIZ in the South China Sea, see John Kerry, "Remarks With Philippine Foreign Secretary Albert del Rosario," December 16, 2013, http://www .state.gov/secretary/remarks/2013/12/218835.htm.

54. See the statement regarding the U.S. defense posture by Evan Medeiros, the Asia director at the White House National Security Council, in Geoff Dyer, "US Blames China for Rising Tensions in South China Sea," *Financial Times*, February 9, 2014, http://www.ft.com /intl/cms/s/0/cdc09e14-91a7-11e3-8fb3-00144feab7de.html#axzz3Alf46gTv; and the testimony by Daniel Russel, assistant secretary of state for East Asia, before the U.S. House of Representatives, in U.S. Department of State, "Maritime Disputes in East Asia," February 5, 2104, http://www.state.gov/p/eap/rls/rm/2014/02/221293.htm.

by asserting its sovereignty claims and also criticized the creation of the ADIZ in the East China Sea.[55]

U.S. pushback against Chinese policy elicited stepped-up Chinese challenges to U.S. allies and another round of Chinese third-party coercion. Shortly after Obama returned to the United States from Tokyo and Manila, China resumed its high-frequency surveillance patrols within the territorial waters of the Diaoyu/Senkaku Islands. It also increased its patrols of these islands' contiguous waters as the Japanese Navy increased its presence in the South China Sea. China also increased its patrols of Philippine fishing activities in disputed waters and its military surveillance of U.S. air and naval activities in the South China Sea. In April 2014 China announced that it would begin drilling for oil in disputed waters near Vietnam.

On the Korean Peninsula, Chinese isolation of North Korea had failed to constrain Pyongyang's nuclear weapons program, and the United States returned to third-party coercion. It strengthened U.S.–South Korea security ties, with implications for Chinese security. In 2015 and 2016 the United States increased its pressure on South Korea to agree to U.S. deployment of the terminal high-altitude area defense (THAAD) missile defense system. Because of its proximity to North Korean launchers, this system cannot defend against North Korean missiles, suggesting that U.S. interest in THAAD for South Korea reflected a political interest in consolidating the US.-South Korea alliance. Moreover, the THAAD system can cover much of Chinese territory, and the United States has insisted that it control the THAAD systems rather than South Korea, thus suggesting to Beijing that Washington's purpose is to integrate the South Korean radar system into the radar grid of its national missile defense system to target Chinese intercontinental missiles and thus undermine China's second-strike capability.

The Chinese ambassador to South Korea warned that if THAAD were deployed in South Korea, China–South Korea relations "could be destroyed in an instant . . . and it would be difficult to restore relations." President Xi personally told President Obama that China was "firmly opposed" to U.S. deployment of THAAD in South Korea.[56]

---

55. The text of Hagel's speech at the May 2014 Shangri-La meeting in Singapore is U.S. Department of Defense, "Secretary of Defense Speech," http://archive.defense.gov/Speeches/Speech.aspx?SpeechID=1857.

56. David Brunnstrom and Lesley Wroughton, "China Calls Obama, Xi Talks 'Constructive,'" Reuters, March 31, 2016, http://www.reuters.com/article/us-nuclear-summit-obama-xi-idUSKCN0WX2RV; Choe Sang-Hun, "South Korea Tells China Not to Intervene in Missile-Defense System Talks," *New York Times*, February 24, 2016, http://www.nytimes.com/2016/02/25/world/asia/south-north-korea-us-missile-defense-thaad-china.html. For a Chinese commentary on these issues, see Liu Chong, "Meiguo Yunniang zai Han Bushu 'Sade' Xitong Banxi" [Analysis of U.S. deployment of "THAAD" system in South Korea], *Xiandai Guoji Guanxi* [Contemporary international relations] 5 (2015): 13–22, 60. For

But Secretary of State Kerry informed Chinese foreign minister Wang that "if we can get to denuclearization, there is no need to deploy THAAD." Deputy Secretary of State Antony Blinken said THAAD "was the latest but not the last defensive step that the Unite States would take if the North Korean nuclear threat persists, and that hopefully it would "motivate China to work with us to change the conduct of the North Korean regime." The United States thus signaled Chinese leaders that U.S. coercive diplomacy was directed as much toward China as it was toward North Korea. And China understood this. It observed that the United States used THAAD to contain China and to pressure it to increase its resistance to North Korea's nuclear program.[57]

In July 2016 South Korea agreed to deployment of the U.S. THAAD system. China observed that the agreement undermines its "strategic security interests" and is "tipping the scale of the regional balance." China further warned that it would "take corresponding measures to safeguard its interests."[58] Whereas after North Korea's January 2016 nuclear test, China had actively cooperated with the United States on new UN economic sanctions against North Korea, after North Korea's September test, China resisted U.S. efforts to pass additional UN sanctions and has pressured South Korea to reconsider its decision to deploy THAAD. From 2014 to 2016 the United States and China engaged in a second round of third-party coercion. U.S. policy on North Korea aimed to coerce China to intervene in North Korea to end Pyongyang's nuclear weapons program. China's policy on the Diaoyu/Senkaku islands cautioned the United States from encouraging Japanese military operations in the South China Sea. In the South China Sea, China raised tension with the Philippines to coerce the United States to restrain Philippine challenges to Chinese sovereignty claims.

The trend in U.S.-China relations is the expected result of the rise of China and the determined emergence of a U.S.-China power transition. Power transitions are inevitably destabilizing, and heightened U.S.-China competition has been anticipated by both scholars and policymakers. Nonetheless, despite the expected difficulty of policymaking, any mistakes in policy will be

---

a similar South Korean perspective, see Sangkeun Lee, "Is the Deployment of THAAD in South Korea a Right Choice?," *Journal of Peace and Unification* 5, no. 1 (2015): 109–16.

57. "Kerry: THAAD Not Necessary if N. Korea is Denuclearized," *Korea Herald*, February 24, 2016, http://www.koreaherald.com/view.php?ud=20160224000363; Michael Martina, "U.S. Challenges China's Imports of North Korean Coal amid U.N. Sanctions," Reuters, October 28, 2016, https://flipboard.com/@flipboard/flip.it%2FCALYEQ-us-challenges-chinas-imports-of-north-k/f-92a9d2a95e%2Freuters.com. Choe, "South Korea Tells China Not to Intervene"; "US Using Deployment of Missile System in ROK as Way to Pressure China," *China Daily*, March 1, 2016, http://www.chinadaily.com.cn/opinion/2016-03/01/content_23692105.htm.

58. See "Foreign Ministry Spokesperson Lu Kang's Regular Press Conference on July 11, 2016," http://www.fmprc.gov.cn/mfa_eng/xwfw_665399/s2510_665401/t1379216.shtml.

costly. After each episode of competition and coercive diplomacy, and as China's capabilities continue to improve, restoring the status quo will be increasingly difficult. Even should relations periodically improve, with each cycle of coercive diplomacy, improved relations may nonetheless be worse than the prior relationship.

Conclusion

East Asia at the Center: Power Shifts and Theory

Øystein Tunsjø

China's rise and the growing allocation of U.S. resources to the Asia-Pacific region are turning East Asia into the center of world politics. Wars in Europe and the Middle East have not reversed this power shift and rebalance. Economic and military power continues to increasingly concentrate in East Asia.[1] China is today the only great power that has regionwide aspirations and, simultaneously, developing capabilities to match those ambitions. The United States is compelled to focus more of its attention on China, its only peer competitor.

While China has not surpassed or obtained power parity with the United States, the relative power distribution between the two nations, and between China and any other third ranking power, has changed in China's favor since the financial crisis in 2007. The power gap between the United States and China has narrowed and China has become even more powerful relative to its neighbors. Events since 2009 suggest that the region is tending toward stronger balancing behavior and more confrontation. Most significant in the new patterns of strategic adjustment are China's growing assertiveness and

---

The title of this conclusion is taken from the study by Warren I. Cohen, *East Asia at the Center: Four Thousand Years of Engagement with the World* (New York: Columbia University Press, 2000).

1. The combined nominal GDP of China, Japan, and South Korea is now roughly twice as large as the combined GDP of Britain, France, Germany, and Italy. See, for instance, International Monetary Fund, "World Economic Outlook Database," http://www.imf.org/external /pubs/ft/weo/2015/01/weodata/index.aspx. If we measure GDP in purchasing power parity, the gap is significantly higher. Asia has been spending more on defense than Europe since 2012. For an account of this trend, see Sam Perlo-Freeman, Aude Fleurant, Pieter D. Wezeman, and Siemon T. Wezeman, *Trends in World Military Expenditure, 2014*, April 2015, http://books.sipri.org/files/FS/SIPRIFS1504.pdf.

the U.S. response to this more assertive behavior. China's economic strength and military modernization have created enhanced capabilities that allow it to assert its interests more forcefully and pursue more ambitious foreign policy objectives. Its challenges to the regional status quo and "the geography of peace" have elicited heightened U.S. concerns about what the current Chinese economic and security behavior pose for U.S. interests.[2]

How China's rise and global power shifts contribute to East Asian (in)stability and prosperity have preoccupied scholars, policymakers, and observers for years.[3] Power shifts and their effect on states patterns of behavior—whereby regional states and the United States are in a process of moving away from extensive hedging and toward either more balancing against or more cooperation (bandwagoning) with China—are exacerbated in each case by the role of nationalism and domestic politics. Adjusting to power shifts and managing a new regional order in the face of inevitable domestic pressure, including nationalism, will be challenging but necessary. Taking into account China's growing strategic weight, the United States has consolidated alliances in East Asia, engaged in closer military cooperation with countries in Southeast Asia, and conducted a more active and provocative diplomacy on sensitive issue such as disputes in the South China Sea. Many regional states have sought closer ties with the United States as a counterweight to China's ascent, but others have adjusted their foreign policy to accommodate China's rising power. Common to all states operating in East Asia, including the United States, is that it is increasingly more difficult to cooperate and confront China simultaneously. East Asia is becoming more polarized.

The various chapters in this volume combine system level factors with an assessment of the role of geography, nationalism, economics, institutions, and political leaders. The contributors to the volume recognize that power shifts or changes in the distribution of capabilities "never tell us all we want to know."[4] International politics can best be understood if the effects of

2. Robert S. Ross, "The Geography of Peace: East Asia in the Twenty-First Century," *International Security* 23, no. 4 (1999): 81–118.

3. Peter Sharman, ed., *Power Transition and International Order in Asia* (London: Routledge, 2015); Elena Atanassova-Cornelis and Frans-Paul van der Putten, eds., *Changing Security Dynamics in East Asia: A Post-U.S. Regional Order in the Making?* (London: Palgrave Macmillan, 2014); Andrew T. H. Tan, ed. *Security and Conflict in East Asia* (London: Routledge, 2015); Robert S. Ross and Zhu Feng, eds., *China's Ascent: Power, Security, and the Future of International Politics* (Ithaca, NY: Cornell University Press, 2008); Kent E. Calder and Francis Fukuyama, eds., *East Asian Multilateralism: Prospects for Regional Stability* (Baltimore: Johns Hopkins University Press, 2008); David Shambaugh, ed., *Power Shift: China and Asia's New Dynamics* (Berkeley: University of California Press, 2005); J. J. Shu, Peter J. Katzenstein, and Allen Carlson, *Rethinking Security in East Asia: Identity, Power, and Efficiency* (Stanford, CA: Stanford University Press, 2004).

4. Kenneth N. Waltz, "Reflections on *Theory of International Politics*: A Response to My Critics," in *Neorealism and Its Critics*, ed. Robert O. Keohane (New York: Columbia University Press, 1986), 343.

structure—that is, if anarchy and the shifts in distribution of capabilities—are added to the unit-level explanations of traditional realism.[5] Structure constrains, but East Asian security is not determined or preordained by structure. As Randall L. Schweller reminds us in chapter 1, enhanced capabilities will permit a country to entertain "aspirations for hegemonic (or, simply, great power) status" but not tell us the purpose of state action or whether and how a state will be able to mobilize its resources in order to respond successfully to structural-systemic incentives and opportunities.

As the contributions to this volume demonstrate, Japan and South Korea have adjusted their respective policies in response to the rise of China and the shifting distribution of capabilities, but whereas Japan has balanced against China and has not been constrained by China's growing economic leverage, South Korean balancing has been constrained by its increasing economic dependence on China, and it has pursued a hedging strategy. The two nations' different responses to the rise of China can also be explained by geographical factors, such as South Korea's closer proximity to China and geographical location on the East Asian mainland versus the water barrier that separates Japan from China. As an island, Japan is more likely to rely on the alliance with the United States. While South Korean leaders seek to sustain the alliance with the United States, South Korea is more constrained by China's growing military capabilities and the threat from North Korea. Thus, geopolitics shapes their respective alliance with the United States and affects their response to the rise of China. Moreover, South Koreans share with the Chinese a memory of Japanese aggression and occupation during the first half of the twentieth century, which allows for history, nationalism, and domestic politics to contribute to Japan's and South Korea's foreign policies differently.

As far back as 2000, Kenneth Waltz wrote that "when external conditions press firmly enough, they shape the behavior of states. Increasingly, Japan is being pressed to enlarge its conventional forces and to add nuclear ones to protect its interests."[6] Japan is increasingly taking steps to enhance its military capabilities and collaborates more closely with regional states in order to confront China diplomatically and militarily, but Japan is not developing nuclear weapons or long-range bombers, missiles, or large aircraft carriers.

5. Kenneth N. Waltz, "The Origins of War in Neorealist Theory," *Journal of Interdisciplinary History* 18, no. 4 (1988): 39–52; Kenneth N. Waltz, *Man, the State and War: A Theoretical Analysis* (New York: Columbia University Press, 1959), 160, 186; Kenneth N. Waltz. *Theory of International Politics*, 60–67, 122–23. For neoclassical analysis, see Randall L. Schweller, chapter 1, this volume; Randall L. Schweller, *Unanswered Threats: Political Constraints on the Balance of Power* (Princeton, NJ: Princeton University Press, 2006); and Gideon Rose, "Neoclassical Realism and Theories of Foreign Policy," *World Politics* 51, no. 1 (1998): 144–72.

6. Kenneth N. Waltz, "Structural Realism after the Cold War," *International Security* 25, no. 1 (2000): 34.

While structural realism correctly suggests that the rise of China will prompt Japan toward balancing, we need to examine unit-level factors to account for the complexity and nuances in states' balancing behavior. Thus, no author in this volume explains shifting patterns of behavior, challenges to the status quo, or increasing instability solely from a structural realist perspective.

This conclusion is divided into two main sections. The first section draws on Robert Gilpin's emphasis on power change to explain the new power dynamics in East Asia. The second section examines the implications of this power change and considers the risk of war and conflict in the region.

China's Rise: Power Change, Not Transition

Power transition theory contends that changes in the power structure and the rise of a great power often lead to war. As A. F. K, Organski and Jacek Kugler note, "If one nation gains significant power, its improved position relative to that of other nations frightens them and induces them to try to reverse this gain by war. Or, vice versa, a nation gaining on an adversary will try to make its advantage permanent by reducing its opponent by force of arms. Either way, changes in power are considered *causae belli*."[7] In contemporary East Asia, the rising power (China) has not gone to war to change the status quo, and the existing leading power (the United States) has not launched a preventive war to preserve the status quo. Power has been redistributed between the United States and China and the power shift continues, but there has not been a power transition between the two. The United States remains the most powerful state within the international system, and China's power in East Asia has not surpassed it. Moreover, power transition and growing asymmetry in China's relations with its neighboring major powers, India, Japan, and Russia, have not contributed to any wars. East Asia has been the most peaceful region in the world for more than three decades.

According to Organski and Kugler, the "power-transition model postulates that the speed with which modernization occurs in big countries is also quite important in disturbing the equilibrium that existed theretofore . . . if growth takes place rapidly, both parties will be unprepared for the resulting shift" and it seems plausible that miscalculation, conflict and wars will occur.[8] Few great powers throughout history have in peacetime risen to power as fast as China has, and in a relatively short period of roughly three

---

7. A. F. K. Organski and Jacek Kugler, *The War Ledger* (Chicago: University of Chicago Press, 1980), 13.
8. Ibid., 21.

decades changed the distribution of capabilities as significantly as China has, without being engaged in any wars. The developments in East Asia and the rise of China suggest that the power transition theory is inadequate in explaining the new power dynamics in East Asia.[9] But the power shift has disturbed the equilibrium.

From a realist perspective, Gilpin's seminal study on war and change in world politics can provide a more nuanced analysis for examining current power shifts and developments in East Asia.[10] Gilpin focuses on different rates of growth of power in the international system and the result of this unevenness, and argues that the "law of uneven growth continues to redistribute power" in a "cycle of growth, expansion, and eventual decline."[11] An enormous amount of writing has been published on China's rise and its growth. China might continue to rise in relative power terms, but instead of focusing on its rise, attention can be shifted to acknowledging that China has reached a stage in its ascent where its enhanced power position starts to change the status quo "as the perceived potential benefits begin to exceed the perceived cost of undertaking a change in the system."[12] China has since 2009 risked undermining its benign security environment by more assertively securing its interests. The United States, the challenged dominant state, responds in order to maintain the equilibrium. As the relative power shift increases, this pattern of action and reaction is reinforced, instability grows, and strategic adjustment becomes necessary.

RULES, SPHERES OF INFLUENCE, AND STATUS QUO

According to Gilpin, the rising state attempts to "change the rules governing the international system, the division of the spheres of influence, and, most important of all, the international distribution of territory."[13] Randall L. Schweller and Xiaoyu Pu have argued that, as the rising power, China—prior to military confrontation and even the threat of such conflict—seeks to delegitimize the dominant power's authority and the existing international order. Full-fledged balancing and global contestation is likely to be the next phase in resisting the unbalanced unipolar structure and the rules governing the international system. But it is not clear to Schweller and Pu whether

---

9. This is consistent with Jack S. Levy's argument back in 2008. See Jack S. Levy, "Power Transition Theory and the Rise of China," in Robert S. Ross and Zhu Feng, eds., *China's Ascent: Power, Security, and the Future of International Politics* (Ithaca, NY: Cornell University Press, 2008), 11–33.

10. Robert Gilpin, *War and Change in World Politics* (Cambridge: Cambridge University Press, 1981).

11. Ibid., 210.

12. Ibid., 187.

13. Ibid.

China will be a "supporter, spoiler, or shirker" of the emerging international order.[14] In chapter 3 of this volume Daniel W. Drezner shows that Chinese leaders do not have a clear vision for an alternative order. This is particularly true in the financial realm, and "China acted like a supporter rather than a spoiler" in macroeconomic policy coordination in the aftermath of the 2007–8 financial crisis. Self-interests were paramount when China introduced large fiscal stimulus packages, "but the salutary effect on the global economy was still significant" and "China largely refrained from challenging the status quo in global economic governance." Drezner not only concludes that China abstained from subverting the existing set of global economic governance rules when the opportunity arose but also warns that observers tend to exaggerate the relative decline of the hegemon and the relative rise of everyone else.

Nonetheless, China has acted more assertive on security and territorial matters in East Asia. As I contend in chapter 2 of this volume, in accordance with Gilpin's law of uneven growth, the division of the spheres of influence in the region is changing, while in chapter 4 Wang Dong emphasizes that a constellation of "two Asias" is emerging. In chapter 2, I argue that the security order established in the aftermath of U.S.-China rapprochement and normalization in the 1970s, with spheres of influences that rested on China's dominance on the East Asian mainland and U.S. superiority in maritime domain, are now challenged by China's greater naval capabilities and more assertive behavior. The nation's growth, and a shift in the distribution of power, allow China to operate in the maritime domain and challenge the United States and its allies in the U.S. sphere of influence in maritime East Asia. Wang's contribution highlights that the rise of China reconfigures the "dual structure" in the region. He notes that East Asian countries look to China for economic growth and to the United States for security guarantees, but such strategies are becoming increasingly irreconcilable. Thus, both Wang and I emphasize that the United States, China, and some regional states are adjusting and revising their hedging strategies in light of current power changes, and this encompasses a growing tendency toward balancing and (re)alignment behavior. In chapter 7, Chung-in Moon also points to the changing geopolitical environment and examines South Korea's strategic positioning and adaptation to changes in the distribution of power. He explicitly asks if South Korea needs to move closer to a rising China, concluding that it can continue to mix cooperation and confrontation and avoiding choosing sides between Beijing and Washington.

China still faces challenges in modernizing its armed forces, and it remains uncertain whether the People's Liberation Army (PLA) will be able to fight

---

14. Randall Schweller and Xiaoyu Pu, "After Unipolarity: China's Vision of International Order in an Era of U.S. Decline," *International Security* 36, no. 1 (2011): 41–72.

and win a war against a modern opponent in the twenty-first century.[15] The United States is still ahead of China in military capabilities, but as the findings of a comprehensive RAND report show, China is closing several military gaps with the United States. In fact, the report concludes, the net change in capabilities is still moving toward China's favor.[16] If another Taiwan Strait Crisis erupts today, the PLA will be much more able to contest the sea, subsea, air, land, and space around Taiwan than it was during the U.S. involvement in the 1995–96 Taiwan Strait Crisis.[17] The findings in the 2015 U.S. Office of Naval Intelligence report on the People's Liberation Army Navy (PLAN) confirm the "significant strides" taken since 2009 in operationalizing and modernizing its force.[18]

Leading experts on the PLAN see the development and deployment of a strong Chinese navy,[19] one that is increasingly modern and regionally powerful, and able to pose a significant "challenge in the Western Pacific to the U.S. Navy's ability to achieve and maintain control of blue-water ocean areas in wartime—the first such challenge the U.S. Navy has faced since the end of the Cold War."[20]

15. Michael S. Chase, Jeffrey Engstrom, Tai Ming Cheung, Kristen A. Gunness, Scott Warren Harold, Susan Puska, and Samuel K. Berkowitz, *China's Incomplete Military Transformation: Assessing the Weaknesses of the People's Liberation Army (PLA)* (Santa Monica, CA: RAND, 2015), http://www.uscc.gov/sites/default/files/Research/China%27s%20Incomplete%20Military%20Transformation_2.11.15.pdf; Dennis J. Blasko, "Ten Reasons Why China Will Have Trouble Fighting a Modern War," February 18, 2015, http://warontherocks.com/2015/02/ten-reasons-why-china-will-have-trouble-fighting-a-modern-war/; Bernard D. Cole, *The Great Wall at Sea: China's Navy in the Twenty-First Century*, 2nd ed. (Annapolis, MD: Naval Institute Press, 2010).

16. Eric Heginbotham, Michael Nixon, Forrest E. Morgan, Jacob L. Heim, Jeff Hagen, Sheng Li, Jeffrey Engstrom, Martin C. Libicki, Paul DeLuca, David A. Shlapak, David R. Frelinger, Burgess Laird, Kyle Brady, and Lyle J. Morris, *The U.S.-China Military Scorecard: Forces, Geography, and the Evolving Balance of Power 1996–2017* (Santa Monica, CA: RAND, 2015), http://www.rand.org/pubs/research_reports/RR392.html; Roger Cliff, *China's Military Power: Assessing Current and Future Capabilities* (Cambridge: Cambridge University Press, 2015).

17. Robert S. Ross, "The Rise of the Chinese Navy: From Regional Naval Power to Global Naval Power?" in Jacques deLisle and Avery Goldstein, eds. *China's Global Engagement: Cooperation, Competition, and Influence in the 21st Century* (Washington, DC: Brookings Institution, 2017).

18. U.S. Office of Naval Intelligence, *The PLA Navy: New Capabilities and Missions for the 21st Century* (Washington, DC: U.S. Office of Naval Intelligence, 2015), http://news.usni.org/2015/04/09/document-office-of-naval-intelligence-2015-assessment-of-chinese-peoples-liberation-army-navy. See also U.S. Department of Defense, *Asia-Pacific Maritime Security Strategy* (Washington, DC: U.S. Department of Defense, 2015), http://www.defense.gov/Portals/1/Documents/pubs/NDAA%20A-P_Maritime_SecuritY_Strategy-08142015-1300-FINALFORMAT.PDF.

19. Cole, *The Great Wall at Sea*, xvi.

20. Ronald O'Rourke, "China's Naval Modernization: Implications for U.S. Navy Capabilities—Background and Issues for Congress," September 21, 2015, https://www.fas.org/sgp/crs/row/RL33153.pdf.

In chapter 9 of this volume, Robert S. Ross argues that China remains unable to challenge the regional balance of power. While China has become more assertive, and developed more capabilities to assert its interests in East Asian waters, the United States has sustained its predominance in the maritime domain and the geography of peace has not been disrupted. In addition, Ross has demonstrated that secondary state economic dependence on a great economic power is an *insufficient* force to compel independently small state realignment. Economic power in the absence of military power cannot determine small state alignments.[21] Australia, Malaysia, and Singapore depend on export to China for economic stability and growth. Nonetheless, these states have sought closer strategic and military cooperation with the United States following China's growing assertiveness and relative power shift. Security concerns and the U.S. superiority in maritime East Asia, rather than economic considerations and Chinese market power, have shaped their alignment preferences.[22] Accordingly, Ross maintains that China's development of significant influence in the international political economy has not trumped the geopolitical realities and the spheres of influence in East Asia. This finding complements Drezner's argument that China's rising economic power has not undermined the existing U.S.-led international economic order.

Gilpin argued that redistribution of territory is the most important of all of the consequences that often accompany relative power shifts. In this case, the dynamic and the extent of change in East Asia differ. Several contributors to this volume point out that China has changed the status quo on the disputed Diaoyu/Senkaku Islands in the East China Sea. No territory has been redistributed, and China has not been able to expand and take control of the disputed islands, but it has maintained a strong presence in the proximity of the islands and challenged Japan's sovereignty, control, and administration through the usage of its growing maritime law enforcement and naval capabilities.

As Ian Bowers and Bjørn Elias Mikalsen Grønning show in chapter 5 of this volume, China's growth makes it difficult for Japan to protect the status quo. China no longer lacks maritime capabilities to protect its interests and can rely on more than diplomatic protests and verbal statements in order to challenge Japan's sovereignty of the contested islands. China is developing a modern navy, and in 2015 operated 205 maritime law enforcement vessels—more than Indonesia, Japan, Malaysia, the Philippines, and Vietnam combined—that can be deployed to underscore its claim over the disputed

21. Robert S. Ross, "Balance of Power Politics and the Rise of China: Accommodation and Balancing in East Asia," *Security Studies* 15, no. 3 (July–September 2006), 355–95.
22. Japan and the Philippines have also strengthened their security ties with the United States, but are not as dependent on the Chinese market as Australia, Malaysia, and Singapore are.

islands. As a result, Japan's position that there is no dispute becomes more questionable. In addition, China's announcement of the Air Defense Identification Zone (ADIZ) for the East China Sea in December 2013 further increased the instability dynamic. As Robert S. Ross writes in chapter 9, these developments forced Japan to reconcile itself to a "new status quo." Nevertheless, China faces in the East China Sea a strong regional power in Japan, which has a highly capable and technologically advanced navy and remains a formal and close ally of the United States, the dominating sea power in the world. This context contrasts with the situation in the South China Sea, were China faces a number of weaker states (some of them very weak) whose relations with the United States are somewhat varied.

To date, China has not established the ADIZ in the South China Sea, but it has gone further in expanding its control over reefs and shoals in these waters than it has in the East China Sea. It succeeded in taking control of the Scarborough Shoal in 2012 during a standoff with the Philippines through the usage of fishing vessels and its civilian coast guard and maritime surveillance vessels. Fearing that an intervention by the U.S. Navy could escalate the conflict, the United States became reluctant and was presented with a fait accompli by China's deployment of its civilian maritime surveillance and coast guard vessels. As M. Taylor Fravel points out in chapter 8, the United States was left with a de facto acceptance of China's control of the shoal. Several of the littoral states around the South China Sea have extended their territory on disputed reefs and shoals through land reclamation. But China's efforts to create a more substantial land mass on Mischief Reef, Fiery Cross Reef,[23] and on other contested reefs and shoals, are unprecedented in scale.

U.S. Defense Secretary Ash Carter stated that the United States is "deeply concerned" and "opposes" any "further militarization" of the disputed waters, reefs, shoals, and islands.[24] During an eleven-day trip to Southeast Asia in April 2016, Carter announced new military agreements with India and the Philippines and visited the carrier *John C. Stennis* operating near the disputed reefs and waters in the South China Sea. Aboard the *Stennis*, Carter stated that the United States will continue to patrol the waters in the region.[25] The tension in the South China Sea has prompted the United States

23. "Chinese Mischief at Mischief Reef," *New York Times*, April 11, 2015, http://www.nytimes.com/2015/04/12/opinion/sunday/chinese-mischief-at-mischief-reef.html?emc=edit_th_20150412&nl=todaysheadlines&nlid=70301755&_r=0.

24. Ash Carter, "A Regional Security Architecture Where Everyone Rises,", May 30, 2015, https://www.iiss.org/-/media/Documents/Events/Shangri-La%20Dialogue/SLD15/Carter.pdf.

25. Michael S. Schmidt, "In South China Sea Visit, U.S. Defense Chief Flexes Military Muscles," *New York Times*, April 15, 2016, http://www.nytimes.com/2016/04/16/world/asia/south-china-sea-us-ash-carter.html?_r=0.

to fly navy surveillance aircraft in close proximity to the reefs and on October 27, 2015, the USS *Lassen* undertook a freedom-of-navigation operation within twelve nautical miles of the disputed reefs in the Spratly Islands to demonstrate that the United States does not recognize any Chinese territorial zone.[26] Such patterns of behavior are heightening tension and risking conflict in the South China Sea.

Finally, China pursued its assertiveness in contested waters in the Paracel Islands through the deployment of the HYSY 981 drilling rig in May 2014. This decision, notes Fravel, signaled China's willingness to pursue, consolidate, and deter others from challenging China's interests and sovereignty claims.

In response to a rising state's attempts to challenge the existing order, undermine the status quo, and expand territorially, the dominant power can counter these challenges through increasing its resources devoted to maintaining the equilibrium or by reducing costs. Domestically, the challenged power can generate new resources through taxation, increase efficiency, improve innovation, and enact more skillful resource management.[27] This volume focuses more on the external measures the United States has pursued in response to China's rise and expansion. There are few signs of a U.S. restraint in its China policy, but a growing concentration of forward U.S. military capabilities on Guam signals a step toward emphasizing offshore balancing and a more secure defense perimeter.[28] Fravel (in chapter 8) and Ross (in chapter 9) clearly show that the United States has not sought any retrenchment against the expanding power of China. Fravel maintains that since 1949, the United States has never been more involved in disputes in the South China Sea than today and Ross contends that the United States has increasingly sought to coerce China.

It is beyond the scope of this volume to assess U.S. grand strategy and overall foreign policy objectives in the post–Cold War era, but the announcement of the U.S. pivot suggests that the administration of President Barack Obama has been seeking to balance commitments and resources.[29] This approach acknowledges that power shifts are under way and then evaluates

26. Jim Sciutto, "Exclusive: China Warns U.S. Surveillance Plane," May 27, 2015, http://edition.cnn.com/2015/05/20/politics/south-china-sea-navy-flight/index.html; Bonni Glaser and Peter A. Dutton, "The U.S. Navy's Freedom of Navigation Operation around Subi Reef: Deciphering U.S. Signaling," *National Interest*, November 6, 2015, http://nationalinterest.org/feature/the-us-navy%E2%80%99s-freedom-navigation-operation-around-subi-reef-14272.

27. Gilpin, *War and Change*, chap. 5.

28. Barry R. Posen, *Restraint: A New Foundation for U.S. Grand Strategy* (Ithaca, NY: Cornell University Press, 2014).

29. Hillary Clinton, "America's Pacific Century," *Foreign Policy*, October 11, 2011, http://foreignpolicy.com/2011/10/11/americas-pacific-century/; White House Office of the Press Secretary, "Remarks by President Obama to the Australian Parliament," November 17, 2011,

priorities and options. The strategic approach embedded in the pivot calls for the United States to bring its objectives into line with its material and political resources and adjust to a new power configuration without weakening its existing commitments and alliances or undermining its prestige and international position. As the Obama administration has experienced, such a strategy of reducing international commitments is politically difficult, and carrying it out is a delicate matter.

The military rebalancing, whereby the United States relatively increased its forward military presence in East Asia and initiated a drawdown of its military presence in Europe, began in the 1990s and was accentuated by the Taiwan Strait Crisis in 1995–96.[30] The war on terror shifted U.S. focus to the wars in Afghanistan and Iraq, although the U.S. military continued to have strong presence in East Asia during the early years of the twenty-first century. Seeking to reduce U.S. commitments and eventually withdraw from the wars in Afghanistan and Iraq, and to shift U.S. priority to the Asia-Pacific region, the Obama administration initiated the pivot in 2011. Russia's aggression and military operations in Ukraine in 2014 and 2015, and the war in Syria and instability in the Middle East, have not reversed the fact that the balance of power challenge for the United States is in East Asia, but these developments have made it more difficult for the United States to reduce its international commitments.[31]

Nonetheless, the U.S. pivot to the Asia-Pacific has not been reversed, and the fundamental premise for a continued rebalance remains. In 2015, according to the International Monetary Fund, China's nominal gross domestic product (GDP) was larger than that of all the countries in East Asia combined—including Australia. Even if we add India and Russia to the equation, China's economic strength would match all these countries. Similarly, according to 2015 data from the Stockholm International Peace Research Institute, China's military expenditure is much higher than all East Asian countries combined and about the same if India and Russia were added. In contrast, Russia is no match for the major European powers in terms of defense spending and GDP. Russia's GDP in 2016 was estimated by the IMF to be about the size of Spain's, about half the size of France's and the United Kingdom's, and just above one-third of Germany's. Russia spends most on

---

https://www.whitehouse.gov/the-press-office/2011/11/17/remarks-president-obama-australian-parliament.

30. Øystein Tunsjø, "Europe's Favourable Isolation," *Survival* 55, no. 6 (2013–14): 91–106; Robert S. Ross, "Bipolarity and Balancing in East Asia," in *Balance of Power: Theory and Practice in the 21st Century*, ed. T. V. Paul, James J. Wirtz, and Michael Fortmann (Stanford, CA: Stanford University Press, 2004), 267–304.

31. U.S. Department of Defense, *Sustaining U.S. Global Leadership: Priorities for 21st Century Defense*, January 2012, http://www.defense.gov/news/Defense_Strategic_Guidance.pdf.

defense in Europe, but the combine defense spending of only two of the major European NATO powers is sufficient to obtain higher defense spending than Russia, and they can outspend Russia on defense with a much lower percentage of GDP. The regional balance of power is only challenged in East Asia and the United States is the only power that can balance China.

Implications and the Risk of War

A dominant power can respond to challenges from a rising power by weakening, containing, or destroying the rising power. The historical record reveals that if status quo powers fail in their attempt to deter the aggressor, incorporate the rising power into the existing order, or sustain the balance of power, the persistent disequilibrium beset by tension and crisis will often be resolved by war. Gilpin calls this a hegemonic war, which changes the system in accordance with the new international distribution of power. It is not inevitable, of course, that there will be a war between the United States and China in the twenty-first century. The rivalry between the two superpowers during the bipolar period of the twentieth century remained a cold war. In the present volume Fravel (chapter 9) suggests that the United States and China will continue "threading the needle" and Schweller (chapter 1) maintains that in the coming decade the situation will likely "continue to simmer" but "not reach a boiling point."

The likelihood of greater tension in U.S.–China relations and throughout the region is the most likely trajectory. The "geography of peace," the primary conditions that have sustained peace and stability in the region for more than three decades, is increasingly undermined. The fact that China goes to sea and is becoming more capable of asserting its interests in the maritime domain suggests that the regional order is in transition. Relations will get worse as the contemporary power shift allows China to continue developing its naval capabilities, spend more on naval shipbuilding, including maritime surveillance and coast guard vessels, and use its growing naval power to consolidate its interests in maritime East Asia.[32]

Robert D. Kaplan has argued that since East Asia is a seascape and the dominant and the rising powers in East Asia are separated by water, "the region will likely avoid the kind of great military conflagrations that took place on dry land in the twentieth century." The assumption is that water is an impediment to invasion. "It is because of the seas around East Asia that the twenty-first century has a better chance than the twentieth of avoiding

---

32. For a comprehensive analysis of China maritime ambitions, see Bernard D. Cole, *China's Quest for Great Power: Ships, Oil, and Foreign Policy* (Annapolis, MD: Naval Institute Press, 2016).

great military conflagrations."[33] Water barriers in East Asia cause significant power projection problems for attacking armies and make China and the United States less vulnerable to a first strike. Water may also prevent a crisis, conflict, or limited war at sea from escalating into a major war or bringing about as much devastation as a land war. But the fact that great power rivalry in the twenty-first century is mainly concentrated at sea makes a limited war more likely. The geography of East Asia suggests that "a future Sino-American competition in Asia will take place in a setting more conducive to war than was Europe during the Cold War."[34]

Schelling writes how geography and physical configurations contribute to the scope of war.[35] A shooting war between the United States and China will clearly come with an added risk of escalation. The main point here, however, is not to speculate about the potential risk of escalation after a limited war erupts. It is an open-ended question; scholarship does not enable prediction of how a conflict might escalate once the superpowers start shooting at one another.[36] Although the risk of armed conflict between two nuclear superpowers remains low, it is higher in maritime East Asia today than it was in the previous bipolar system concentrated on continental Europe.

The geopolitics of East Asia is more dynamic and unstable than the static East-West divide in continental Europe during the Cold War. A third world war, including the use of nuclear weapons, was seen as possible if the militaries of either the Warsaw Pact countries or the North Atlantic Treaty Organization had crossed into their opponents' respective spheres of influence. An invasion posed an existential threat, and the stakes of inadvertent escalation were so high that they effectively stabilized the European continent during the Cold War. In contrast, the contested areas in East Asia today are in the maritime domain, where a battle at sea could largely be confined to East Asian waters and not pose a direct existential threat in the form of a land invasion. Under such conditions, decision makers might risk a war over maritime disputes in East Asia or a first strike against an opponent's navy, calculating that the possibility of a full-scale invasion or major war is less likely when the great powers are not located on the same landmass.[37] The

33. Robert D. Kaplan, *Asia's Cauldron: The South China Sea and the End of a Stable Pacific* (New York: Random House, 2014), 6–7, 175.

34. John J. Mearsheimer, *The Tragedy of Great Power Politics*, 2nd ed. (New York: Norton, 2014), 395–98; Øystein Tunsjø, "The Cold War as a Guide to the Risk of War in East Asia," *Global Asia* 9, no. 3 (2014): 15–19.

35. Thomas C. Schelling, *The Strategy of Conflict* (Cambridge: Harvard University Press, 1980), 74–77.

36. Thomas C. Schelling, *Arms and Influence* (New Haven, CT: Yale University Press, 1966), 48–49, 105, 123.

37. Tunsjø, "The Cold War as a Guide."

risk of escalation to the use of nuclear weapons is, therefore, less likely, and this might paradoxically increase the risk of conventional war at sea.

Moreover, water barriers suggests that U.S. maritime allies in East Asia can behave more recklessly in their confrontation with China because the stopping power of water protects them from China's superior land power. West Germany and other U.S. allies in Europe were so afraid of Soviet invasion that they sought to avoid brinkmanship and instead sought to engage and accommodate the Soviet Union. Rather than diminish the likelihood of war, East Asia's geography increases the risk of war. Finally, as John J. Mearsheimer emphasizes when comparing the U.S.-Soviet rivalry, "no territorial dispute between the superpowers—Berlin included—was as laden with intense nationalistic feelings as Taiwan [and sovereignty claims in the East and South China Sea are] for China. Thus, it is not hard to imagine a war erupting over Taiwan, though the odds of that happening are not high."[38] As a result of East Asia's geopolitics, the contemporary conflicts and risks becomes more difficult to manage and deter. It is more difficult to draw red lines and trip wires at sea.[39] There is no East-West divide, Berlin Wall, or Checkpoint Charlie in East Asian waters. There are no trip wires or commitments that are not inescapable. Instead, U.S. commitments regarding potential flashpoints in the South China Sea, the East China Sea, and the Taiwan Strait and are more uncertain. It might be contended that a battle at sea in maritime East Asian does not represent a hegemonic war, but the control of East Asian waters and sea lanes is at the heart of the twenty-first century's contest over regional hegemony in East Asia.

The outlook for East Asian stability is uncertain. The revival of China as a dominant regional power brings new forms of competition and forces us to ask whether the existing U.S.-China power relationship can be preserved or whether the growth of China's power reflects an underlying instability in the system whereby the status quo dominant power will persist in balancing against the aspiring rival. A combination of factors that include economic, military, and technological power shifts, in addition to nationalism and geography, produces a changed equilibrium and rising pressure for the remaking of a new regional order that redefines the status quo and spheres of influences. Whatever maybe the underlying causes of international conflict, the combined explanatory factors and causes applied by the contributors to this volume enhance our knowledge of U.S.-China relations, the most important bilateral relationship of our time, and provide guidance for understanding future developments in East Asia, the strategically most vital region in the world.

38. Mearsheimer, *The Tragedy*, 397.
39. Schelling, *Arms and Influence*, 47–48, 71.

Index

Abbott, Tony, 125–126, 167
Abe, Shinzo (administration of): alliances, 38, 124–125, 160–168; China and, 178, 185, 187, 194, 275; constitutional reforms, 157–159; military strategy and reforms, 10, 37–38, 140–142, 146, 149–162; nationalism of, 17, 37–38, 120, 146–149; Yasukuni Shrine visits, 178, 185, 221
Afghanistan, 110
Ahn Jung-geun statue, 221
Air Defense Identification Zone (ADIZ), impact of, 24, 60, 104, 120, 145, 250, 252–253, 281, 293
Altman, Roger, 71
Aquino, Benigno, 240, 244
Article 9 (Japanese Constitution), 158–159
ASEAN: cooperation with China, 106–107, 109, 127; hedging by, 127–128; Japan and, 163, 193; South China Sea disputes and, 240–241, 245, 249, 257. *See also individual members*
Asian Infrastructure Investment Bank (AIIB), 6, 82, 107
Australia: China and, 6, 125–126, 292; Japan and, 120–121, 163, 166–167; U.S. and, 6, 104, 119, 120–121, 125, 292

Bader, Jaffrey A., 53–54, 237, 268
Bajoria, Jayshree, 30
balancer role, 206–207, 211
balancing, 35–40; in bipolar era, 8, 41–42, 59–67, 91, 285, 286; conditions favoring, 47–49, 52–53, 198–199; external, 198–199; Japan and, 287; South Korea and,

198–199, 201, 215–216, 217, 225, 226; underbalancing, 36–37
bandwagoning: conditions favoring, 43, 199; hedging *vs.*, 51–52; rhetorical, 209–210; South Korea and, 199–200, 201, 206, 208–210, 224, 226–227
Ban Ki-moon, 185
Beijing consensus, 76–78, 84–86
Biden, Joe, 53, 221, 223–224
bipolar era, 57–68; balancing in, 8, 41–42, 59–67, 91, 285, 286; China-U.S. relations in, 8, 61–65, 62–63, 113–119, 122–123; possible trajectories, 130–134
Blinken, Antony, 283
Booth, Ken, 57
Bo Xilai, 17, 32, 87, 177, 183
boycotts and embargoes: consumer, 188–191; rare earth embargoes, 74, 84, 148, 188–189
Bremmer, Ian, 34
Breuilly, John, 28–29
BRIC nations, 71, 82–83
Brooks, Stephen G., 43, 65
Brown, Gordon, 75
Brunei, 248, 249
Bush, George W. (administration of): China and, 114–115, 117–118; South Korea and, 56, 205, 206, 208, 209, 227, 266, 267
Buzan Barry, 51–52
Búzás, Zoltán, 36

Campbell, Kurt, 241, 242, 244, 275
Carter, Ashton, 122, 257, 293
Chan, Steve, 36, 226

Cheng-Chwee Kuik, 45–46
Chen Shui-bian, 56, 59
Cheonan (ship), 215
China: assertiveness of, 24–26, 59–63, 97,
    108–110, 243–246, 250–260, 281–283,
    286–298; Australia and, 6, 125–126, 292;
    coercive diplomacy, 261–284; domestic
    politics in, 17, 23–26, 32–34, 86–90;
    economic capabilities/growth of, 72–73,
    86–99, 101–103, 138–139; economic
    coercion by, 73–74, 83–84, 148, 170, 180,
    187–196, 273–274; economic policies of,
    67–90, 97–99; economic *vs.* military
    power, 8–9, 42, 292; foreign loans and
    development banks, 6, 73, 82, 107,
    255–256; foreign strategy (overall),
    106–117; hedging by, 41, 43, 56–59, 101,
    107–108; Japan and, 24, 60, 144–149,
    169–195, 272–279, 292–293; anti-Japanese
    sentiment in, 30, 32, 148, 149, 169–172,
    175–187, 194; land reclamation/creation
    by, 61, 104, 145, 250–251, 254, 255,
    256–260; maritime capabilities/strategies
    of, 2–3, 104–105, 276–277, 280–281,
    291–293; military capabilities/strategies
    of (general), 42, 138–140, 143–146,
    290–291; nationalism in, 21–22, 25–26,
    29–33; North Korea and, 18–19, 130, 215,
    219, 265–266, 268–272, 282; Russia and,
    57, 108, 111–113, 130–131; South China
    Sea disputes and, 59–61, 104, 145,
    233–260; U.S. and, 8, 41–68, 73–74, 83–84,
    113–123, 261–284. *See also* Diaoyu/
    Senkaku Islands disputes
China 2030 project, 87–88
China Development Bank, 255
Choe Thae Bok, 265
Chongqing Model, 87
Chung, Jae Ho, 201
Chu Shulong, 193
CICA Conference, 113–114
CLCS (UN Commission on the Limits
    of the Continental Shelf), 235–236, 239, 251
Clinton, Hillary, 18, 72, 237–239, 242–243,
    244, 264, 275, 279
coercive diplomacy, 261–284; concept,
    262–264; Japan, China, and U.S., 272–279,
    283; North Korea, China, and U.S.,
    261–262, 265–272
co-evolution, 132–133, 229
Cold War, 47, 58, 64–65, 66–67, 263, 297–298
Cole, J. Michael, 184
"comfort women" dispute, 212, 221, 222
congagement, 44
constitutional reform, in Japan, 157–159
Cooper, Zack, 49
Copeland, Dale, 34
Cowpens (ship), 252, 281

Cui Tiankai, 240
currency reserves, 73, 95–96
currency swaps, 78–79, 179–180

Dai Bingguo, 116, 178
defense spending, 42, 66n82, 138–140, 153,
    295–296
Del Rosario, Albert F., 240
democracy, 21
Dempsey, Martin, 222, 255, 270
Deng Xiaoping, 23, 106
Denney, Steven, 38
development banks, 6, 82, 107, 255–256
Diaoyu/Senkaku Islands disputes:
    China-Japan relations and, 24, 60,
    147–149, 180–183, 186–187, 272–279,
    292–293; rare earth embargoes, 74, 84,
    148, 188–189; U.S.-China relations and,
    1, 56, 272–279, 283; U.S.-Japan relations
    and, 111, 161–162, 267, 272–279, 281
Dokdo dispute, 212, 221
domestic politics, 15–40; economic
    interdependence and, 32–35; realist
    theories and, 27–29, 32, 35–36, 198;
    second-image explanations, 20–26, 32–33;
    third-image factors, 23, 26; uncertainty
    and, 15–16. *See also* nationalism
Dongmaengpa school of thought, 224
Donilon Thomas, 119, 250, 278–279
Downs, Erica Strecker, 172
dual structure/two Asias, 100, 104, 129,
    133, 201

earthquakes, 179
East China Sea disputes. *See* Air Defense
    Identification Zone; Diaoyu/Senkaku
    Islands disputes
economic coercion, 73–74, 83–84, 148, 170,
    180, 187–196, 273–274
economic policies: of China, 67–90, 97–99;
    of U.S., during financial crisis, 78–80
economic strength: of China, 72–73, 86–99,
    101–103, 138–139; of U.S., 92–97, 103, 133
embargoes and boycotts: consumer boycott,
    188–191; rare earth embargoes, 74, 84,
    148, 188–189
entrapment, 11, 205, 263, 268, 279, 280
exchange rate policies, 79–80, 81
exports, 93–94, 102, 174, 202, 292

Fallon, William J., 118
Fan Changlong, 255
Fang Fenghui, 270
Feigenbaum, Evan A., 104
Feng Wei, 190
Ferchen, Matt, 86
Fiery Cross Reef, 293
fifth column, 192–194

financial crisis (2008), 24; China's response to, 79–87, 97–98; perceived threats to global order, 69–78; U.S. response to, 78–80
financial sector, 94–96
Finlandization, 199
Fisman, Raymond, 189
FONOPs (Freedom of Navigation operations), 257, 258
Foot, Rosemary, 56–57
Freidhoff, Karl, 38
Friedberg, Aaron, 22, 44
Fujitsu employee arrests, 274
Fukuyama, Francis, 74, 77
Fu Ying, 244, 247

G-20 monitoring, 79–80
Gao Hucheng, 194
GDP: Asian vs. European, 285n1; of China-ASEAN free trade area, 106–107; China vs. U.S., 72; Chinese growth in, 101–102, 138, 295; deceptiveness of, 94; defense spending as percent of, 42, 66n82, 138–140, 153, 295–296; fiscal spending as a percent of, 81; international distribution of, 64
GDP (Gross Domestic Product), 139fig
geography: China strategies and, 287; Japanese security strategy and, 140–142, 145–146; military conflicts and, 40, 66–67, 296–298
Gill, Bates, 219
Gilpin, Robert, 24, 96, 137n2, 170, 288, 289–290, 292, 296
global financial crisis. See financial crisis (2008)
Goh, Evelyn, 45, 46n18
Goldstein, Avery, 56, 59, 106
Green, Michael, 218
Greenspan, Alan, 75
Guam, 118–119, 294
gyunhyong oigyo, 217

Hagel, Chuck, 221, 281–282
Hagström, Linus, 188–189
Hainan Province, 252
Halper, Stefan, 76–77
hedging: by China, 41, 43, 56–59, 101, 107–108; concept and theory of, 44–53, 105; conditions favoring, 46–47, 50–53, 105–106; extensive, 43, 46–48; negative moderate, 43, 46–48; by regional states, 41, 43, 101, 123–128, 129, 133; shift away from, 8, 41, 59; by South Korea, 287; by U.S., 41, 43, 53–56, 101, 117–123
hegemonic wars, 296–298
high-speed rail program, 175
Hirschman, Albert, 33, 191–192

Hughes, Christopher, 37
Hu Jintao, 114, 175, 178, 210
human rights, 20–21
HYSY 981, 254, 294

Ikenberry, G. John, 48, 67
Impeccable (ship), 237
India, 163, 166, 167–168, 293
internal balancing, 198
Iran, 264–265, 280
Ishihara, Shintaro, 148, 182, 274

Jacques, Martin, 77
Jajoopa school of thought, 205, 208, 224
Japan: Australia and, 120–121, 163, 166–167; balancing by, 287; China and, 24, 60, 144–149, 169–195, 272–279, 292–293; coercive diplomacy and, 272–279, 283; constitutional reform, 157–159; foreign strategy (overall), 36–39, 160–168; GDP, 139fig; military capabilities/strategy, 140–142, 145–459, 153, 282, 287; nationalism in, 7, 17, 37–38, 138, 146–149; South Korea, China, and, 179–180; South Korea, U.S., and, 211, 212, 214, 220–224; U.S. and, 111, 120–121, 160–162, 267, 272–279, 281, 287. See also Diaoyu/Senkaku Islands disputes
Jiang Weizeng, 190
Jiang Zemin, 203
Jin Baisong, 190
Johnston, Iain, 97

Kahler, Miles, 85
Kang, David, 129, 225
Kaplan, Robert, 40, 296–297
Katz, Richard, 173, 174
Kennedy, Scott, 86
Kerry, John, 270, 271–272, 278, 279, 283
Kim Dae-jung, 203
Kim Jong-Il, 265
Kim Jong-un, 18
Kim Young-sam, 207, 214
Kirshner, Jonathan, 33–34
Kissinger, Henry, 132, 229
Kleine-Ahlbrandt, Stephanie, 184, 220
Koizumi, Junichiro, 175
Kugler, Jacek, 288
Kupchan, Charles, 78
Kuwajima, Hiroaki, 192

Lampton, David, 21–22
land reclamation/creation, 61, 104, 145, 250–251, 254, 255, 256–260
Layne, Christopher, 71
lebensraum, 31
Lee Hsien Loong, 127–128
Lee Myung-bak, 197, 210–216, 224–225

Le Yucheng, 84–85, 150
Li Bin, 207
Lieberthal, Kenneth, 72, 77
Li Keqiang, 86, 87, 88, 90, 107, 248, 249, 270
Lim, Darren J., 49
Liu Junhong, 192
Liu Weimin, 110, 112
Li Yiqiang, 185–186, 255
Li Zhaoxing, 176–177
Luo Yuan, 266

Malaysia, 236, 239, 253, 292
Manicom, James, 179
Manning, Robert A., 104
Mastanduno, Michael, 67, 78
Ma Xiaotian, 265–269
McNally, Christopher, 82
Mearsheimer, John, 131, 199, 298
Medeiros, Evan S., 45, 53–54, 253
military strategies and capabilities.
    See individual country
Ming dynasty, 196, 197, 229
Ming Wan, 175
Min Gyo Koo, 173
Mischief Reef, 256, 293
missile defense system (MD), 220, 222–224,
    282–283
Mitsui OSK Lines, 191
Morgenthau, Hans, 4, 28, 65, 197
motivational uncertainty, 15, 16

Naoto Kan, 148
Nathan, Andrew, 77
nationalism: anti-American sentiment in
    South Korea, 202, 205; anti-Japanese
    sentiment in China, 30, 32, 148, 149,
    169–172, 175–187, 194; anti-Japanese
    sentiment in South Korea, 10, 39–40, 202,
    220–221; in China, 21–22, 25–26, 29–33; as
    counterpart to structural realism, 28–29;
    hypernationalism, 30; impact of on policy,
    8, 35–38; in Japan, 7, 17, 37–38, 138,
    146–149; rise of across region, 6–7; in
    South Korea, 38, 202; as tool for elites,
    7, 21–22, 36–38
National Security Council (Japan), 150
National Security Council (South Korea),
    205–206, 210
National Security Council (U.S.), 53–54
National Security strategy (Japan), 151–152,
    163, 166
Nazi Germany comparisons, 31
neoliberalism, 70, 74–75, 89–90, 92
networkization, 101, 120–122, 124
neutrality, 200
New Development Bank (NDB), 82–83
nine-dash line, 236, 238, 251, 253
Noda, Yoshihiko, 182, 274

North Korea: China and, 18–19, 130, 215,
    219, 265–266, 268–272, 282; China-South
    Korea relations and, 202, 210, 211–216,
    218–220, 224, 227; South Korea and, 204,
    208, 210, 211–216, 218, 220, 265; South
    Korea-U.S. relations and, 201, 202,
    211–212, 214–215, 222–224; U.S.-China
    relations and, 261–262, 265–272;
    U.S.-North Korea relations, 205. See also
    Six-Party Talks
Nye, Joseph S., 48, 117

Obama, Barack (administration of): China
    and, 53–56, 122–123, 262, 278–280, 282;
    economic leadership of, 78–80; global
    management strategies of, 17–18; Japan
    and, 111, 119, 161–162, 253, 278–279;
    Philippines and, 281; pivot to Asia, 55,
    61–62, 104–105, 119–123, 212, 221,
    294–295; South China Sea disputes and,
    237–239, 242, 247, 250, 251–252, 253, 256,
    258; South Korea and, 213, 267, 281–283.
    See also Clinton, Hillary; Kerry, John
oil drilling, 165, 166, 241, 250, 254, 282,
    294
One Belt, One Road initiative, 82
Organski, A.F.K., 288

pacifism, in Japan, 37, 138, 147, 159
Panetta, Leon, 122, 246, 267–268
Paracel Islands, 61, 145, 236–237, 239, 246,
    254, 294. See also South China Sea
    disputes
Park Geun-hye, 126–127, 197, 217–224, 225,
    270, 271, 272
Pew surveys, 71–72, 77–78, 103, 128–129
Philippines: Japan and, 163, 164–165; U.S.
    and, 111, 119, 239–252, 253, 257, 281, 293;
    Vietnam and, 236
pivot to Asia, 104–105, 119–123, 212, 221,
    294–295; Chinese response to, 234; dual
    structure and, 100, 103; hedging and,
    45, 55, 59; neutrality and, 56; Philip-
    pines and, 243; rebalancing and, 66;
    Russia-China relations and, 111; TPP
    and, 18; trilateral cooperation and, 212,
    220–221
positive moderate hedging, 46–48
power: continued U.S., 92–97, 103, 114, 115,
    133, 288; shifts in, 3–4, 285–298; apparent,
    69–78, 170; sources of, 26–29
Pu, Xiaoyu, 86, 91, 289–290
public opinion surveys. See surveys
Puri, Rajinder, 31
Putin, Vladimir, 111, 112, 222

Qin Gang, 185, 211
Qing dynasty, 196, 197, 229

RAND reports, 44, 291
rare earth embargoes, 74, 84, 148, 188–189
realist theories: domestic politics and, 27–29, 32, 35–36, 198; Japan-China relations and, 170, 191–192, 288; law of uneven growth, 24–25, 289, 290; U.S.-China relations and, 41–42
Regional Comprehensive Economic Partnership (RCEP), 6, 9, 107
renminbi (RMB): as currency of exchange, 102; exchange rate policies, 79–80, 81; as reserve currency, 73, 95. *See also* land reclamation/creation
Republic of Korea (ROK). *See* South Korea
reunification (of Korea), 216, 219
RIMPAC (Rim of the Pacific Exercise), 123
Rodman, Peter, 118
Roh Moo-hyun, 197, 203–210, 224
Ross, Robert, 25, 35, 206
Roubini, Nouriel, 34
Rumsfeld, Donald H., 118, 205, 206
Russel, Daniel, 253, 256
Russia, 57, 108, 111–113, 130–131, 295–296

Samuels, Richard J., 45
Sansha City, 242, 245, 246
Saunders, Phillip C., 172
Scarborough Shoal, 11, 61, 74, 242, 243–245, 246, 293. *See also* South China Sea disputes
Schelling, Thomas C., 297
Schweller, Randall. L., 43, 86, 91, 289–290
Scobell, Andrew, 77
sea lines of communication (SLOCs), 141–142, 145
second-image explanations, 20–26, 32–33
Senkaku Islands disputes. *See* Diaoyu/Senkaku Islands disputes
Shambaugh, David, 85
Shanghai Cooperation Organization (SCO), 108, 109
Shangri-La Dialogue, 120, 122, 257
Shen Danyang, 190, 193
Silk Road Fund, 255
Singapore, 62, 103, 104, 292
Six-Party Talks: Chinese attitudes towards, 218, 219–220, 265, 271, 280; South Korean attitudes towards, 209, 213, 215, 220; U.S.-China relations and, 56, 265; U.S.-South Korea relations and, 202, 215
Sohn, Injoo, 180
South China Sea disputes, 233–260; increasing US involvement in, 62, 104, 235–243, 252–255, 256–259, 281–282, 293–294; Chinese assertiveness, 59–61, 104, 145, 243–246, 250–260, 281–283, 293; mutual restraint, 246–250; Japan-China relations and, 144, 145–146, 164–165; land

reclamation/creation, 61, 104, 145, 250–251, 254, 255, 256–260
South Korea: anti-American sentiment in, 202, 205; balancing by, 198–199, 201, 215–216, 217, 225, 226; bandwagoning by, 199–200, 201, 206, 208–210, 224, 226–227; China, U.S., and, 6, 10–11, 199–229; coercive diplomacy and, 265–272, 282–283; hedging by, 287; Japan, China, and, 179–180; Japan, U.S., and, 211, 212, 214, 220–224; anti-Japanese sentiment in, 10, 39–40, 202, 220–221; Lee administration, 210–216, 224–225; military capabilities/strategy, 205–209, 211, 222–224; nationalism in, 38, 202; North Korea and, 204, 208, 210, 211–216, 218, 220, 265; Park administration, 217, 220–224, 225; Roh administration, 204–210, 224
Soviet Union, 58, 64–65
Spratly Islands, 1, 61, 145, 164, 294. *See also* South China Sea disputes
Starrs, Sean, 93–94
state capitalism, 76–77
status quo: China and, 289; definition, 137n2; Japan and, 137–138, 168, 292–293; South Korea and, 200–201, 225–226
Steinberger, James, 53–54
Stokes, Doug, 95–96
Strausz-Hupé, Robert, 28
structural theories, 15–16, 22, 35–36, 68, 287
Subi Reef, 256
Subramanian, Arvind, 72
Suisheng Zhao, 26
Sukhee Han, 201
surveys: Chinese attitudes to Japan, 183–184; Chinese attitudes to U.S., 77–78; on global power, 71–72, 103, 128–129; South Korean attitudes to U.S. and China, 226–229
Syria, 63, 264, 280

Taiwan, 56, 59, 74, 263n4, 298
Tang Jiaxuan, 192
taoguang yanghui policy, 106–109, 204
tariffs, 81–82
THAAD (Terminal High Altitude Area Defense), 222–224, 282–283
Thayer, Carl, 166
third-image factors, 23, 26
third-party coercive diplomacy. *See* coercive diplomacy
tianxia international order, 129
trade and investment: China's global role, 81–82; economic interdependence and, 32–35; exports, 93–94, 102, 174, 202, 292; free trade agreements, 6, 9, 18, 106–107; Japan and China, 173–178, 187–188, 191–194; South Korea and China, 204, 216

Trans-Pacific Partnership (TPP), 6, 9, 18
trilateral cooperation, 120–121, 166–168, 179–180, 211, 212, 214, 220–224
Trump, Donald, 18
Truong Tan Sang, 248

uncertainty, 15–16, 46–55, 105–106, 144, 198–199
UN Commission on the Limits of the Continental Shelf (CLCS), 235–236, 239, 251
unipolarity: as condition favoring hedging, 51–53; era of, 47–49, 52–59, 91–93, 98–99; hedging during, 47–49, 53–59; shift away from, 63–68, 91–93, 98–99
United Nations Resolutions on North Korea, 19
United States: Australia and, 6, 104, 119, 120–121, 125, 292; China and, 8, 41–68, 73–74, 83–84, 113–123, 261–284; economic leadership of, 78–80; hedging by, 41, 43, 53–56, 101, 117–123; Japan and, 111, 120–121, 160–162, 267, 272–279, 281, 287; low-cost foreign strategy of, 17–18; missile defense system, 220, 221–224, 282–283; North Korea and, 205; Philippines and, 111, 119, 239–252, 253, 257, 281, 293; pivot to East Asia, 55, 61–62, 104–105, 119–123, 212, 221, 294–295; power of, 92–97, 103, 114, 115, 133, 288; South China Sea disputes and, 62, 104, 233–260; South Korea and, 6, 10–11, 199–229, 265–272, 282–283; strategic flexibility doctrine, 205–209; trilateral cooperation, 120–121, 211, 212, 214, 220–224; Vietnam and, 56, 104, 120, 121–122, 238–239
UN Security Council seat, 176
U.S. dollar, 73, 95–96

Vietnam: Japan and, 163, 165–166; South China Sea dispute and, 236–241, 246, 248, 254–255, 282; U.S. and, 56, 104, 120, 121–122, 238–239

Walt, Stephen, 225–226
Waltz, Kenneth, 16, 57, 67, 234, 287
Wang Jisi, 72, 77
Wang Yi, 192, 223, 248, 249, 270
war, power changes and, 4, 66–67, 288–289, 296–298
Washington Consensus. *See* neoliberalism
Weis, Jessica, 172
Weitz, Richard, 223
Wen Jiabao, 86, 89, 175, 178–179, 182
Wheeler, Nicholas J., 57
Will Yinan He, 171
Wohlforth, William C., 43, 65, 67, 99
Wolfer, Arnold, 22
WTO, 75, 81–82, 88, 89, 92–93
Wu, Junhua, 188
Wu Dawei, 270

Xi Jinping, 87; *China 2030* project, 87; Japan and, 187; new security concept, 113–114; North Korea and, 270, 271–272; on peaceful development, 109, 115–116; Russia and, 111; South China Sea disputes and, 248–249, 250, 255, 258; South Korea and, 127, 218–220, 221, 222, 271–272; U.S. and, 262, 278–280, 282
Xu Dunxin, 193

Yahuda, Michael, 172–173
Yang Jiechi, 185, 255, 273
Yang Xing, 174
Yan Xuetong, 31, 112, 130–131
Yasukuni Shrine, 149, 175, 178, 185, 221
Yeonpyong Island, shelling of, 211, 212, 215, 224, 227
Yoon Byung-se, 218

Zhao Tingyang, 129
Zhou Yongkang, 182
Zhou Yongsheng, 189
Zhu Ni, 174
Zhu Rongji, 203–204
Zoellick, Robert, 70, 114, 117–118

www.ingramcontent.com/pod-product-compliance
Lightning Source LLC
Chambersburg PA
CBHW022302280326
41932CB00010B/948